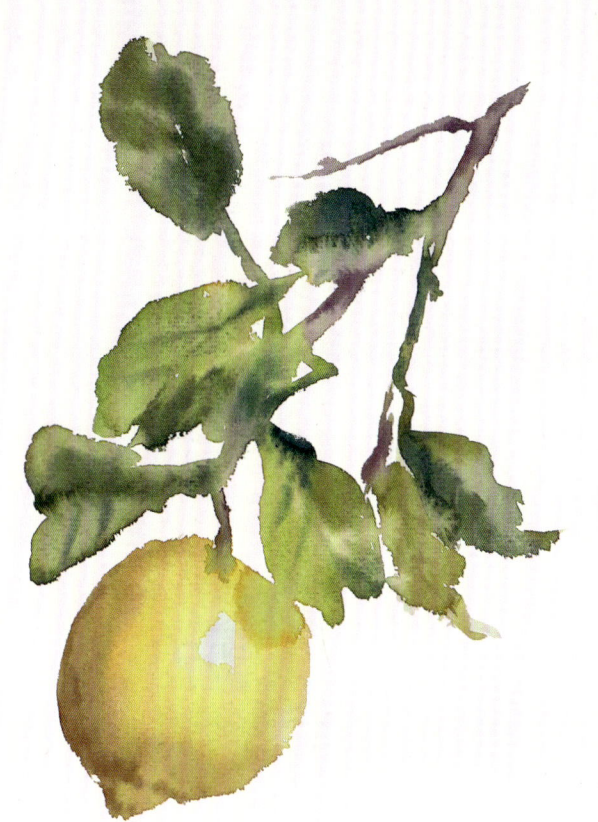

The Big Book of
WATERCOLOUR

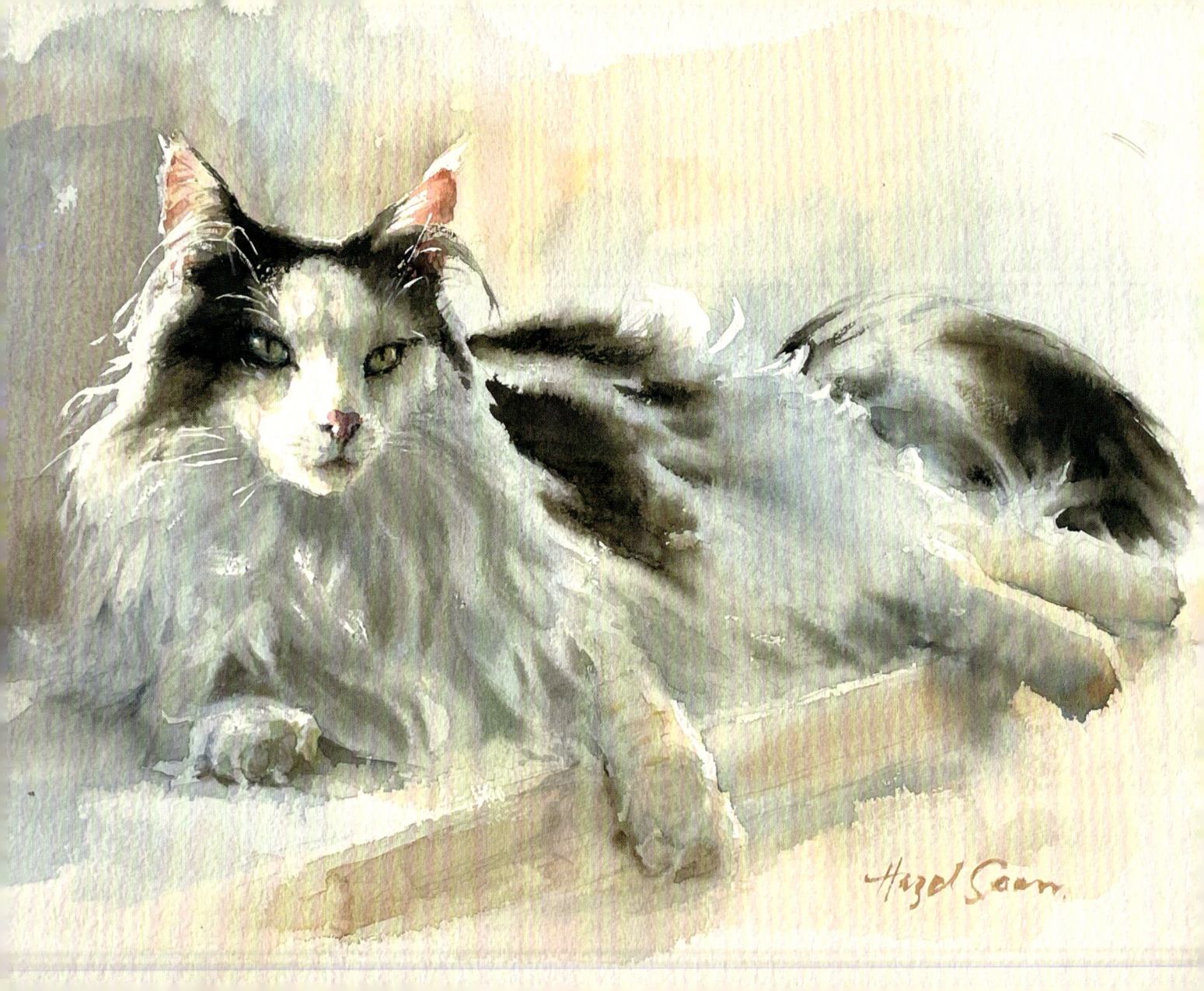
Hazel Soan.

The Big Book of
WATERCOLOUR

Hazel Soan

BATSFORD

First published in the United Kingdom
in 2025 by
Batsford
43 Great Ormond Street
London
WC1N 3HZ

An imprint of B. T. Batsford Holdings Limited

Copyright © B. T. Batsford Ltd 2025
Text and images copyright © Hazel Soan 2025

Originally published as three separate titles:
*Learn Watercolour Quickly, Learn Watercolour
Landscapes Quickly* and *Learn to Paint People Quickly.*

ISBN 978 1 84994 964 4

A CIP catalogue record for this book is available from
the British Library.

10 9 8 7 6 5 4 3 2 1

Reproduction by Rival Colour Ltd, UK
Printed and bound by Dream Colour, China

This book can be ordered direct from the publisher at
www.batsfordbooks.com, or try your local bookshop

To all who share in this watercolour journey.

Acknowledgements

I would like to thank Nicola Newman, Eoghan O'Brien and Lee-May Lim
for compiling this comprehensive guide to watercolour from the Learn
Quickly series. As ever, working with the team at Batsford has been a pleasure.
My special thanks go to the proofreader, Katie Hewett, for checking on any
unnecessary repetition. Watercolour remains my passion and sharing it is
such a joy; I thank my publishers and readers for making this possible.

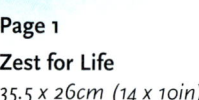

Page 1
Zest for Life
35.5 x 26cm (14 x 10in)

Page 2
Bucky
43 x 56cm (17 x 22in)

Contents

About this book

Watercolour has captivated artists and viewers alike for centuries. Its unique ability to represent light, atmosphere and emotion through translucent layers of pigment set it apart from other mediums, making it beautiful to behold and challenging to master. This compendium is designed to be a comprehensive guide to enable you to embark with confidence on your own creative journey, offering insight, techniques and inspiration through a variety of subjects.

The book is divided into three parts. It begins with the essential materials and basic techniques that make watercolour such a delight to pursue, advocating that the subject should be used to paint the watercolour rather than the watercolour used to paint the subject. The second part takes the journey into landscape painting, exploring the art of illusion, space and depth, patterns of light and shade, and the use of perspective. In the third and final section the reader is guided gently through the exciting challenge of painting people, simplifying the process of representation and showing how the inclusion of figures imparts life into paintings.

With such broad content, this one book will equip you to paint watercolour with the knowledge and skills needed to bring your artistic vision to life. Welcome to the journey, as we discover the endless possibilities this rewarding medium has to offer ...

▷ **Rose to the Occasion**
38 x 51cm (15 x 20in)

Flowers are always a reliable subject through which to explore the thrill of watercolour. The translucent petals and glorious colours lend themselves perfectly to the medium.

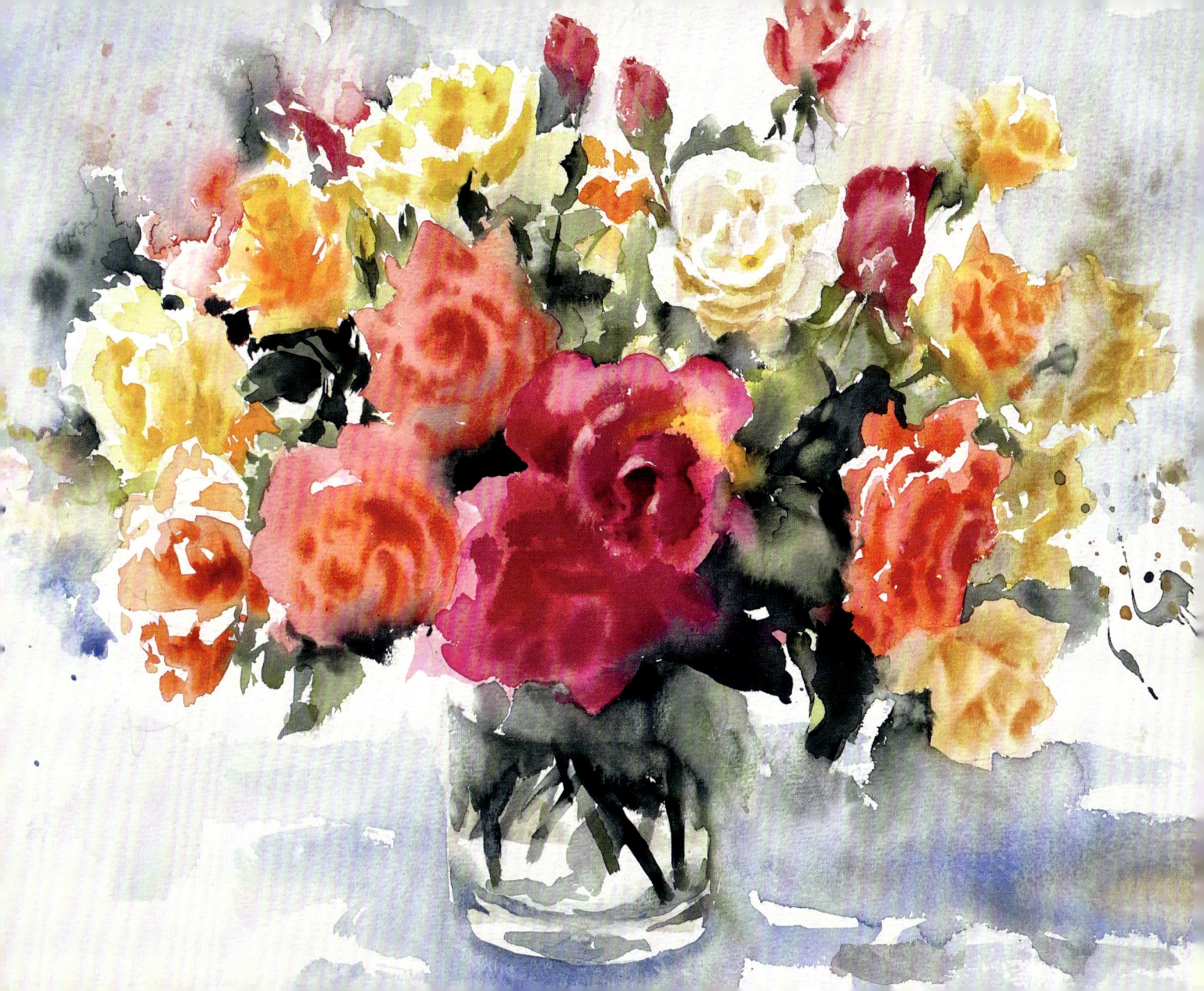

Learn Watercolour
Quickly

Introduction

This section of the book introduces you to the watercolour medium, the paint, the pigments, the brushes, the paper and a whole range of techniques for laying this lovely medium on paper to make your heart sing. You can read this section in about 30 minutes, and will be ready to start painting even before you reach the chapter on how to choose your subject, so I suggest you take it slowly and start painting as early on in the book as possible, practising what you learn as you read. Painting is a verb before it becomes a noun, and you will learn quickly the more you lay paint on paper.

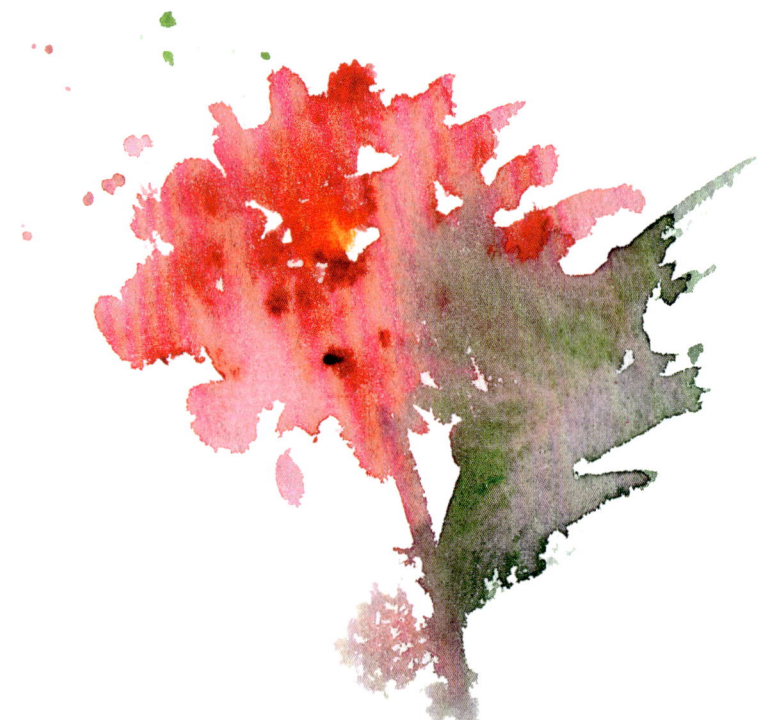

▷ **Floating By**
15 x 20cm (6 x 8in)
Watercolour is a medium that can very quickly catch the essence of a subject.

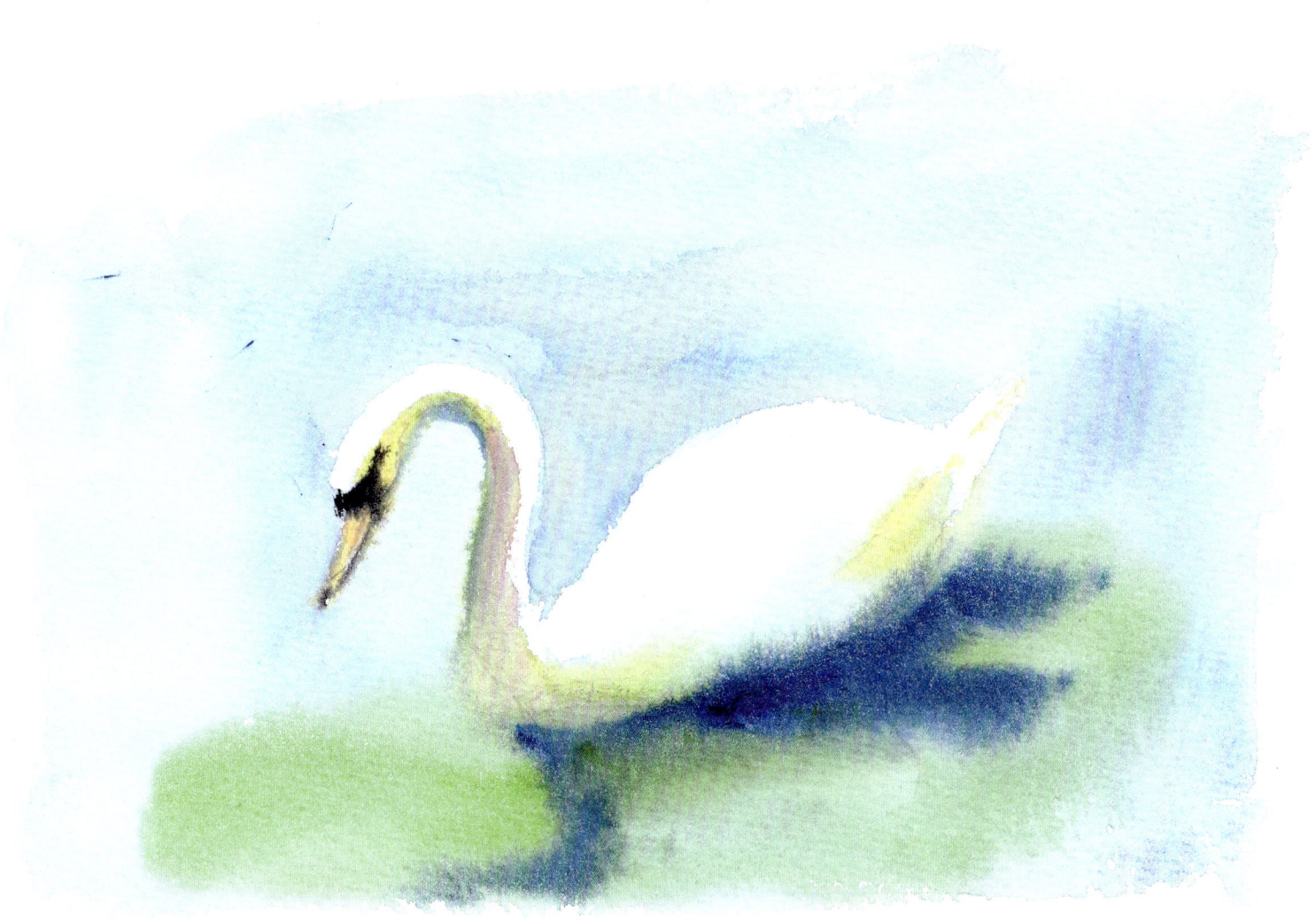

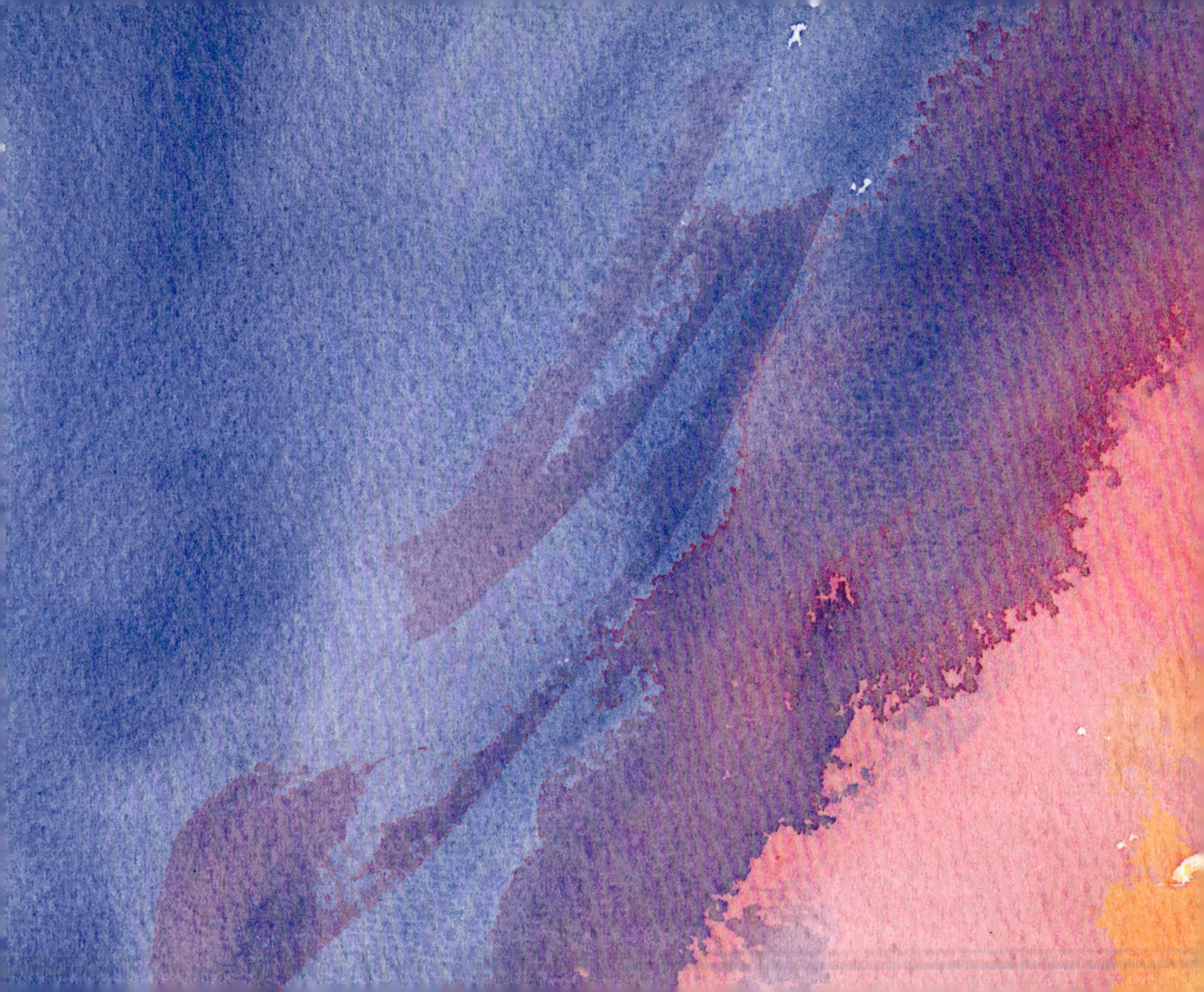

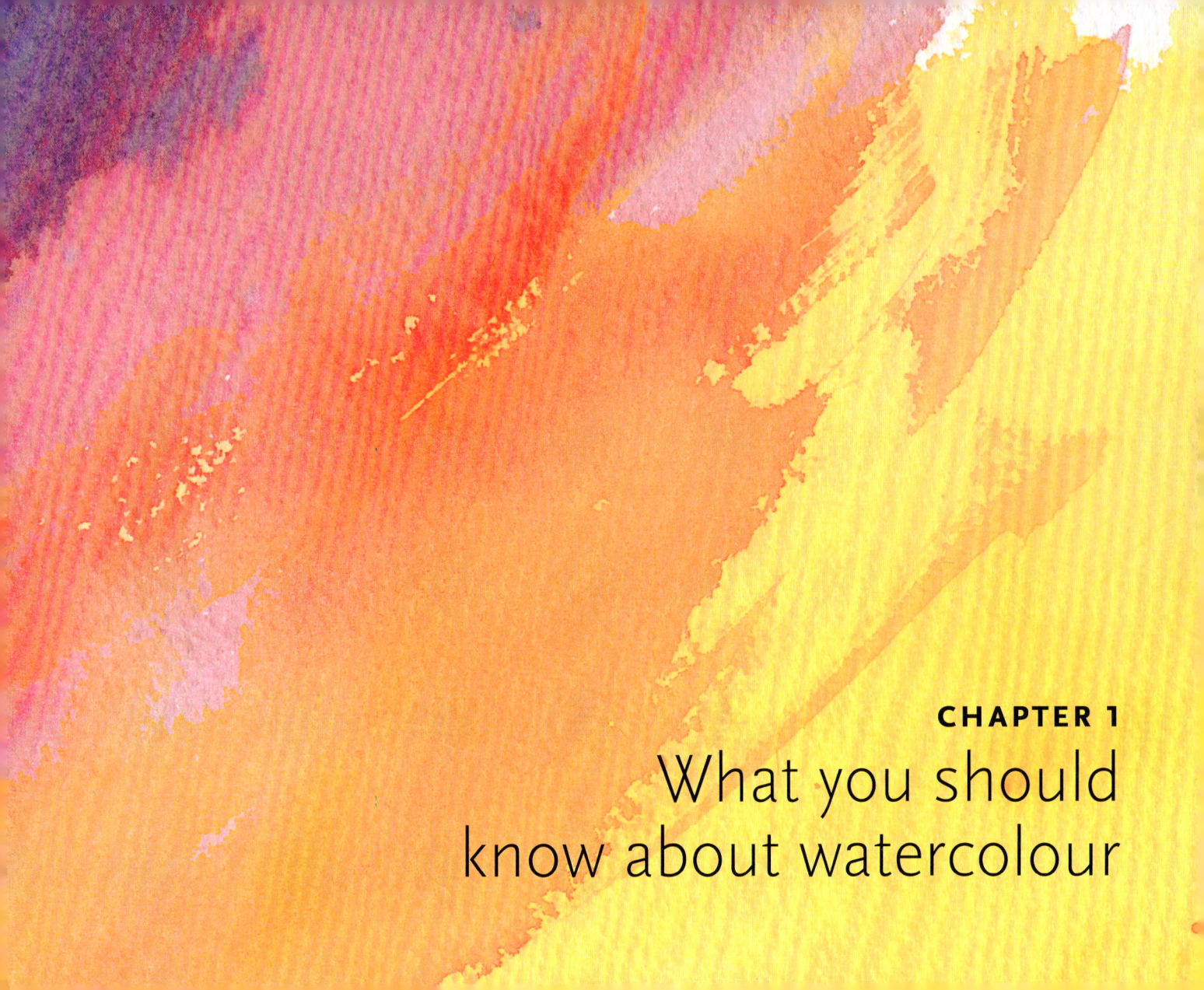

CHAPTER 1

What you should know about watercolour

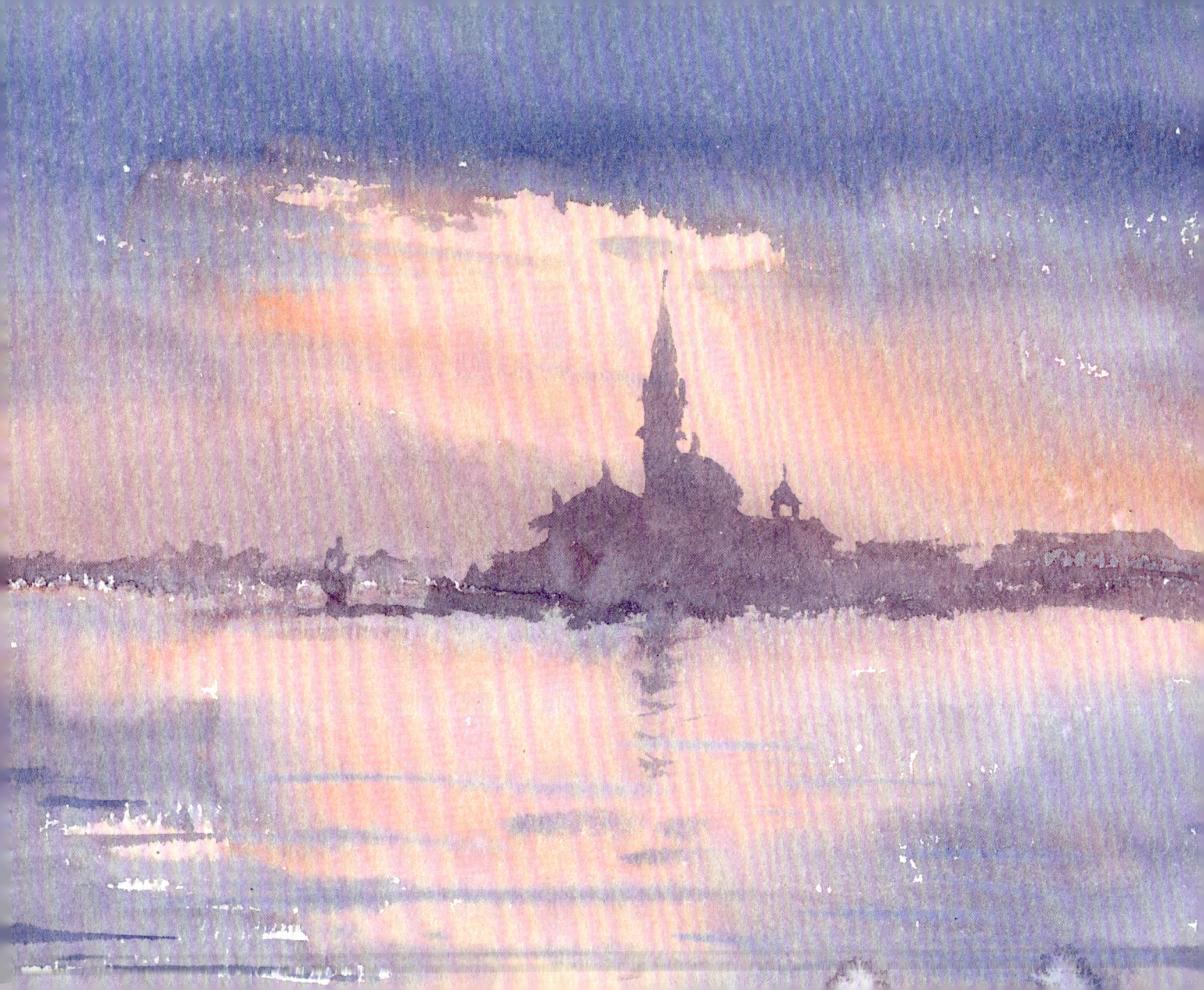

The medium of watercolour

Watercolour is a transparent painting medium that is diluted with water, mixed on a palette with a brush and then applied to paper. The light in a watercolour painting is represented by white paper, the painter paints the shade and tints the light. Watercolour paper is heavier than cartridge paper to prevent it from buckling when wet. You can use any tool to apply watercolour, but the brushes that are made especially for this medium make it much easier to get satisfying results.

◁ **Jewel of the Adriatic**
28 x 38cm (11 x 15in)

With just two colours, Light Red and Ultramarine Blue, the captivating medium of watercolour is able to evoke the glorious light of the rising sun over a majestic silhouette in Venice.

You need only the desire

Watercolour is known for its radiant washes and clarity of colour. The appearance of the watercolour is more important than the content it conveys – grasping this concept allows even a beginner to achieve attractive results. As mentioned earlier, always bear in mind that you are using the subject to paint a watercolour rather than watercolour to paint the subject.

It is true that mastering watercolour to a high level of expertise will take time, even a lifetime, but the beauty of this medium can be found as soon as you start, just by letting the lovely pigments and papers do their stuff and not worrying too much or trying too hard.

▽ **The Student**
28 x 35.5cm (11 x 14in)

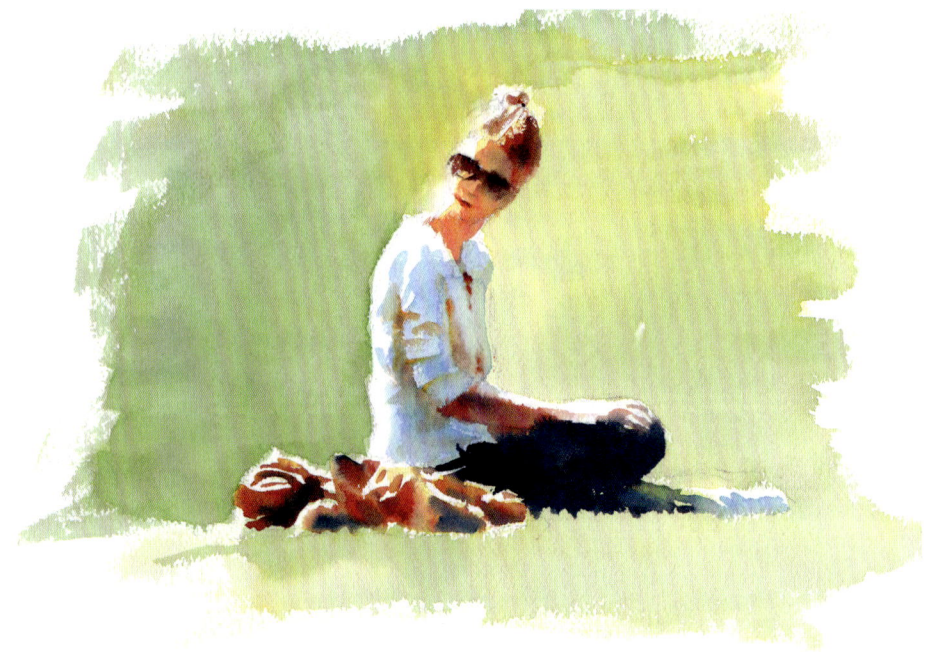

Be curious

Inquisitive people learn fast; art does have rules, but there are no boundaries. Here is a medium that benefits from thought before action and enjoys concentration. 'Less is more' should be the watercolourist's motto and being succinct often takes more preparation and care than being long-winded.

Do not be afraid to experiment even though you may waste paper in doing so, and don't be afraid to break the rules. Most great discoveries are made by mistake, so get out of your comfort zone and explore the medium. As much as is possible, paint from life rather than from photographs. Great pleasure is found in the process of painting and if you produce a worthwhile result, bliss will be your reward. The exciting thing about watercolour is that it actually does provide an adrenaline rush because of the precariousness that can be involved in using this medium.

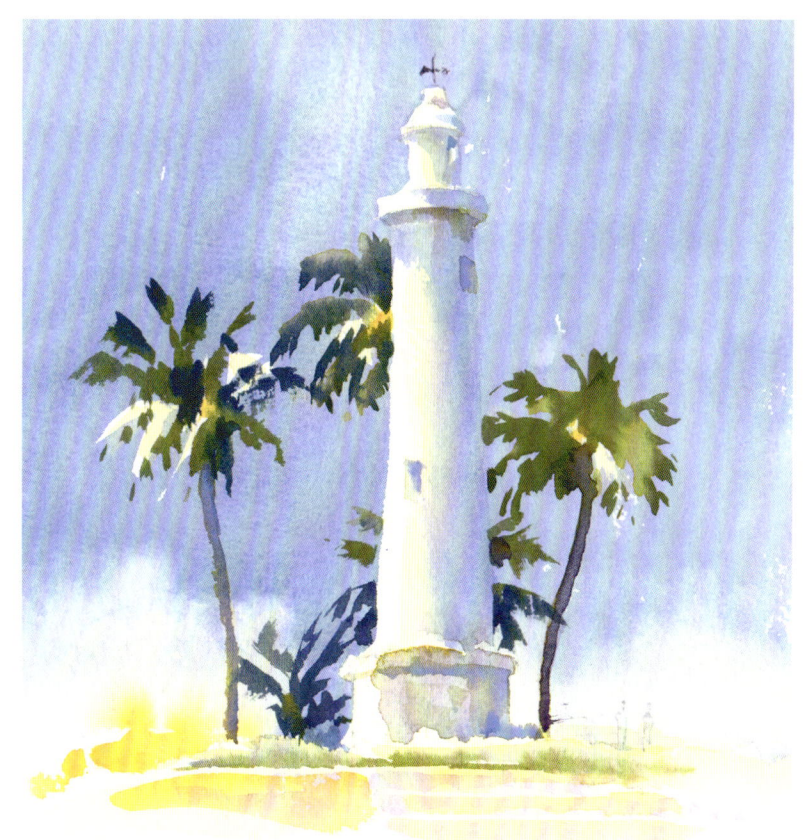

△ **The Lighthouse**
25.5 x 25.5cm (10 x 10in)

Creation and failure are interlinked

Creation and failure are inescapably linked: without doubt, among your successes there will be failed watercolours. These are part of your creative archive and are just as important as the paintings you come to cherish: get used to it, don't let it get you down, just carry on.

Watercolour can be unforgiving, but usually only when it is overworked and loses its fresh and lively appearance – as you haven't got much time, you are unlikely to fall into this trap! If it goes wrong it is only a piece of paper, so simply get a fresh piece and start again.

▷ **Crossing the Kalahari**
23 x 30.5cm (9 x 12in)
You need very few colours and little time to paint a watercolour. Here Ultramarine Blue, Yellow Ochre and Permanent Rose are used in combination to create this desert scene in just a few minutes.

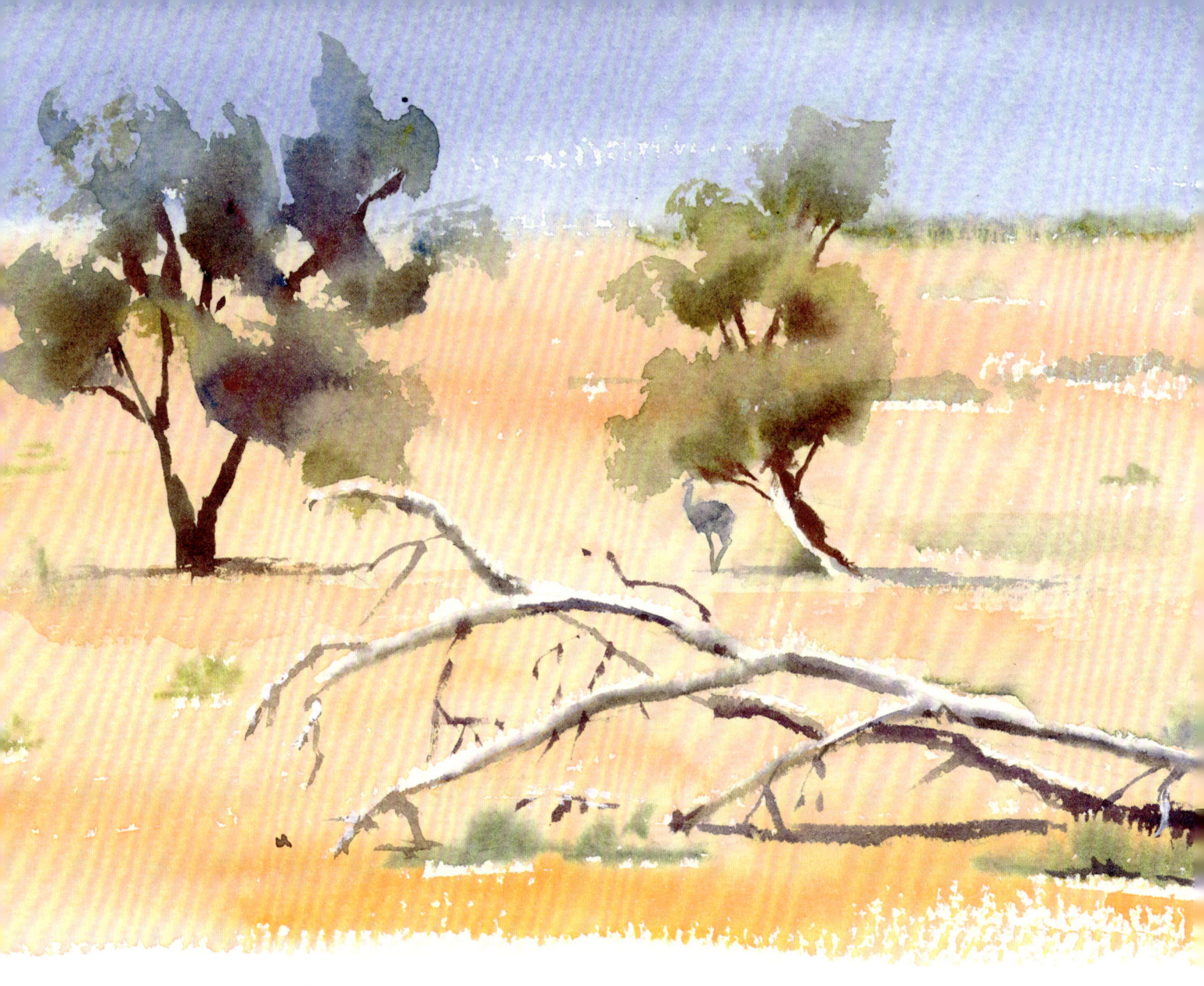

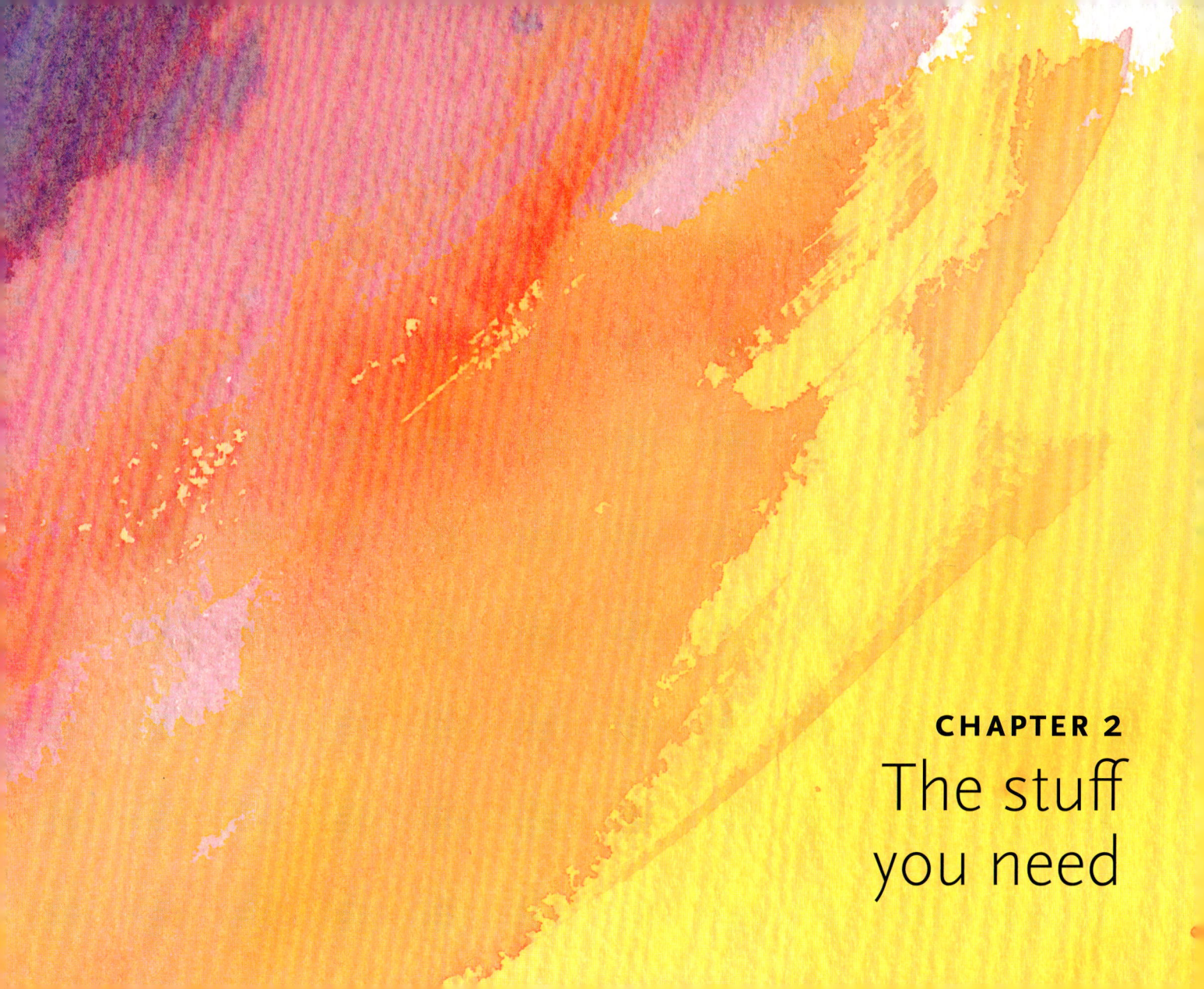

CHAPTER 2

The stuff
you need

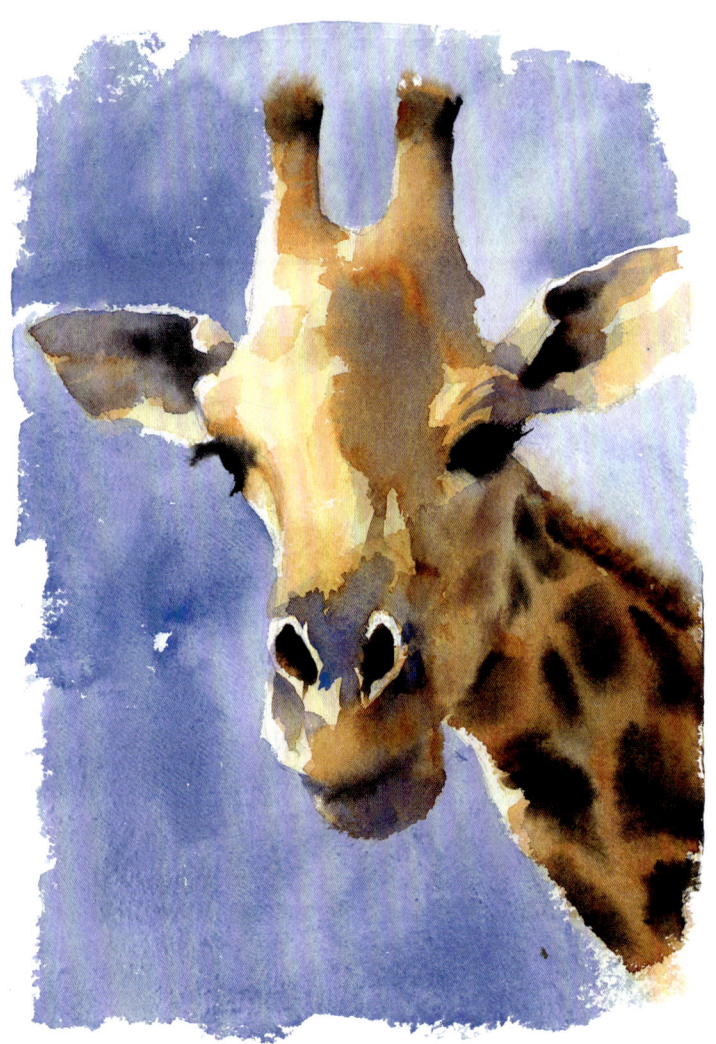

Less is more

You do not need many materials to paint good watercolours. 'Less is more' is the watercolourist's maxim and applies to the materials as well as the actual painting.

Art shops can be overwhelming. All you need to start with is one fairly large or medium-sized natural hair brush, three to six tubes of paint, a palette to mix on, watercolour paper, water and some kitchen towel. If you want to work more upright, a lightweight, portable, folding easel is ideal as it can be carried outside. Alternatively, work flat; sit on a seat or stool and hold your painting on your knees or work at a table – you can't then tilt your paper in any direction.

◁ **Curious Giraffe**
56 x 38cm (22 x 15in)
I worked flat to ensure the paint for the patches on the neck could spread out evenly in all directions.

Don't buy cheap products

Do yourself a favour: buy artists'-quality materials. These may be more expensive, but buying cheap watercolour paints is a false economy – it makes the painting process more difficult, and the paint doesn't go so far or bring such good results.

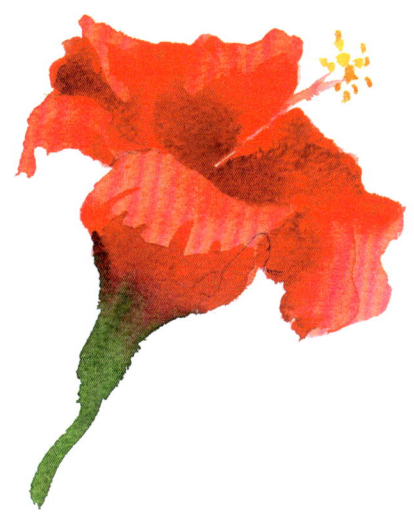

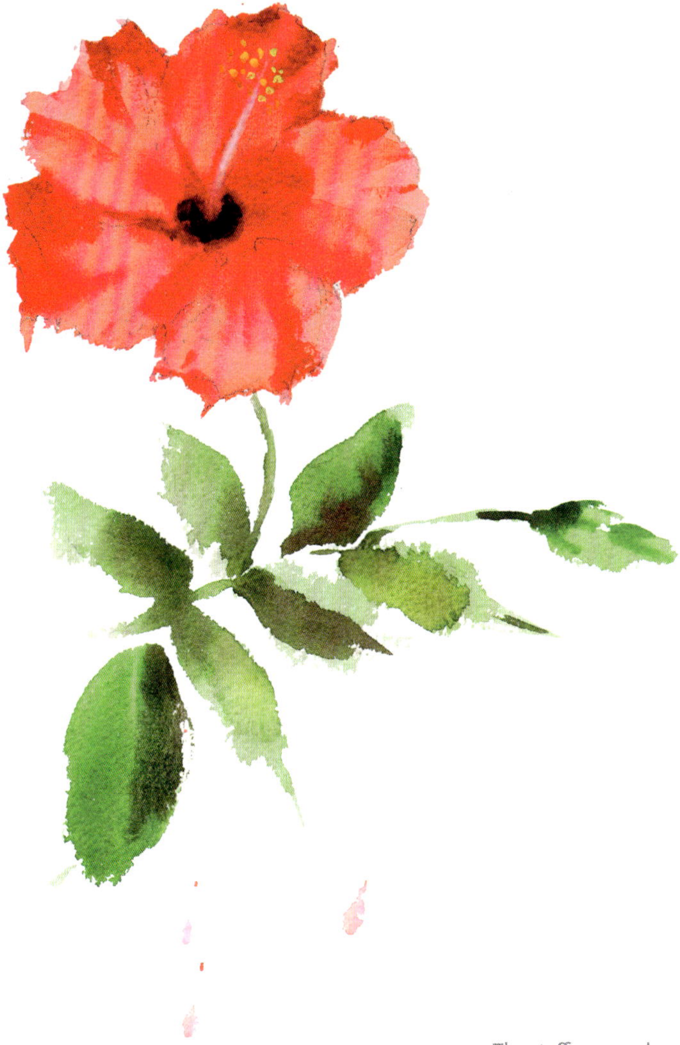

△ The purity and intensity of artists'-quality pigments make rich, glowing colours.

Brushes

Choose natural hair brushes, as they are easier to use than synthetic nylon brushes. Also, with natural hair you can manage with just one brush, whereas with nylon you would need several to make the same brushmarks. Start with one round natural hair brush – size 12, 10 or 8 depending on the size of paper you want to work on (see box, right). It will be more expensive than a nylon equivalent, but it is much more versatile, it will come to a fine point for detail and has a broad body that can carry lots of paint for larger washes, and it will last for many years. Research stockists online to find the best-value products.

If you want to add another brush at this stage, a 20mm (¾in) flat natural hair brush would be useful and costs less than a round brush. If you fall in love with this medium, you can add more brushes at a later date, including a thin, narrow brush for fine, even lines called a rigger.

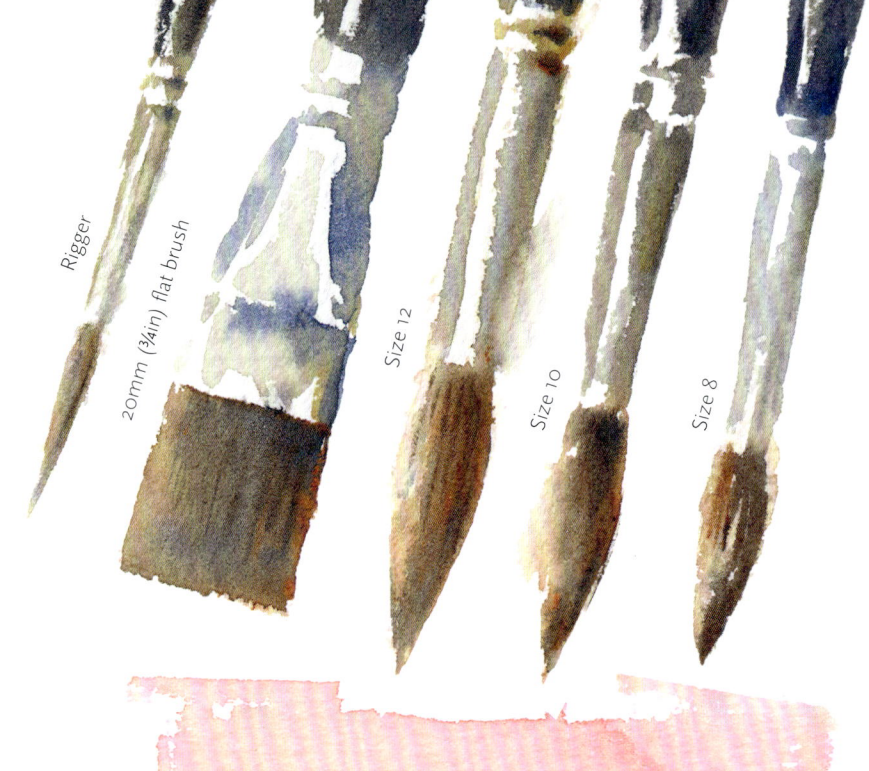

Rigger

20mm (¾in) flat brush

Size 12

Size 10

Size 8

Brush sizes
I suggest the following sizes of natural hair brush for particular paper sizes, but aim to use the biggest brush possible:
• Paper 51 x 41cm (20 x 16in) and larger: size 12 to 14 brush
• Paper 41 x 30.5cm (16 x 12in): size 10 brush
• Paper 30.5 x 20cm (12 x 8in) and smaller: size 8 brush

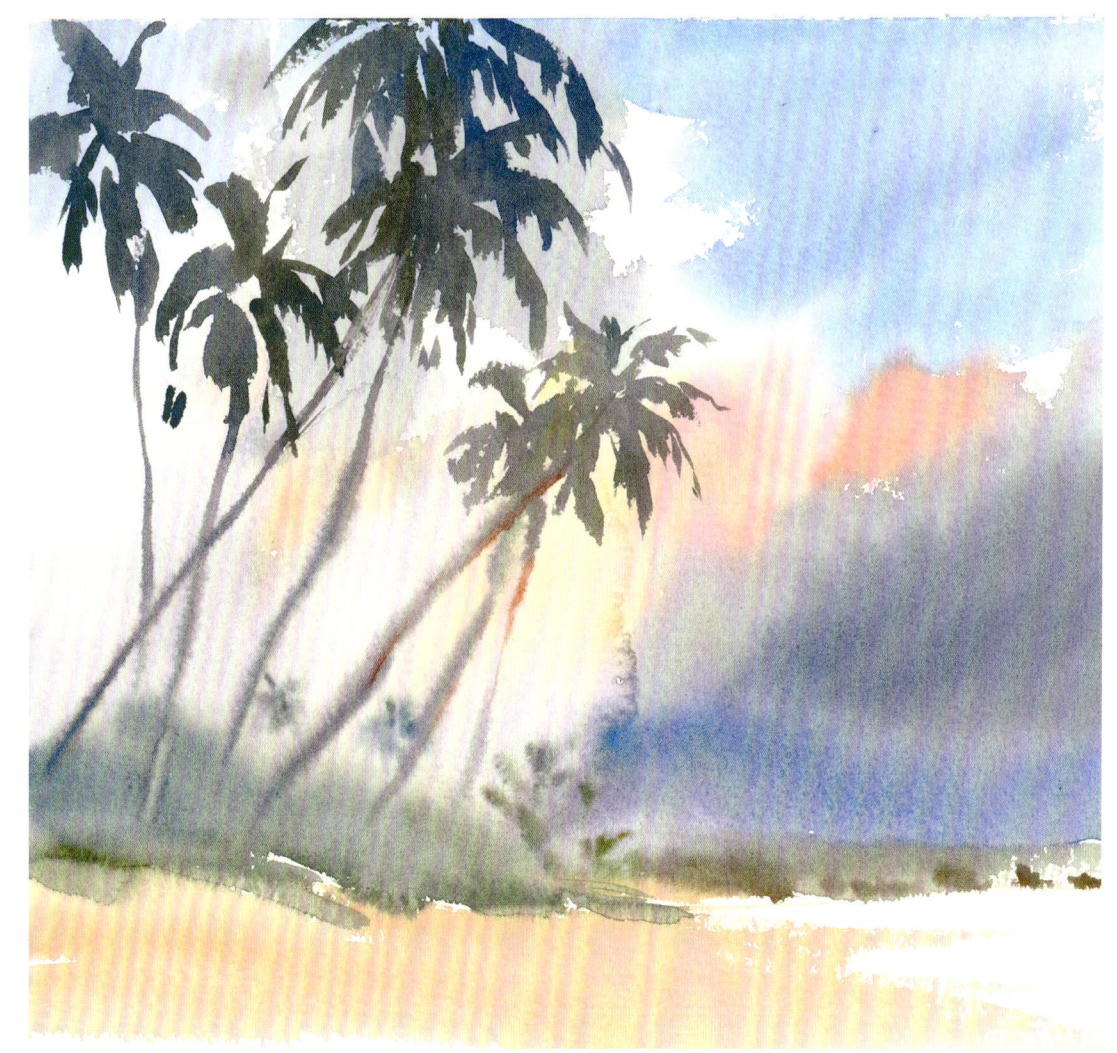

▷ Bending to the Song of the Wind

25.5 x 28cm (10 x 11in)

The natural hair brush can shape a frond or suggest a coming storm; the tip is used for detail, the body of the brush for broad washes.

Paints

Artists'-quality watercolour paints are purer and go a lot further than students'-quality colours, and will make for more radiant paintings. With watercolour, the fewer colours you use, the better the results. Artists' watercolour is such an intense pigment that you need very little, and even a small tube lasts a long time. Since watercolour is essentially a transparent medium, you will be surprised at how little pigment you use for the majority of a painting (see page 46 for the colours I suggest you buy).

◁ This little sketch is painted with the same tube colours as shown in the picture: Ultramarine Blue, Alizarin Crimson and Aureolin (yellow).

Palette

When it comes to palettes, a china or enamel palette is easier to mix on than a plastic palette (but heavier to carry if working on location). A palette with several sloping wells is ideal so the water can pool at the bottom and remain drier up the slope.

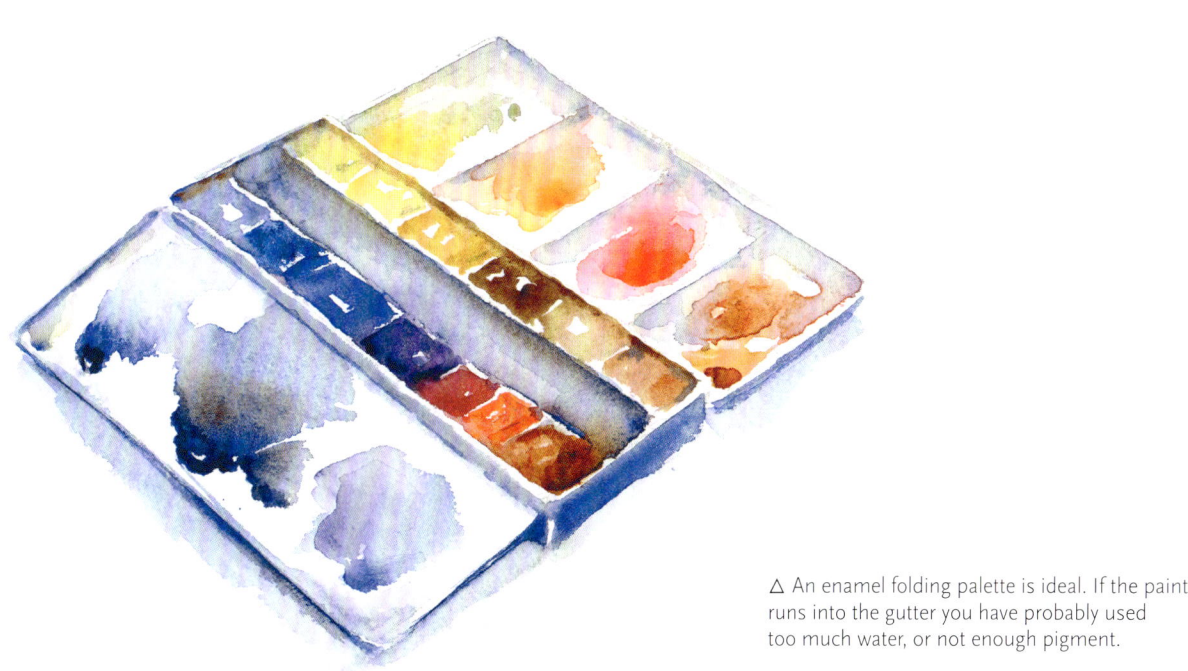

△ An enamel folding palette is ideal. If the paint runs into the gutter you have probably used too much water, or not enough pigment.

Paper

The main ongoing cost in watercolour painting is that of the paper, but since you can only learn to paint by actually painting on the paper, it is rather essential!

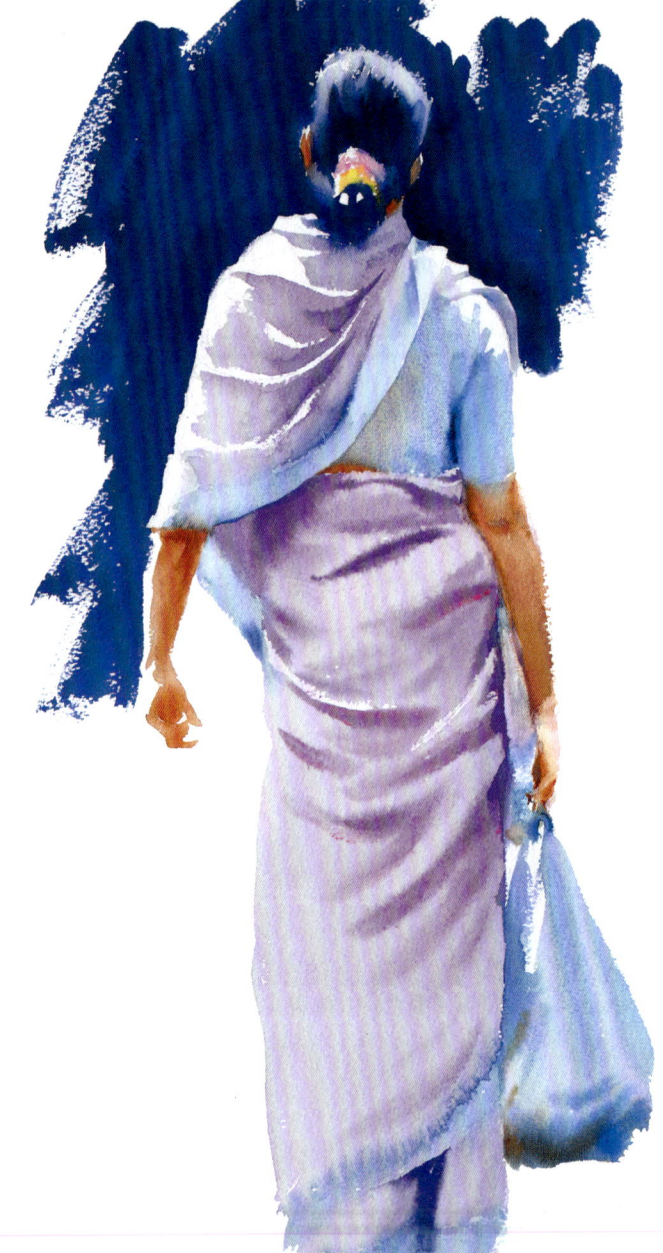

▷ **Lilac Sari**
56 x 30.5cm (22 x 12in)
The uneven surface texture of watercolour paper gives pleasing edges to the brushmarks of the background in this painting as the paint dances over the rough grain.

There are two main types of watercolour paper: paper made with cotton and paper made from wood pulp. The paintings in this book are all made on 100 per cent cotton paper, mostly with a rough surface, so if you like their appearance I suggest you use the same. Later, you can experiment with different papers. Paper thickness is categorized by its weight per ream. Choose heavier weight paper – 300gsm (140lb) or thicker. Forget thin paper as it buckles too much.

Surface texture
There are three main choices of surface texture:
• Rough: the grain has a prominent tooth.
• NOT (cold-pressed): the tooth is less pronounced.
• HP (hot-pressed): the surface is very smooth.

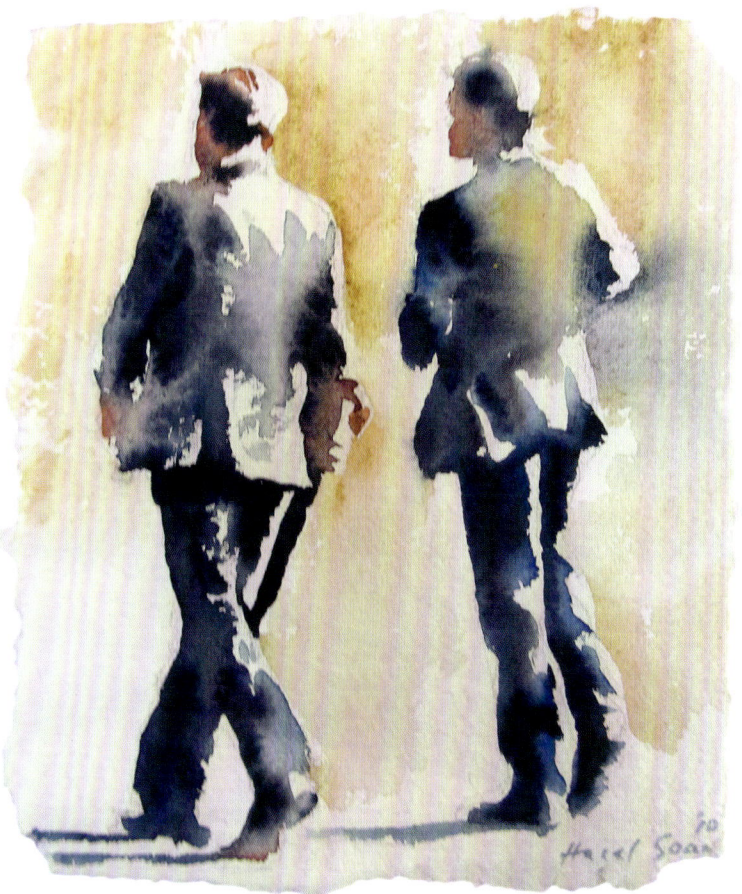

△ **City Duo**
20 x 15cm (8 x 6in)

These city suits were painted on rough khadi paper, which is made with long-fibre cotton and therefore holds the water longer than most papers.

Water and kitchen towel

Water is needed to mix with the paint to break down the gum-arabic binder, thus allowing the paint to float on the paper and set when dry. It's a good plan to have two to three small pots of water – this allows you to use a couple for rinsing off paint and one clean-water pot for making the radiant tints. You will also need kitchen towel, or a sponge or cotton rag to mop up excess water.

Pencil and eraser

It is not always necessary to draw before painting except when you need a guide for the brush. For this you need a softish pencil (2B or 4B) or a graphite stick. It does not matter if pencil marks show under a watercolour but, if corrections are to be made before painting, use a putty rubber rather than an ordinary eraser so that you do not scuff the surface of the paper.

▷ Watercolours often require very little drawing before applying the paint. Here, only the outline of the zebra is sketched because the versatile natural hair brush can make specifically shaped strokes to delineate the stripes and thus shape the animal perfectly.

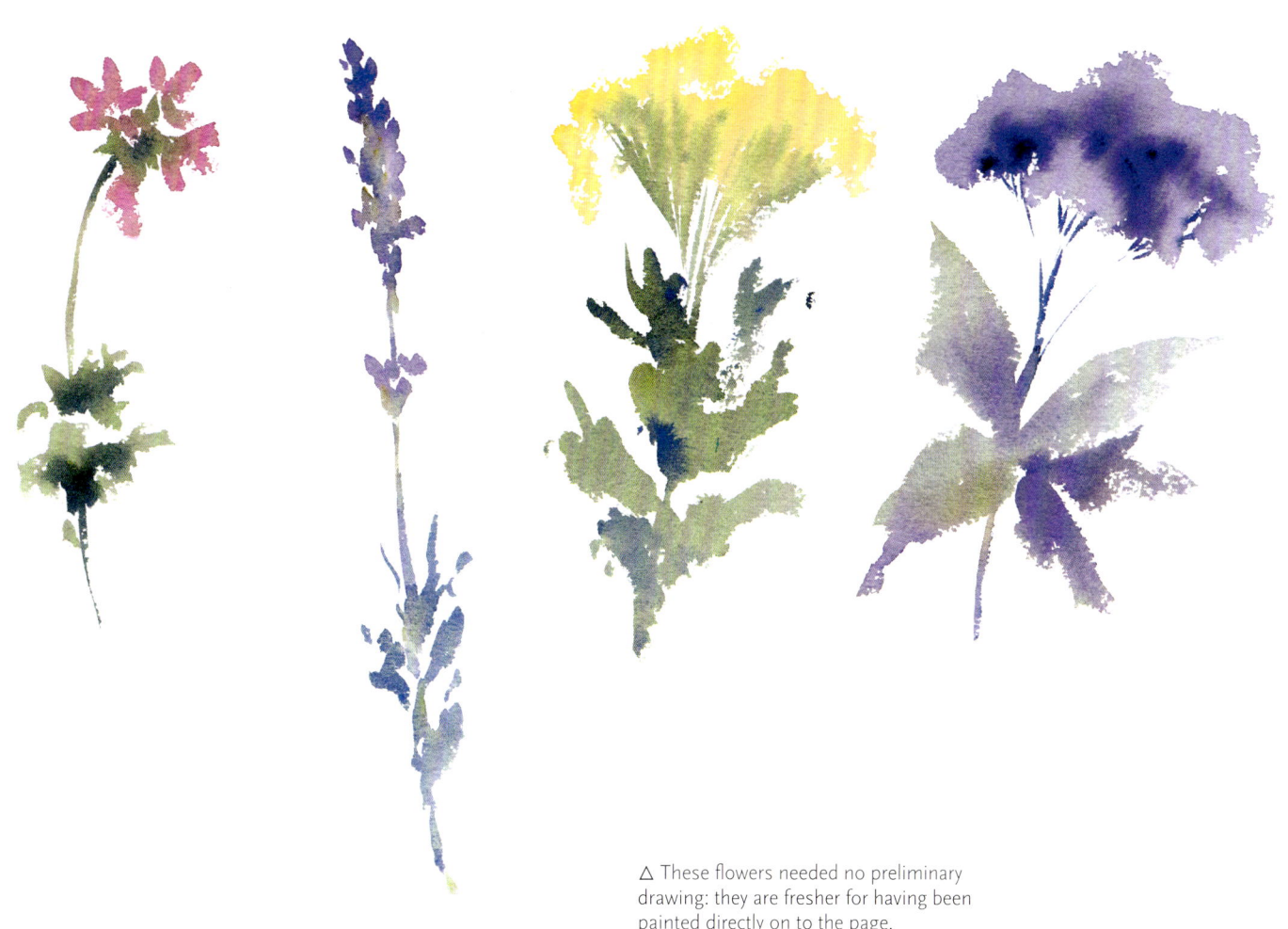

△ These flowers needed no preliminary drawing: they are fresher for having been painted directly on to the page.

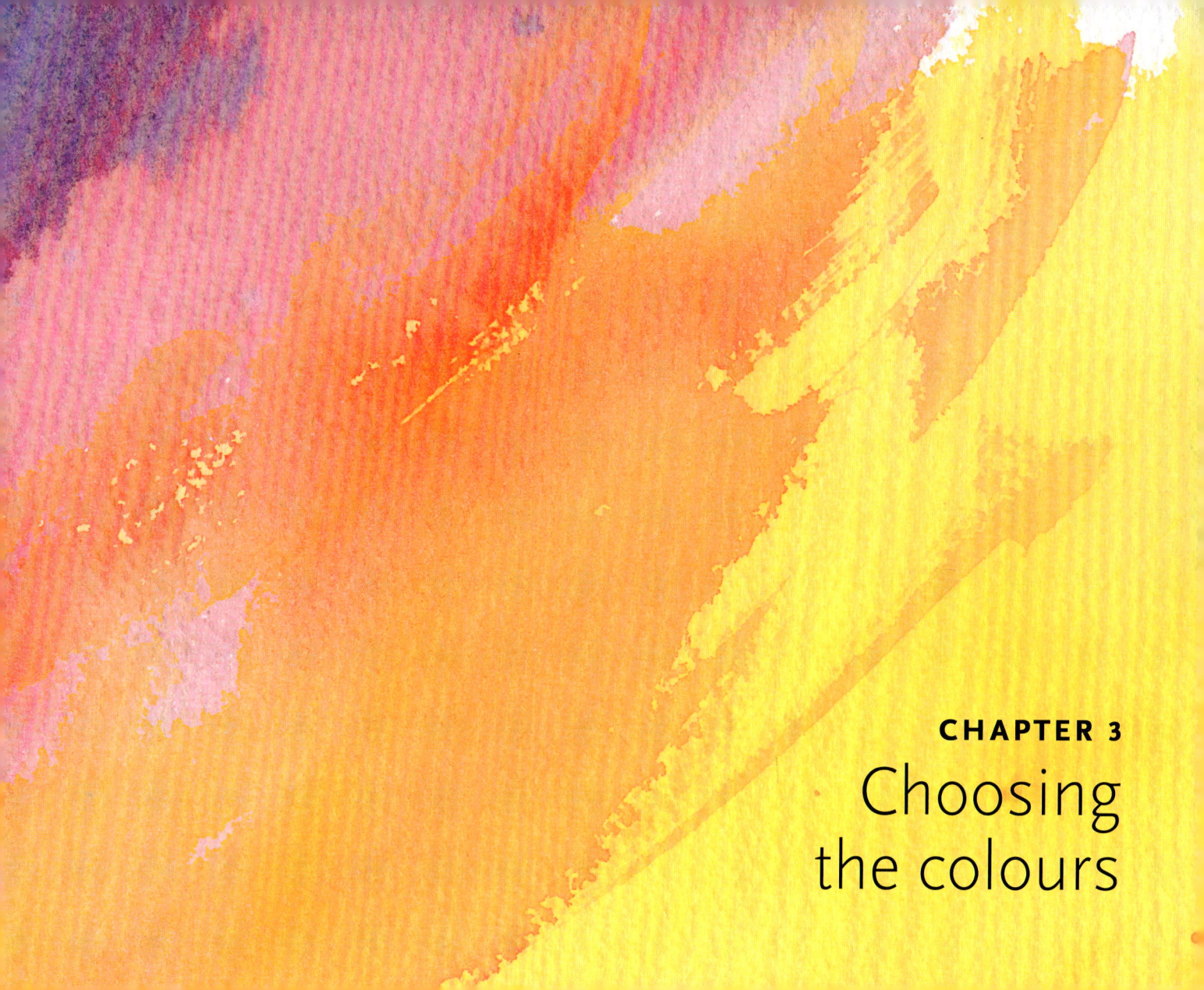

CHAPTER 3

Choosing
the colours

The primary colours

There are three main colours in painting – red, yellow and blue. These are known as primary colours and can be mixed together to make all other colours. There are many different reds, yellows and blues available in watercolour, so it is possible to make many variations with combinations of a red, a yellow and a blue.

At the end of this chapter (see page 46), I recommend a set of colours to start painting with, but do aim to use as few as possible in any one painting.

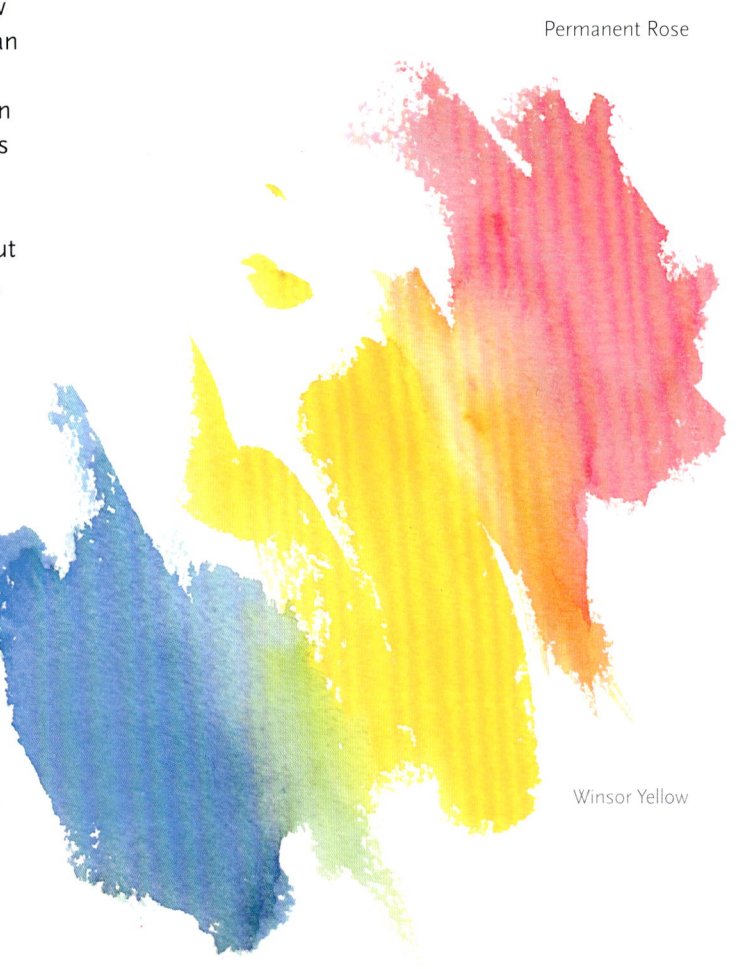

Permanent Rose

Winsor Blue

Winsor Yellow

▷ A blue, a yellow and a red mix to make a full range of colours.

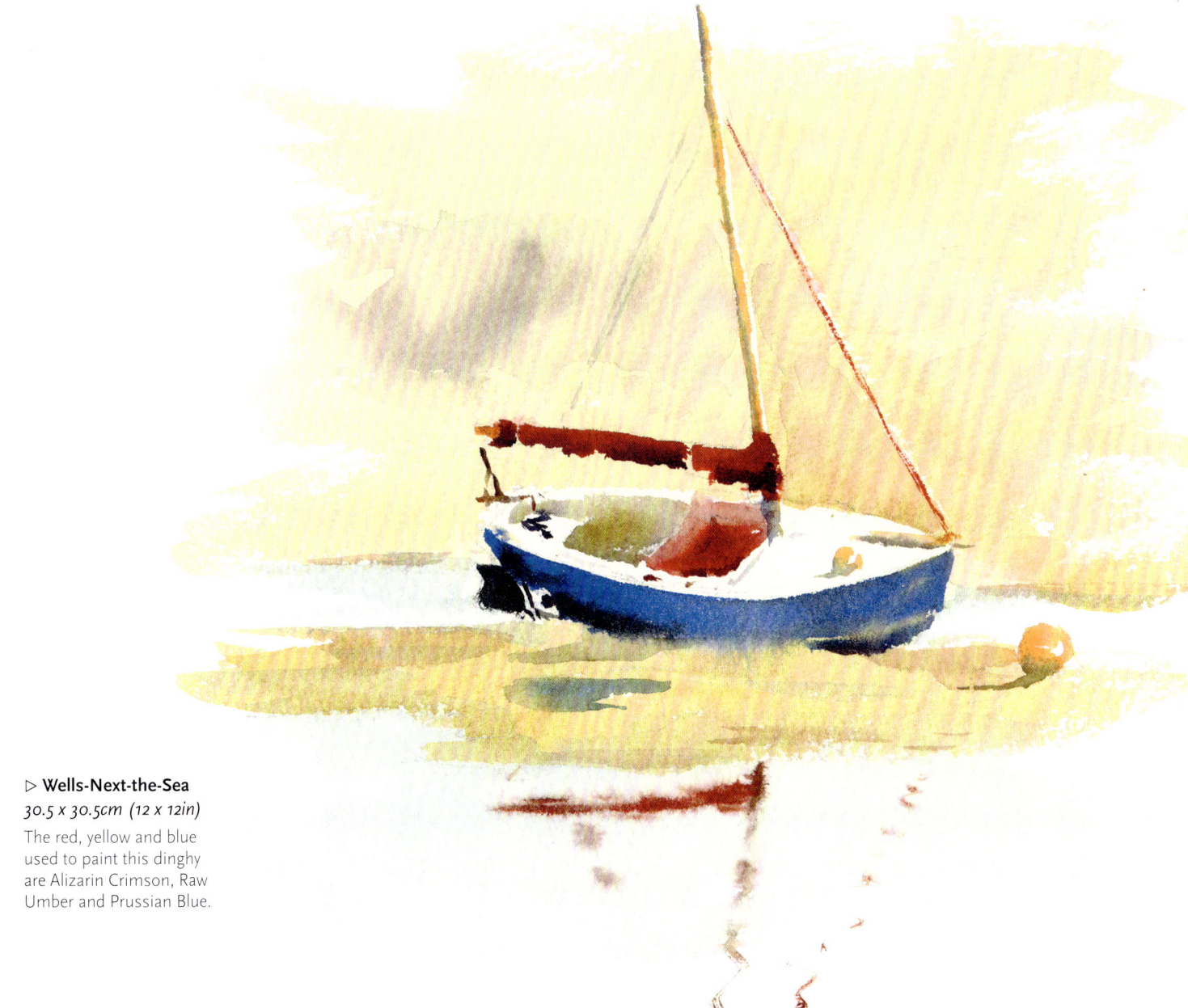

▷ **Wells-Next-the-Sea**
30.5 x 30.5cm (12 x 12in)
The red, yellow and blue
used to paint this dinghy
are Alizarin Crimson, Raw
Umber and Prussian Blue.

Secondary colours

By mixing pairs of primary colours together you will make three more colours: these are called secondary colours. Red and yellow make orange, blue and yellow make green, and blue and red make violet.

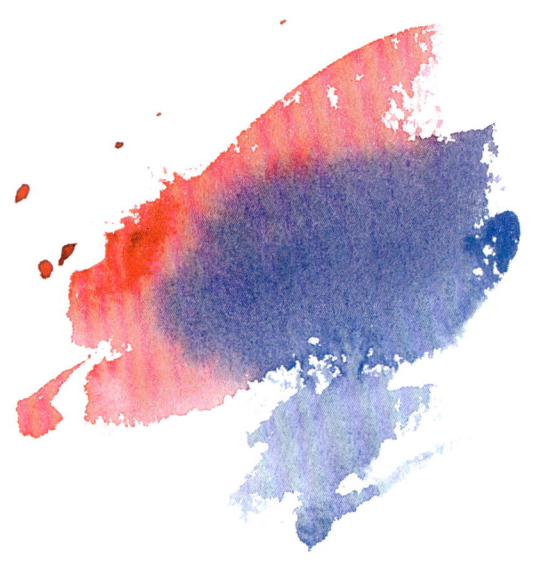

△ Cobalt Blue and Permanent Rose make violet; here the colour is made by mixing the two together on the paper.

△ Blue and yellow make green; here the green is made by layering Winsor Yellow over Winsor Blue.

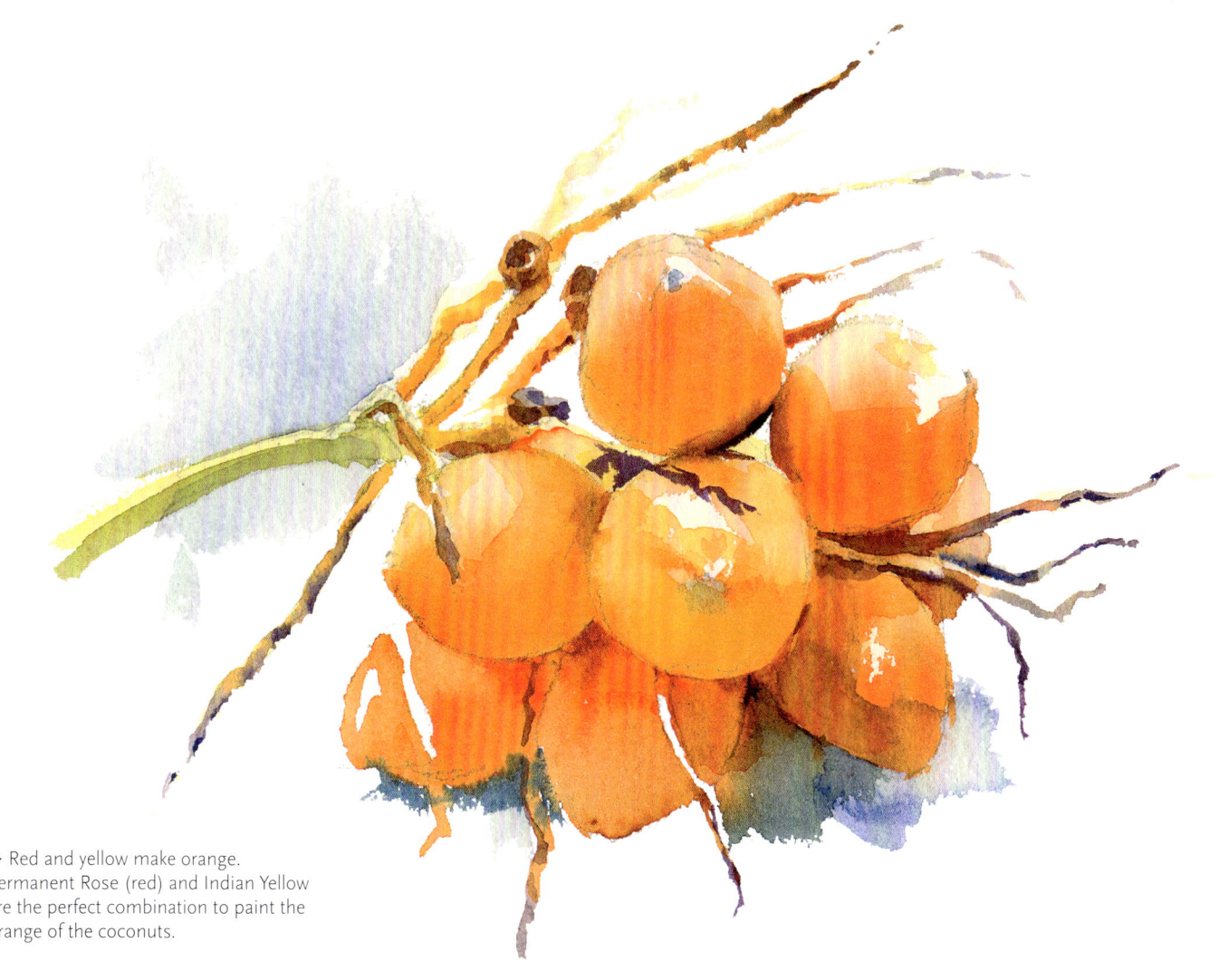

▷ Red and yellow make orange.
Permanent Rose (red) and Indian Yellow
are the perfect combination to paint the
orange of the coconuts.

Tertiary colours

When a primary colour (e.g. blue) is mixed with the secondary colour made from the other two primaries (e.g. orange, which is made from red and yellow), browns, greys and blacks result. These are called tertiary colours as they result from a third stage of mixing. Because watercolour paints come in a broad range of colours, mixing blacks, browns and greys can also be achieved by using ready-made secondary colours, such as Viridian (green) and Schmincke Violet. Some examples of two colour combinations are shown on this page.

Over the page, in the watercolour of an elephant, you will see how layers of yellow, blue and red combine and mix together to make all the colours required for the painting.

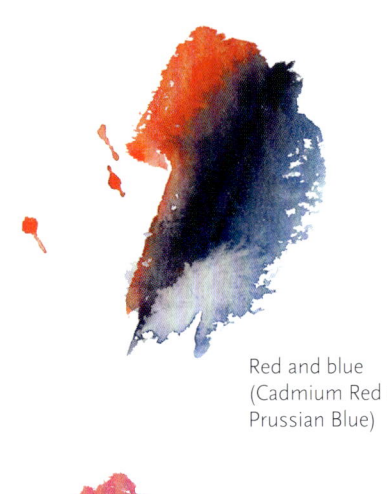

Red and blue
(Cadmium Red and
Prussian Blue)

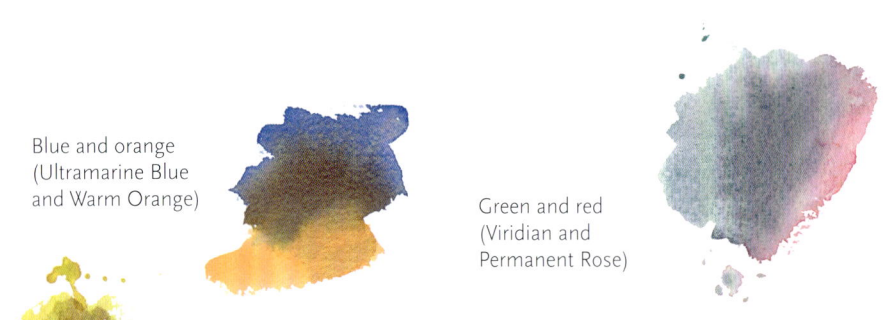

Blue and orange
(Ultramarine Blue
and Warm Orange)

Green and red
(Viridian and
Permanent Rose)

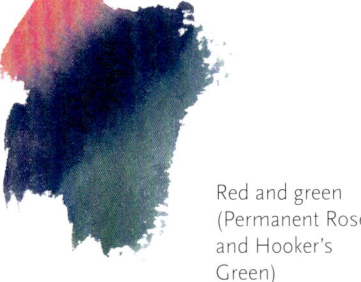

Red and green
(Permanent Rose
and Hooker's
Green)

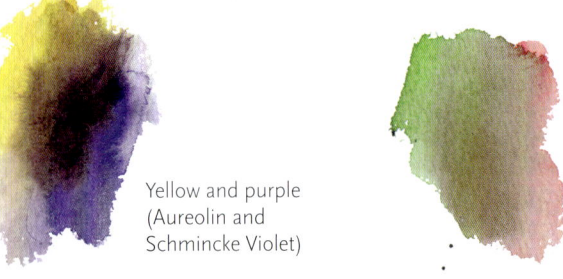

Yellow and purple
(Aureolin and
Schmincke Violet)

Green and red
(Permanent Sap Green
and Alizarin Crimson)

▷ **The Sun Gets Up With Great Earliness**
20 x 28cm (8 x 11in)

The three colours used to make the greys in the sky and the black silhouettes in this dawn sketch on the river are Aureolin (yellow), Ultramarine Blue and Burnt Sienna (a red-brown).

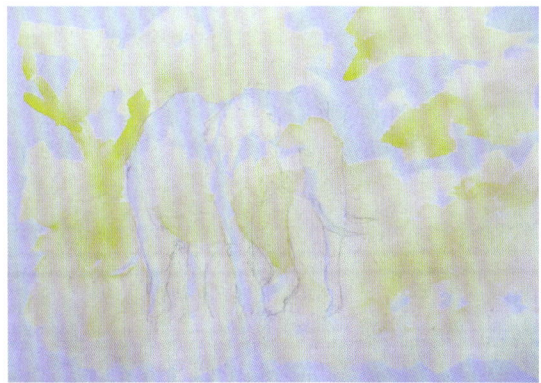

Demonstration stage 1: The first wash is the yellow of Aureolin, which goes under any colour that has yellow in it, i.e. any greens, oranges, browns and greys.

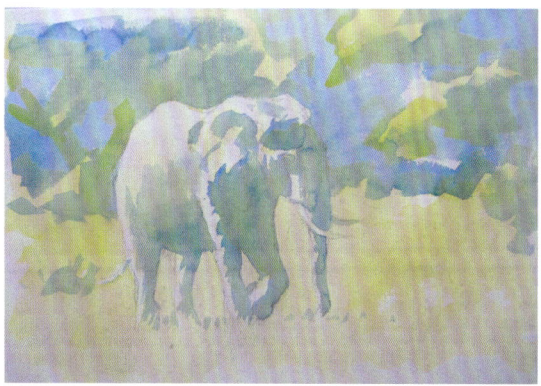

Stage 2: Prussian Blue follows, painting any area that has blue in it, such as the sky and the shadows and the green of the trees.

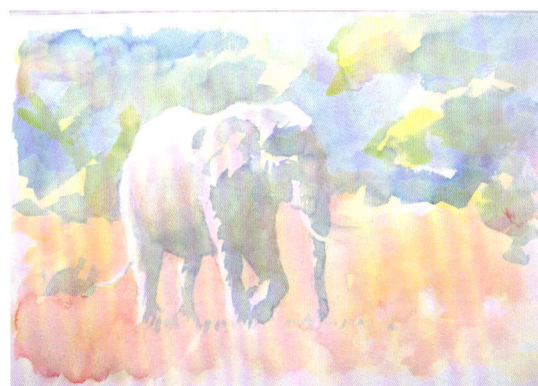

Stage 3: Now it's the turn of the red. Alizarin Crimson is diluted to a pale pink and goes over the yellow of the grass to turn it to orange and over the shadows on the elephant to turn them to grey.

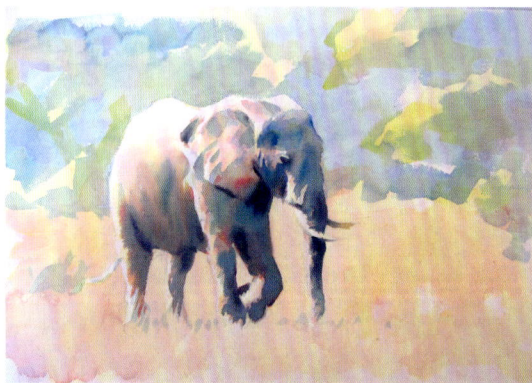

Stage 4: The same three colours are now used either individually or mixed together to darken the tones of the elephant and ...

▷ ... then in the trees to make the dark browns of the branches. So you see – with just three colours you can make a full range of colours and tones.

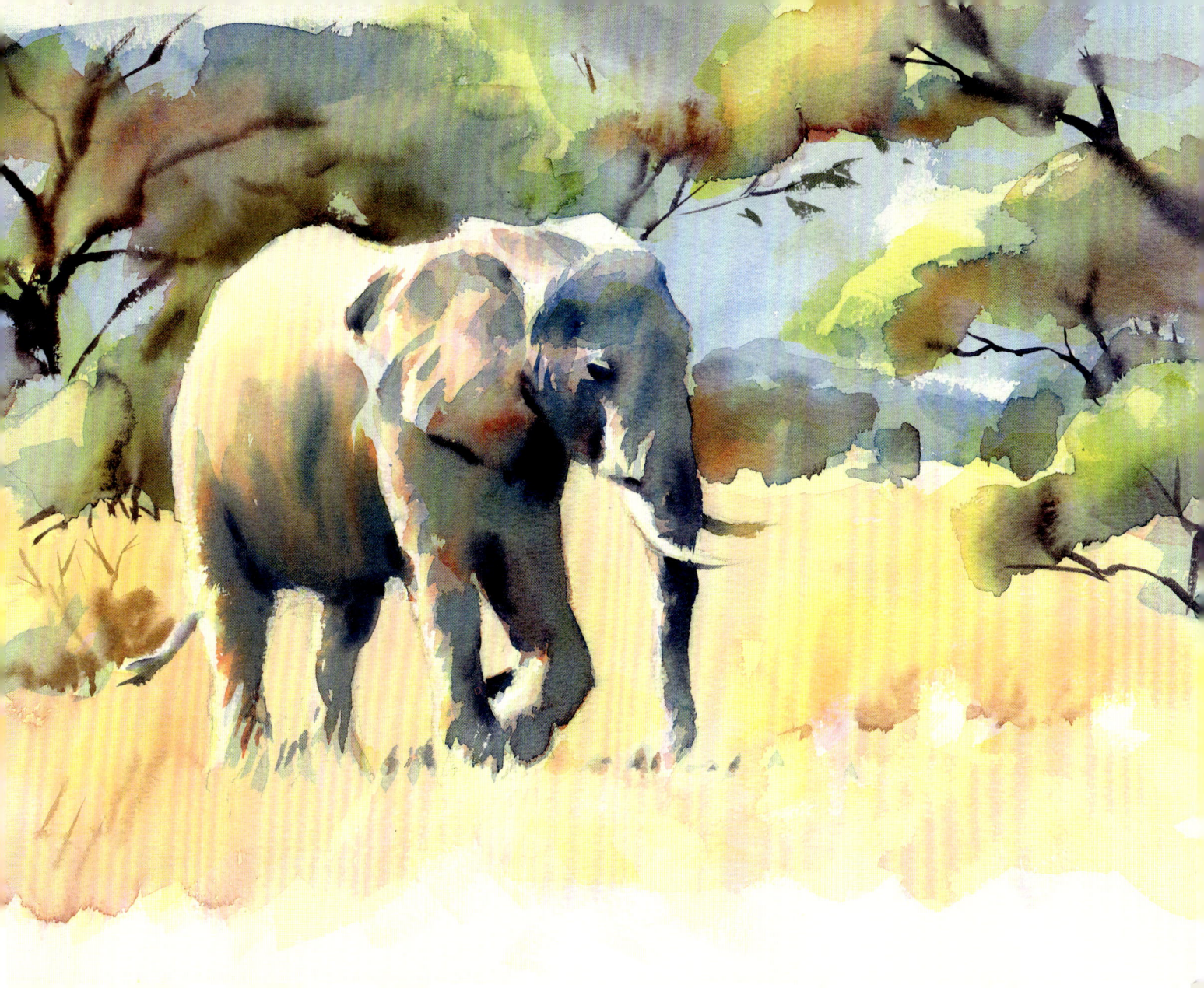

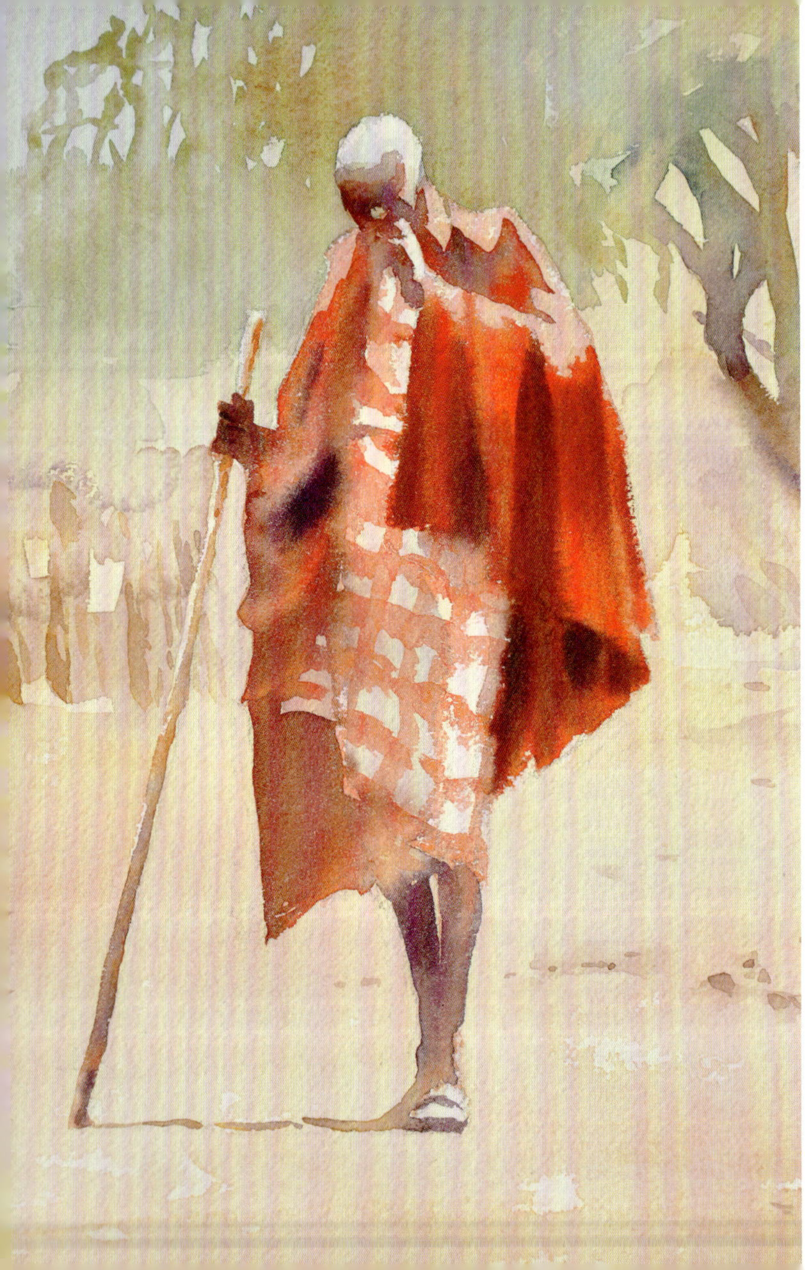

Transparency

The transparent, thin films of paint in watercolour are called tints and glazes. Because they are transparent, they can be overlapped to make an unlimited number of colours and shades. When diluted, all the colours are transparent, but in their concentrated form, some pigments are less transparent than others and some are actually opaque, providing a denser covering.

In a full palette you would need colours of all types, but, as it is often the misuse of opaque colours that causes muddy mixtures, to start with I suggest you use mainly transparent colours, and add opaques for punches of bright or lighter colour instead of mixing with them.

◁ **Belonging**
30.5 x 25.5cm (12 x 10in)
The reds used to paint the cloak and sarong of this Maasai chief are fully transparent pigments: Quinacridone Red with Brown Madder for the deep folds and shadows.

The fabric of the colours

Watercolour is made of the finely ground grains of real pigments; some of these are from the earth, some from carbon and some from metals and other minerals. The heavy metal cadmium gives us an opaque red, which is essential for its brilliant hue.

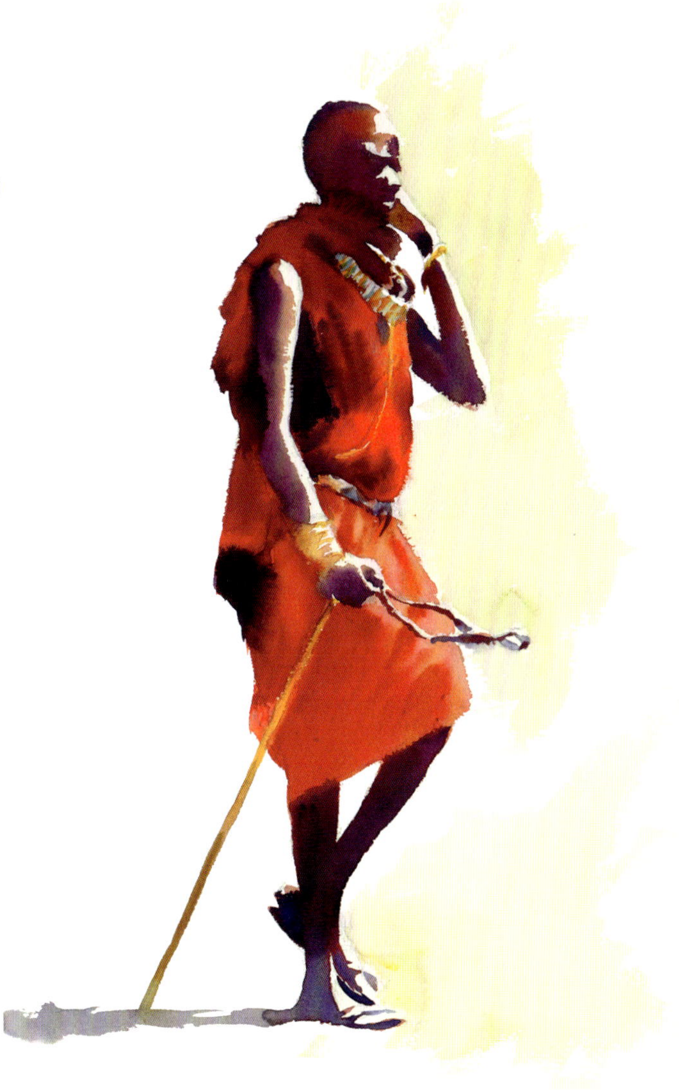

▷ Cadmium Red is used for the robe of this Maasai warrior – it is an opaque colour and delivers a bold, brilliant, dense red. You can see the difference compared to the transparent red opposite.

Colours have temperature

It may seem strange, but colours have temperature. Red is considered warm and blue is cold. The many variations in each hue also veer either to red or blue, giving us warm or cool versions of each colour. Artists call this the temperature bias and use it to alter the mood of a painting. Warm colours create a cheerful, upbeat mood; cool colours are more subtle and serious. Reds also jump forward, while blues recede.

In these two paintings, you can see how different the appearance of a warm blue and yellow appear as compared with a cool blue and yellow.

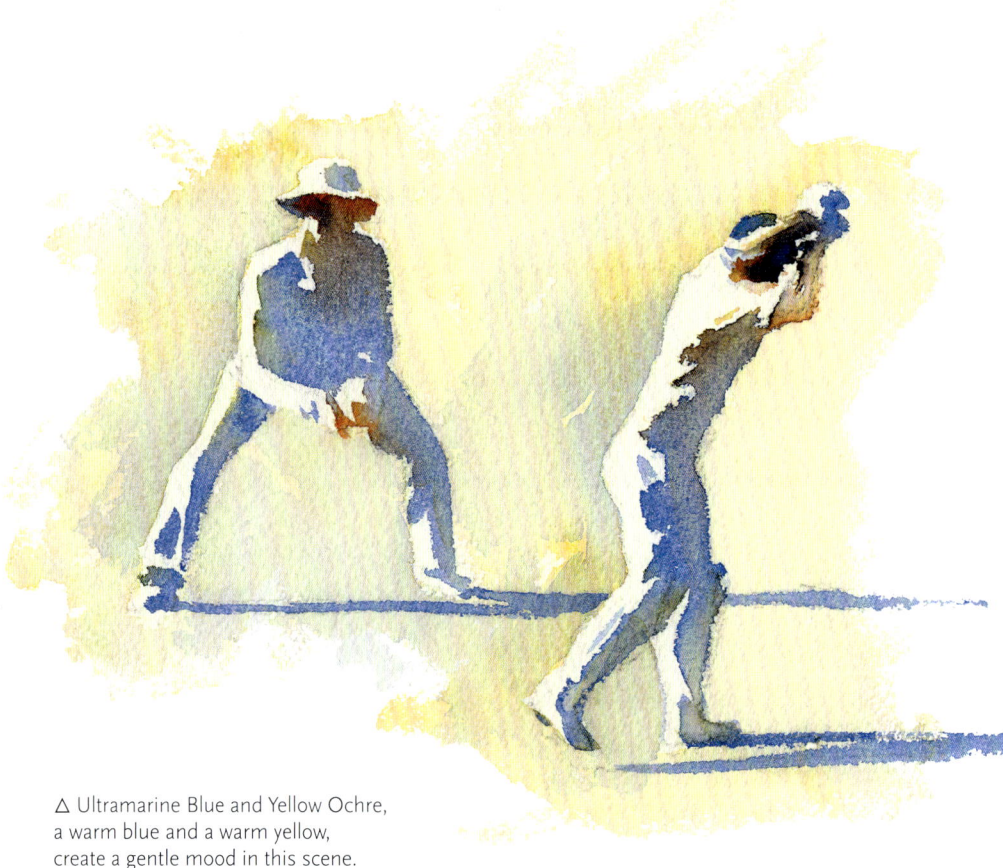

△ Ultramarine Blue and Yellow Ochre, a warm blue and a warm yellow, create a gentle mood in this scene.

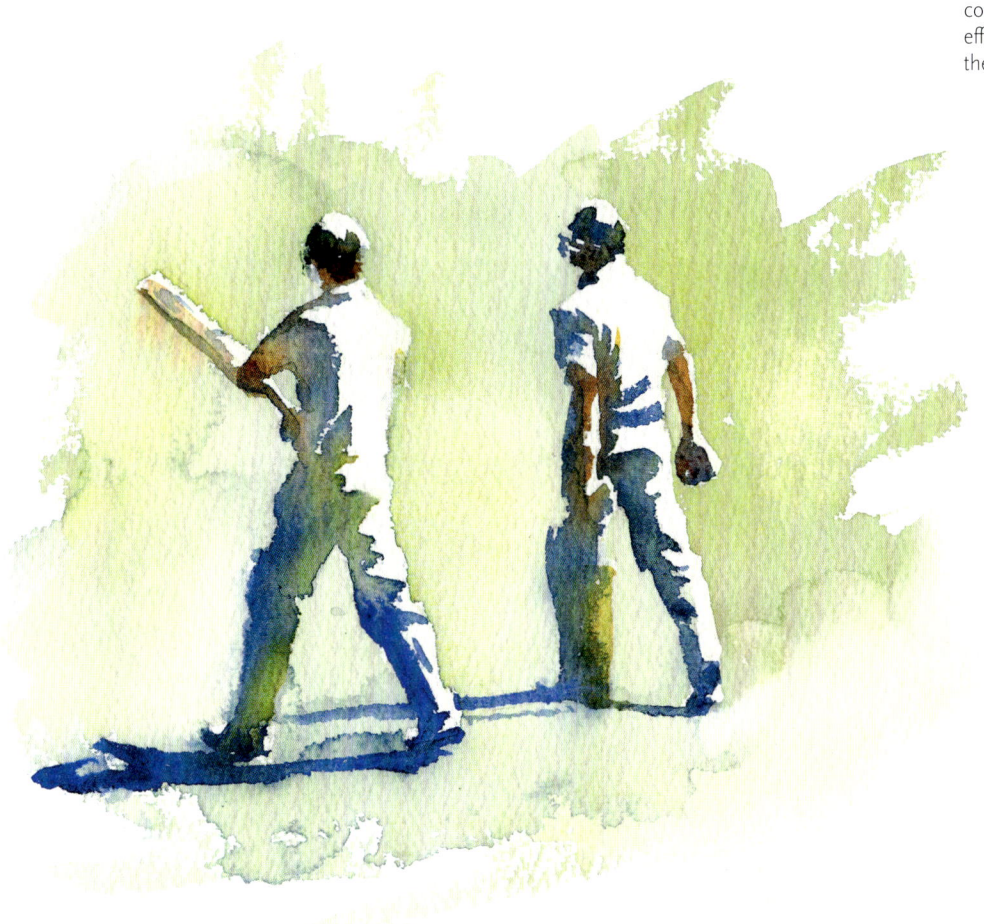

◁ Prussian Blue and Aureolin are the cool blue and cool yellow used here. The effect is brighter but more 'severe' than the warmer image shown opposite.

Your first set of colours

When you choose a set of colours, ideally you want to include both a warm and a cool version of each of the three primaries – red, yellow and blue – and then you can indeed mix all the colours in an infinite number of ways. This collection of 11 colours is a great starter set.

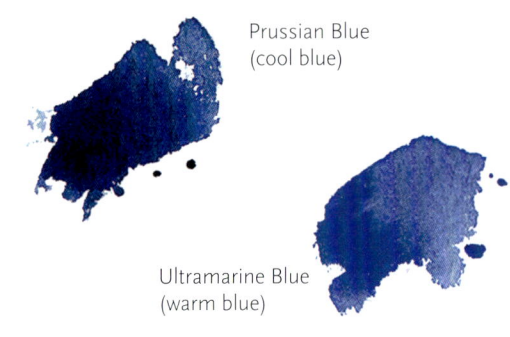

Prussian Blue
(cool blue)

Ultramarine Blue
(warm blue)

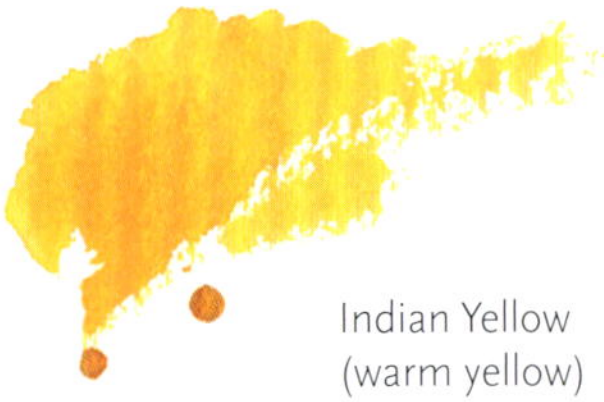

Indian Yellow
(warm yellow)

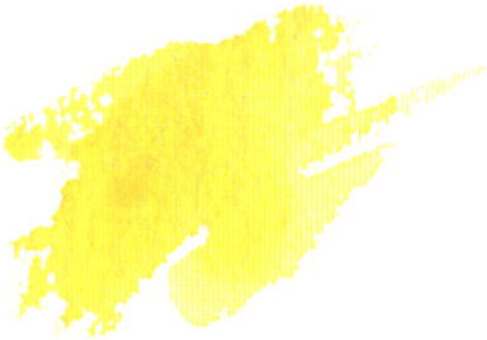

Aureolin (cool
yellow)

Yellow Ochre

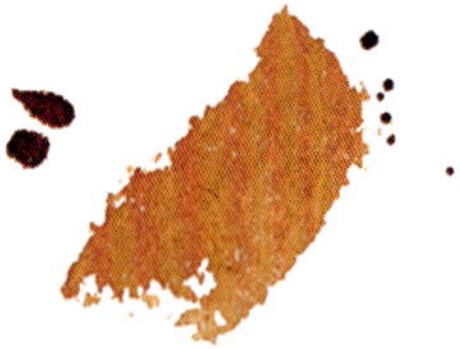

Burnt Sienna

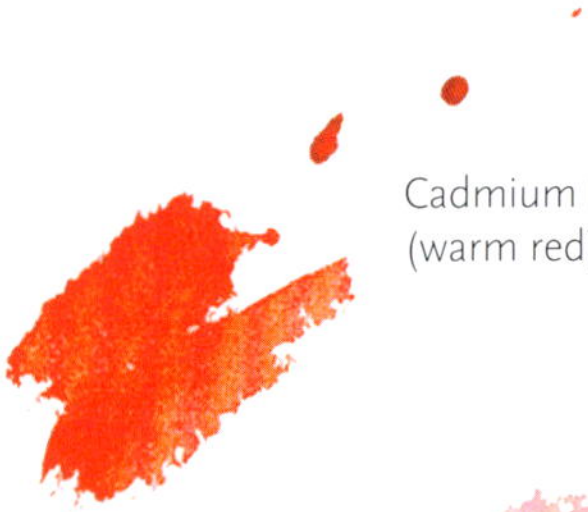

Cadmium Red
(warm red)

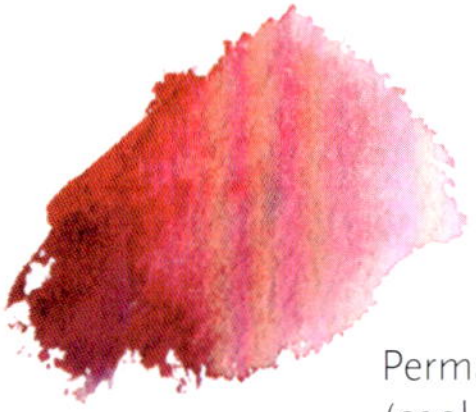

Permanent Rose
(cool red)

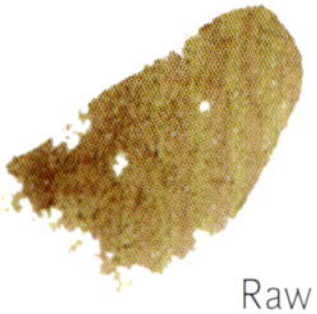

Raw Umber

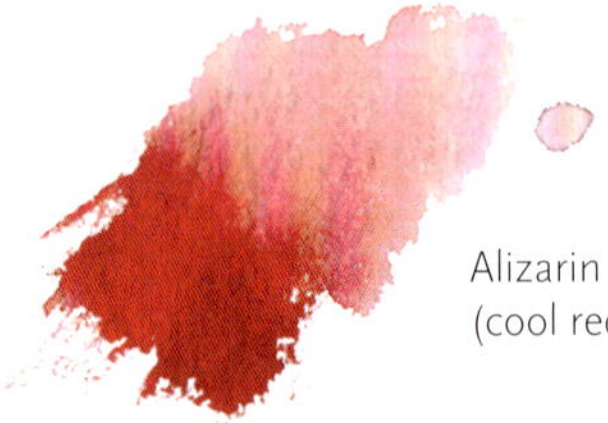

Alizarin Crimson
(cool red)

Burnt Umber

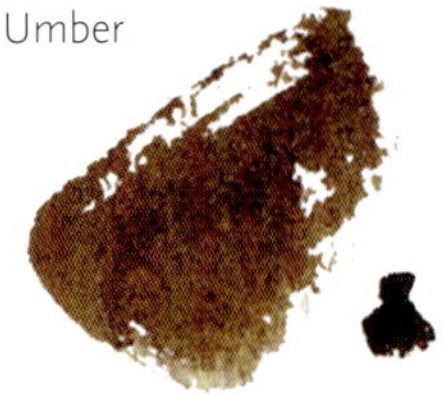

▷ **On the Sunny Side of the Street**
41 x 51cm (16 x 20in)
Yellow Ochre, Permanent Rose, Ultramarine Blue and Cadmium Red, with a dash of Prussian Blue and Aureolin for the bright greens.

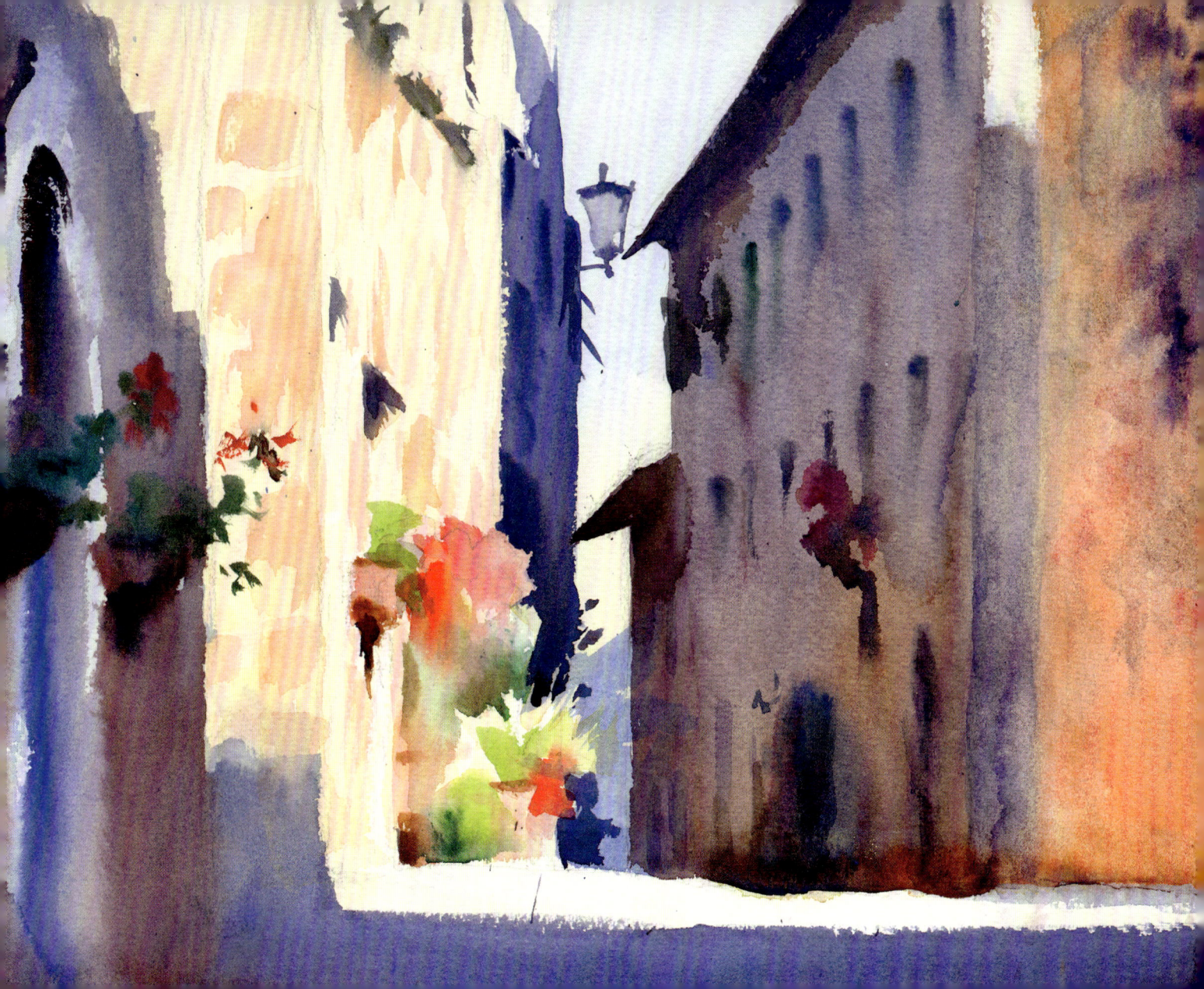

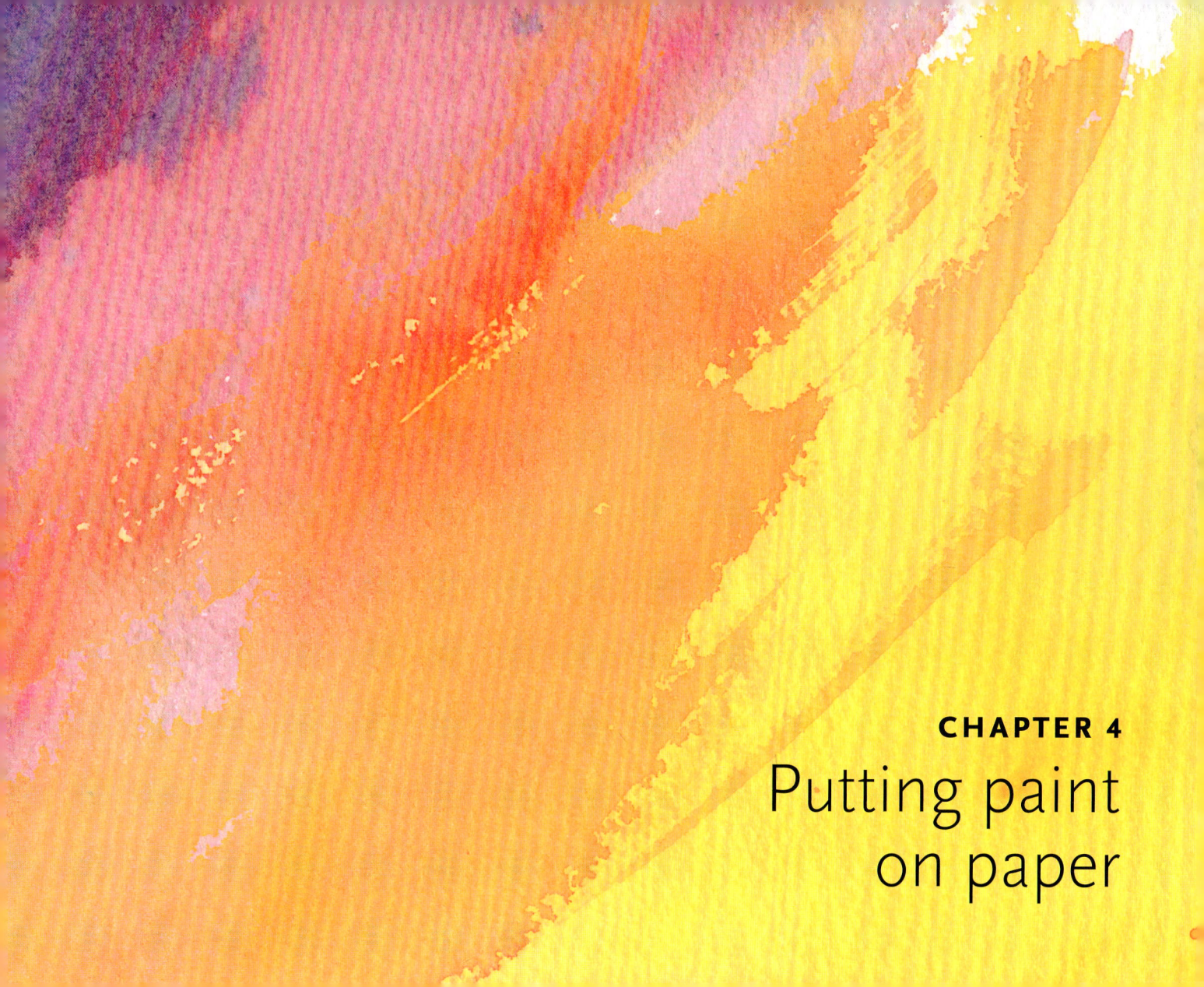

CHAPTER 4

Putting paint
on paper

Mixing on a palette

The idea of mixing paint on a palette is to get it to the right colour, consistency and quantity before loading the brush for the strokes ahead.

If you are using tubes of paint, squeeze just a little on to the palette. Don't put it in the middle, as this is where you will be mixing; place it at the edge or up the slope of the palette. Dip your brush in the water pot and fully load it with water, then tap off the excess on the side of the pot. Touch the tip of the brush into the edge of the squeezed-out paint to pick up a small amount of pigment and then mix it on the palette in a circular motion to create an even consistency.

If you are using watercolour pans, work the wet brush on the dry pan until it yields sufficient colour, then bring it on to the palette to mix evenly.

▷ Look carefully at these Christmas baubles to see how the colour on each has been diluted to make the lighter areas, and deepened to paint the shaded areas. Differing amounts of water are needed to reach each consistency.

The right amount of water

The more water you use, the more dilute the paint will become. Avoid using too much – if it all runs into the gutter of the palette, instead of a sparkling glaze you will only have tinted water!

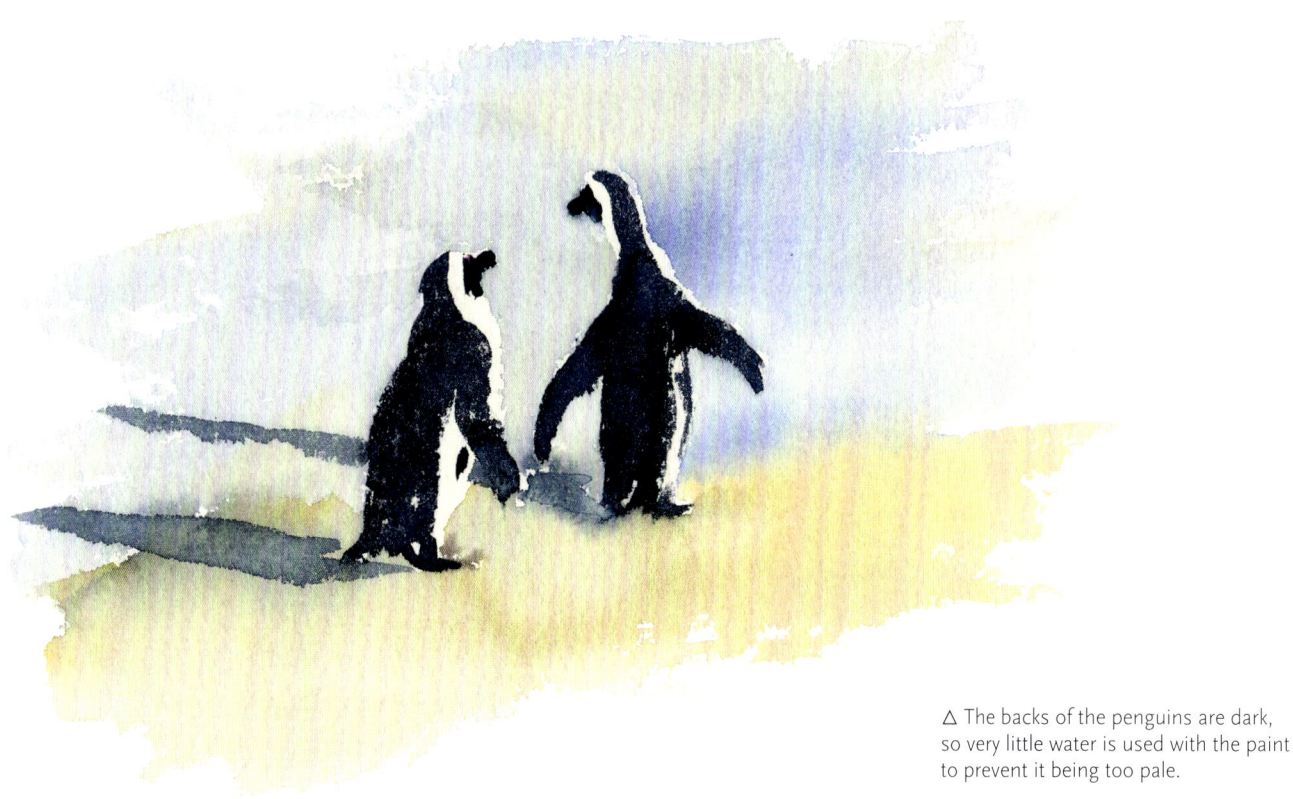

△ The backs of the penguins are dark, so very little water is used with the paint to prevent it being too pale.

The brushmarks

Watercolours are painted with brushstrokes that join up, overlap and stand alone. The secret is to use as few strokes as possible to give the most information. Individual brush strokes, shown right, join to make the hockey players below. Once again, less is more. Learning to use the brush with dexterity will bring early success to your paintings.

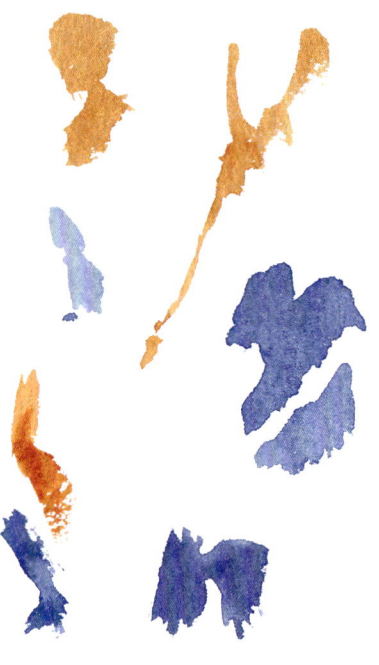

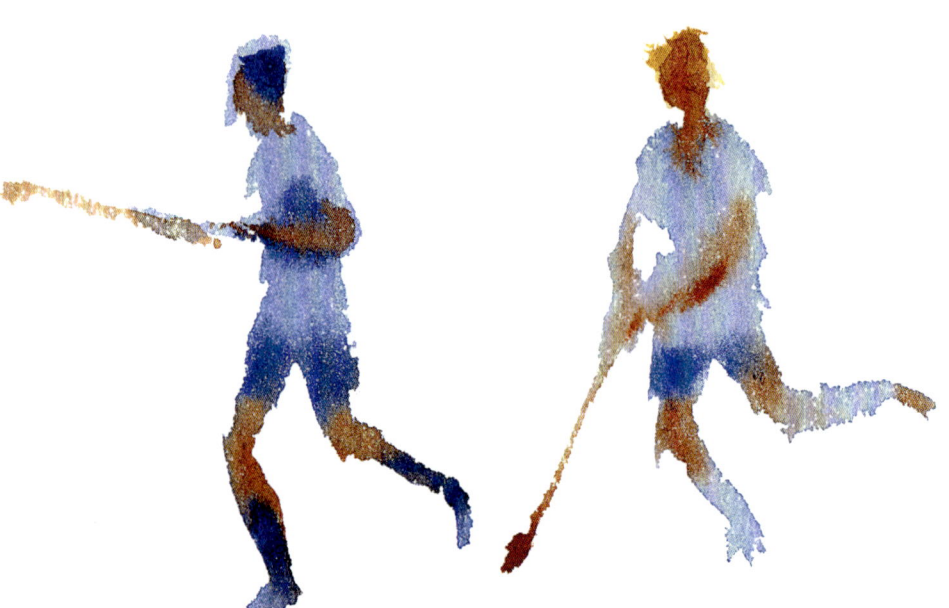

▷ **Lovely Weather for Ducks**
20 x 28cm (8 x 11in)

The shapes of the ducks are painted with quite precise brushstrokes; the ripples, on the other hand, are freely applied, along with the broad washes that tint the water.

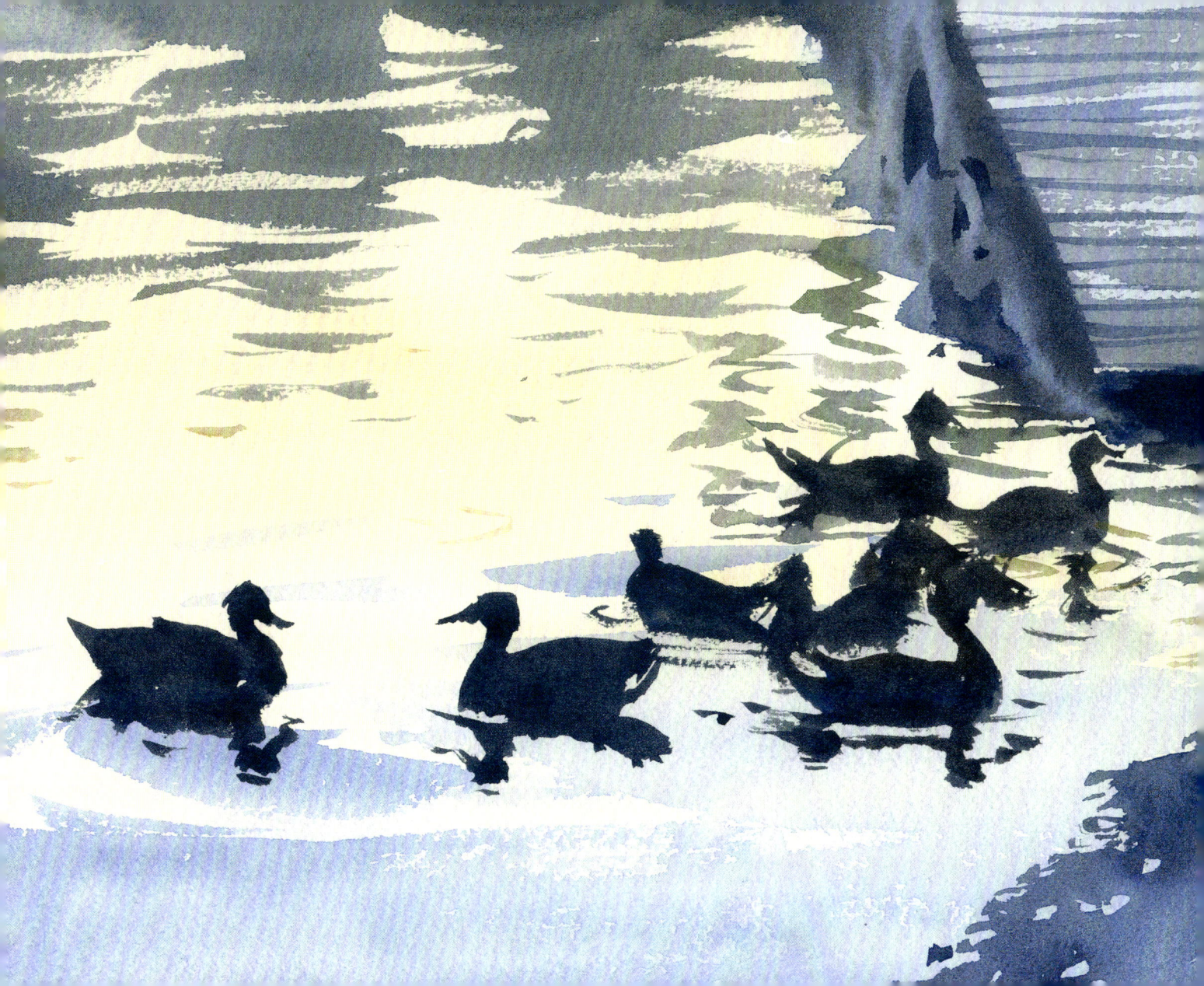

Using the brush

The tip and body of the round natural hair brush enable you to make brushmarks in any number of shapes and sizes. Intricate shapes, fine details and broad patches can all be made with a loaded brush. Hold the handle of the brush with your thumb and forefingers around the fattest part. In this position, you will get free but controlled movement at the brush head. Use the tip to make fine marks and lines, and press down the body of the brush to make broader marks. Get used to rolling the brush handle between your fingertips so you can twist and turn the brush to make marks for specific shapes.

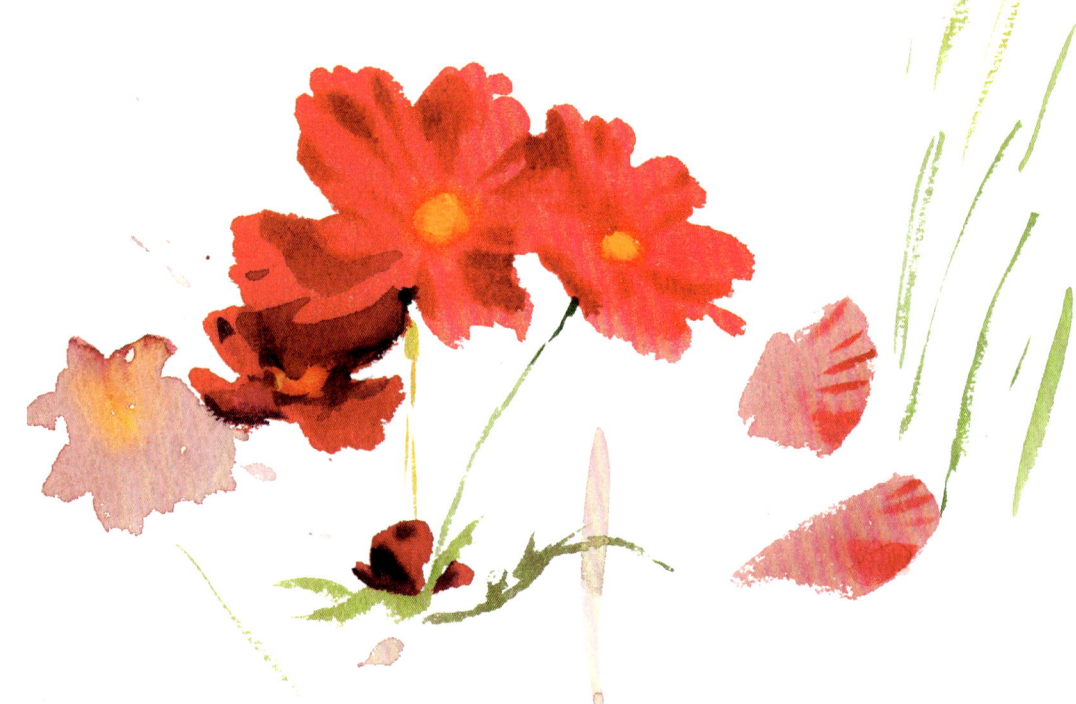

▷ Pressing the brush down releases more paint to make the broad petal shapes. Using just the tip draws the narrow lines. Dabbing in touches of yellow paint with the tip of the brush indicates the stamens.

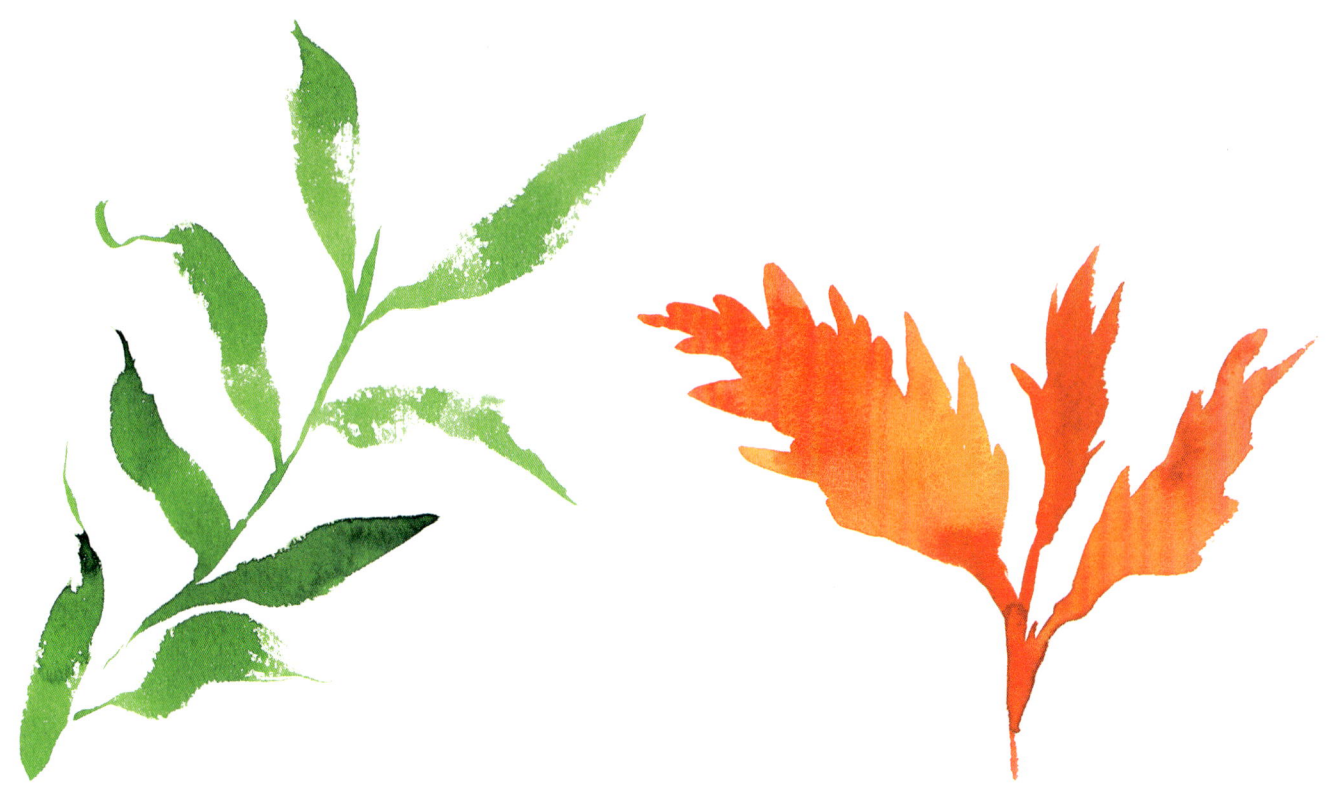

△ To make these leaf shapes, bring the tip of the brush to a point by rolling it in the palette; hold the brush at an angle to the paper as you make the stroke – press down to release more paint in the middle of the leaf, twist it again to bring it back to a point, and lift off at the end of the leaf.

△ To make more complex shapes like these red leaves, the brushstrokes are joined up: the wet paint from each stroke blends together to make a seamless shape.

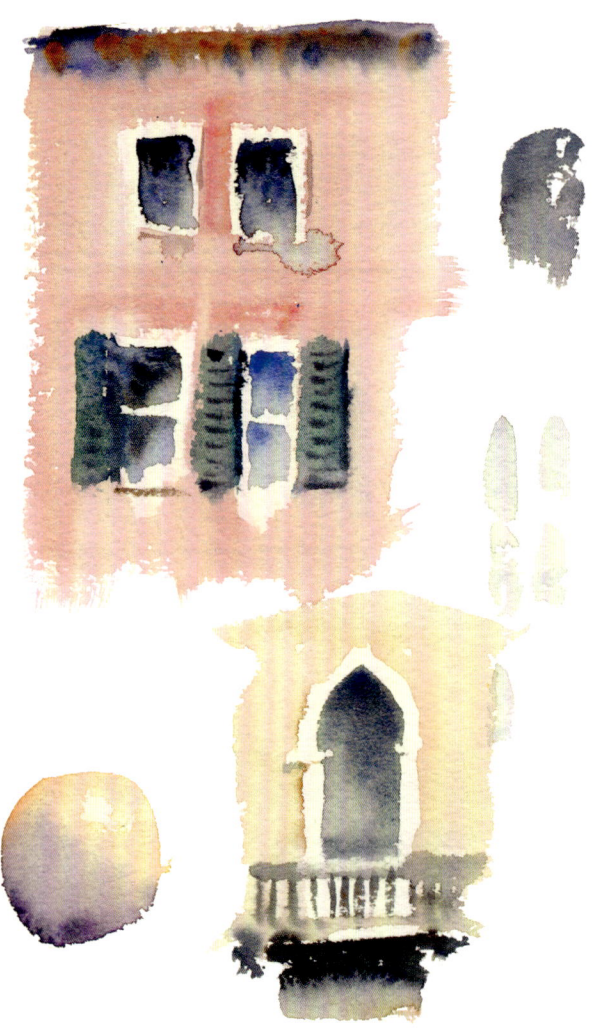

Try the flat brush too

The flat natural hair brush is a versatile tool that allows for panels of colour, broad strokes and also narrow lines. You can lay washes and make marks of almost any shape and size. All the marks on this page are made with a 20mm (¾in) flat brush.

▷ **Dawn Rush Hour on the Grand Canal**
35.5 x 51cm (14 x 20in)
This painting of Venice is painted entirely with a flat brush. The large brush head is great for keeping your approach loose and bold.

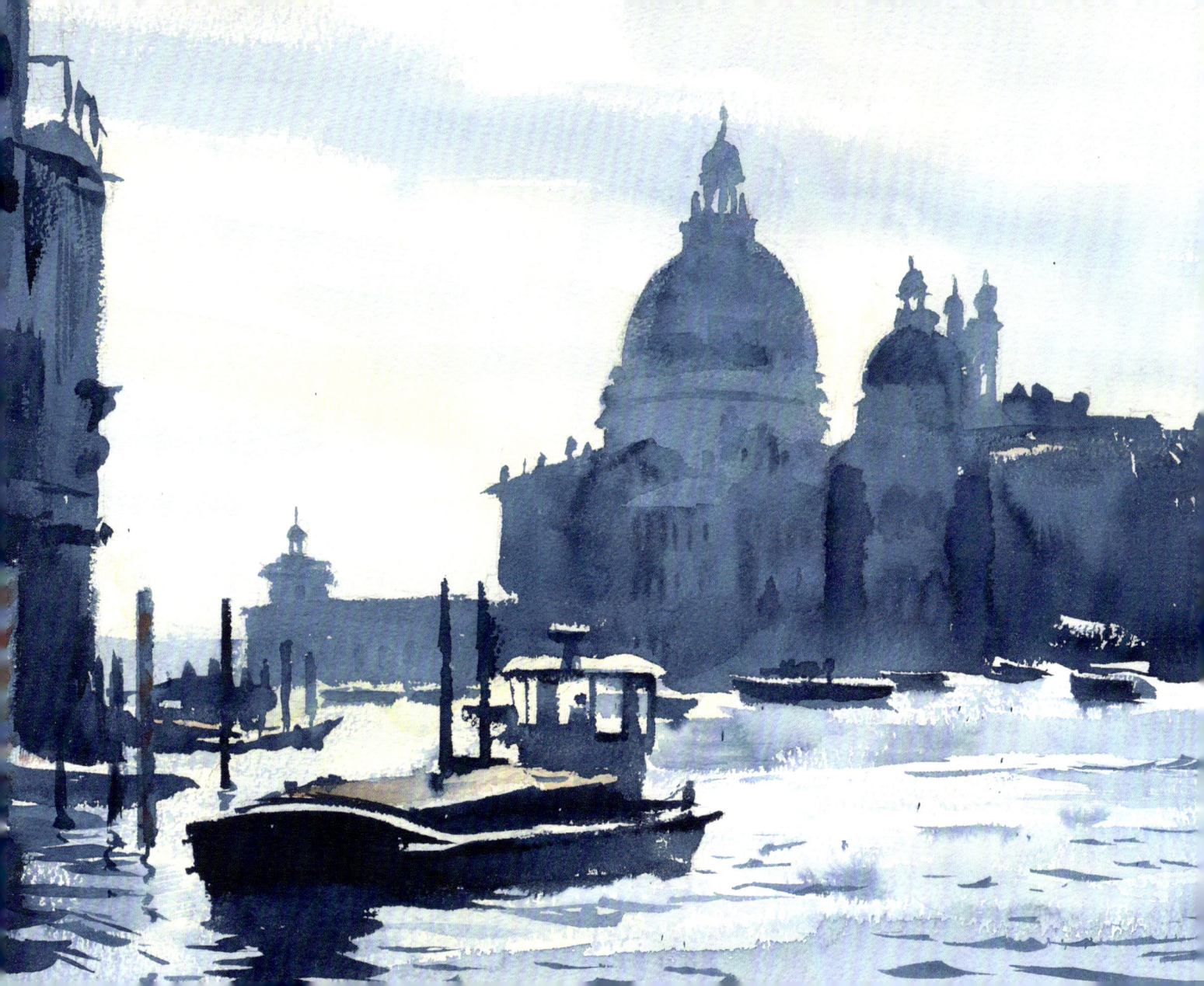

Painting techniques

There are three main techniques for applying paint to paper in watercolour and each has a rather obvious name: wet on dry, wet into wet, and dry-brushing. The next few pages explain these techniques and also show you how to make seamless washes for large areas of colour such as skies.

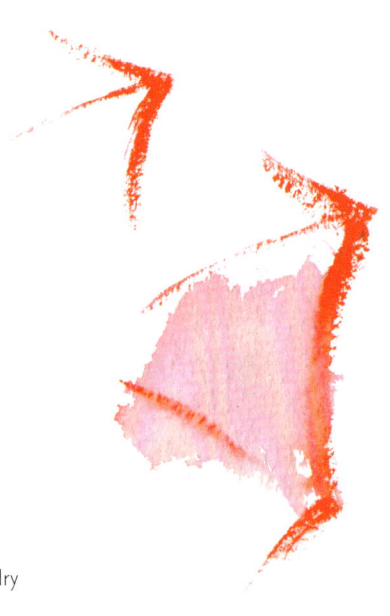

▷ **Lady in Red**
18 x 8cm (7 x 3in)
The border and fine lines on the umbrella are added into the wet wash with dry brushstrokes.

▷ ▷ **Passionate About Pink**
28 x 35.5cm (11 x 14in)
Two of the main techniques used in watercolour can be clearly seen here in the petals of the bougainvillea: wet-on-dry layering and wet-into-wet blending.

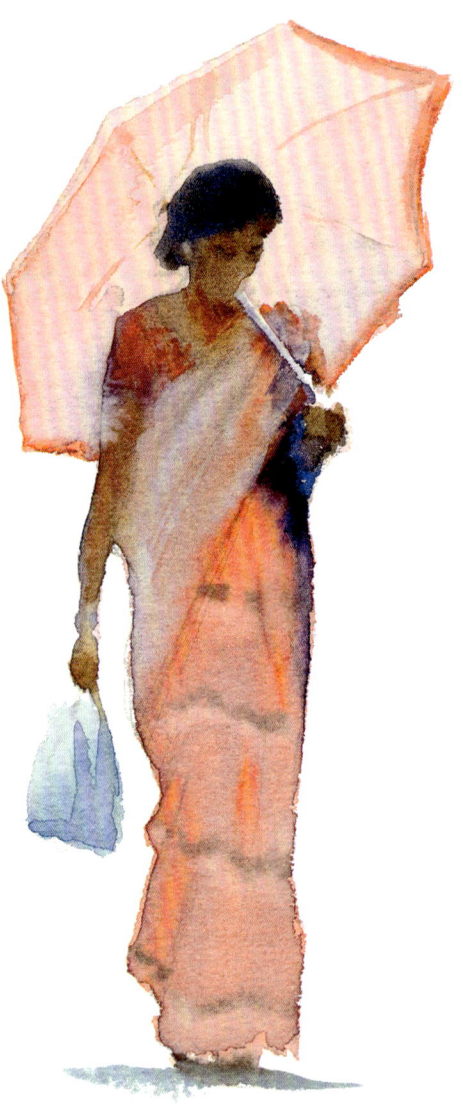

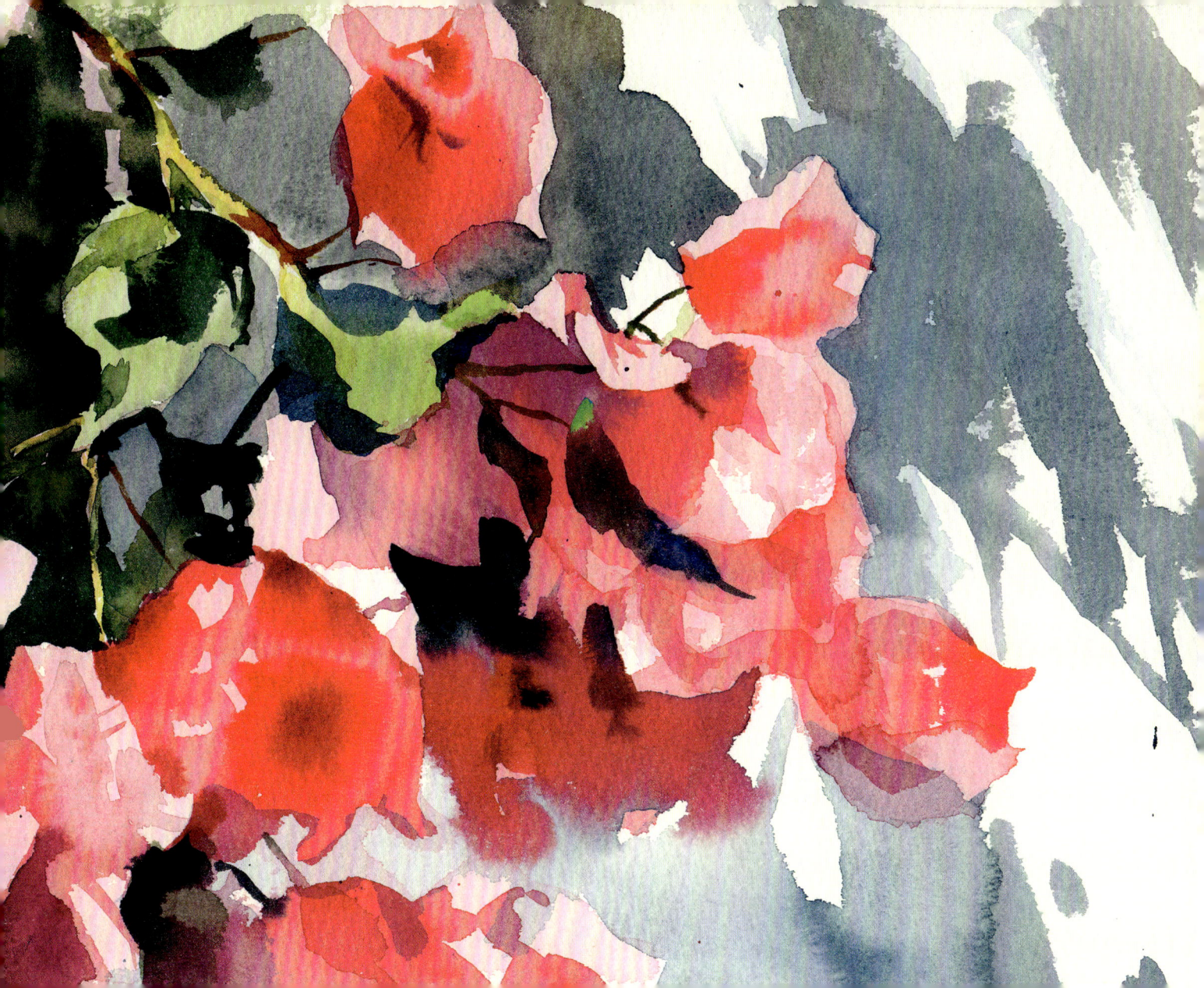

Wet on dry

In this technique, the wet paint is applied to dry paper, giving a crisp edge to the laid brushstroke. When dry, subsequent layers of transparent colour can be added on top in a series of overlapping tints and glazes. Because watercolour is a transparent medium, this layering of colours creates a whole variety of new colours and tones from just a few pigments.

To avoid disturbing the drying particles of pigment underneath, each layer of paint must be allowed to dry completely before the next is added.

◁ The transparent tint of Ultramarine Blue over the pink of Permanent Rose makes a charming violet; laying Indian Yellow over the same pink makes a vibrant, translucent orange.

▷ **Dallas Skyline**
28 x 35.5cm (11 x 14in)
Working wet on dry is ideal for suggesting angular forms such as the skyscrapers in this city, as it clearly defines the edges to the washes and brushstrokes.

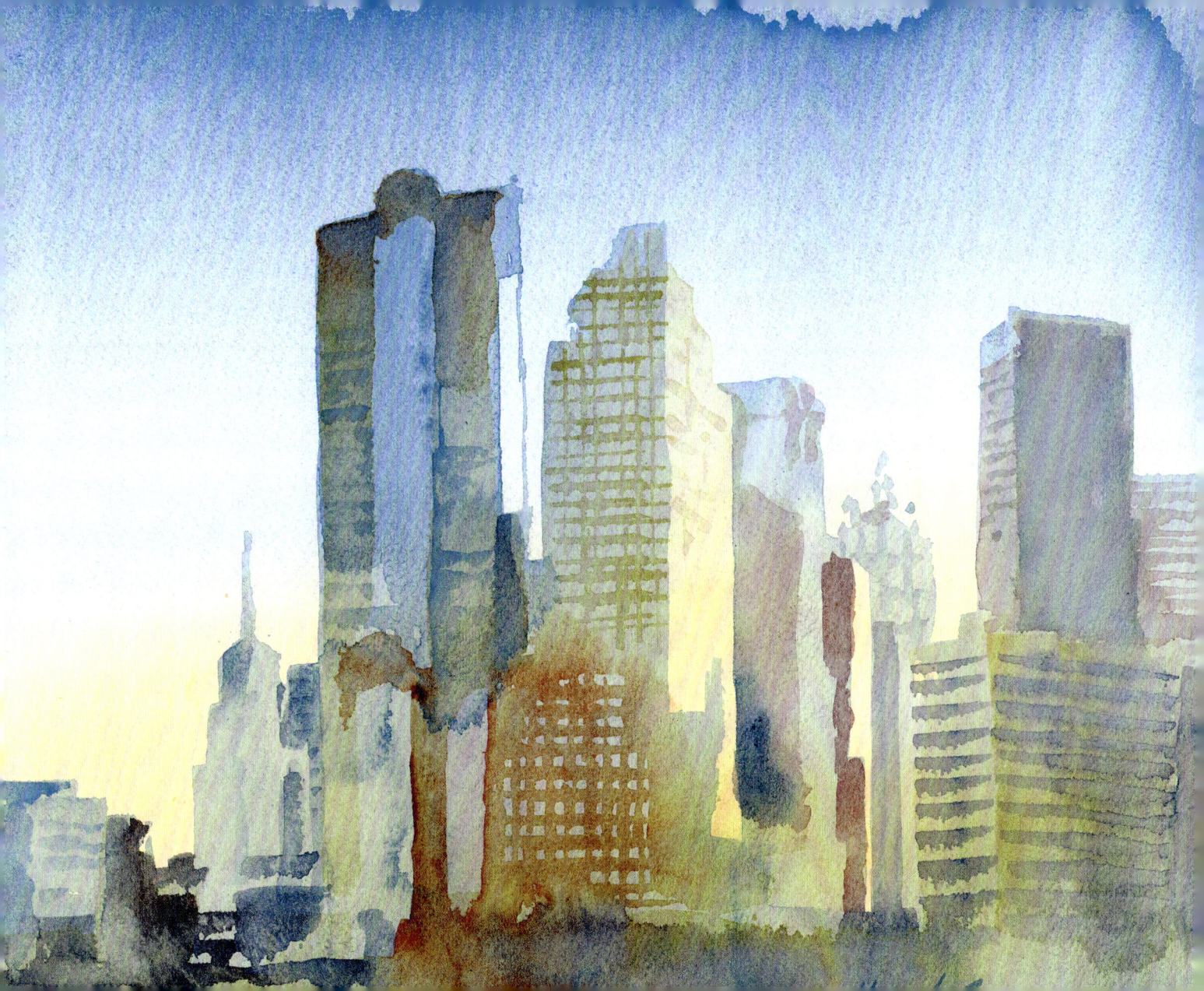

Mixing by layering

The colours created by layering vary according to the order in which the colours are laid. Even from the same two colours, the result will differ depending on which colour is put down first. Since each mix is unlikely to be exactly the same as the one before, these differing tones add to the endless variety you can achieve.

Layering is used frequently in watercolour landscapes. The sky is painted first and is often extended under the foreground features to provide an undertone, which encourages harmony in the painting and enhances the mood. Sky washes must be allowed to dry if a crisp skyline is required.

▷ When colours are overlapped, the colour looks different depending on which colour is on top. On the left, Yellow Ochre is laid over Ultramarine Blue and on the right, Ultramarine Blue is laid over Yellow Ochre.

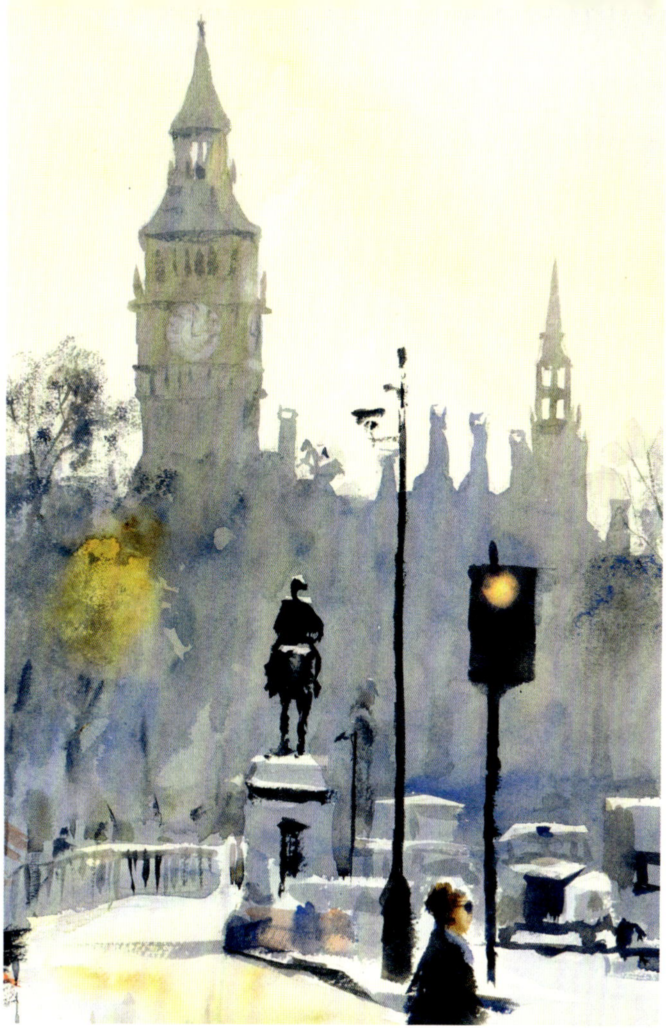

London Calling *56 x 38cm (22 x 15in)*

Stage 1: The pale sky wash of Yellow Ochre and Prussian Blue is painted as an undertone to the whole painting.

Stage 2: The London skyline is only added when the wash for the sky has dried. The yellow undertone shimmers through the grey mix laid on top.

Wet into wet

In this technique the paint is applied to paper that has been either dampened with clean water or is damp from a previous, still-wet wash or brushmark. Paint is introduced with a gentle stroke and spreads out into the damp surface or wash, giving soft edges to the brushmark and creating gradual blends where wet colours mingle with each other. Successive applications of paint must each be more concentrated than the last to take into account that there is already water on the paper from the previous wash. The drier the colour, the less it will spread.

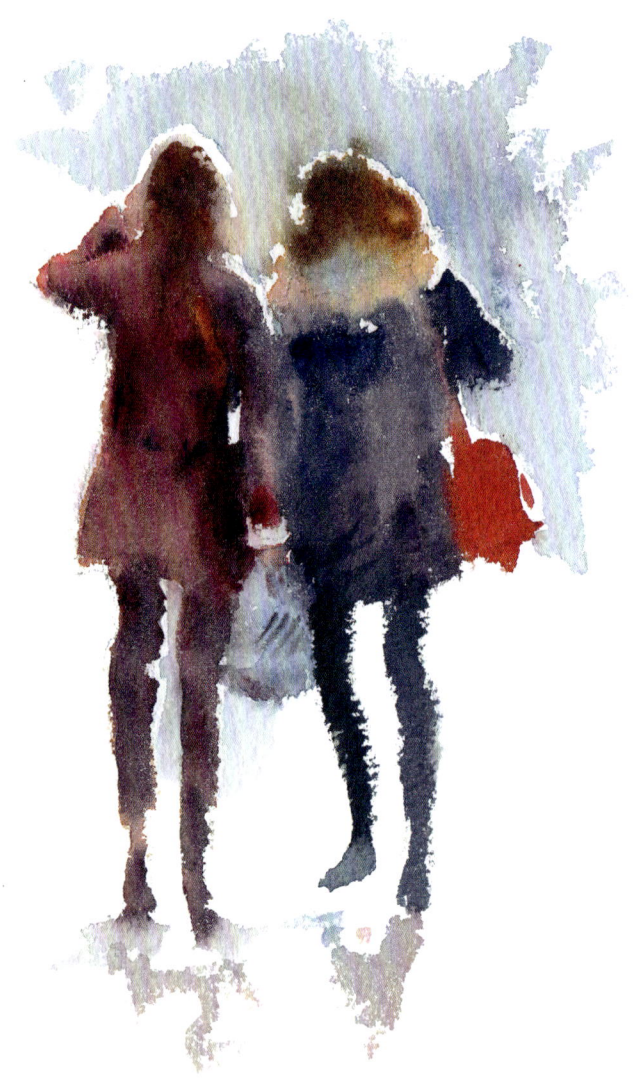

▷ **Retail Therapy**
25.5 x 15cm (10 x 6in)
The girls in this sketch would look rather static if their details were clearly defined. By adding the colours wet into wet, the pigments blend into one another and the watercolour appears more lively.

▷ ▷ **Spring is Sprung**
20 x 28cm (8 x 11in)
The yellows of the daffodils are gradually deepened by adding more concentrated (and therefore drier) colour, wet into wet. This technique is ideal for painting organic subjects such as flowers.

Mixing on paper / blending on paper

With a wet-into-wet technique a touch of ambiguity is created as the colours blend together on the paper more freely than when they are applied with wet-on-dry brushstrokes.

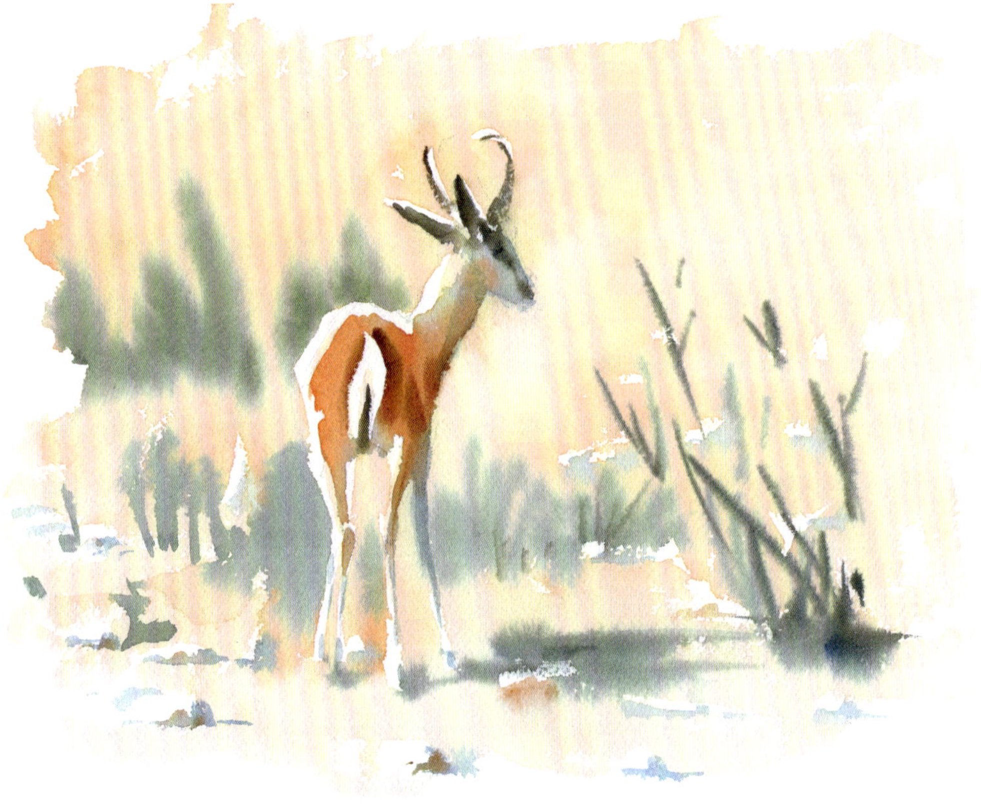

◁ Springbok
20 x 28cm (8 x 11in)

The scrubby foliage is dashed into the background with energetic brushstrokes while the wash is still wet, suggesting more interesting foliage than if it had been applied with regular wet-on-dry brushstrokes.

Backruns

If the mix of paint in the added brushstroke is too wet, the water will flow into the previous wash and cause a backrun, a mark that resembles a cauliflower! Watery paint that pools in a wash can be sucked up with the tip of the brush. However, don't be afraid of backruns: they are one of the lovely characteristics of watercolour and although they may happen by mistake, they can also be used purposefully.

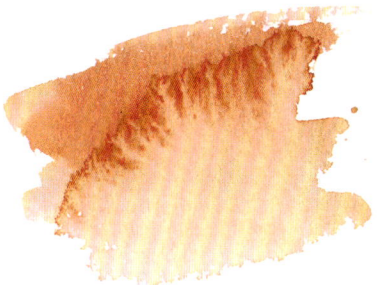

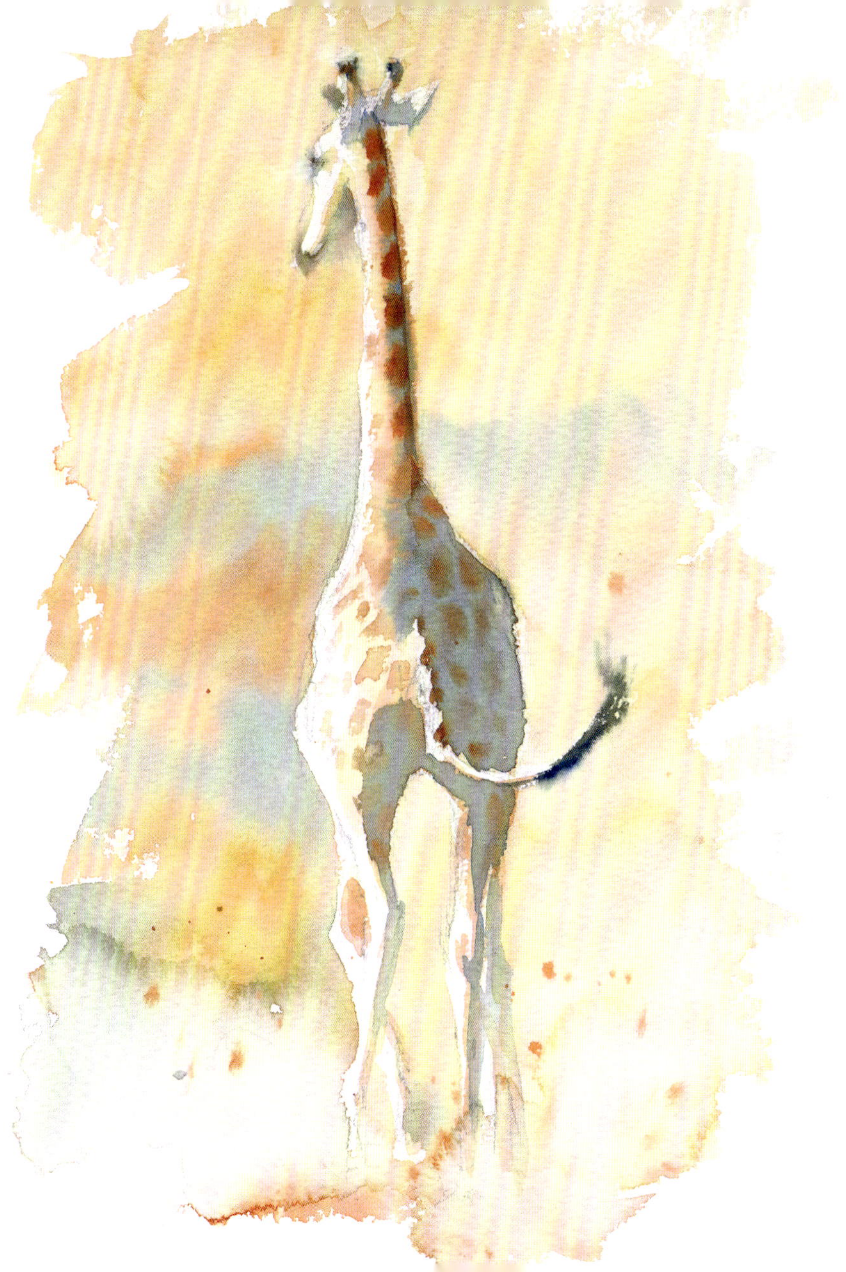

▷ **Giraffe**
38 x 28cm (15 x 11in)

An attractive suggestion of dust kicked up by the giraffe is created by engineering a backrun.

Working at speed

Adding colours wet into wet is a technique for speed as you do not have to wait for paint to dry. The rich dark tones of this elephant walking through the bush are quickly arrived at by painting wet into wet.

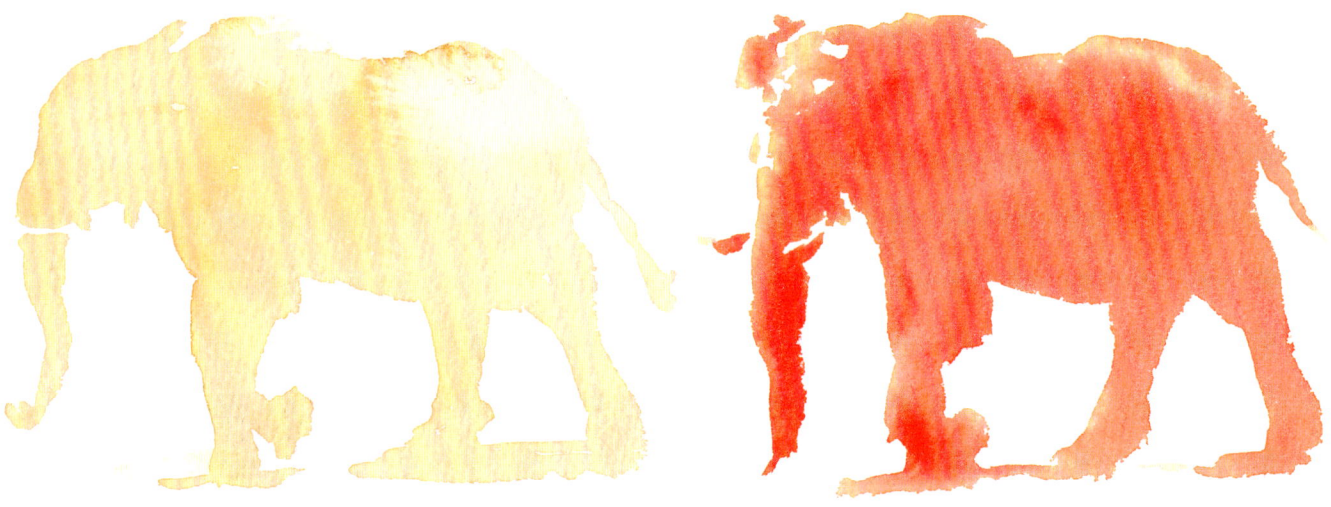

Stage 1: First the shape is painted with a pale wash of Quinacridone Gold.

Stage 2: Next Quinacridone Red is added, leaving the lighter topmost parts untouched.

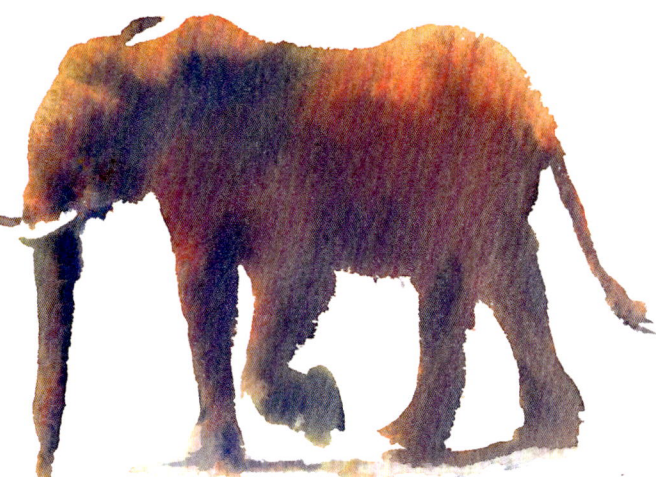

Stage 3: Then Indanthrene Blue is touched in, leaving more of the top-lit area untouched. The colours have blended together to make a warm purple-grey.

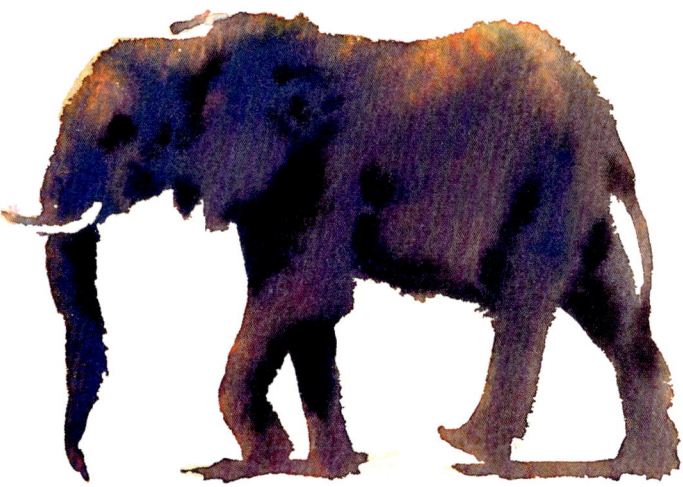

Stage 4: Lastly, a neat consistency of all three colours is mixed together in the palette to make a black, and touched in from the shadiest sides to give some definition.

Dry-brush

The neat paint applied by a dry brushstroke provides a certain energy, as the action of the stroke is visible. The paint is not always concentrated – sometimes the brush is just barely loaded with paint and brushed sideways across the surface of the paper to create an uneven wash or brushstroke.

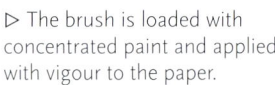
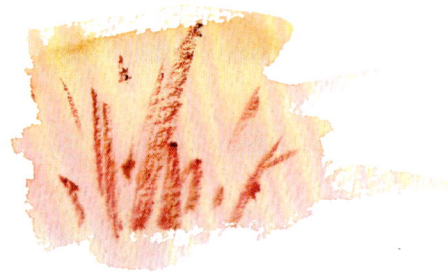

▷ The brush is loaded with concentrated paint and applied with vigour to the paper.

△ Dry-brush is more effective on a rough paper as the brush deposits paint on the bumps and skips over the troughs, leaving an attractive broken texture.

Splaying hairs

Pinching the hairs of the brush between your fingers and splaying them apart makes each hair deliver its load of paint in a single strand. You can use this method to make a series of fine lines. Hot-pressed or NOT paper is better for this technique.

▽ The patina of wood is created by splaying the hairs of the brush as it is brushed over a background wash.

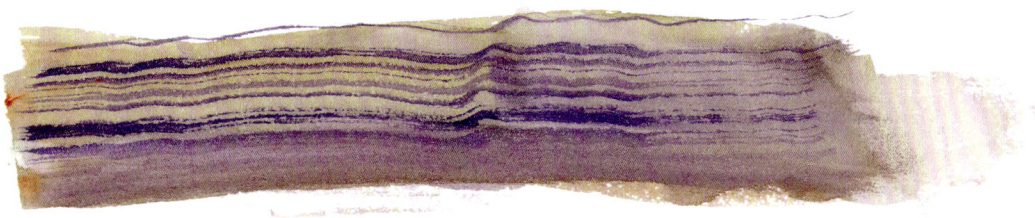

Other useful techniques

Paint can be applied with any tool, even your fingers. Artists often use sponges to apply watercolour to make a speckled patina, or spatter paint from the brush to make attractive random splashes, or even spray it from a toothbrush to make a fine-grained splatter.

▽ **Spatter**
Paint is flicked from a brush to give the random impression of footsteps along a beach.

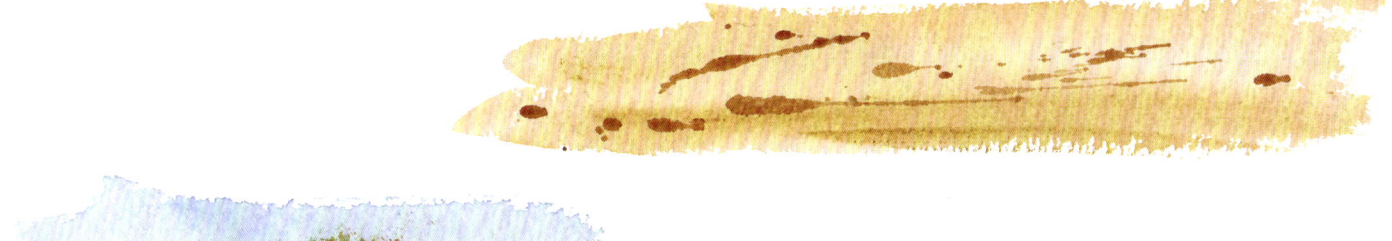

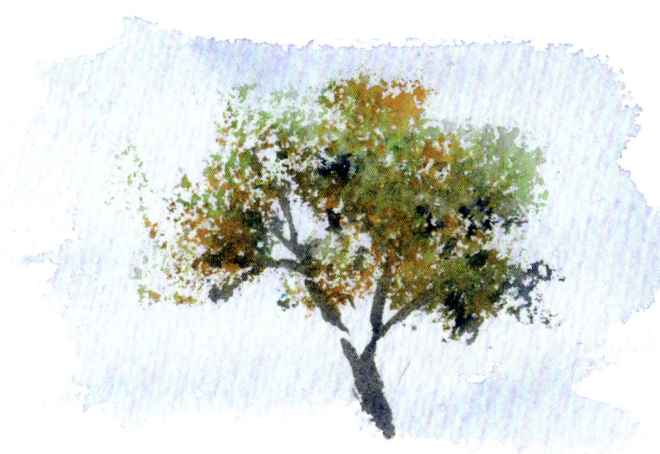

△ **Sponge**
This pattern of speckled foliage is achieved by applying paint with a natural sponge.

△ **Splatter**
Running your finger backwards across a toothbrush loaded with paint releases a fine spray of paint, ideal for representing a gravelly texture.

Reserving the white paper

In watercolour, the white of the paper represents the light, so it is a very important factor in a painting. The watercolourist leaves highlit areas untouched, tints light areas and paints the shade, usually building from light to dark tones. As a result, watercolourists rarely need white paint, except to add small details of light, to correct small areas, or to mute strong colours.

Drawing a pencil sketch to mark the lightest areas of your subject before you start painting provides a guide for the brush, telling it where it can and cannot go.

◁ **Living Streets, Verona**
28 x 20cm (11 x 8in)

A pencil guide enabled me to brush in the buildings' shapes with confidence and leave out the highlights on the roofs of the cars.

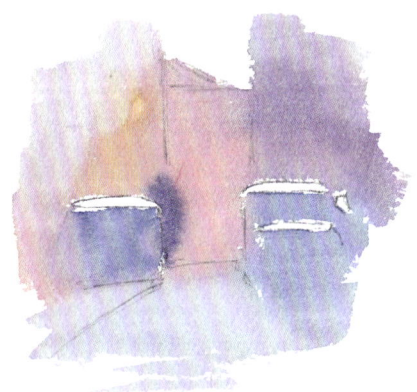

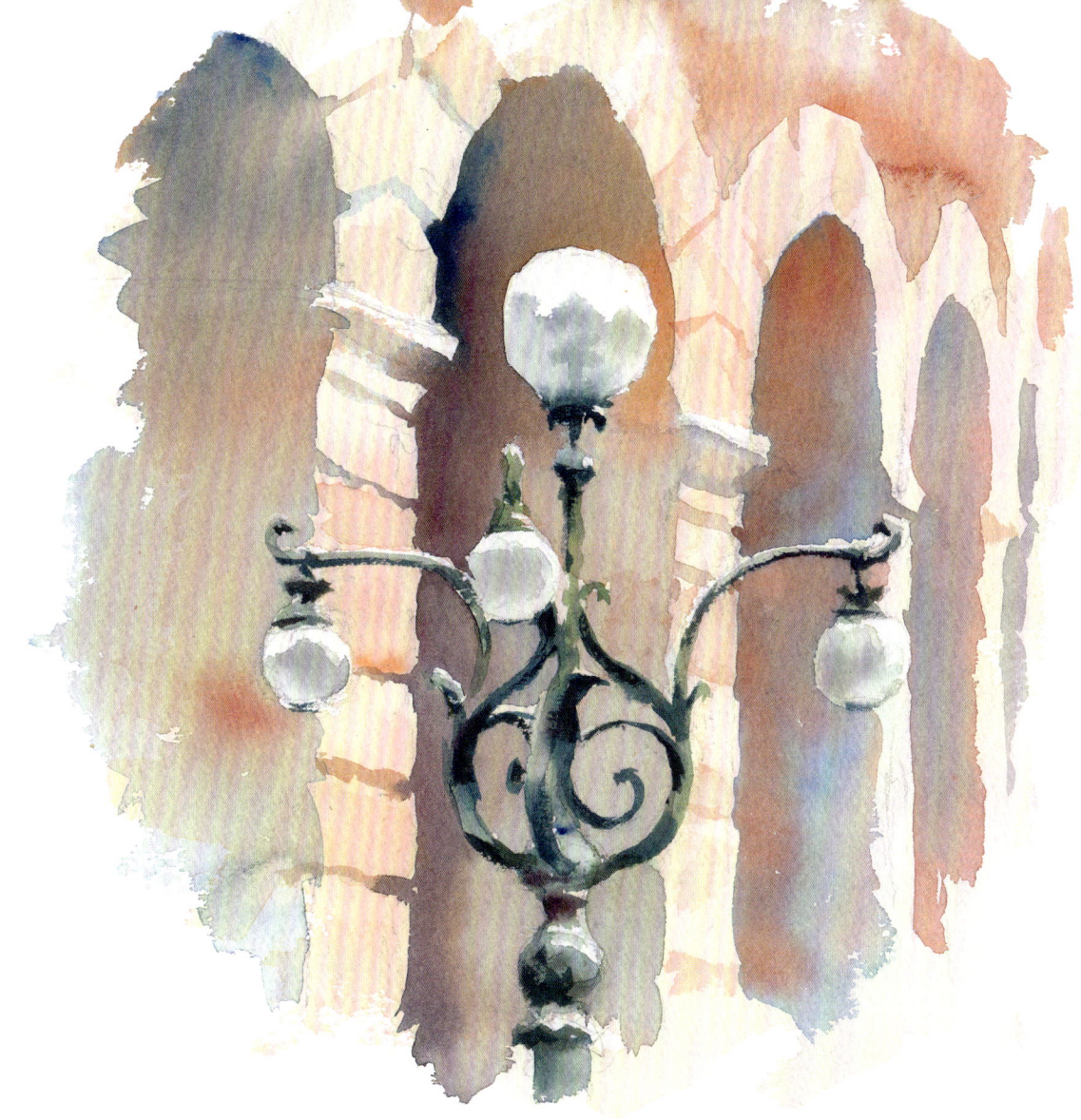

◁ When a subject in the foreground is lighter than the background, like these lamps against the arches of the arena in Verona, a pencil guide helps to paint the wash safely around it and reserve highlights on the framework of the lamp.

Masking fluid

Art suppliers sell a useful aid for reserving fiddly areas of light: a pale-coloured latex liquid called masking fluid. It is applied to areas you want to preserve as highlights, painted over when dry, and then rubbed off when the paint itself is dry to reveal the untouched paper.

Warning
Never use your best brushes to apply this fluid, as it ruins brushes as soon as it dries. Use a cheap brush or an old, worn-out brush, the end of a brush or a dip pen.

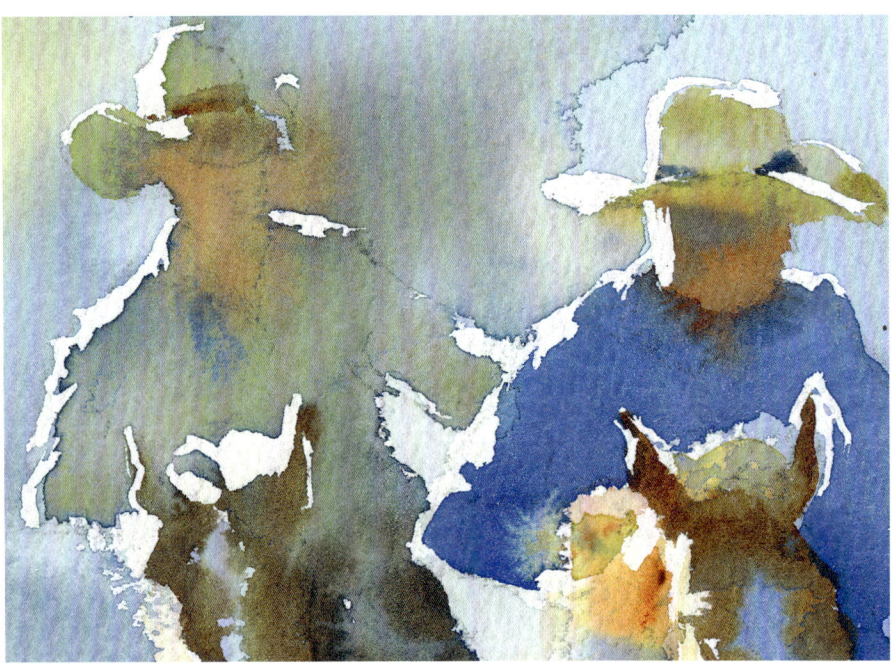

▷ **Texas Rodeo**
30.5 x 41cm (12 x 16in)
Masking fluid has been used to reserve the highlights and the swish of the reins in this glimpse of rodeo action.

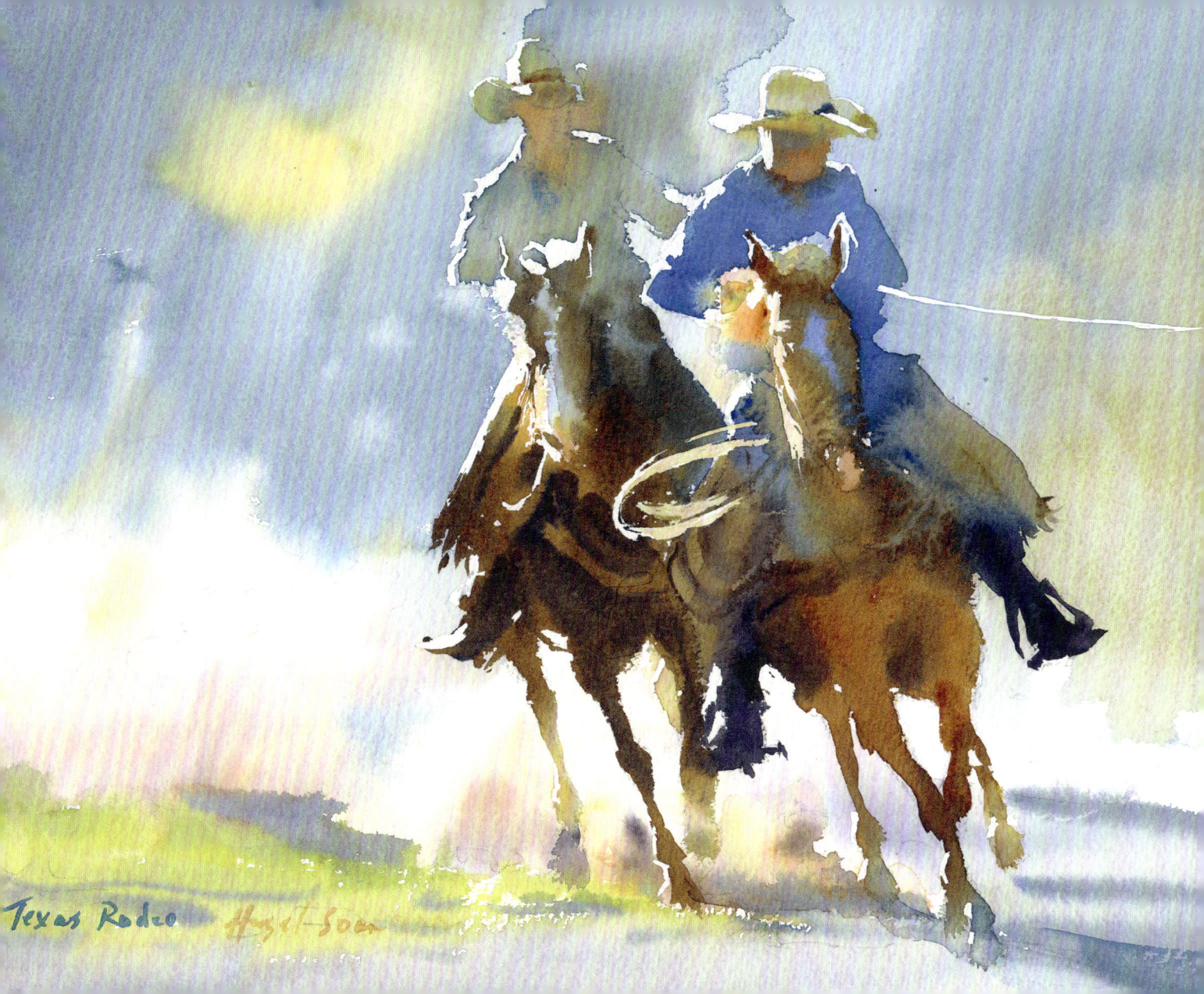

Texas Rodeo   Hazelwood

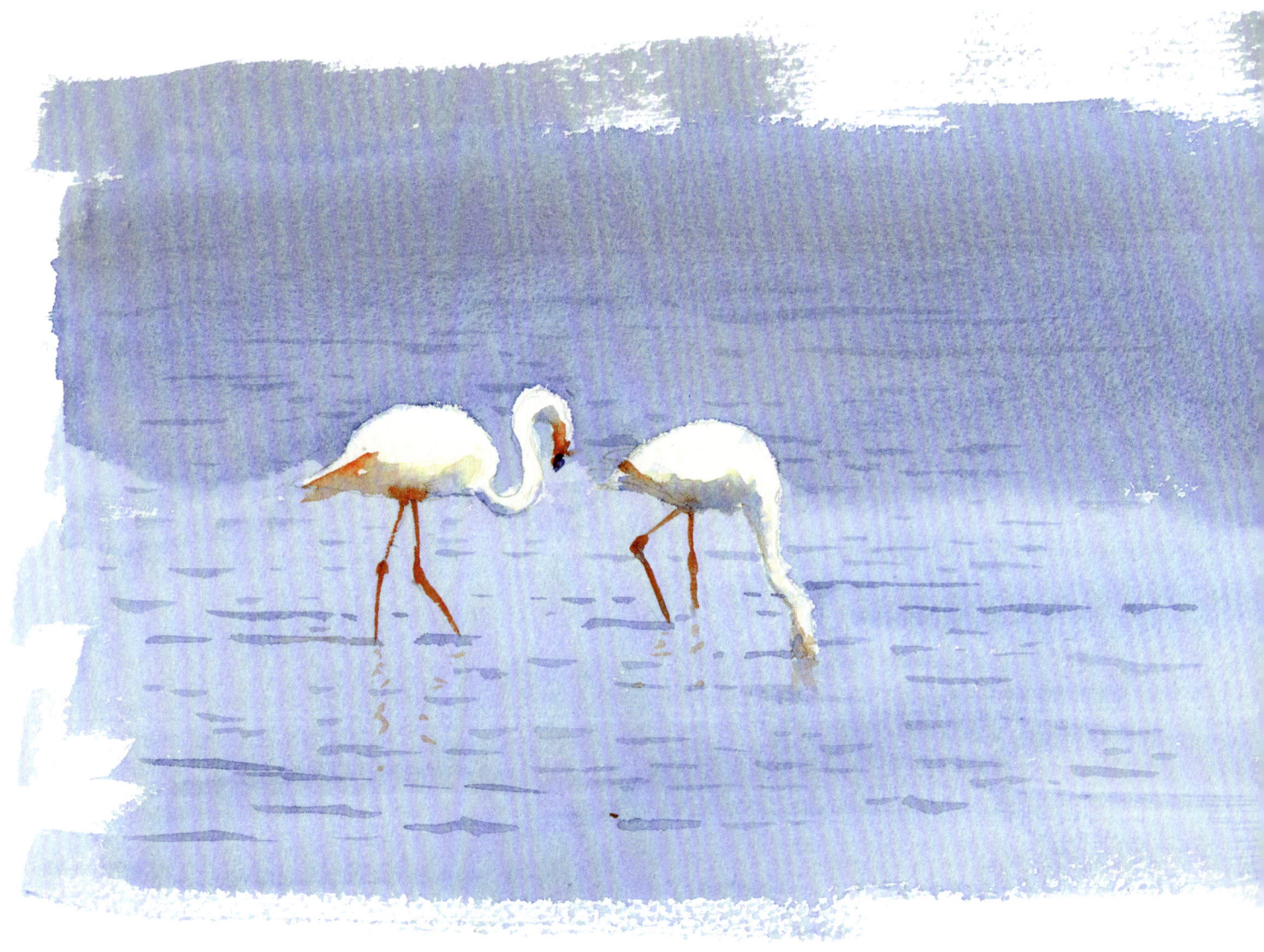

Washes

Large areas of a colour or a blend of colours are achieved by laying broad, overlapping brushstrokes, and allowing them to blend together seamlessly. This is called a wash.

The first wash is the freshest

Even though many watercolours are built up in layers, watercolour marks are by default at their most transparent in a single film, so try to make your initial washes in a single, seamless layer.

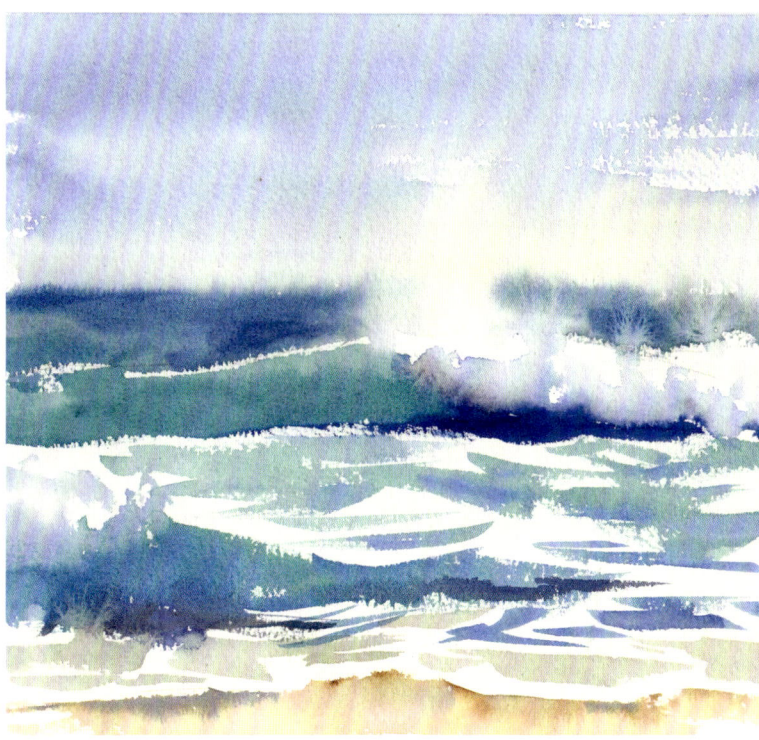

◁ **Duet**
28 x 35.5cm (11 x 14in)
Ultramarine Blue has been painted in broad, overlapping brushstrokes made with a flat brush to create a smooth background wash for the water surrounding the flamingos.

△ **The Green Sea**
25.5 x 28cm (10 x 11in)
This painting is created from top to bottom with narrow, linear washes of single layers of pigment. White paper is left between brushmarks within the washes, creating a vigour in the painting.

How to paint a wash

Load your brush with paint (use either a round or flat brush). Brush it across from one direction, gradually coming down the paper and letting each subsequent stroke slightly overlap the previous one, so that the brushstrokes blend along their length. Continue until the required area is covered. Try to resist taking the brush back and forth like a house-painting brush: the freshest wash is the one in which the particles of paint are allowed to dry undisturbed. Don't fiddle with the wash while it is drying either – any aberrations are unlikely to be noticeable once the rest of the painting is in place.

Lift any pooled water out with the tip of the brush or the corner of a piece of kitchen towel so as not to disturb the drying wash. Do not dab: it will spoil the appearance.

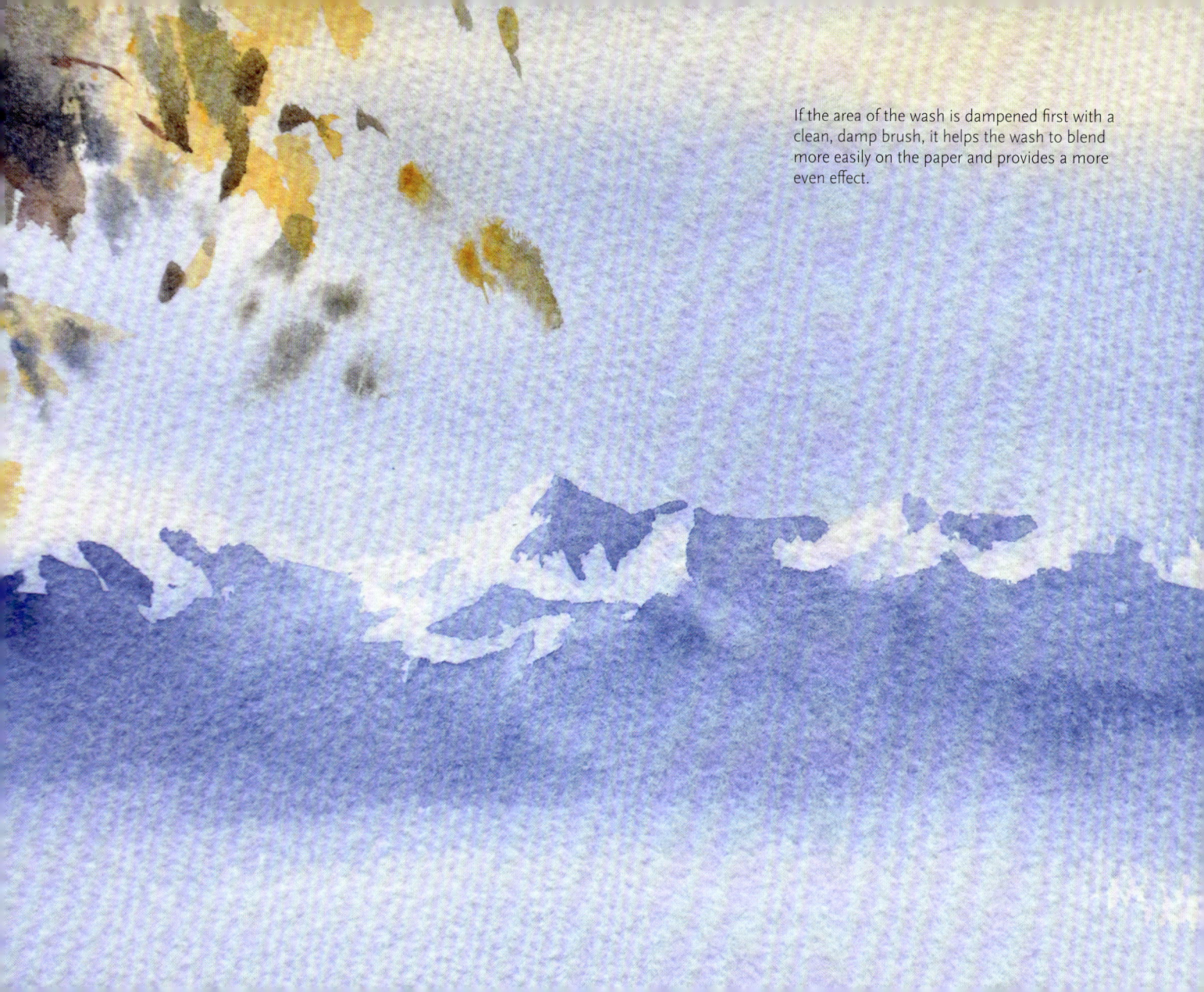

If the area of the wash is dampened first with a clean, damp brush, it helps the wash to blend more easily on the paper and provides a more even effect.

Graduated wash

A graduated wash is one that varies in tone from top to bottom. To make a wash that gets lighter towards the bottom, such as you might need for a sky, allow the natural offloading of the pigment to lighten the colour for you or gradually dilute the paint as you come down the page.

△ Lay it and leave it – a happy wash is painted and left well alone.

△ If you mess with a wash you will disturb the drying paint and lose the freshness.

△ If you allow paint to pool in the corners it will back up and cause a backrun.

Variegated wash

A wash of more than one colour is one of the most attractive passages of colour in watercolour. This is called a variegated wash. Dampen the paper before you start; it will encourage the colours to blend together and create a seamless wash.

The Dragon Soon Sleeps, Sri Lanka
20 x 28cm (8 x 11in)

The colours blend on the damp paper to evoke the soft, dusky glow of the humid equatorial sunset.

Drifting wash

Gravity is your friend when you want
to make colours drift into or through
a wash. Tilt the paper to encourage the
flow of paint and lay it flat as soon as
you have achieved the desired effect.

▷ Wet the paper before applying the paint.
Tilt the paper in the desired direction and
allow the paint to drift into position.

▷ ▷ The drifting blends of watercolour
create an evocative atmosphere as a shaft
of light parts the clouds above this beach.

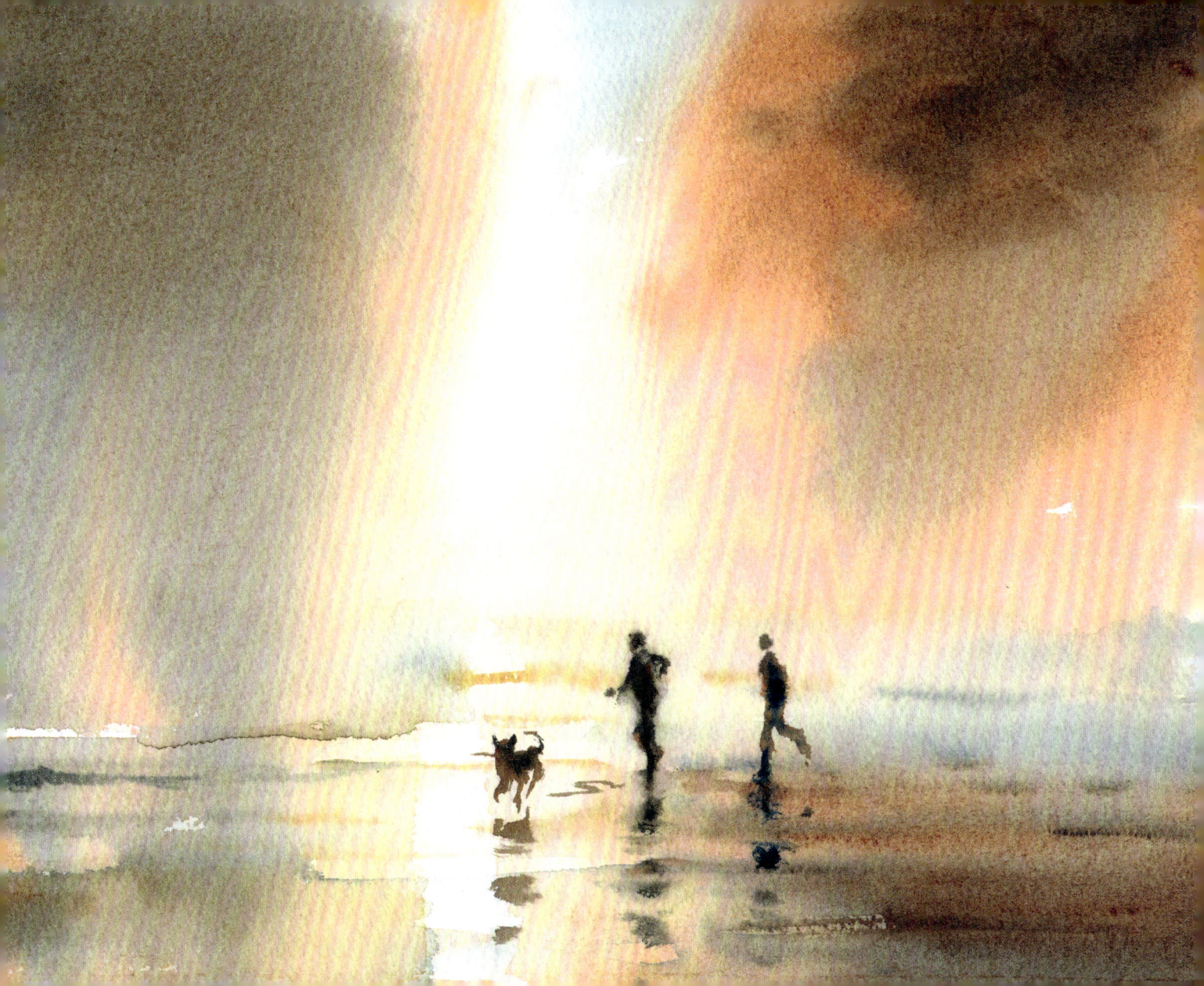

Restoring light in watercolour

The aim in watercolour painting is to keep the painting as fresh as possible. If you overwork washes they lose their transparency, which cannot usually be regained, and it is often quicker to start again rather than try to correct. However, small corrections can be made and highlights added with white watercolour paint because it is opaque.

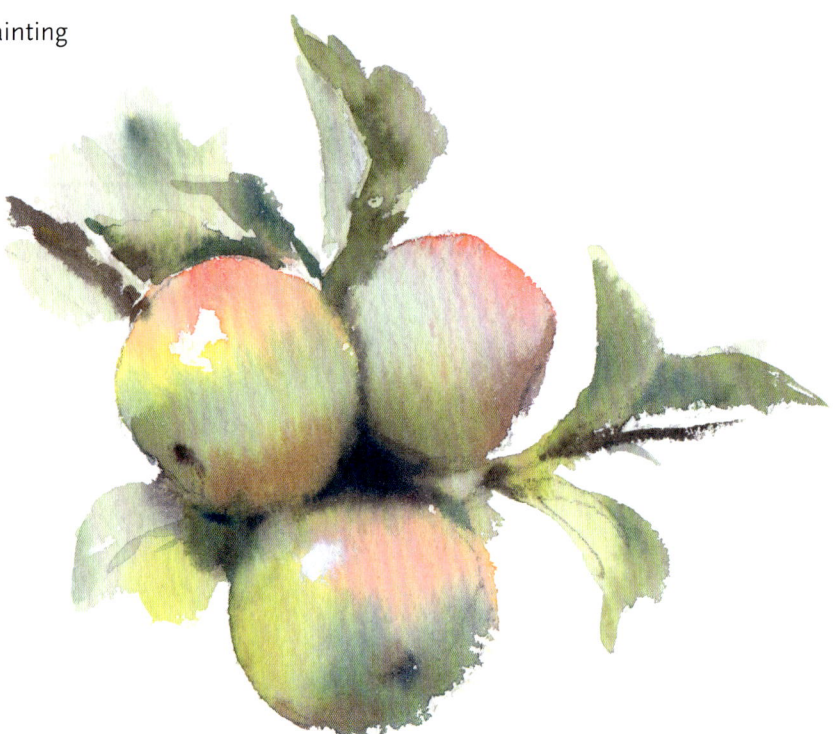

White paint

In watercolour, white paint cannot replicate the white paper, but it can be used to regain highlights in small areas, and especially if positioned amid darker tones.

△ The highlight on the lower apple has been restored with white paint and looks almost as fresh as the untouched white paper highlight on the apple above.

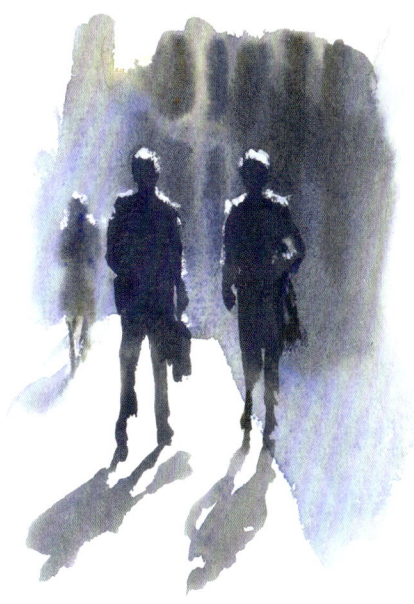

△ White paint has been used to restore the highlights on the figures and stands out well against the dark background.

▷ **Homage to Winslow Homer**
76 x 56cm (30 x 22in)
Several highlights on the coconuts are restored with white paint, some of which is tinted with an Indian Yellow glaze to re-create the orange glow.

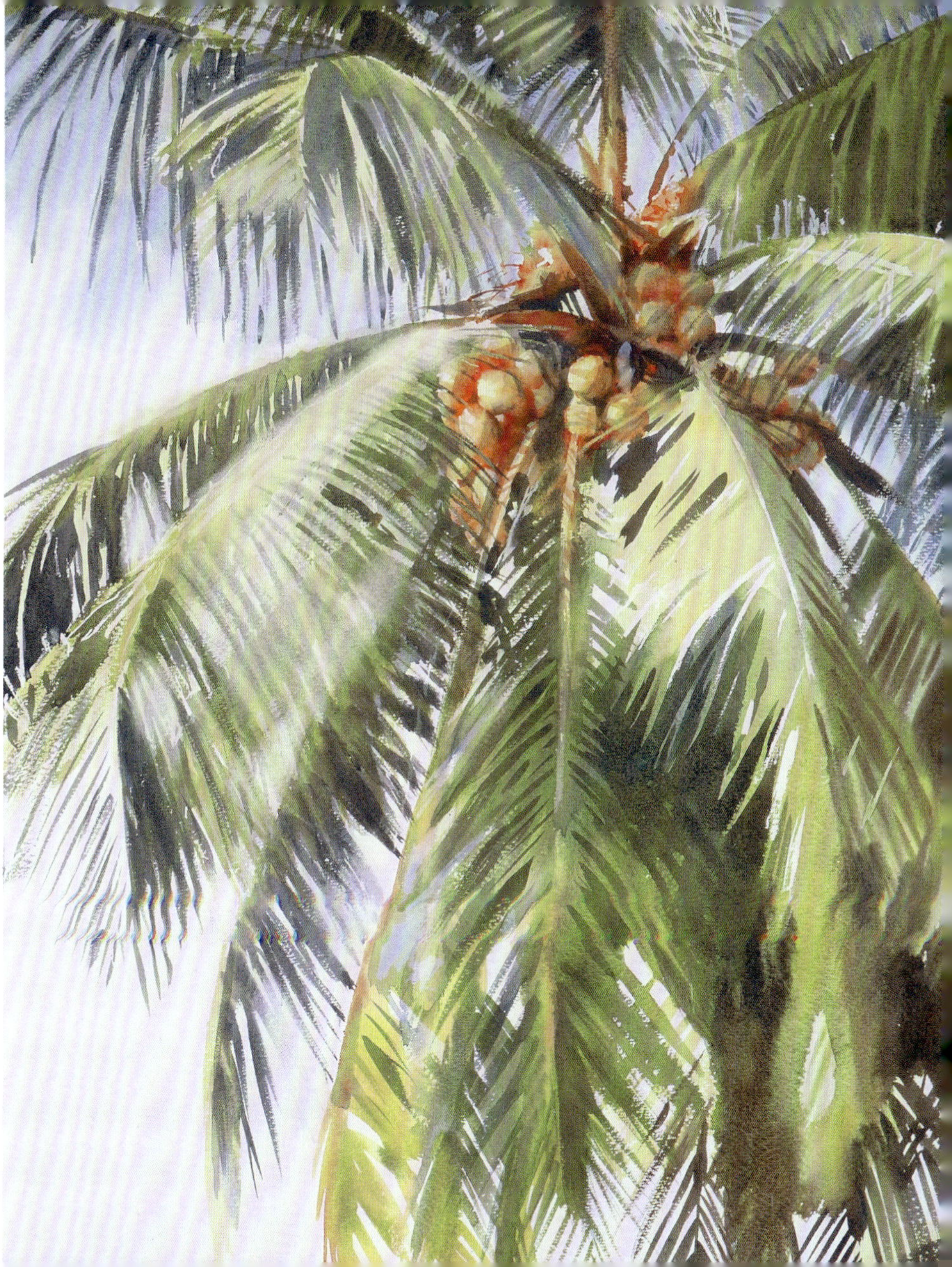

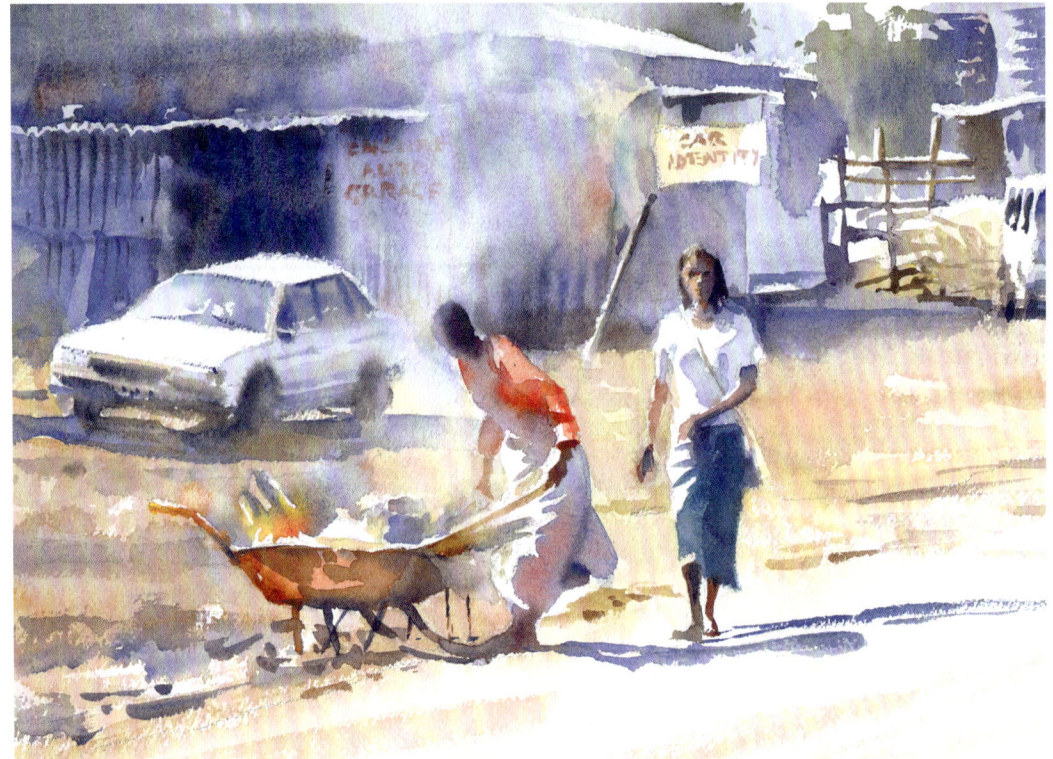

Kenyan Wheelbarrow
30 x 41cm (12 x 16in)
The smoke is created by lifting off the Ultramarine Blue paint of the background with a clean, damp sponge.

Lifting off

There are some pigments that are called 'lifting colours' because they do not stain the paper. They can be lifted off with a clean, damp brush or sponge, even when completely dry. Useful examples are Ultramarine Blue, Burnt Sienna and Burnt Umber.

28 x 38cm (11 x 15in)

The colours used here are Ultramarine Blue and Burnt Sienna, both 'lifting colours'. The white sail has been lifted off with a sponge wiped between a stencil cut to the shape of the boat, then dabbed dry.

Scratching off

Because watercolour paper is thick and fairly robust, you can scratch the paint off small areas of a finished painting with a sharp blade to reveal the white paper.

▷ A scalpel blade is drawn across the surface of the paper to scratch out the ripples on the water.

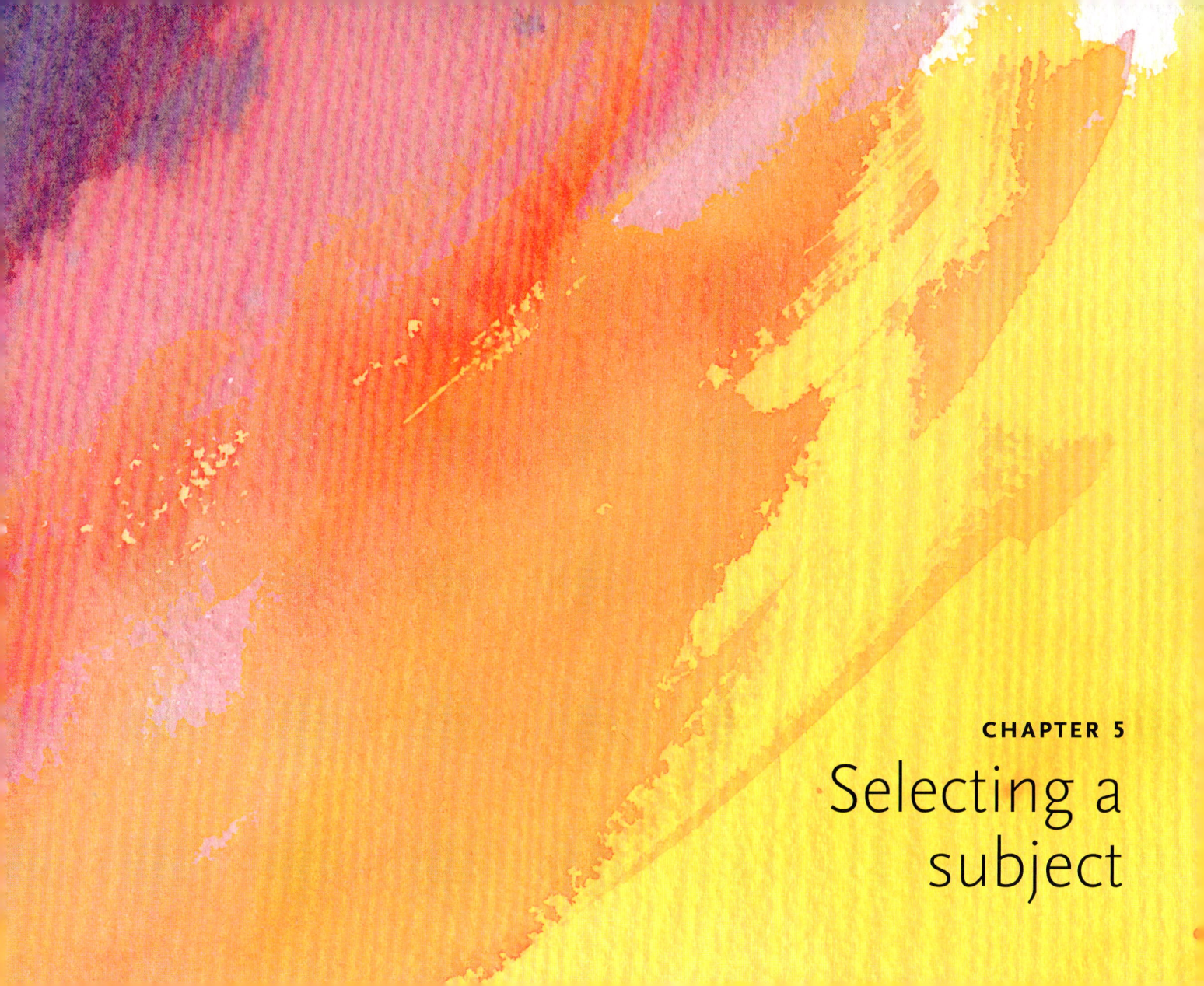

CHAPTER 5
Selecting a subject

What makes a good subject?

Representational watercolour painting makes a pattern of colours work together on flat paper to suggest, or look like, something that exists in three-dimensional form in the real world.

The artist has a set of tools at his or her disposal in order to achieve this – line, shape, light and shade (known in 'art-speak' as tone or value), perspective, proportion and colour. A picturesque view does not necessarily make a good painting unless there is a convincing pattern of light and shade going on, or an interesting composition of shapes and lines. Likewise, a mundane subject can turn into a marvellous painting when blessed with a light that turns it into an attractive design of light and shade.

Things to look for
- **Lines** that lead the eye into the painting or towards the focus
- **Shapes** that vary and make interesting brushmarks
- **Light** that enlivens and breaks up areas of darkness
- **Shade** that suggests form, offers a touch of ambiguity and provides areas of peace
- **Perspective** to imply depth, distance and narrative
- **Proportion** to enhance scale and a sense of space
- **Colour** that entertains the eye

▷ **Rainy Day in Verona**
20 x 23cm (8 x 9in)
A dull, wet afternoon springs to life with the contrasting shapes of dark figures and their brollies, thus making an interesting pattern of light and shade and a good subject for a painting.

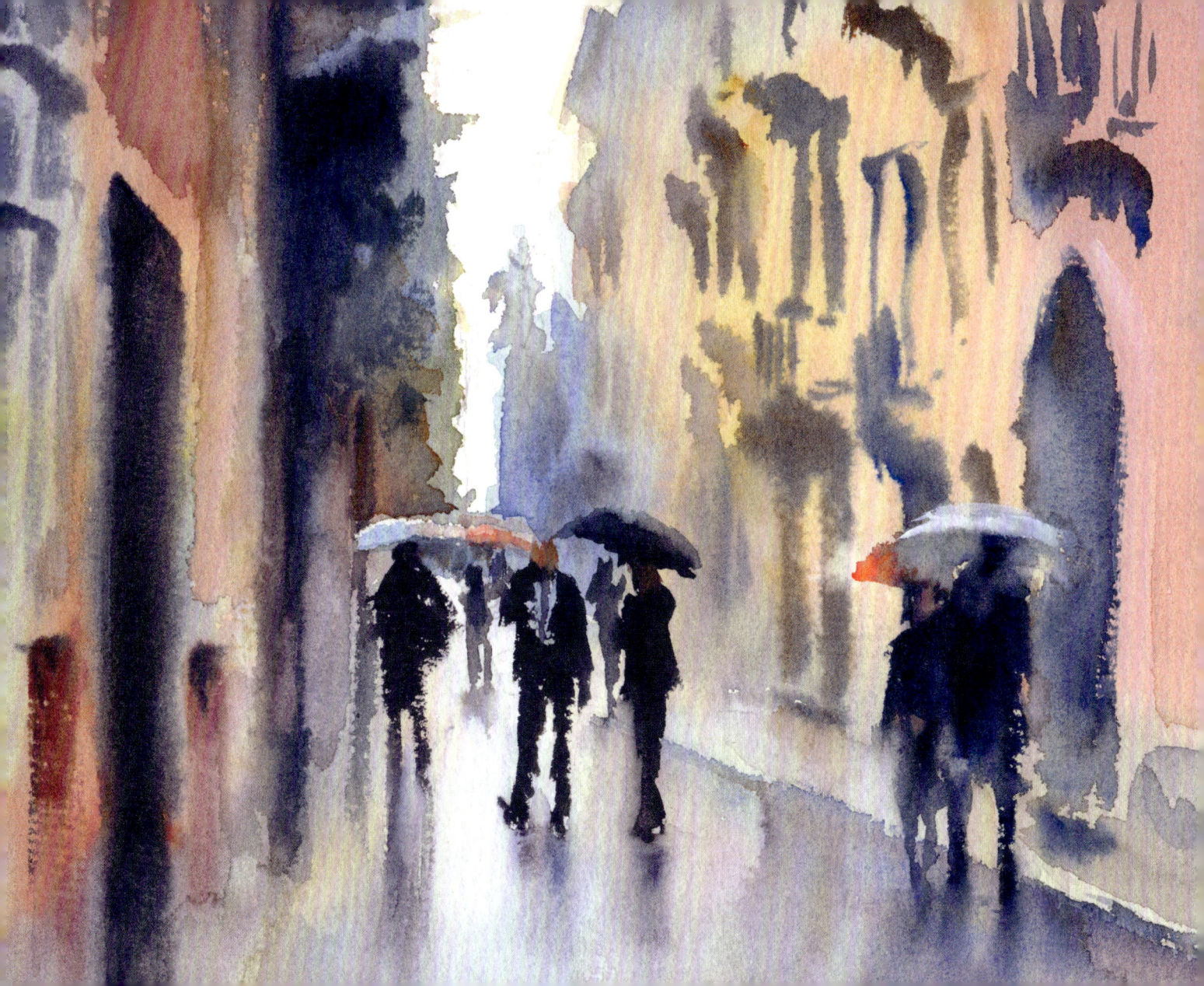

Shape

Shape is hugely important to painting watercolour: intriguing shapes will captivate your audience and entertain the eye. An interesting or arresting shape is always a good subject. The shape delineates the space of an object and enlivens the surrounding area. When painting a shape, avoid presumption and generalization, and take advantage of the irregularities and intricacies of the outline to make sure you have maximized the entertainment value.

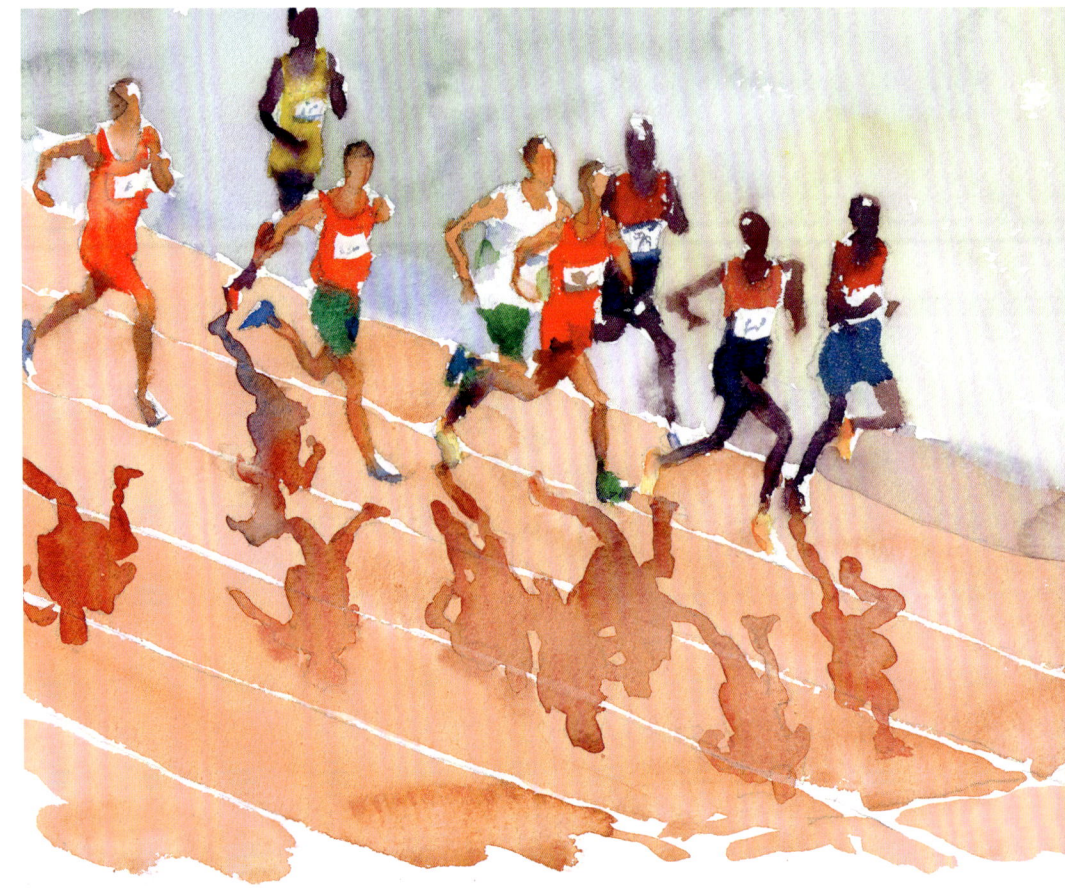

△ **Prospecting for Gold**
28 x 38cm (11 x 15in)
The runners and their reflections all enjoy slightly different shapes as they sprint for home, making them a lively subject for watercolour.

Silhouette

Against the light, shapes fall into silhouette and become easier for the watercolourist to paint. Being darker than their surroundings, they can be painted without drawing first and with positive brushstrokes. As always, take care to seek out the essence of the shape.

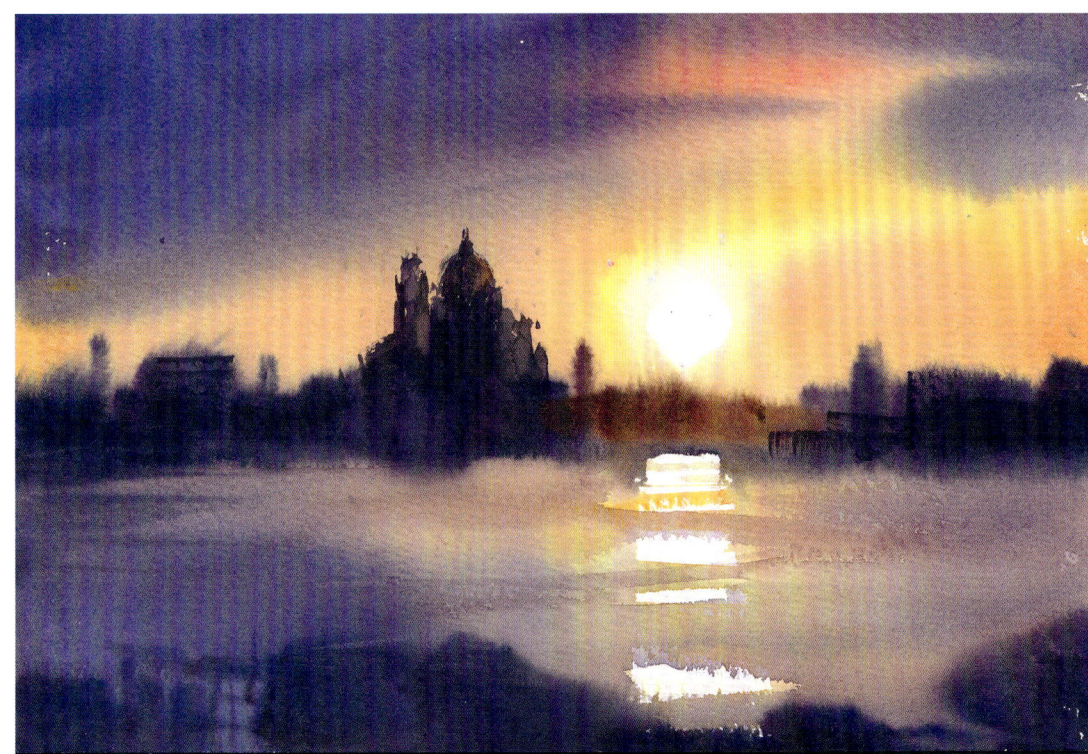

▷ **Lagoon**
20 x 28cm (8 x 11in)

When a complex building like Santa Maria della Salute in Venice falls into silhouette against the setting sun, it becomes much less daunting to paint.

Negative spaces

The eye orientates itself to that which is tangible, but the spaces between and around objects are just as important and interesting to the flat world of painting. These areas are often termed the negative spaces.

Because you are painting on a flat surface with transparent colours, the background and foreground are not really separate things; they get built up together. Get used to thinking of them in conjunction with each other. For example, a background might be needed to show up the light on the side of a subject, because without a background the light could not be seen, so it is painted along with the subject.

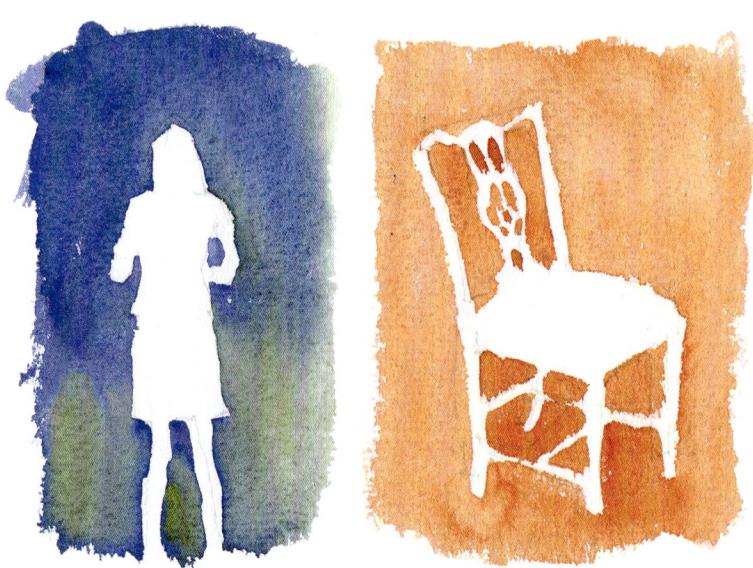

◁ The spaces around and between things are also termed negative shapes.

▷ **Freedom of the City**
20 x 28cm (8 x 11in)

The spaces under the arches, the gaps between the figures and the haloes of light over their heads are just as interesting as the silhouettes themselves – maybe more interesting.

Light and shade

Strong light and shade make exciting watercolours, and so too does subtlety. Light and shade announce form, depth and space, and in a painting these are interesting allusions. An object will be lighter on the lit side and darker on the shady side even if it is of one colour in 'real life'. This variation in tone over the surface of objects is delightful to paint and persuades the viewer of the shape of the subject being represented.

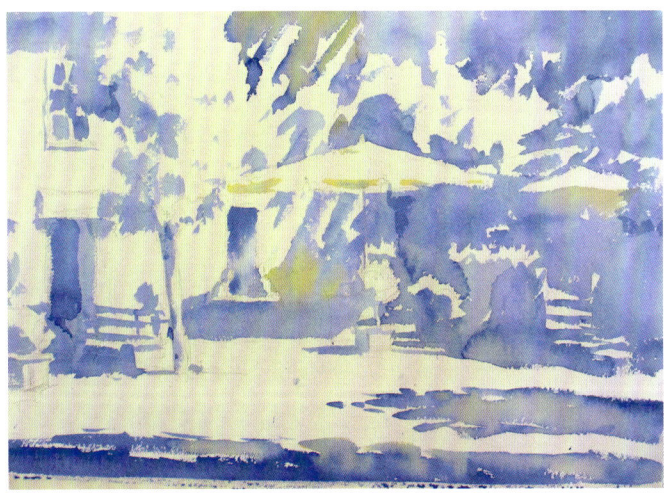

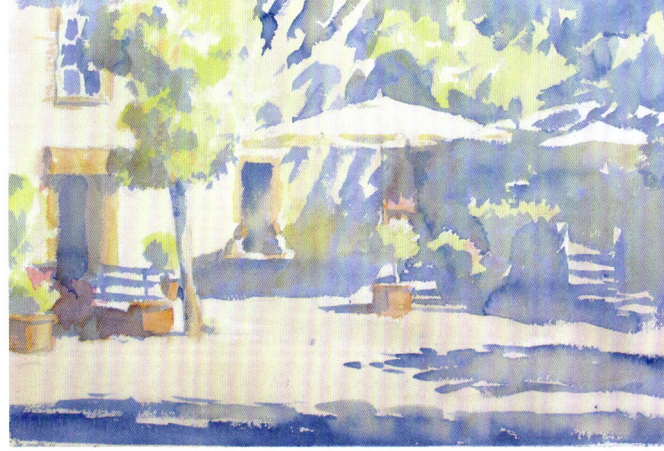

Demonstration stage 1: A sunny subject can be composed by painting just the areas in shade with a blue. Immediately, the structure is obvious, because in painting the shade you thereby establish the forms.

Stage 2: The colours of the painting are laid in glazes over the blue shadows, which remain visible below the transparent layers, reinforcing the structure of the painting.

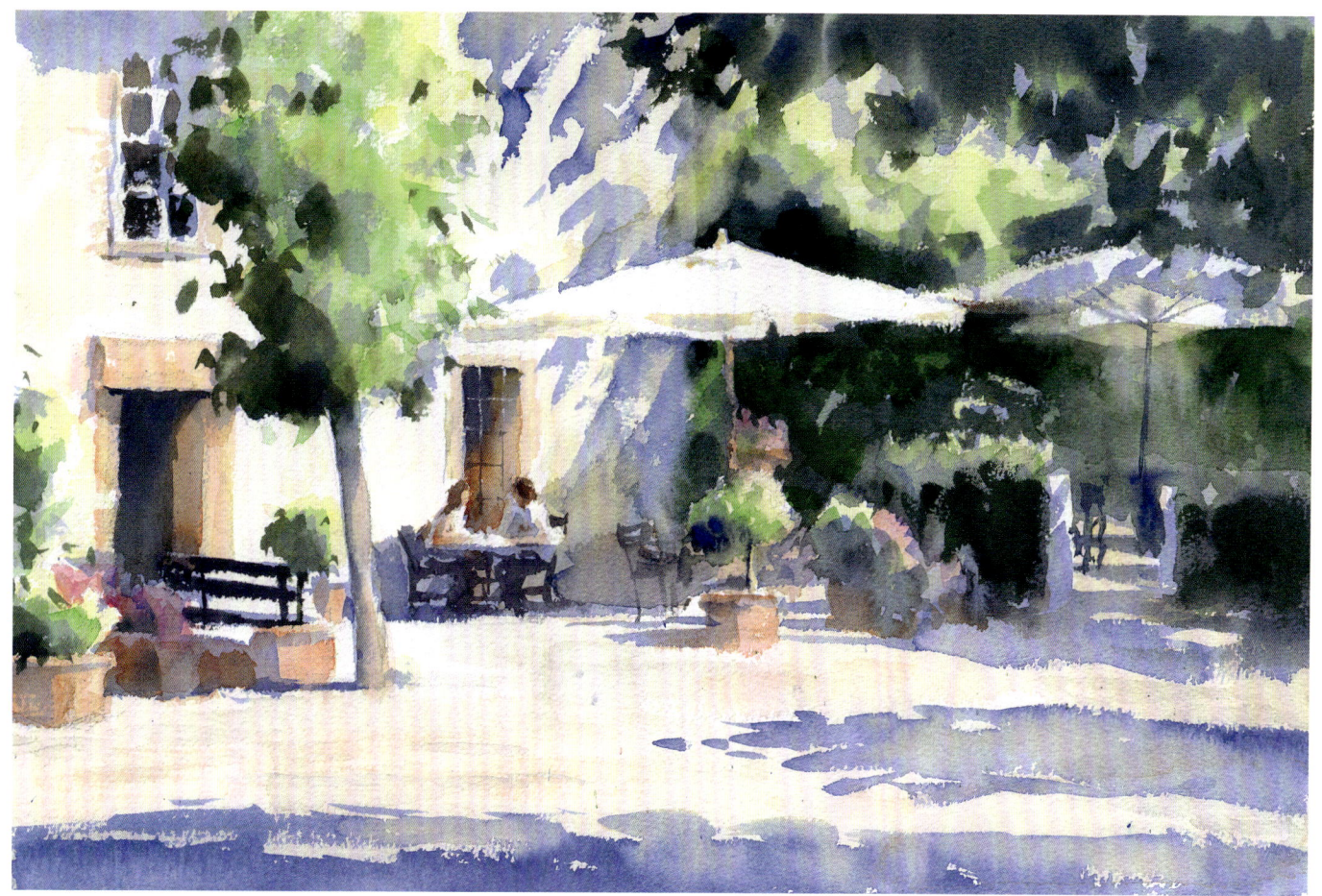

△ **Bathing in Sunshine**
38 x 56cm (15 x 22in)
The darkest areas are strengthened in tone and details added in, always maintaining the same counterchange of light and shade established from the start.

Form

The changing shade of a colour around a form is always an interesting subject to paint. To demonstrate three-dimensional form in painting use a light tone, mid-tone and dark tone.

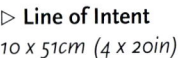

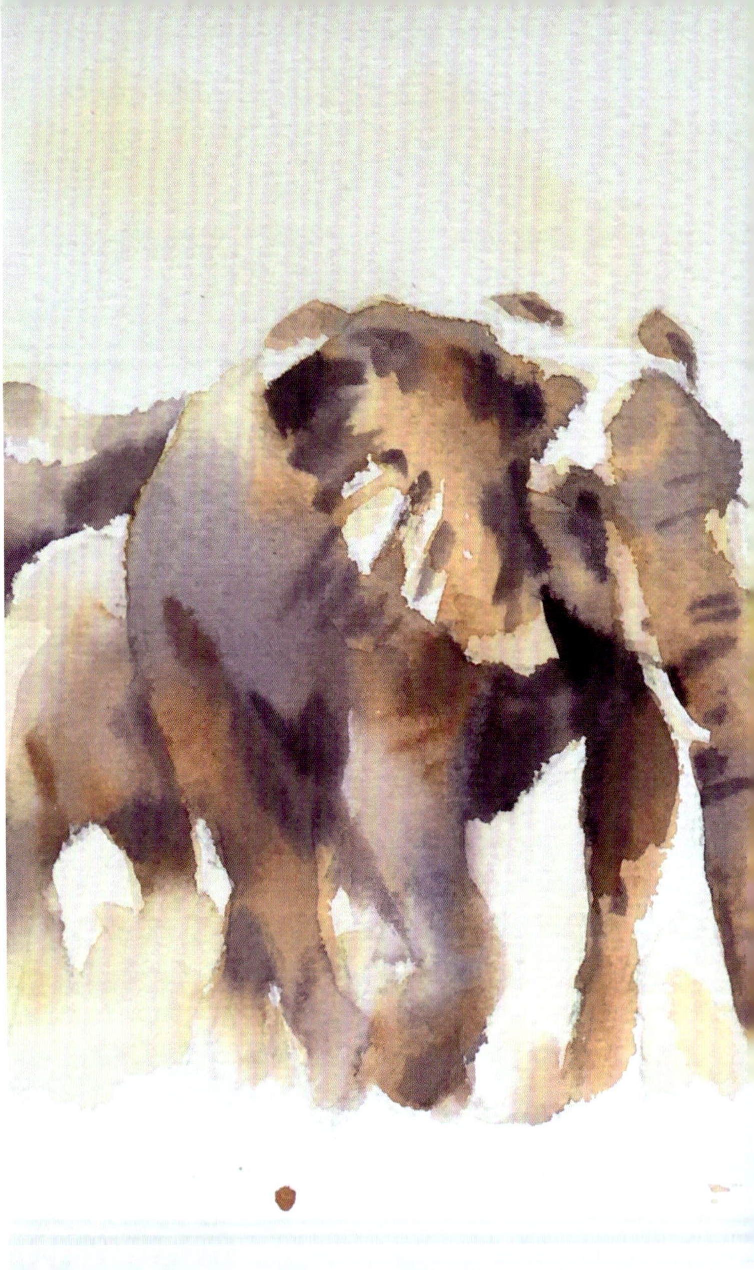

▷ **Line of Intent**
10 x 51cm (4 x 20in)
The lightest tone is the highlight on the backs of the elephants, showing us that these face upward towards the sun. The mid-tone is the bulk of their bodies, which receives less light than their backs, and the darkest tone is their undersides, which turn away from the light into shadow. This gradual change in tone tells us they have rounded forms.

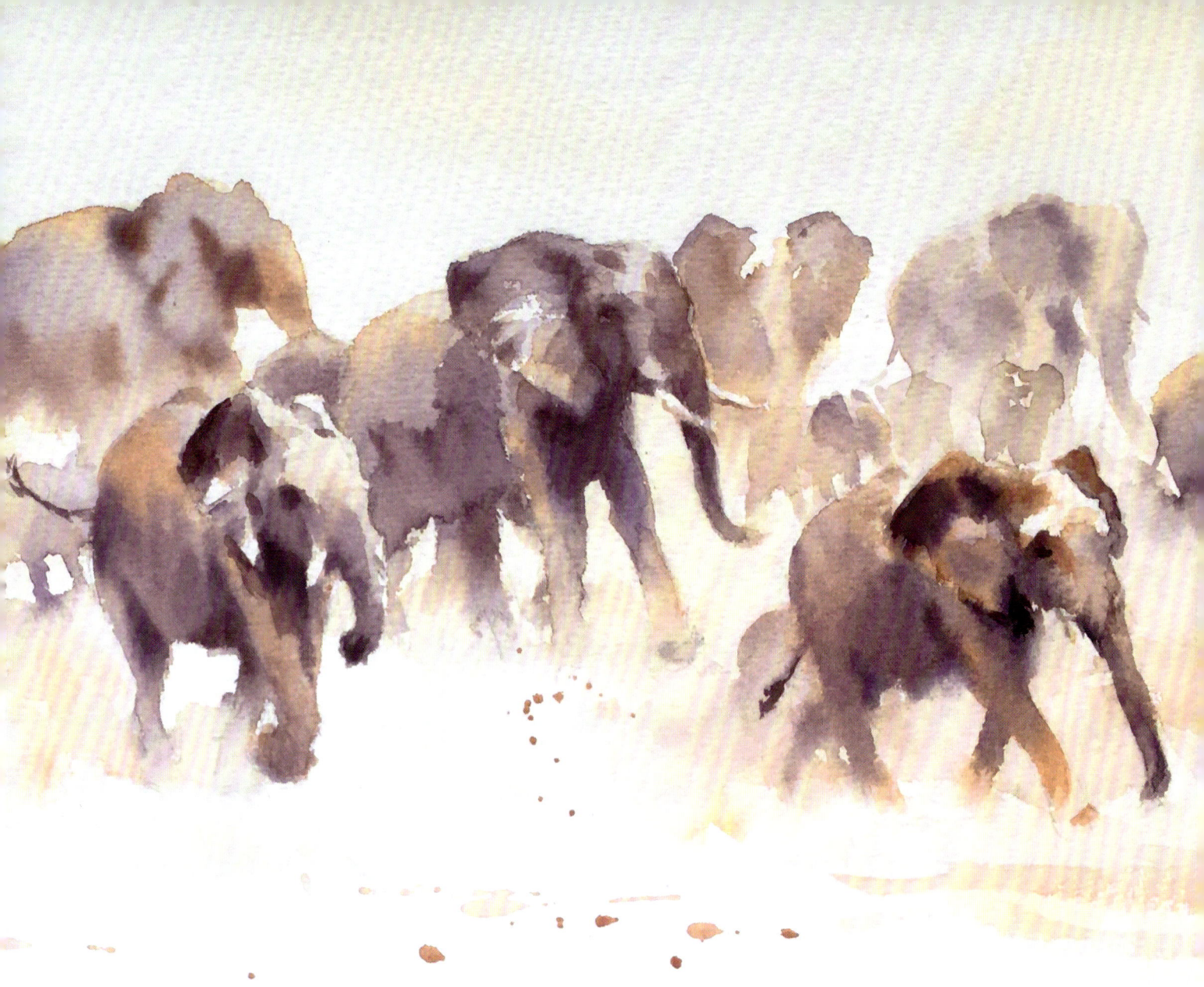

Rounded forms

A gradual change from light to dark implies a rounded form. Wet into wet is therefore the best technique to show roundness as the blends graduate.

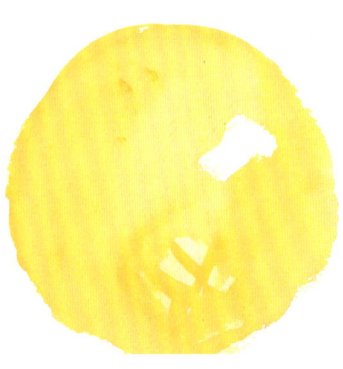

Stage 1: Untouched highlights are left out of a circular wash of Indian Yellow.

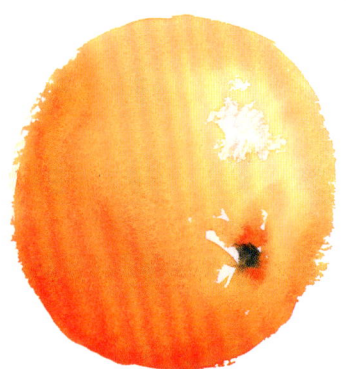

Stage 2: An orange colour made from mixing Permanent Rose with Indian Yellow is touched into the damp wash from the darkest side, and more intense colour is gradually added until the required strength is achieved to make the orange fruit appear spherical.

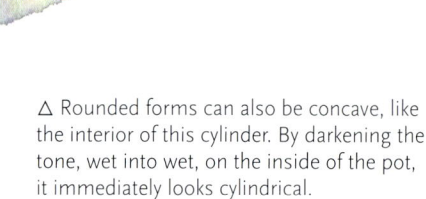

△ Rounded forms can also be concave, like the interior of this cylinder. By darkening the tone, wet into wet, on the inside of the pot, it immediately looks cylindrical.

Angular forms

Angular forms have defined edges, so the wet-on-dry technique can delineate these perfectly (see page 60).

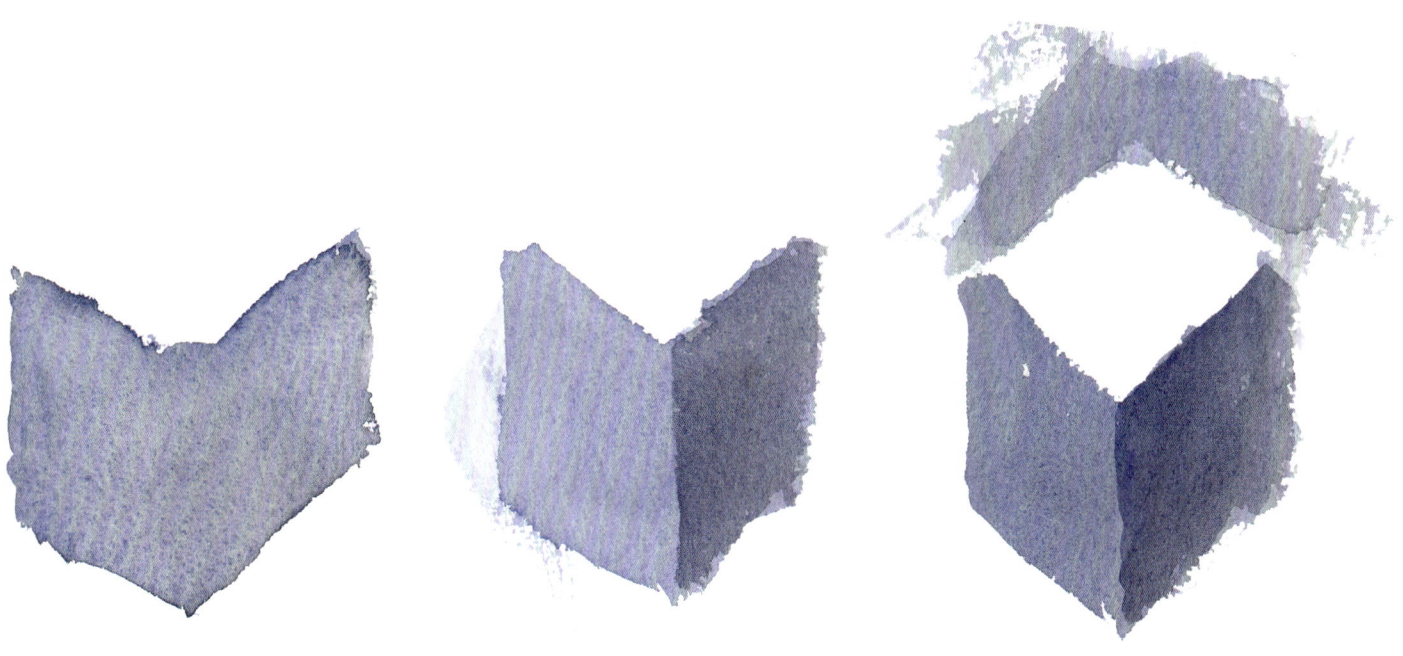

△ A wet-on-dry tint over the chevron shape, plus the hint of background, immediately suggests the angular form of this cube.

Space and depth

Space can be alluded to in painting, and makes an interesting watercolour. The illusion of space can be created through the careful use of light and shade and by perspective.

◁ Usually the lightest and darkest tones are in the foreground with less contrast in the distance. By pitching a darker tone adjacent to a lighter tone, the darker tone implies that it goes behind the lighter area in front of it.

▷ **Boston Skyline**
20 x 28cm (8 x 11in)

When a subject is back-lit, the furthest distance will appear paler and more muted than closer objects, which become darker as they approach. The difference in tone suggests distance.

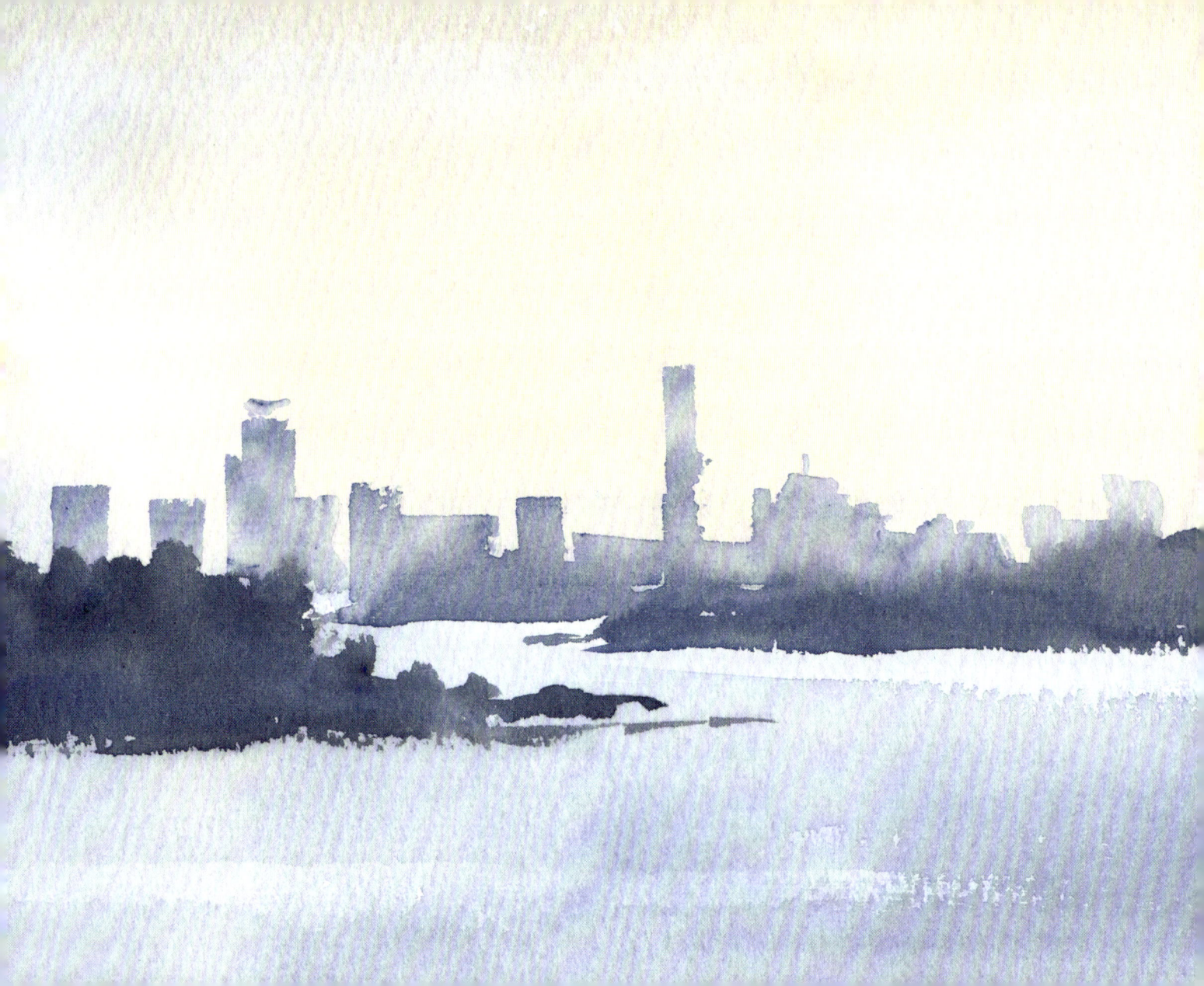

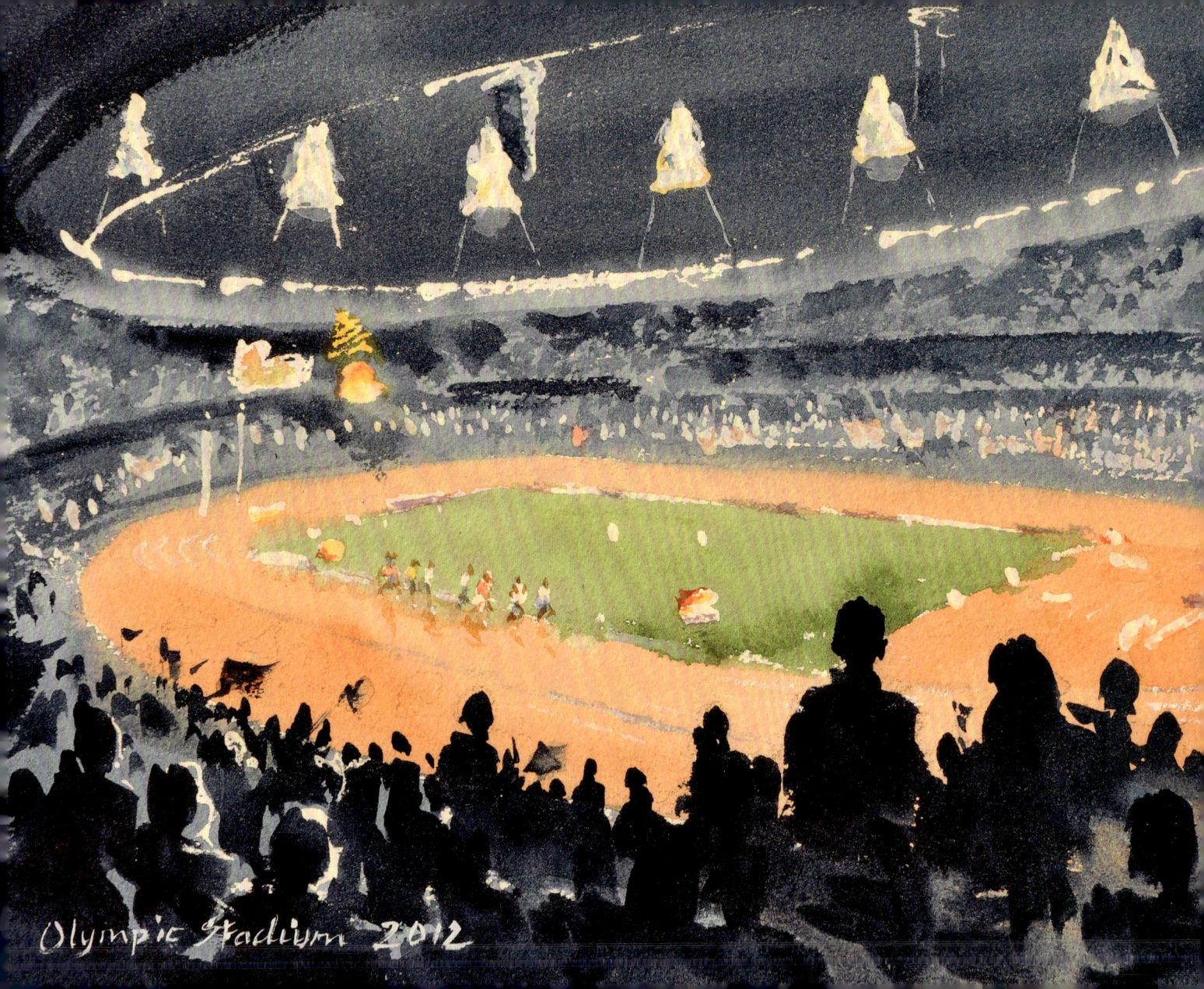

Olympic Stadium 2012

Perspective

Perspective can be used to imply space or distance. Objects made smaller appear to be in the distance, larger objects appear closer.

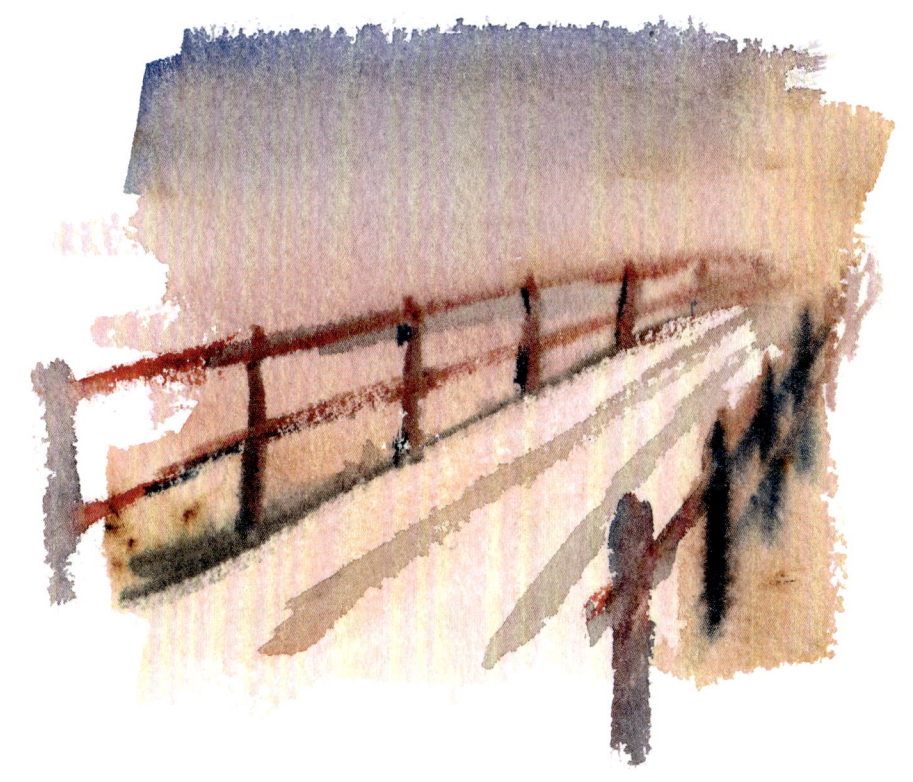

▷ The fence posts diminish in size as they go further away, and the parallel ruts in the road come closer together, creating a sense of distance and space.

◁ **Ring of Excellence**
25.5 x 30.5cm (10 x 12in)

The vast scale of the Olympic Stadium in London is created on a small piece of paper by showing the figures in the far distance as very small, and those in the foreground as much larger.

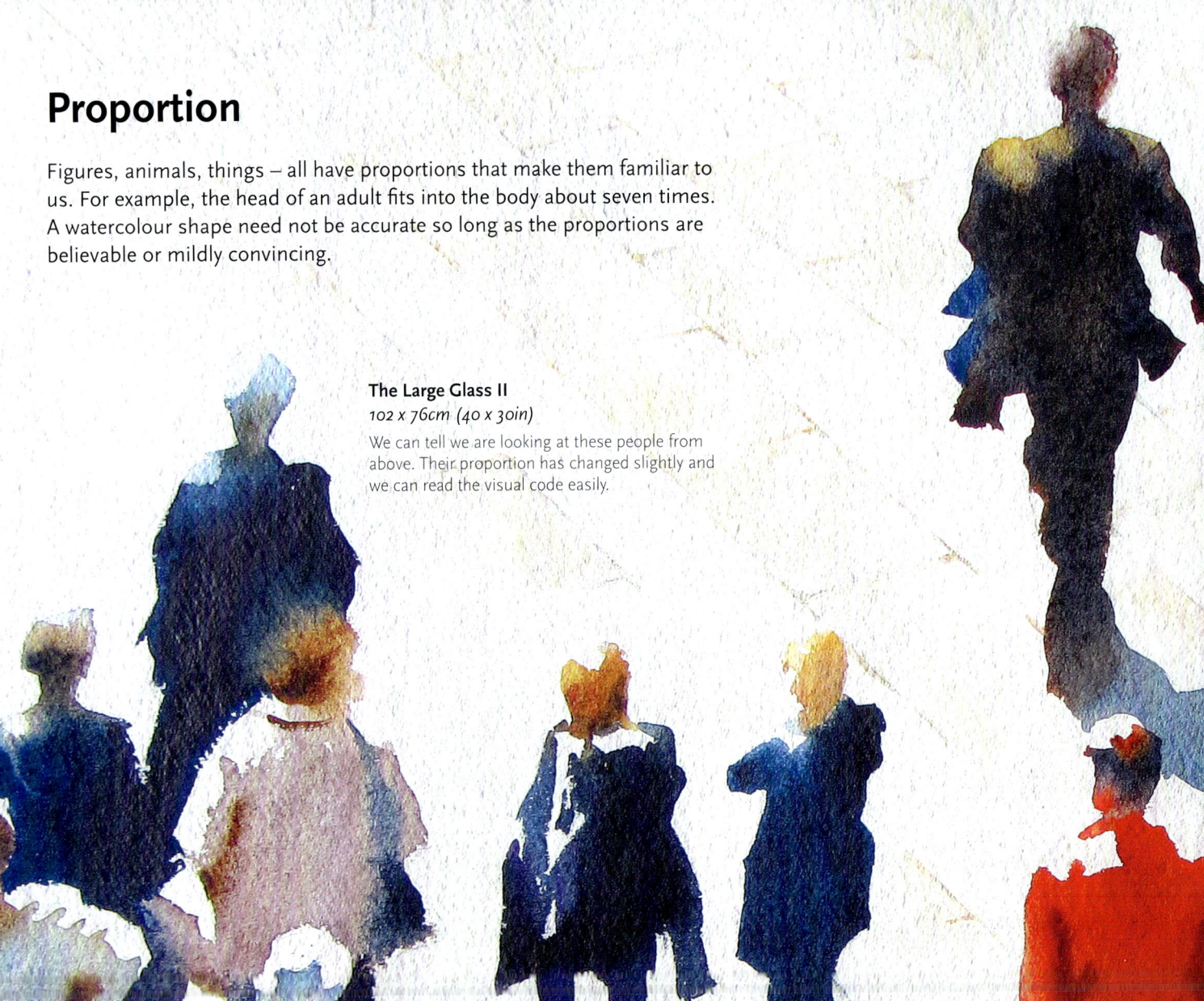

Proportion

Figures, animals, things — all have proportions that make them familiar to us. For example, the head of an adult fits into the body about seven times. A watercolour shape need not be accurate so long as the proportions are believable or mildly convincing.

The Large Glass II
102 x 76cm (40 x 30in)
We can tell we are looking at these people from above. Their proportion has changed slightly and we can read the visual code easily.

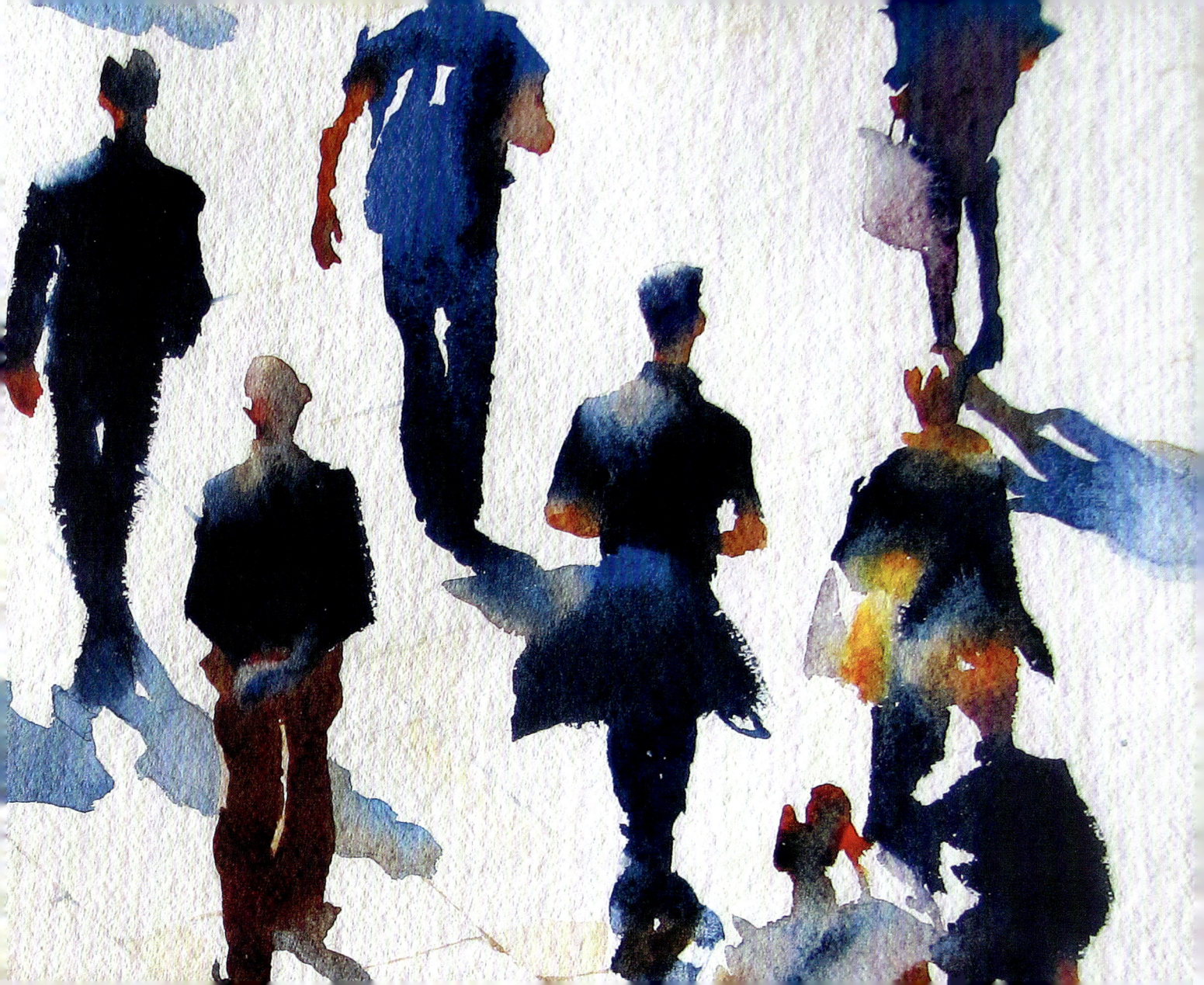

Designing the picture

A watercolour painting does not have to be complicated or full of activity to succeed. Watercolour welcomes simplicity. The beautiful passages of blending and overlapping colours are attractive enough in themselves. Most paintings do, however, benefit from a focus, which will usually be what drew your attention to the subject in the first place and what you are most interested in.

As a rule of thumb, it is better not to position main features bang in the middle; placing them to the right or left of centre will make a more interesting composition. The same applies to the horizon. The 'rule of thirds' (see opposite) works well in general, but remember that rules in art are also made to be broken.

Don't be a slave to veracity

Don't try to copy your subject exactly; it is the inspiration for your watercolour and you are under no obligation to mimic it. A painting has a life of its own; it is a new creation and you can change anything in the subject to suit your watercolour. Oscar Wilde puts it perfectly: 'Art begins where imitation ends.'

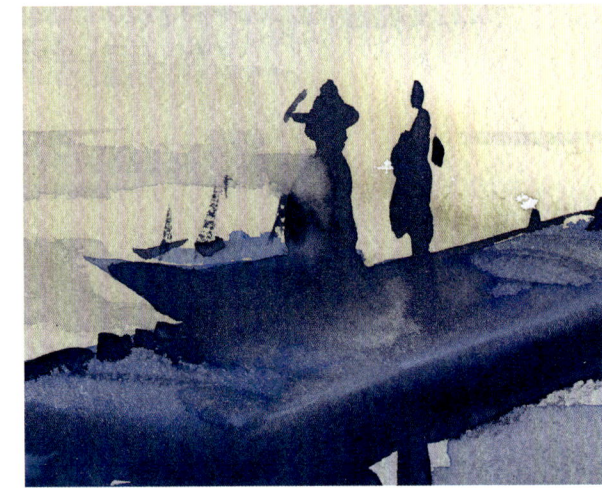

▷ In this detail these are just blobby brushmarks but, even so, we interpret them as two women conversing by a boat.

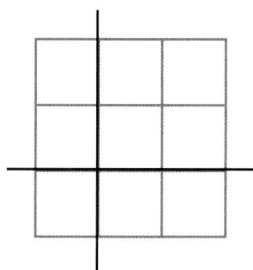

△ **Rule of thirds**

Positioning your focus or feature a third in from the left or right makes for a better composition balance than right in the centre.

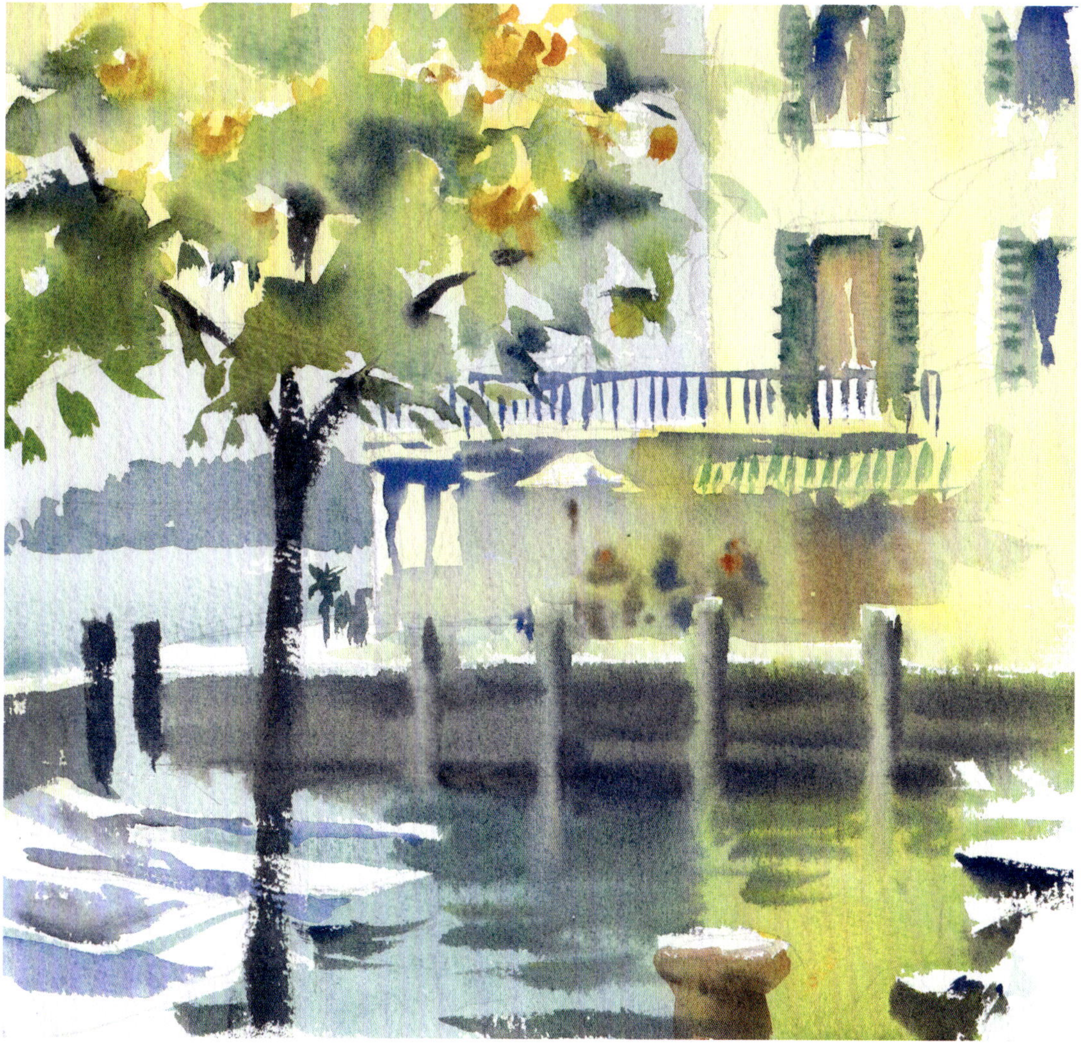

▷ **Gargnano**
25.5 x 28cm (10 x 11in)

In this quick sketch, the vertical line of the tree is about a third in from the side and the harbour wall about a third up, giving a satisfying balance to the composition.

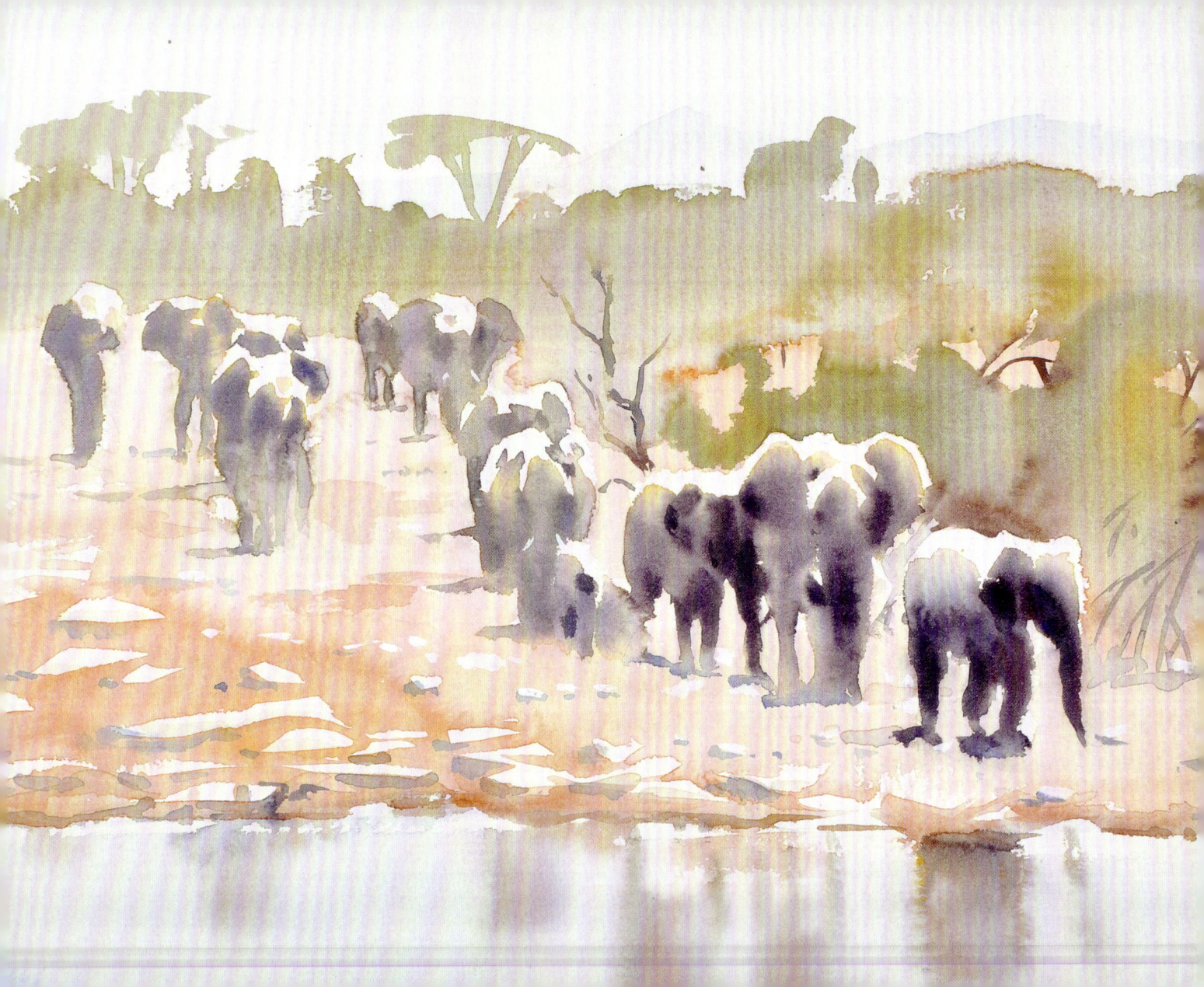

Knowing when to stop

If the watercolour on the paper looks lovely, you can stop at any time. You do not have to 'finish' a watercolour. Because it is on paper, you can crop off anything that doesn't work anyway and even change the focus of the painting.

Don't try to 'tidy up' your watercolour: ambiguity is one of the lovely characteristics of blending. The technique termed 'lost and found' exploits the vanishing substance of features as they melt in hazy shadow and gain definition in the light.

Most of all, do not fiddle. Overworking watercolours kills off freshness. If I am unsure whether something is finished or not, my motto is: 'If in doubt, chicken out!'

◁ **The Attraction to Water**
30.5 x 41cm (12 x 16in)

The herd of elephants approaching the water is implied by shapely but fairly vague brushmarks and alternating light and dark tones. Proportion, shrinking size and fading tone suggest distance ... but most is left to your imagination.

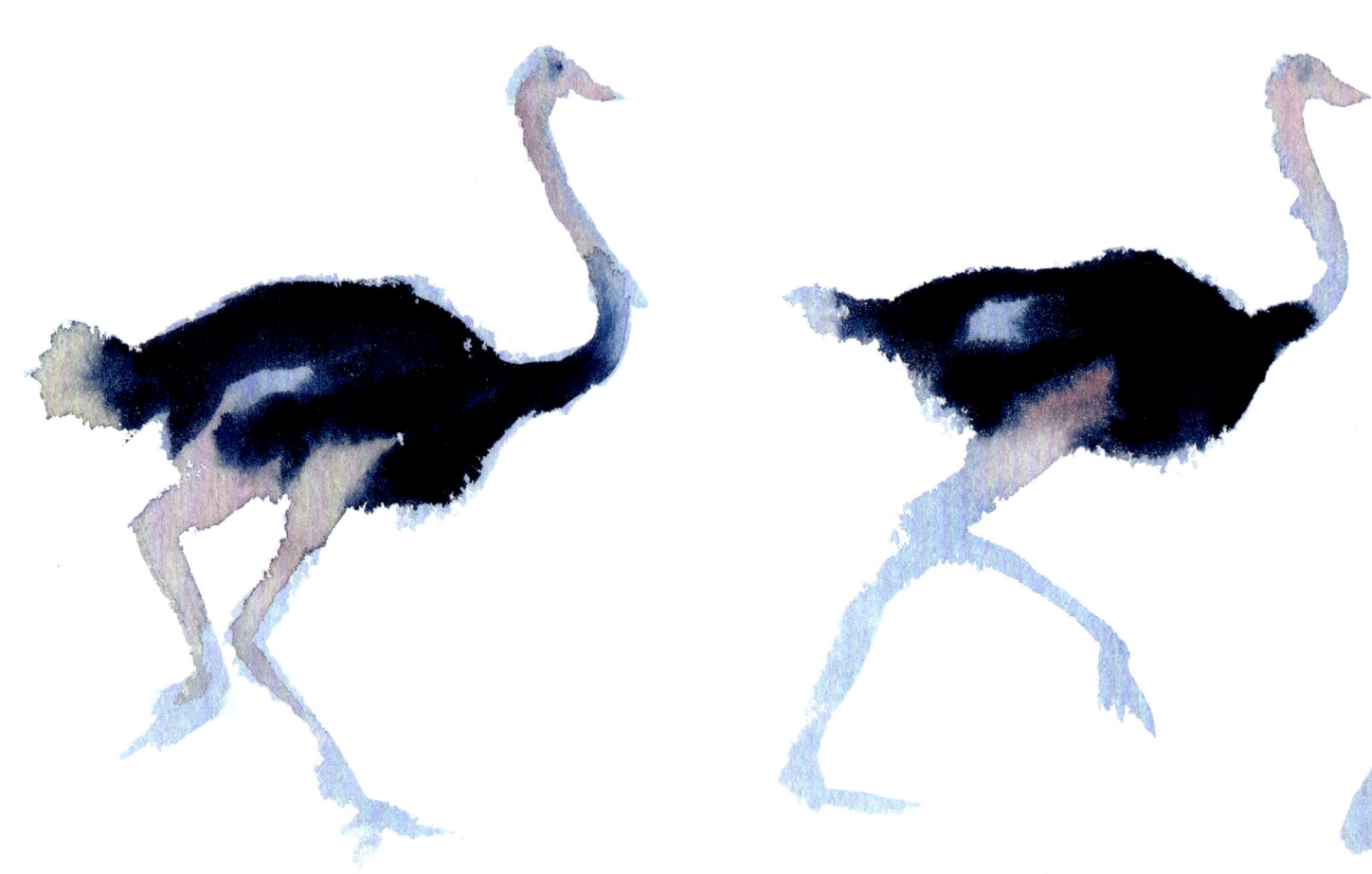

Go for it!

Have fun, relax and enjoy! The process of painting is seeing, mixing, laying brushstrokes and blending colours – the rest will come in time.

Gaining confidence

You have reached the end of the first section, and may already have made some sketches and paintings. Watercolour is a medium you can use anywhere. It is direct, quick-drying and requires a minimum of tools and materials that are lightweight and easy to transport. You have seen how the medium is so attractive in itself that you can get wonderful results right from the start, even if you just mix colours on a palette. Experience comes with practice and with practice comes excellence, but you are now on a roll, you know the basics and are ready to continue the journey – watch out for the adrenaline rush!

▷ **Running for Joy**
56 x 76cm (22 x 30in)

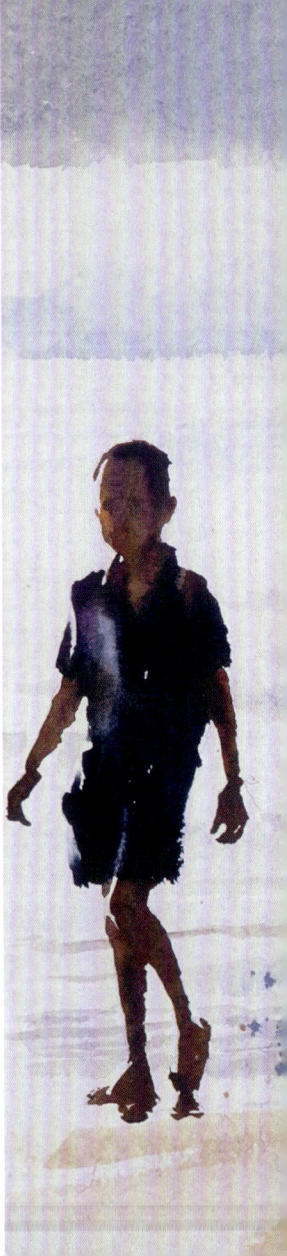

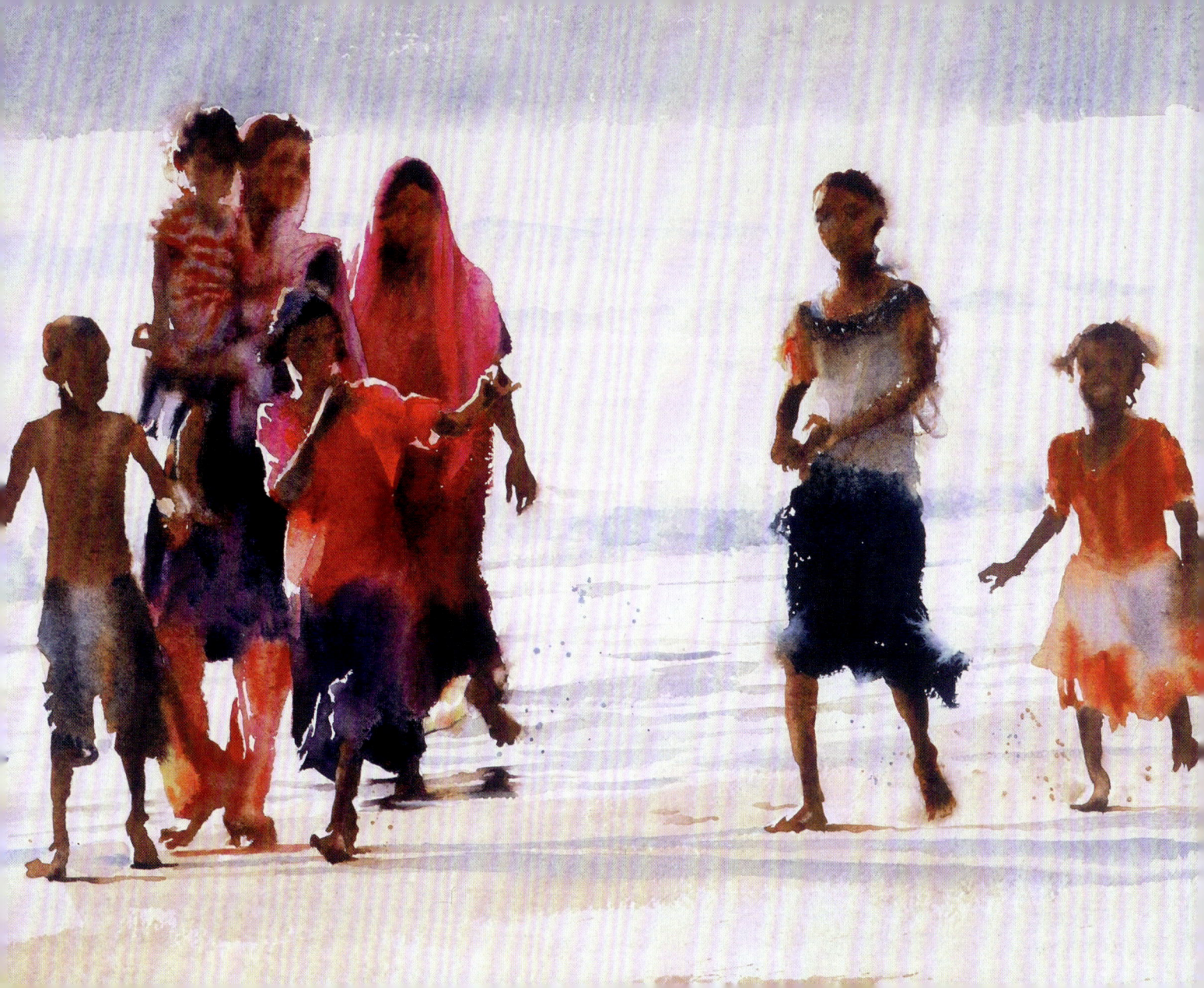

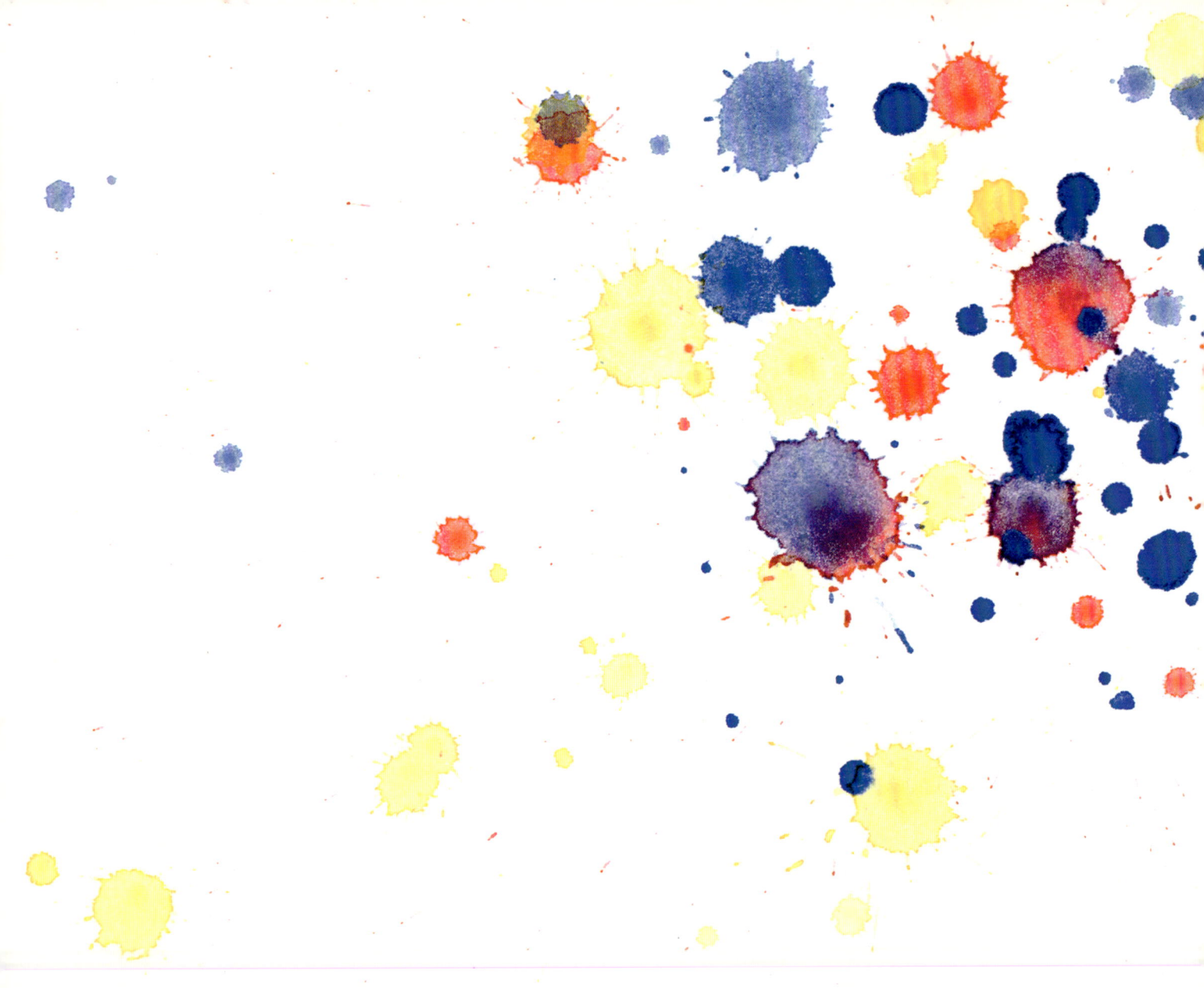

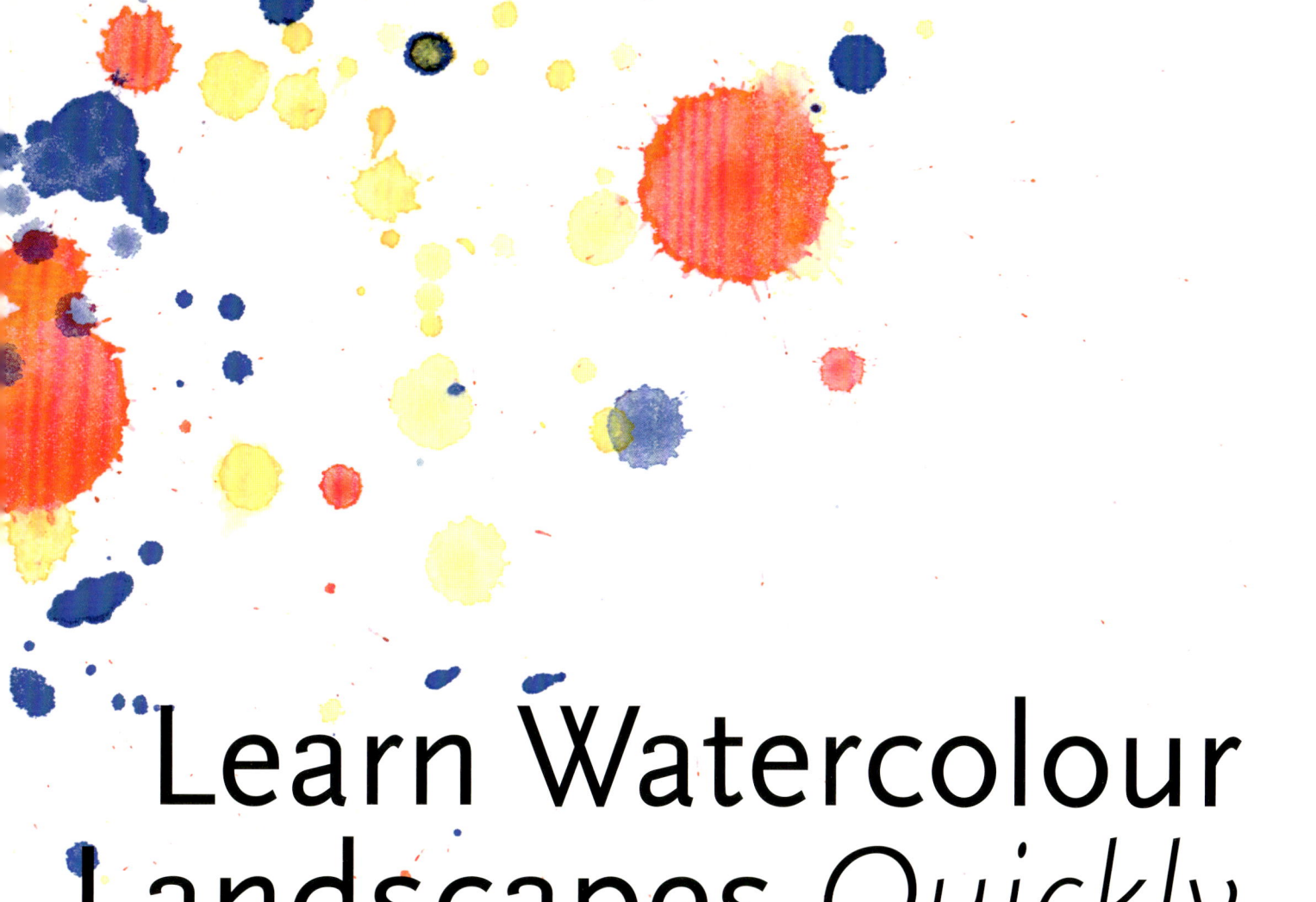

Learn Watercolour Landscapes *Quickly*

Introduction

Watercolour landscape painting is an exciting process. It takes a piece of the huge wide world, shrinks it to paper size, flattens it into two dimensions and creates something that did not exist before. Though it may resemble the landscape the artist sees, it is not the landscape, nor is it a copy – it is a new creation, a watercolour painting. I find this creative metamorphosis rather magical. How is it possible? Read on and find out.

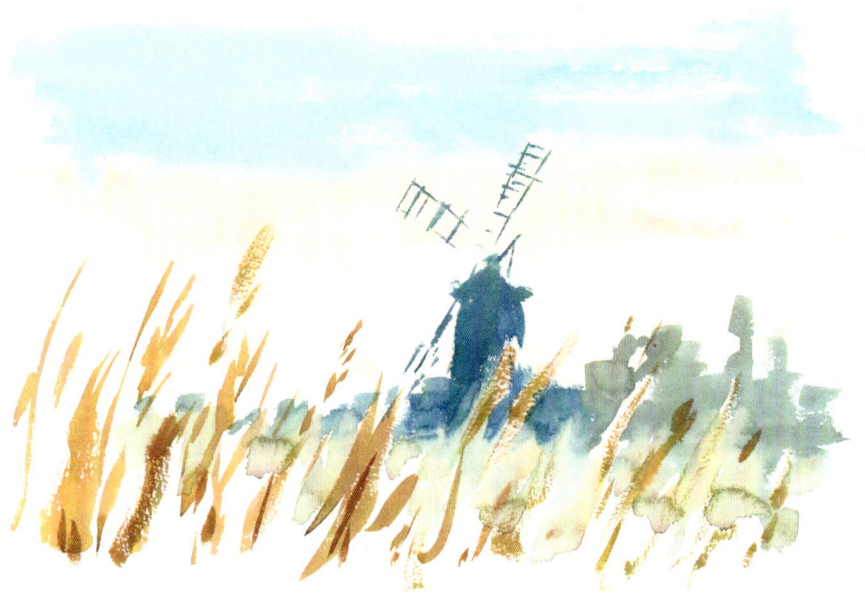

◁ Little is needed to suggest a landscape.

▷ **West Virginia Byway**
28 x 38cm (11 x 15in)

The characteristics of the watercolour medium are so attractive in themselves that a mundane subject, such as these two roadside sheds, makes an enjoyable painting with just three colours – Alizarin Crimson, Aureolin and Ultramarine Blue – and a play of light and shade.

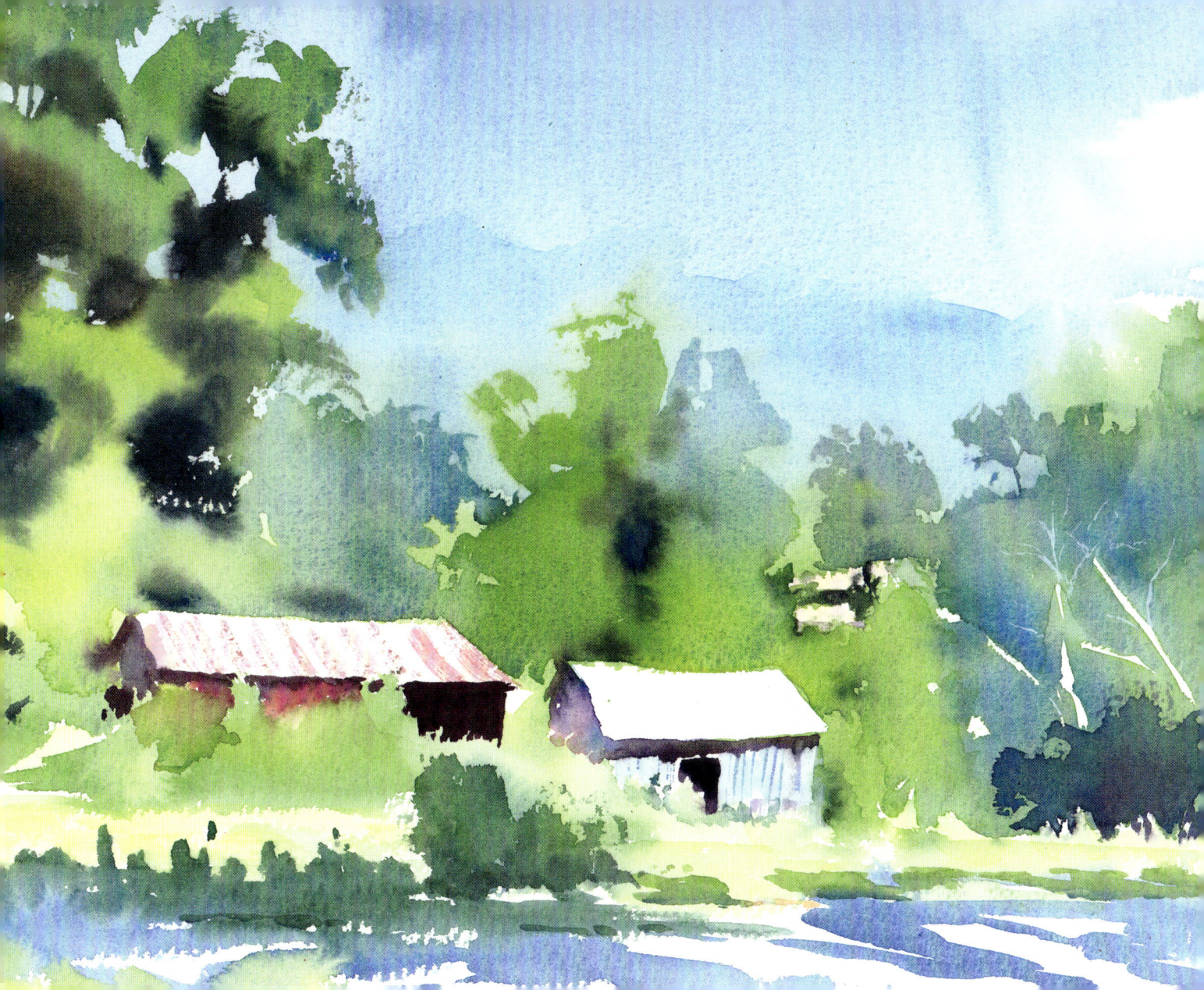

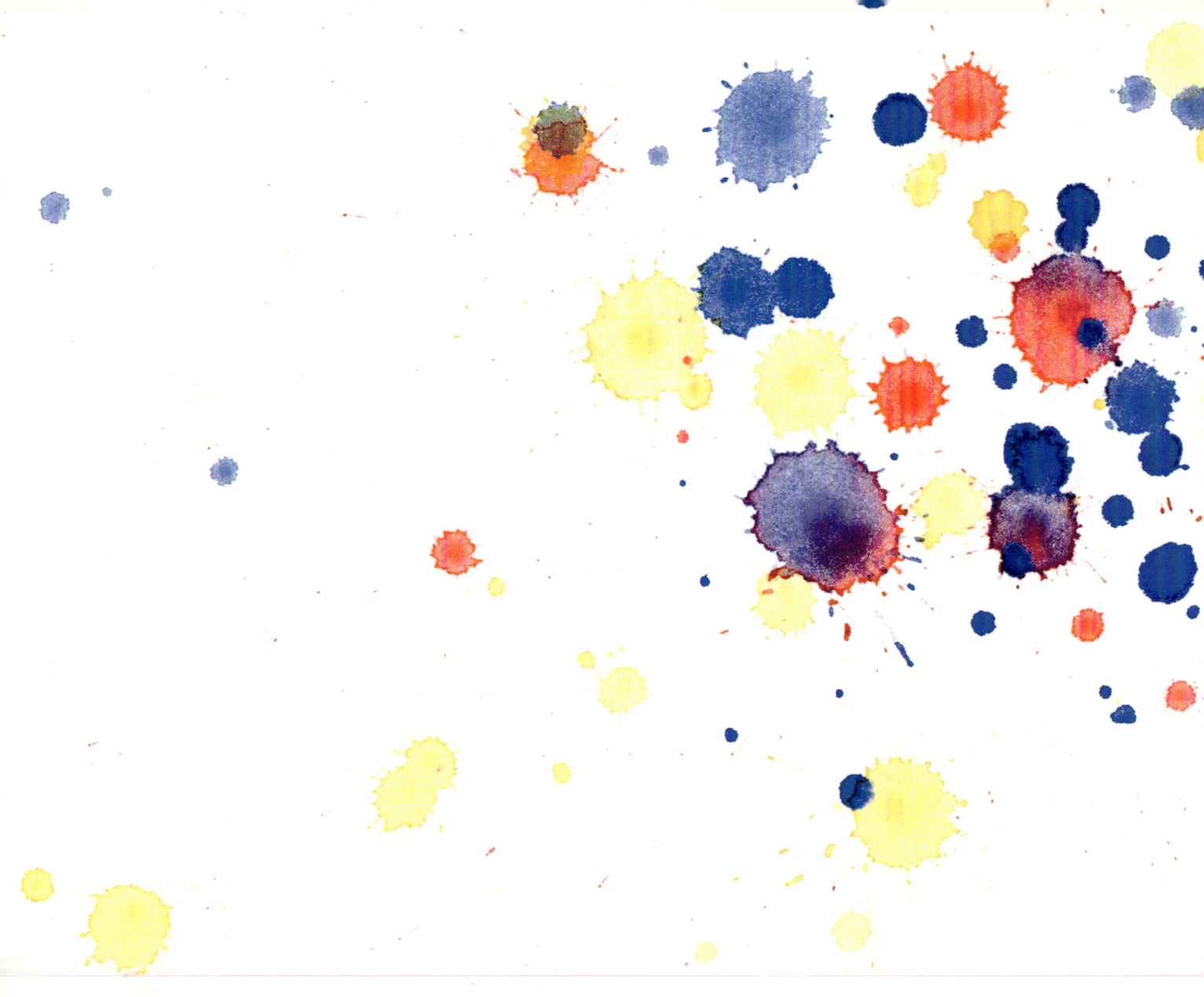

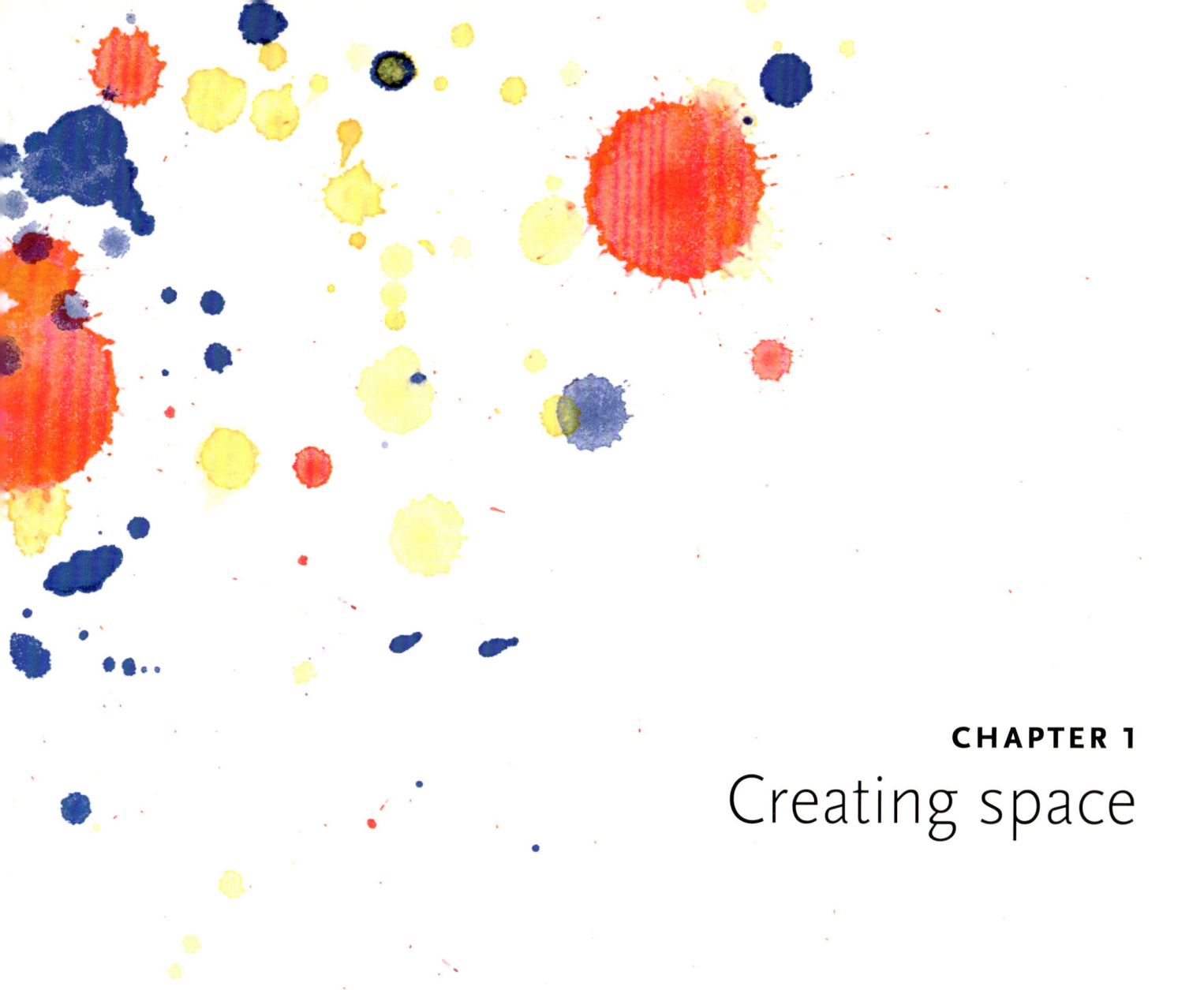

CHAPTER 1

Creating space

The art of illusion

The magic that makes landscape painting possible is the art of illusion. With the use of tone, colour and perspective, the artist has the means to convince the viewer that a three-dimensional world is reinvented on the flat surface of the paper. Watercolour is the perfect accomplice in this illusion; lightweight and easy to carry to any location, it is quickly applied and dries fast.

Three-dimensional illusion, however, is only the means to an end. Successful watercolours are not a matter of reproducing exactly what you see on paper – they are about making something new in the form of a painting. A watercolour may be inspired by the landscape but should inherit a life of its own. Before you start, instead of thinking that you are using watercolour to paint a landscape, rather think 'I am using the landscape to paint a watercolour.' This simple adjustment of mindset will free you from imitation and allow you to be creative.

Delete copy
Happily, you can remove the word 'copy' from your painting vocabulary. A painter cannot possibly 'copy' a landscape – no piece of paper would be large enough and the landscape is overwhelmingly three-dimensional!

▷ **Summertime in Wargrave**
25.5 x 33cm (10 x 13in)
Watercolour is a very practical medium for painting outside and can be applied quickly or slowly, at any size, to accord with how much time you have available. Here my time was limited, so I chose a small fragment of the garden scene.

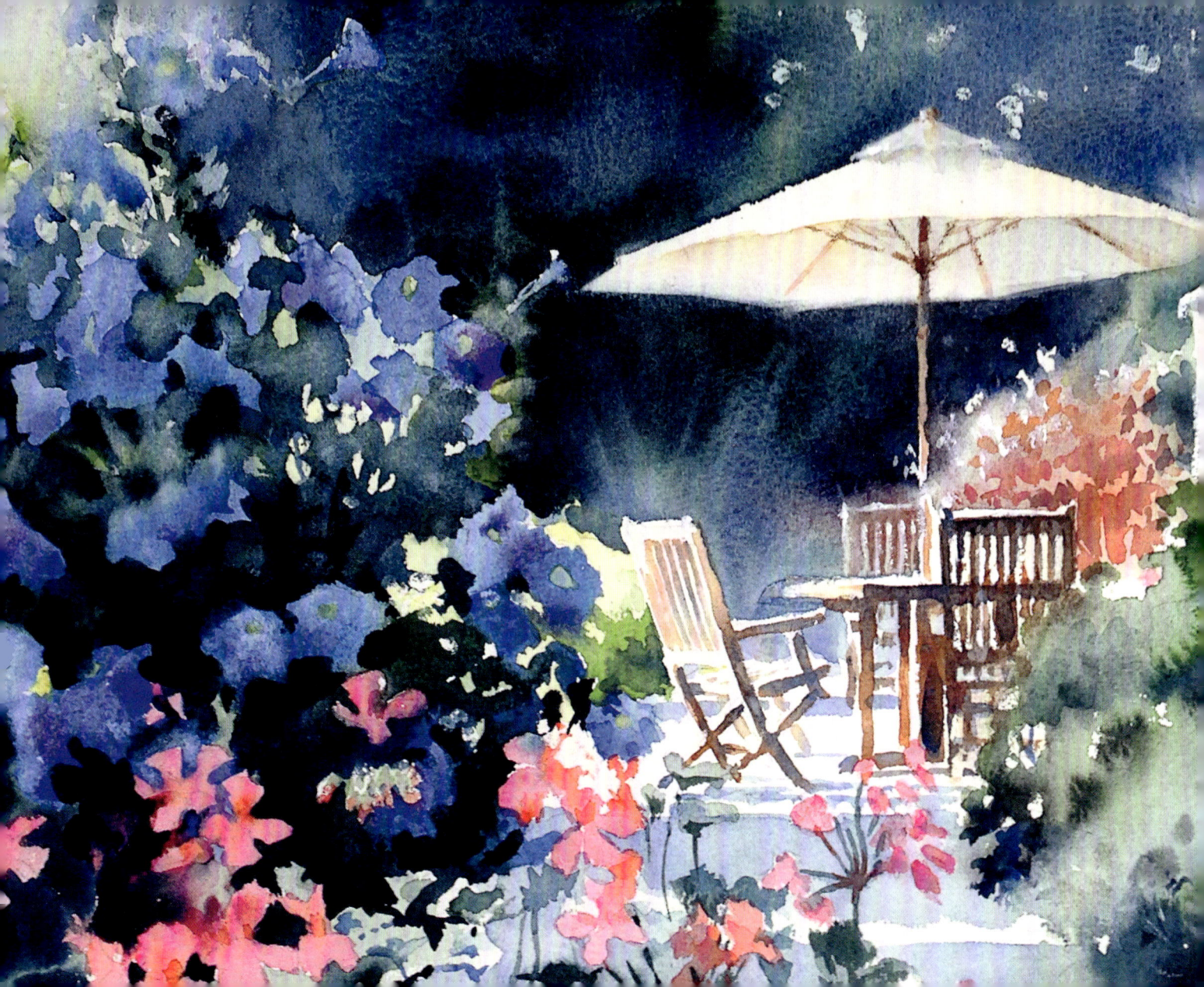

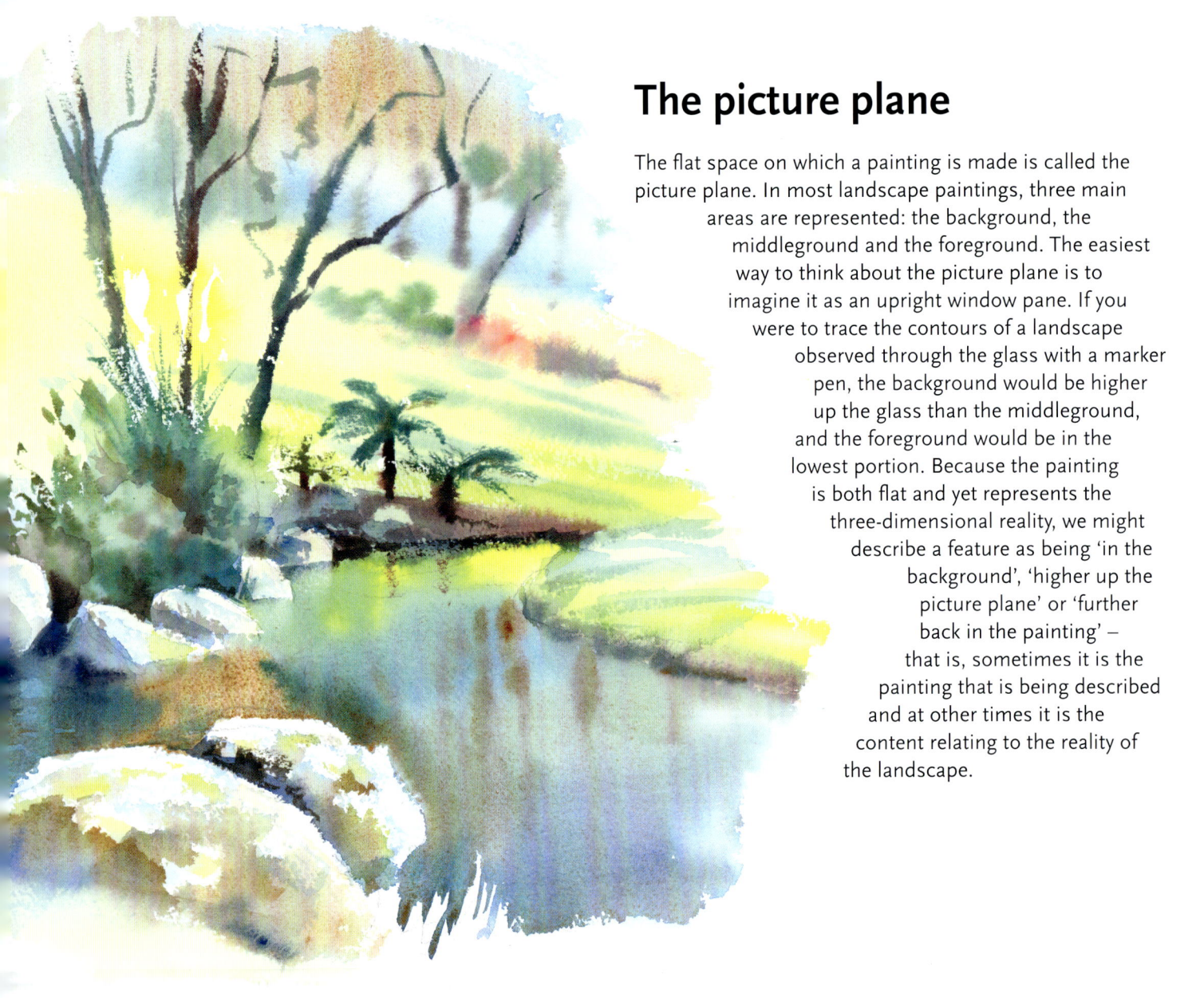

The picture plane

The flat space on which a painting is made is called the picture plane. In most landscape paintings, three main areas are represented: the background, the middleground and the foreground. The easiest way to think about the picture plane is to imagine it as an upright window pane. If you were to trace the contours of a landscape observed through the glass with a marker pen, the background would be higher up the glass than the middleground, and the foreground would be in the lowest portion. Because the painting is both flat and yet represents the three-dimensional reality, we might describe a feature as being 'in the background', 'higher up the picture plane' or 'further back in the painting' – that is, sometimes it is the painting that is being described and at other times it is the content relating to the reality of the landscape.

▷ **Coming Back by Boat, Venice**
38 x 28cm (15 x 11in)

Water fills both the foreground and the
middleground – about two-thirds of
the picture plane. A boat in the distance is
coming towards the middleground but is still
high up the picture plane, and the distant
ferry and buildings are in the background,
in the top third of the picture plane.

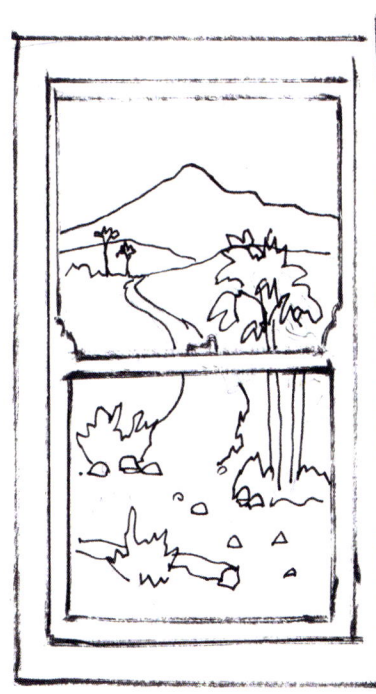

◁ Background

◁ Middleground

◁ Foreground

The horizon

The horizon is always at our eye level no matter what the vantage point and whether it is visible or not. At sea level we can see almost 4.8km (3 miles) before the Earth's curve obscures our view. From a height we can see further; if we stand on a hill at an elevation of 30m (100ft) our view extends to just over 19km (12 miles).

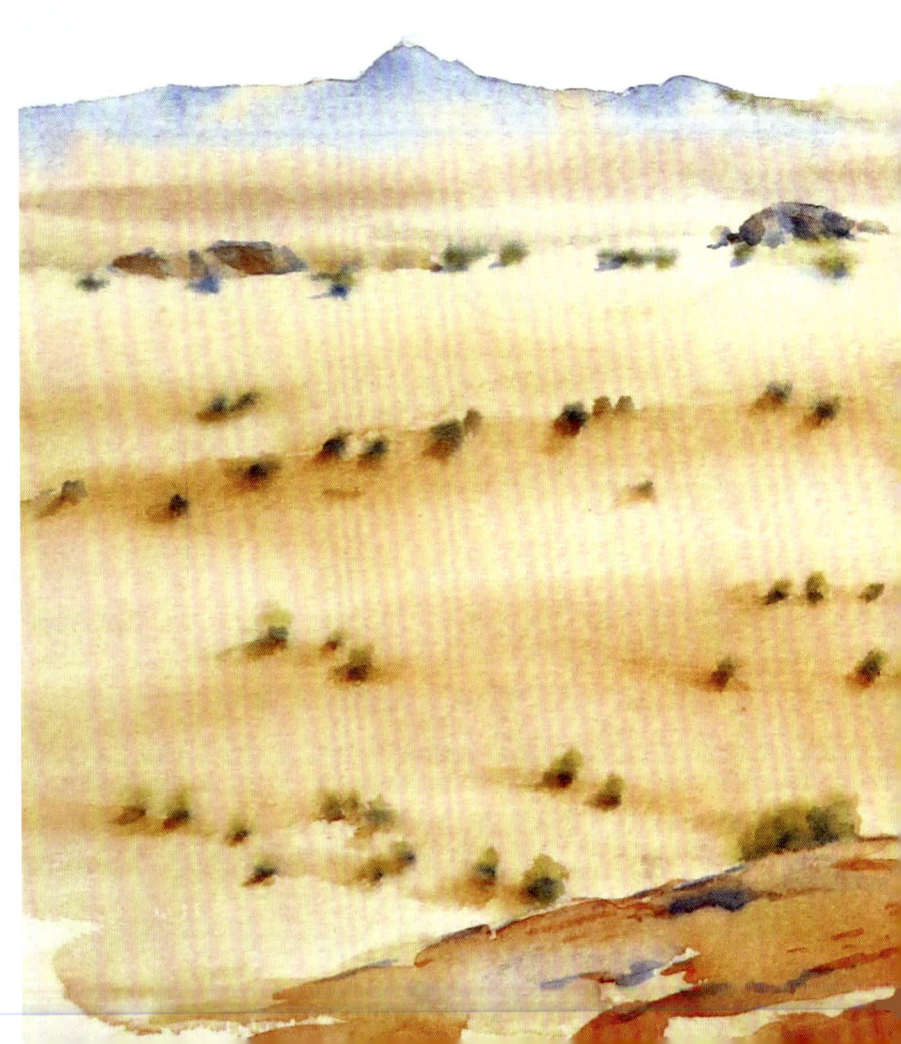

Ed and Aimée in the Marienfluss
30.5 x 66cm (12 x 26in)

The horizon is always at our eye level, whether we are looking across an expanse of landscape or at something close. Our visual acuity is so good that we can see hundreds of kilometres from a mountaintop if the air is completely clear.

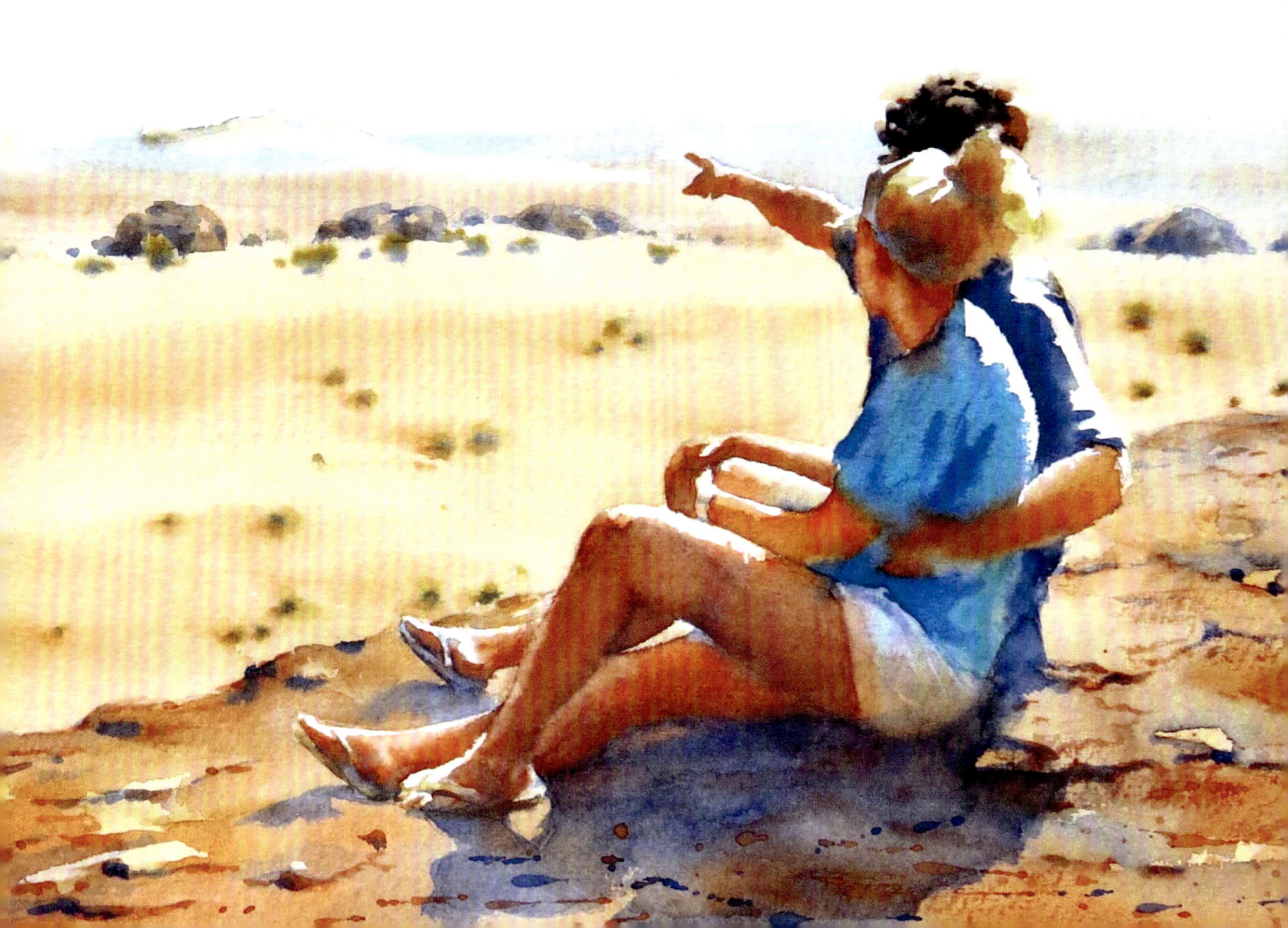

Depth, distance and space

The landscape space we see before us starts at our feet, travels to the horizon and returns overhead in the arc of the sky. Atmospheric perspective takes place within this concave space, making things smaller, bluer and less defined in the distance. The terms background, middleground and foreground refer to the depth of the space, which can be deep or shallow depending on the portion of the view we choose to paint. The physical features within the space, such as hills, trees, bushes, buildings, figures and animals, are mainly bulky, rounded or cuboid forms, with their relative size found by linear perspective. Painters have several tools to create the illusion of depth on the flat picture plane of the paper: these are scale and perspective, strength of tone, colour temperature, definition and counterchange.

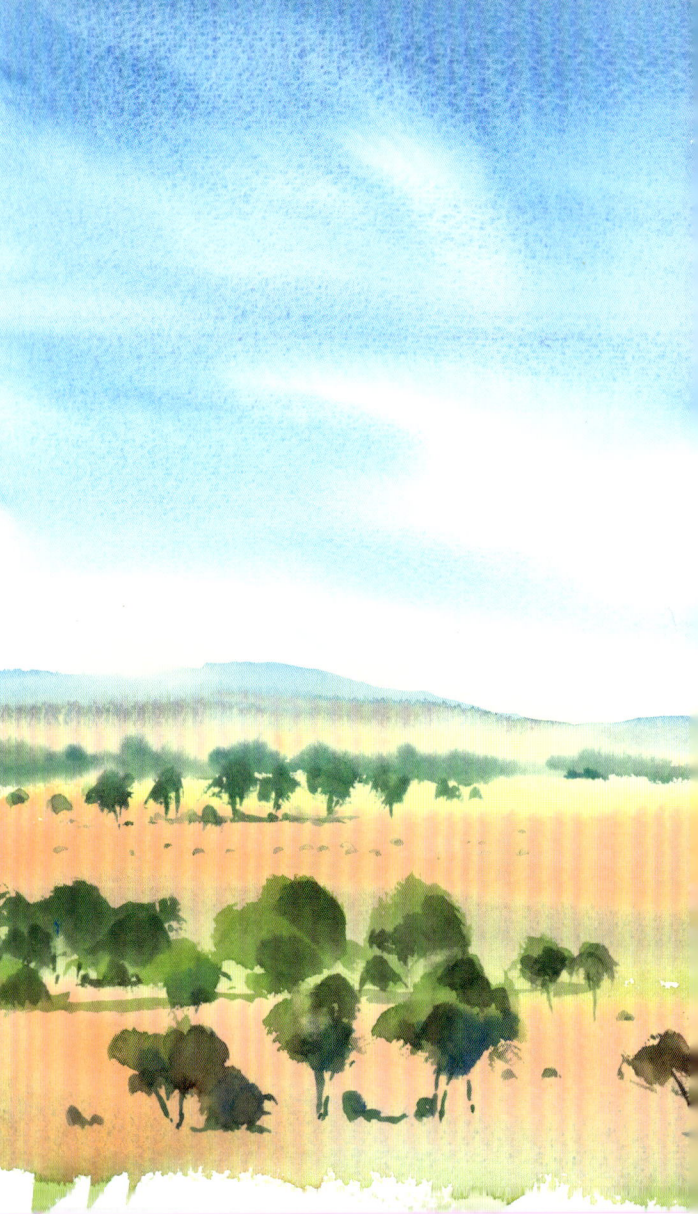

▷ **Mara Landscape**
38 x 28cm (15 x 11in)

The comparison between the size of the trees at the bottom of the painting and the diminished size of those higher up the picture plane implies the vastness of an African plain.

▷ **Lone Tree, Mara**
38 x 28cm (15 x 11in)
The strong tones of the foreground tree bring it forwards in contrast to the paler background, creating a sense of distance between the two elements.

IN THE DISTANCE

Tones are paler

Colours are cooler (more blue)

Scale makes similar-sized trees appear smaller

Less distinction and detail are visible

IN THE FOREGROUND

Tones are stronger

Hues are warmer and brighter

Size and scale are larger

Greater distinction and detail are visible

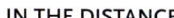

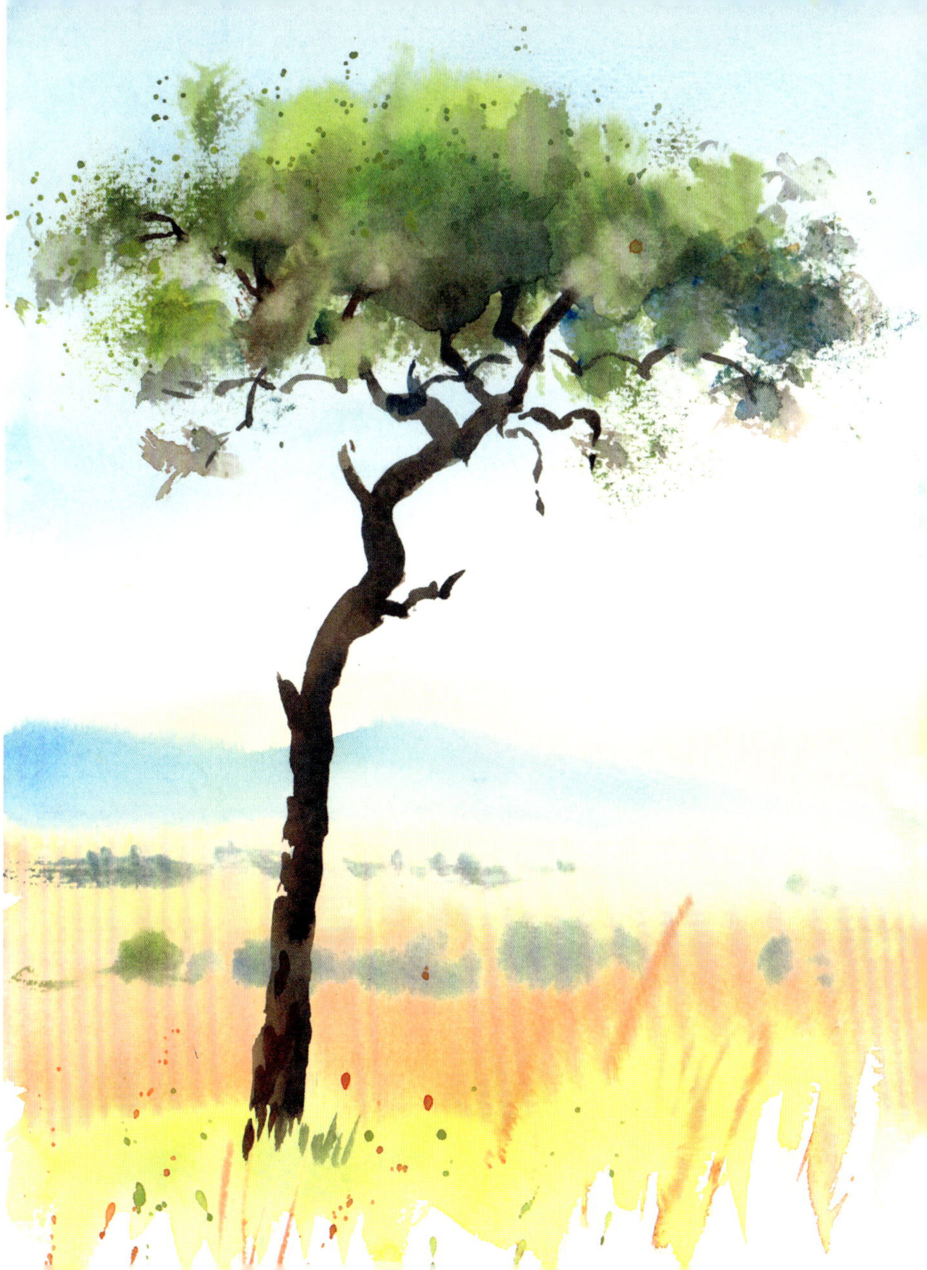

Scale and perspective

When items in the foreground are painted larger in scale than similar ones in the background, an immediate impression of depth and distance is created. An understanding of linear perspective enables you to represent features in the landscape at the right height, width and depth in relation to each other, thus providing spatial illusion on the picture plane.

Linear perspective uses parallel lines drawn from the viewer's line of sight converging to a vanishing point on the horizon line. A painting can have any number of vanishing points, one for each set of parallel lines angling across the picture plane.

With careful observation, comparing and measuring objects relative to each other, you can work out the relative proportion and scale of the features in your landscape without drawing perspective lines, but they are very useful for working out the angles of buildings in the foreground or middle distance, particularly rooflines, arches, windows and doorways.

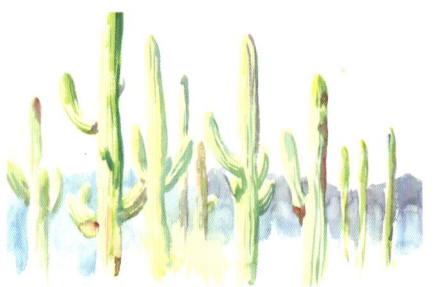

◁ **Scale**

The eye compares the relative scale of the larger cacti in the foreground with the smaller cacti in the background, and concludes that some are in front of others.

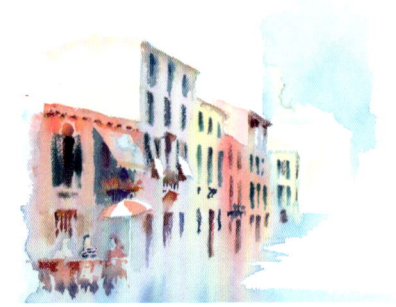

◁ **One-point perspective**

This shows a single vanishing point on the horizon, directly ahead. Any lines parallel to the line of sight will recede towards this vanishing point.

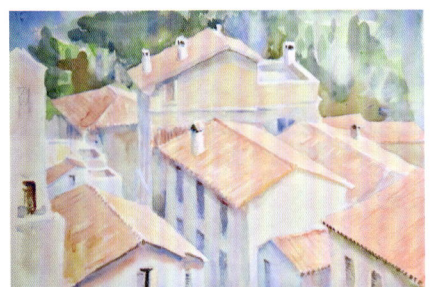

◁ **Two-point perspective**

A cubic form such as a building has two main sets of parallel lines running to the horizon.

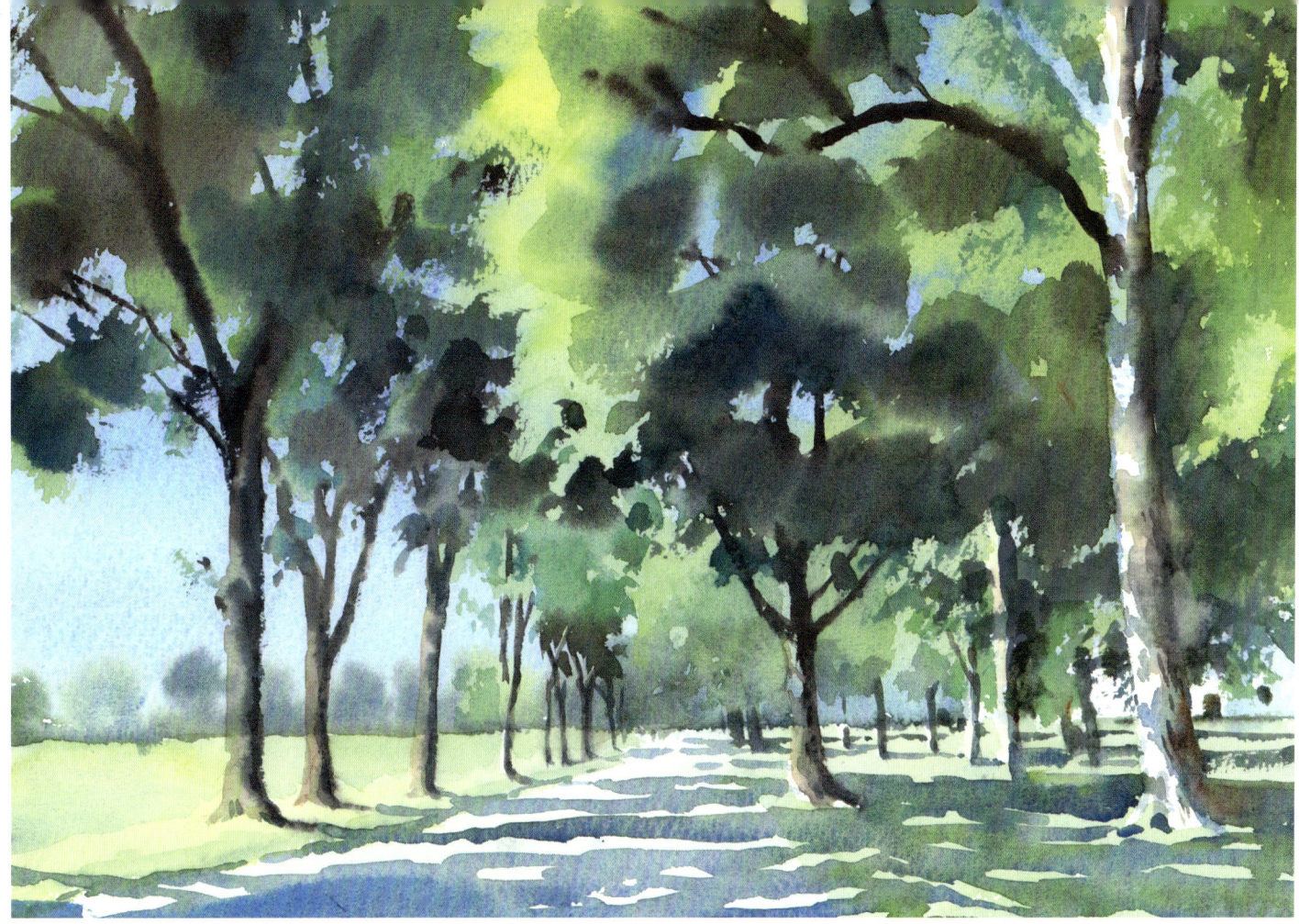

Avenue of Green

28 x 38cm (11 x 15in)

This is an example of one-point perspective, with the parallel lines of the road
and the trees converging towards a single vanishing point on the horizon line.

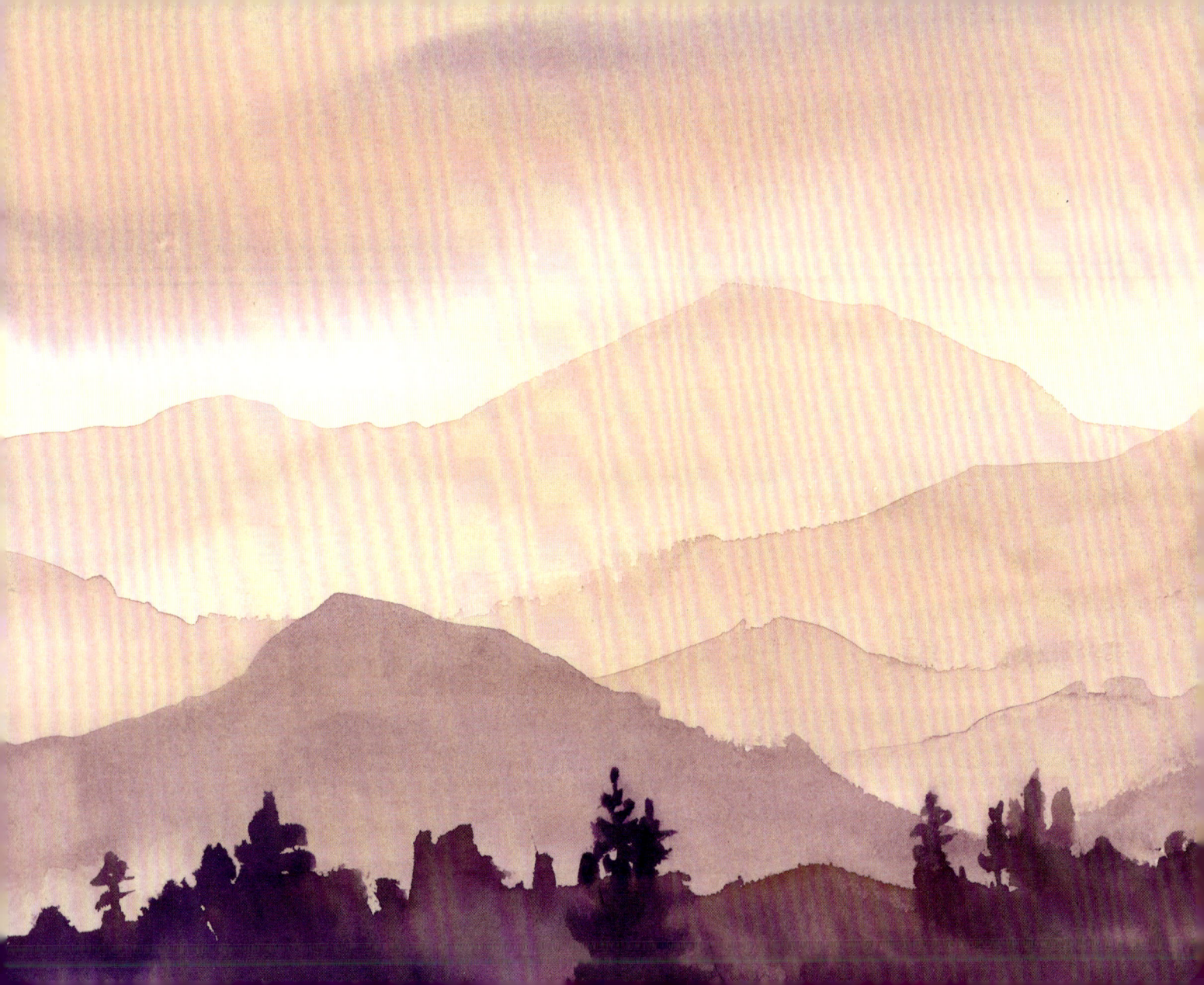

Strength of tone

Colours are made up of both hue and tone. Hue is their colour classification (for example red, yellow, blue) and tone is their shade. Tone has a vast range from the lightest light to the darkest dark, and is a powerful tool in the painter's box of tricks as it enables the eye to perceive depth. Strong tones advance while pale tones recede, so a decrease in the strength of tone, from strong in the foreground to pale in the background, enables the viewer to read the flat surface of the picture plane as a representation of space.

The distant hills are pale, the foreground features dark. Just the layering of successively darker tones convinces the viewer that an immense space exists between foreground and background.

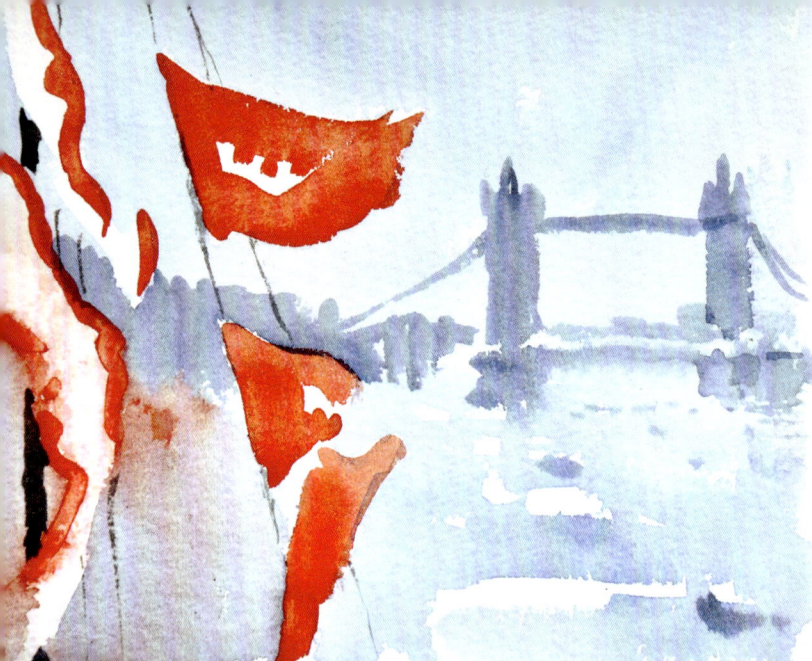

◁ **Red Flags for the Jubilee**
12.5 x 15cm (5 x 6in)
In this small painting the red of the flags attracts attention and advances on the picture plane.

Colour temperature

Colours come in many hues and shades and also have a temperature bias. Those towards the red end of the spectrum have a warmer temperature bias than those towards blue. Warm colours advance on the picture plane and cool colours retreat (you have probably noticed how distant hills often appear blue due to the atmosphere). Consequently, by increasing the warmth of features in the foreground you bring them forwards, while using cooler versions of colours in the distance helps them to recede. Since red advances it can also act to draw attention to the focus of a painting – for example, a figure in red will stand out. Use warmer versions of greens, yellows, blues and browns in foreground features and bluer, cooler versions for the distant features.

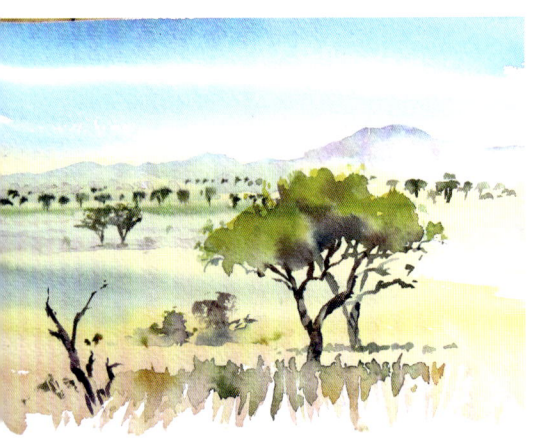

◁ The brown and yellow colours of the foreground and the bright yellowy-green of the tree foliage are warmer than the bluer greens, mauve and blue of the background hills. The temperature bias enhances the impression of distance already set up by scale and the decrease in tone and definition.

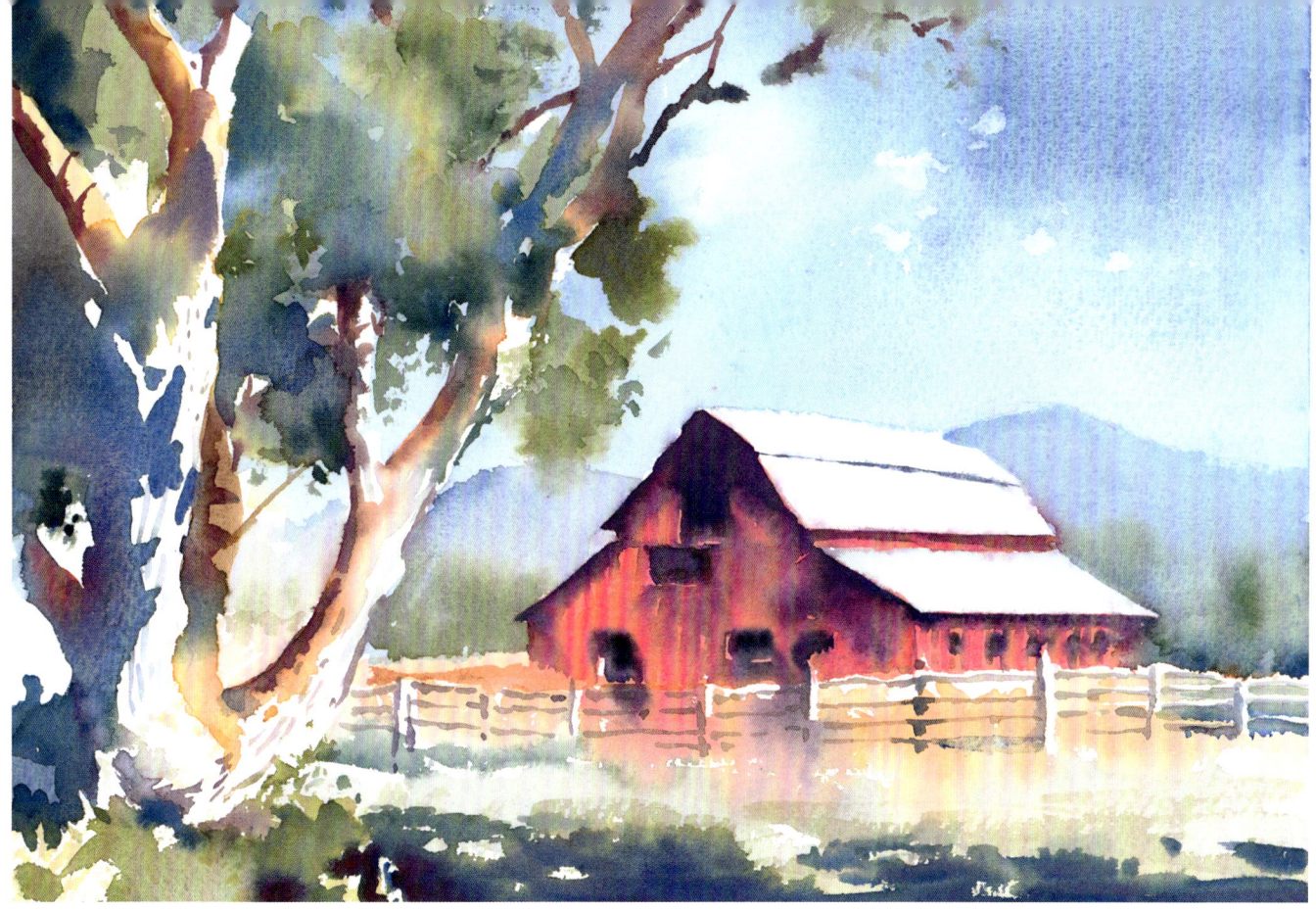

△ The Red Barn
28 x 38cm (11 x 15in)

Even though the tree in the foreground is closer to the viewer, larger in scale and stronger and brighter in tonal contrast, the red barn easily asserts its presence as the focus of the painting because the warm red colour draws attention.

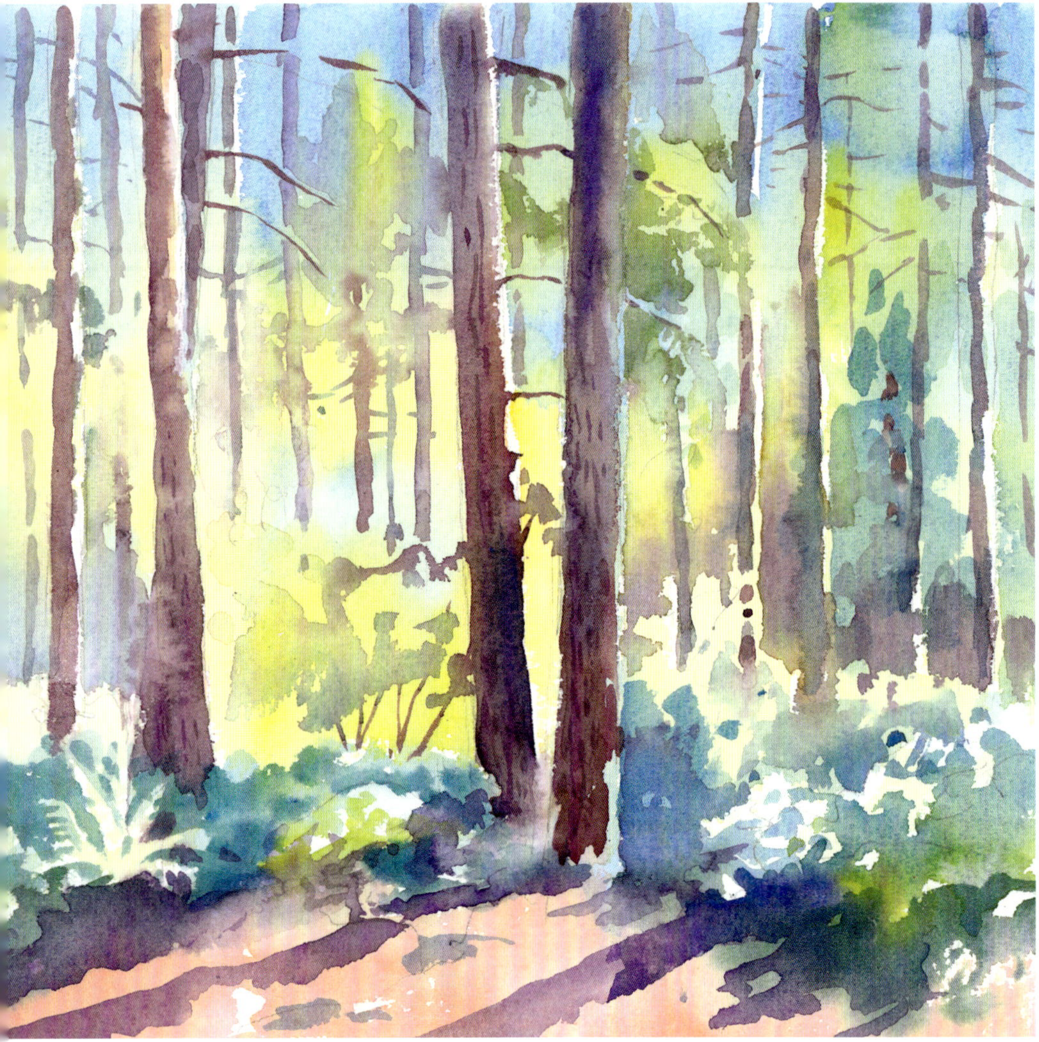

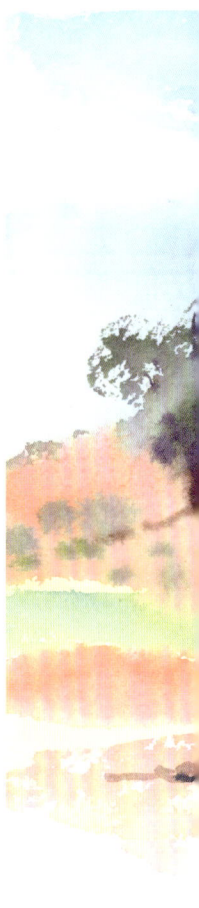

◁ **Bridlewood**
25.5 x 28cm (10 x 11in)

By painting the foremost tree trunks with a little more definition and the distant trunks with less, as well as showing them paler and narrower, a sense of the space in the forest is created.

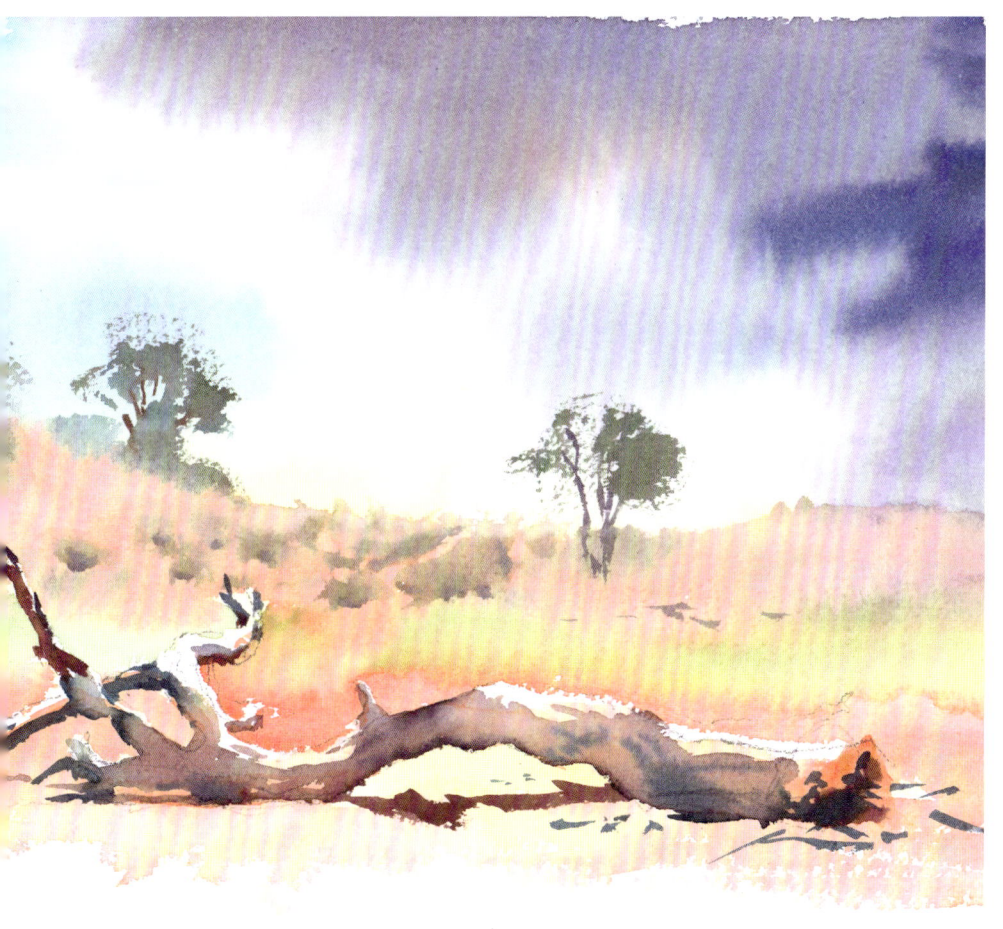

Definition

As you observe the three-dimensional landscape you will notice that objects in the distance gradually lose definition the further away they are, so it is no surprise that this works in painting too. Lack of definition suggests an item is in the background; conversely, increased definition brings it forwards. Brushstrokes and washes applied in a well-defined manner with crisp edges tend to advance towards us on the picture plane, whereas vague, blurred areas step back.

◁ **Waiting for the Lion to Appear, Kalahari**
23 x 28cm (9 x 11in)
Detail and definition advance on the picture plane. By defining the brushmarks in the foreground log and softening the brushmarks in the more distant trees, the space between them is made easy for the eye to comprehend.

Counterchange

A difference between adjacent tones on the picture plane helps to define spatial relationships, showing that features lie one in front of another. The pencil lines drawn for a composition usually demarcate where the eye discerns individual objects, a perception which is due largely to tonal register. In principle, therefore, there should be an exchange of relative tone either side of a pencil line. This lighter than/darker than counterchange sets up the illusion of space between objects overlapping on the picture plane. If your painting looks flat, the way to give it depth and contrast is to increase and even exaggerate the counterchange, darkening the tones against lighter tones and vice versa. Having established individual areas of tonal exchange, make sure the overall balance makes visual sense, with the tones in the foreground brighter and stronger than those in the background.

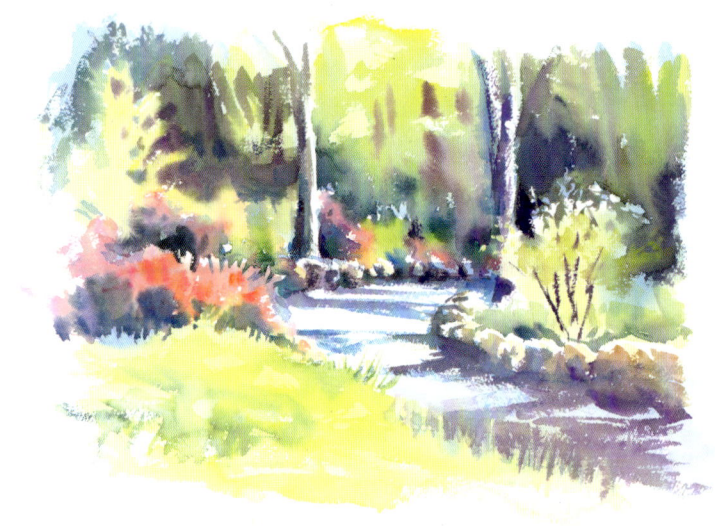

△ In this mosaic of alternating tones, light is contrasted against an adjacent darker tone and vice versa, so that the eye can clearly comprehend what lies in front and what lies behind.

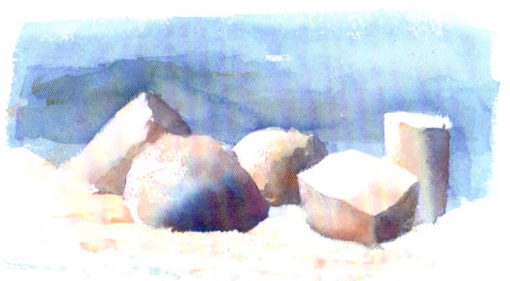

◁ It can help to see features in the landscape as geometrical shapes one in front of the other. Here a pile of rocks similar to those in the painting opposite has been approximated to a wedge, hemispheres, a cube and a cylinder.

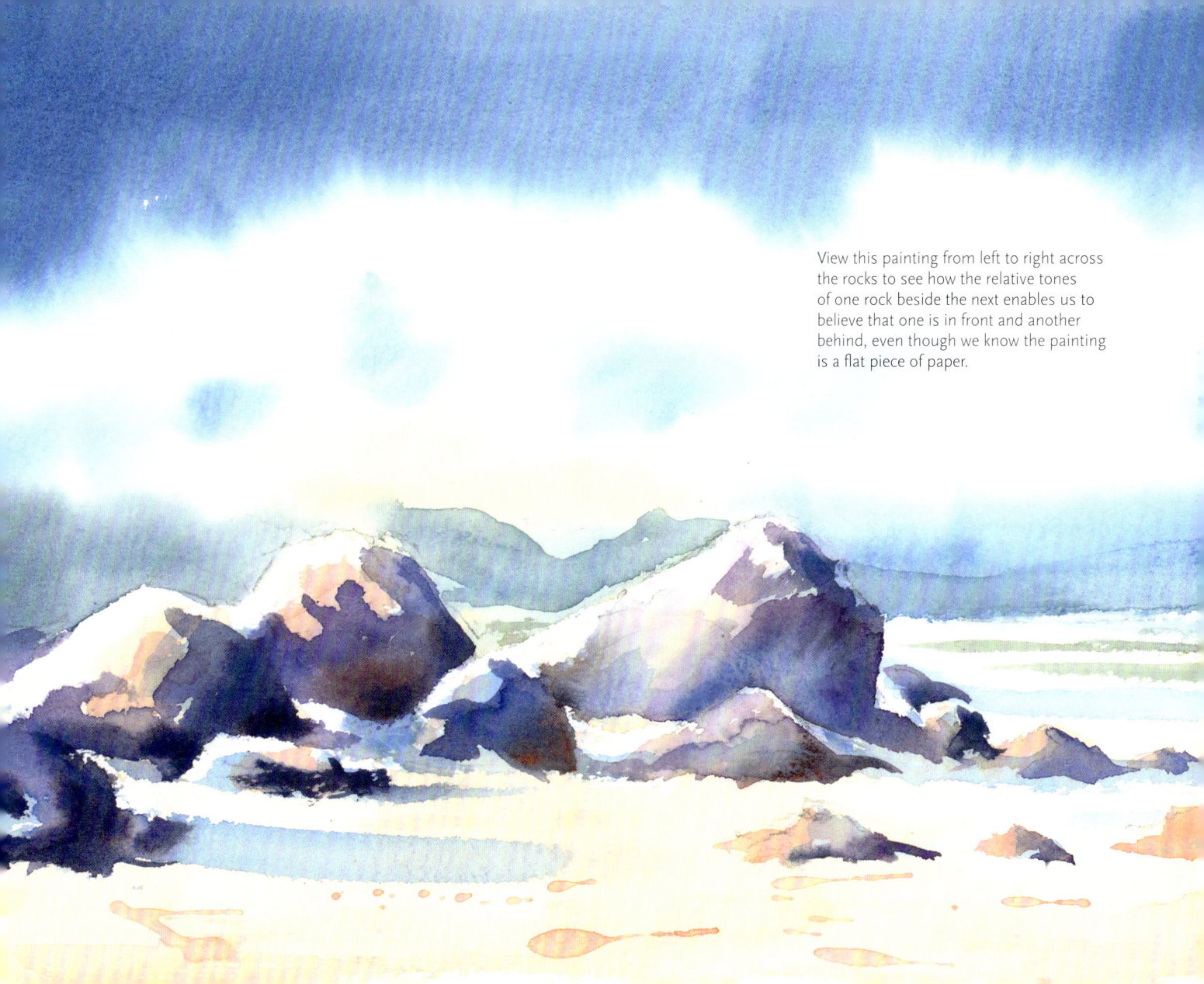

View this painting from left to right across the rocks to see how the relative tones of one rock beside the next enables us to believe that one is in front and another behind, even though we know the painting is a flat piece of paper.

Summing up the basic rules

Following the basic rules of creating space in landscape painting produces the illusion that three dimensions exist on the flat surface of the paper. Let's sum them up:

• Scale and perspective make similar features appear larger close up, smaller in the distance.

• Strong tones advance, pale tones recede.

• Warm, bright colours advance, while cool, muted colours recede.

• Definition brings objects closer; lack of definition sends them into the background.

• Counterchange establishes spatial relationships, showing that one item lies in front of, or behind, another.

Summer at Gravetye Manor
28 x 38cm (11 x 15in)

The distance across the lawn of this garden is not great. The flowers in the right-hand foreground are larger in scale, stronger in tone and warmer in hue than the border behind, and although not a lot of detail is shown, the brushstrokes in the foreground are more defined and pronounced than in the background. The counterchange between the lit table and the shrubs behind enables us to deduce immediately that it sits in front.

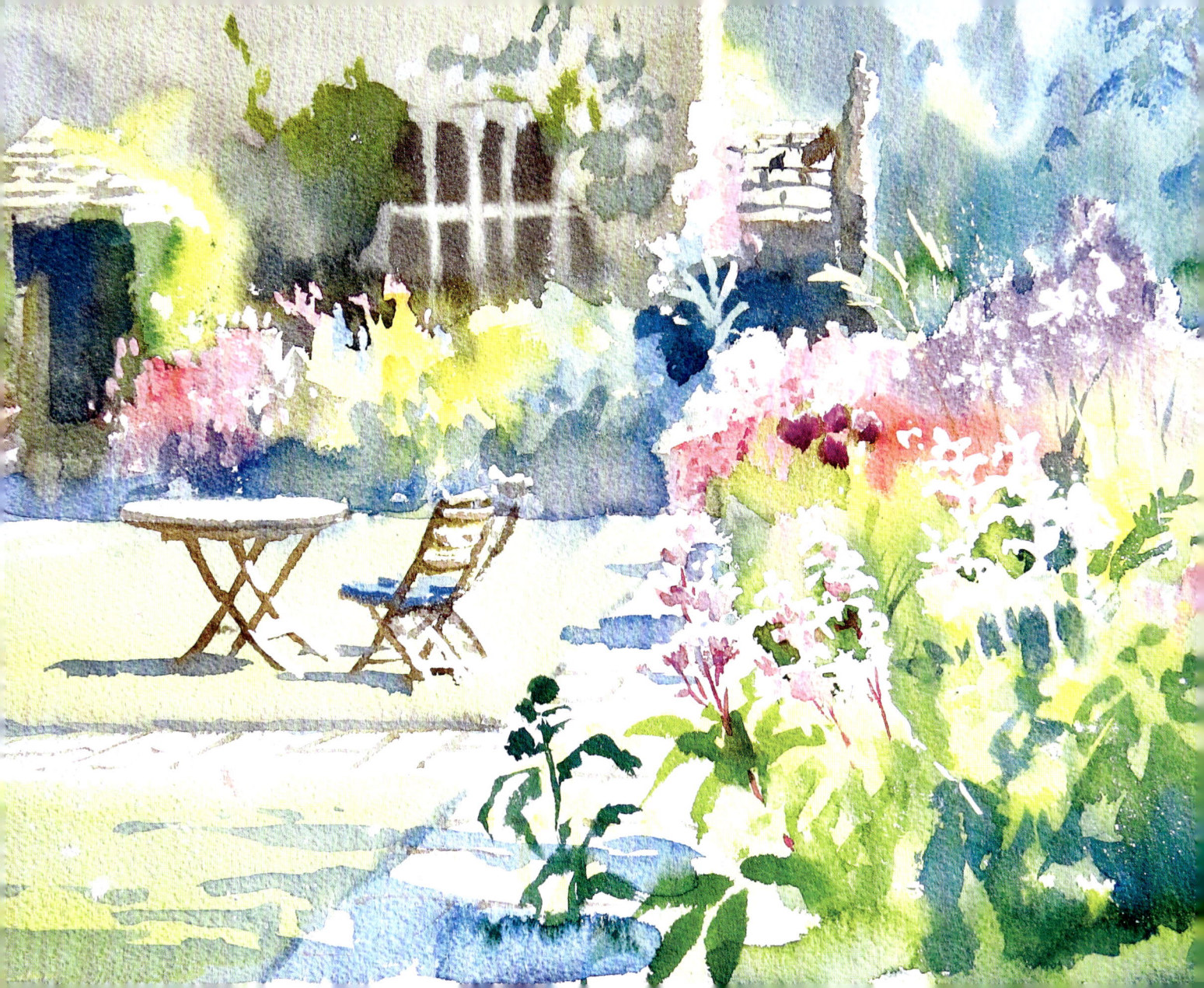

Start-up materials

I expect you are itching to paint, so let's get you equipped. You don't need masses of equipment, and it's best to keep it lightweight so that you can easily carry it into the landscape. My suggestions are below. Add an art bag to contain them. A portable easel and stool are optional for comfort – if you don't want to carry them you can just take a plastic bag to sit on.

Paper

I recommend watercolour blocks (where the sheets of paper are glued together at the sides, so there is no need to stretch them to avoid cockling when water is applied) and spiral-bound sketchbooks of 100 per cent cotton paper, with a Rough surface, weight 300gsm (140lb) plus. The size is up to you – anything from small (about 18 x 28cm/ 7 x 11in) to as big as you can handle, for example 61 x 45.5cm (24 x 18in).

Pencils

You will not always draw before painting, but pencils are essential in your kit as a drawing guides the brushstroke. I recommend using HB and 2B or 4B pencils. Add a putty rubber, which is softer than an ordinary eraser, and does not scuff the paper surface. Pack a pencil sharpener or a craft blade (also useful for separating the sheets of paper from a block).

Paints

There is no definitive list of colours for landscape painting – every artist uses a different set. The important thing is to become familiar with the ones you have. I suggest both pans and tubes of artists'-quality watercolour. Start with six colours – a warm and cool version of each of the primaries – and add some earth colours too. My suggestions are shown below.

Blue

Ultramarine Blue
Warm, transparent and lifting

Prussian Blue
Cool, transparent and staining

Yellow

Indian Yellow
Warm and almost transparent

Aureolin
Cool and almost transparent

Red

Cadmium Red
Warm, opaque and granulating

Alizarin Crimson
Cool, transparent and staining

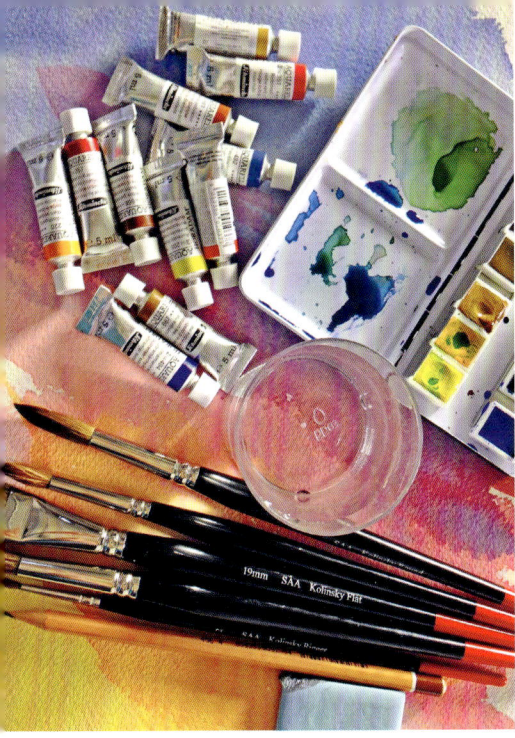

Palette

I use a travelling metal enamel palette and fill it with my chosen pans. I carry tubes of paint in a small pouch.

Brushes

While pure natural hair brushes are expensive, they are worth it because they can carry large amounts of pigment and allow control over its release. I favour round brushes in large sizes (12 and 10), and the smaller 6 and 8 (sizes vary somewhat between brands). If the brushes have good tips the only small brush you will need is a rigger, which has long hairs ideal for making thin, linear strokes for branches. Add a large flat brush (approx. 20mm/¾in), which you can use to lay washes and wet the paper in preparation.

Miscellaneous

Of course you will need water pots, and a water reservoir (a plastic bottle). Also pack some rags or kitchen paper.

Keep painting materials as lightweight as possible, since water and paper are heavy in themselves.

Earth colours

Yellow Ochre
Warm and semi-opaque

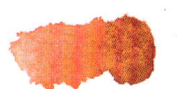

Burnt Sienna
Warm, transparent and lifting

Raw Sienna
Cool, transparent and granulating

Raw Umber
Cool and granulating

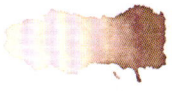

Burnt Umber
Warm and transparent

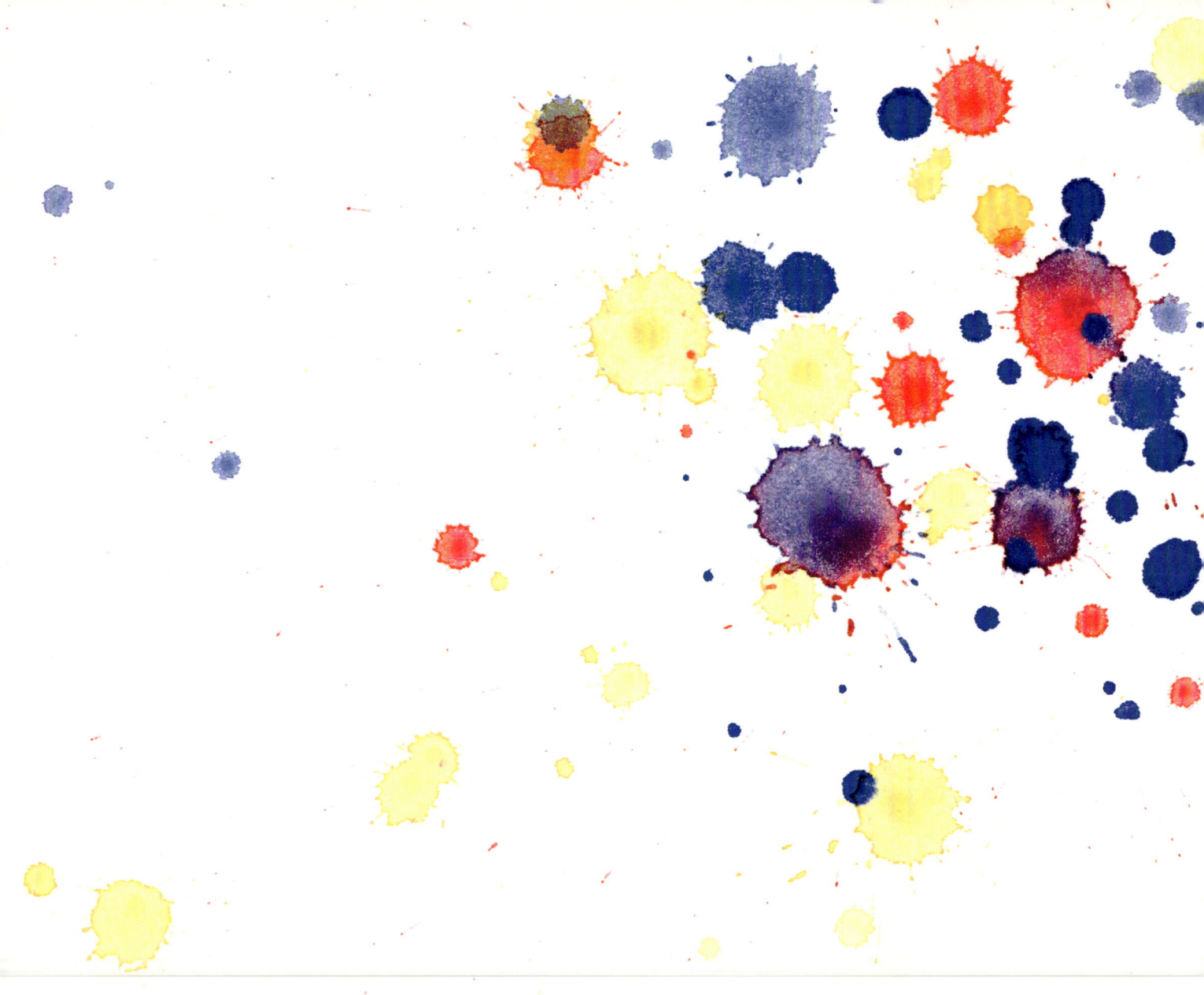

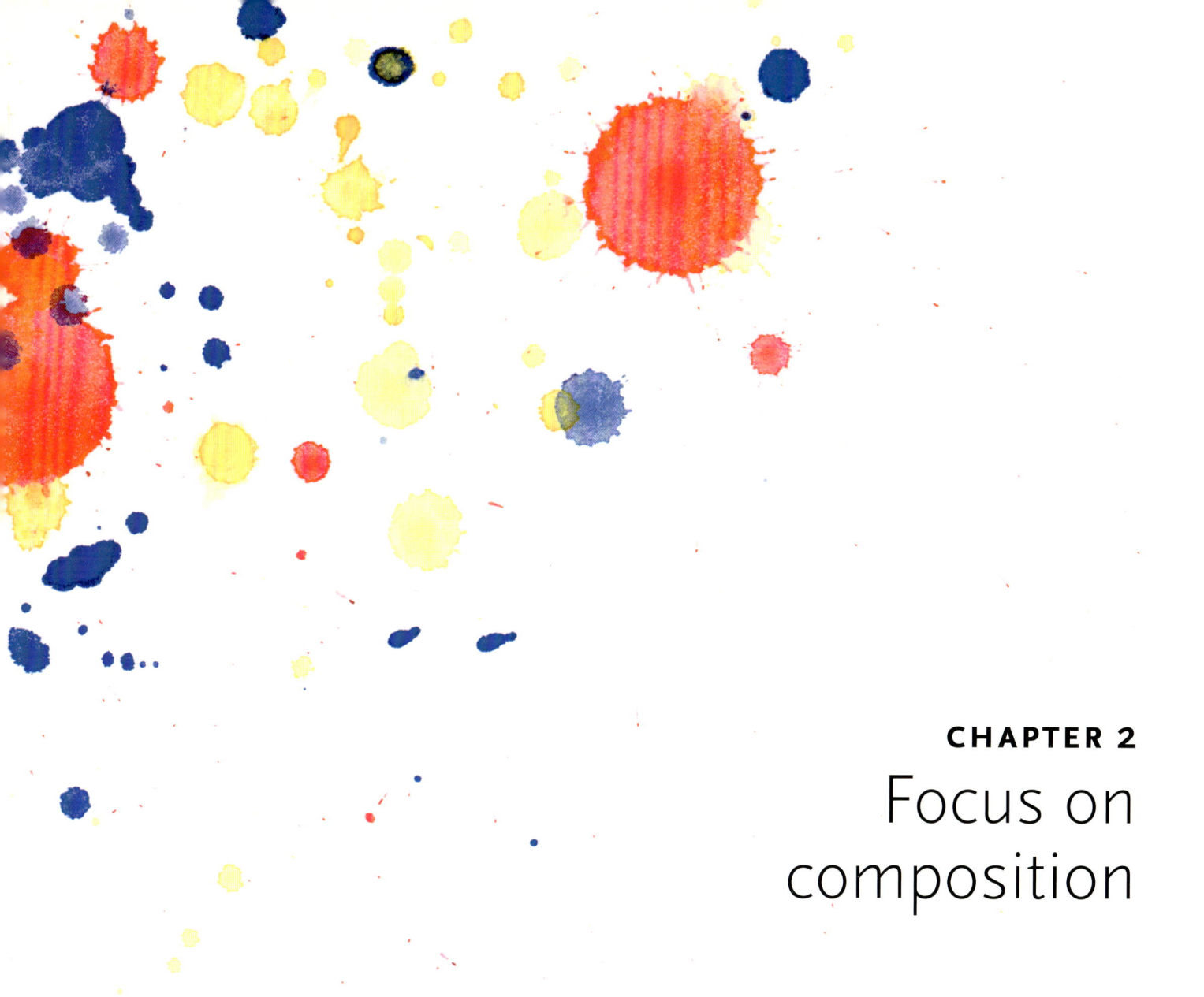

CHAPTER 2
Focus on
composition

Finding your focus

The design of a painting is called the composition. This can be simple or complex and benefits from a focus. When you come across a view that prompts the desire to paint, ask yourself what in particular has attracted you. Make this your focus. Not only will it bring coherence to the painting but it takes the pressure off the definition, or even inclusion, of less important elements.

Few landscapes, even the most picturesque, offer an immediately obvious composition. A sweeping panorama may look tempting to paint, for example, but it may lack structure. Find a focus or a leading line, such as a river or a road, and the panorama then becomes a candidate. Feel free to juggle things around to help balance the layout. Good positioning of principal features turns views into workable compositions. Abstract elements, such as the pattern of light and shade, weather or a particular atmosphere, can also provide the focus.

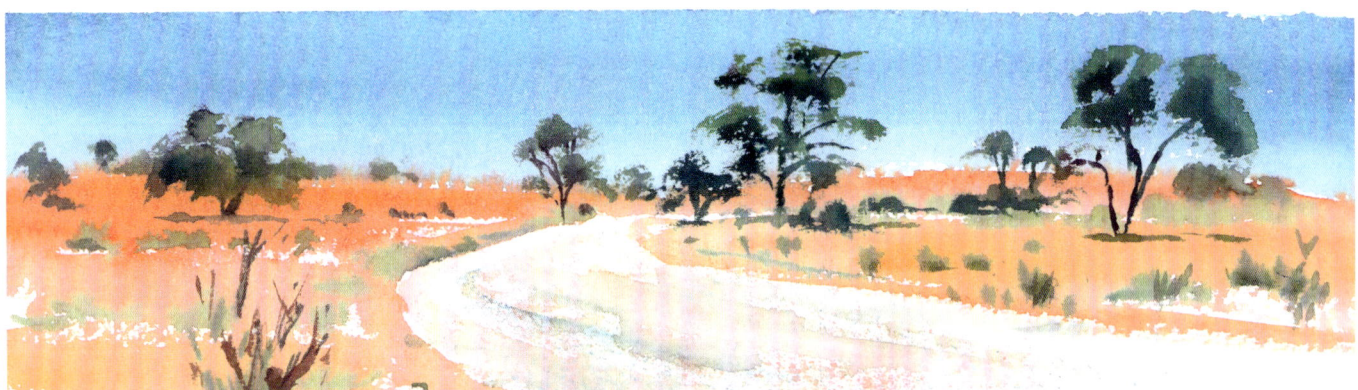

King's Road in the Rain
28 x 38cm (11 x 15in)

The rainy day and the reflections were the focus of this composition, with the bus and the cyclist drawing the eye into the scene.

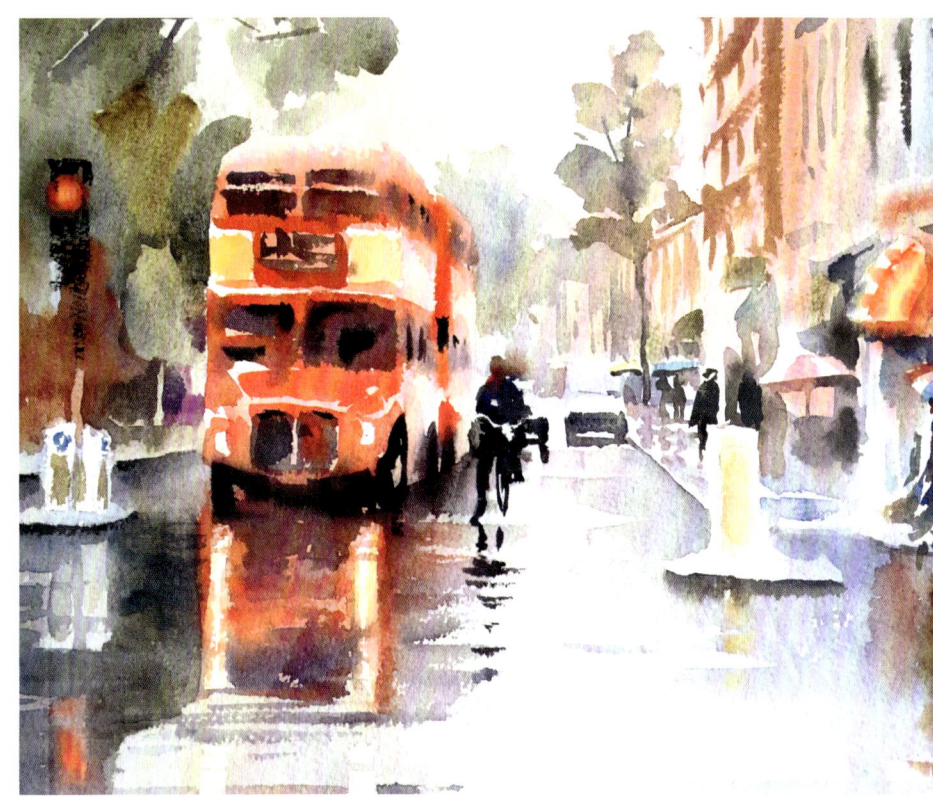

◁ The focus here is the road going off into the distance, the curve of the tyre track leading the eye into the painting and beyond. Watercolour is such a lovely medium in itself that attractive blends of pigment are often enough to make a painting succeed.

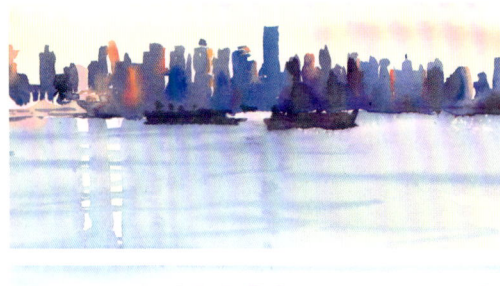

Horizon placed above the centre line

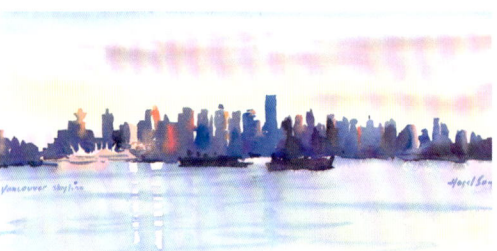

Along the centre line

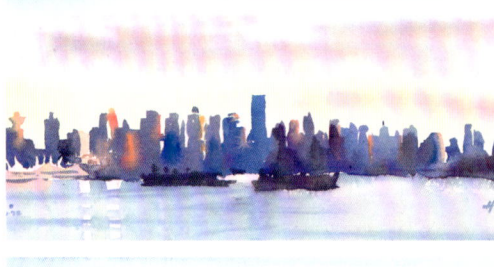

Below the centre line

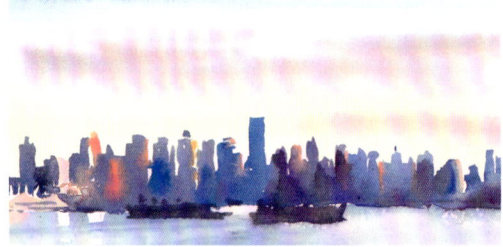

Further below the centre line

The horizon line

Whether visible or not, the horizon line is always at your eye level, so the first decision in planning the composition is to decide where to place it on the paper. As a rule of thumb it is better to position it above or below the centre line to prevent the painting from being split in half, but straight across the middle can also work so long as the composition looks balanced (and paper can always be cropped if you change your mind!).

◁ **Sky Rise, Vancouver**

12.5 x 41cm (5 x 16in)

Here the shoreline of Vancouver is my horizon line. Altering its placing on the paper changes the balance of the composition. Which do you prefer? I like the third version best, as it gives the buildings a space to rise into and enough light tone below to balance the dark tones above.

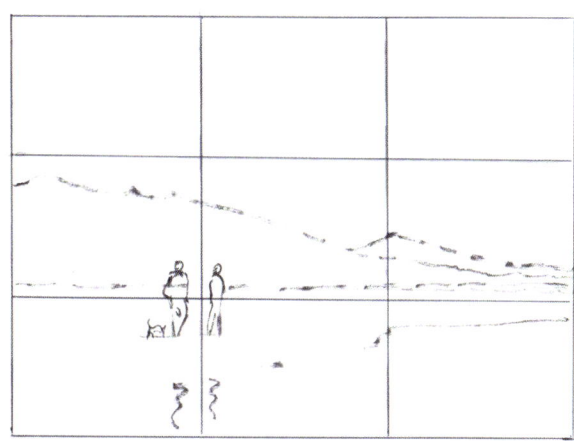

▷ Mentally divide the picture plane into thirds along both orientations and design your painting with this grid in mind; it will help to balance your composition.

The rule of thirds

Positioning the focal point is an important consideration. A central feature can split a composition in two halves; placing it off-centre usually makes for a more striking composition. A good way to arrive at a balanced composition is to divide the picture plane into thirds with equally spaced imaginary lines, two horizontal and two vertical. Align the important elements of your composition, for example the horizon line and predominant subject, along or near these lines and in the vicinity of their intersection points, then juggle the elements until you get a pleasing balance.

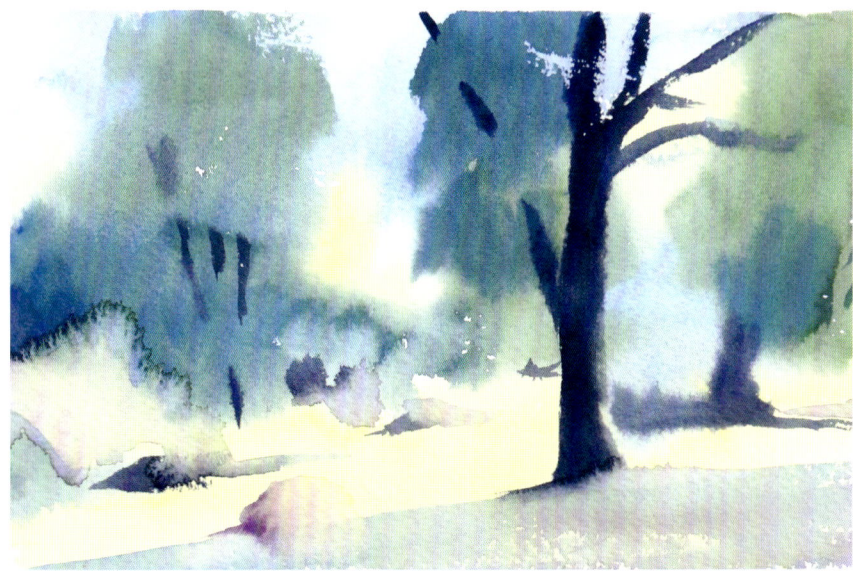

◁ A vertical subject such as this tree can split a painting in two if placed in the middle, hence it is better placed off-centre. The level of the horizon follows the 'rule of thirds', creating a balanced and pleasing layout.

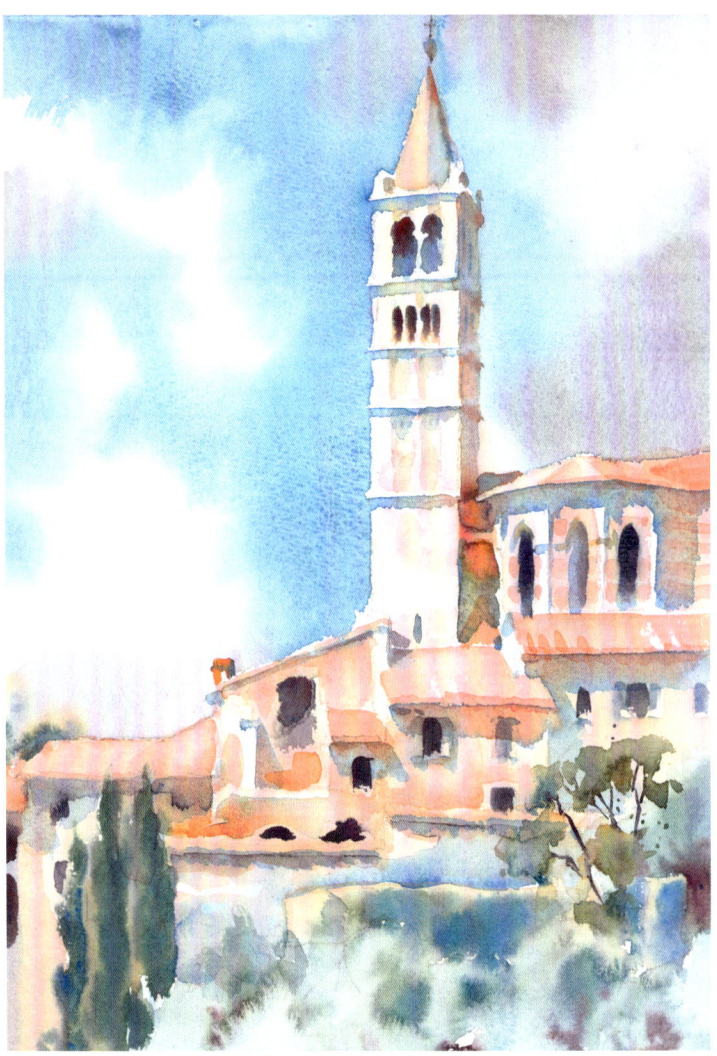

Selection and orientation

Many landscape paintings are painted in a landscape format, but most views offer a choice between portrait, square or landscape orientation. Looking through a viewfinder helps make the decision. You can cut an aperture out of card but the most flexible viewfinder is literally at your fingertips. Touch the forefingers and thumbs of both hands together to form a roughly rectangular-shaped aperture, which can be elongated or squared at will, moved back and forth, and orientated vertically or horizontally.

Roam the landscape looking through this aperture, seeking a section you find pleasing or interesting in composition. When you settle on your view, note the left and right extent, lower one forefinger towards the centre of the aperture, note the corresponding point in the landscape and use this as a reference for the mid-point of your composition.

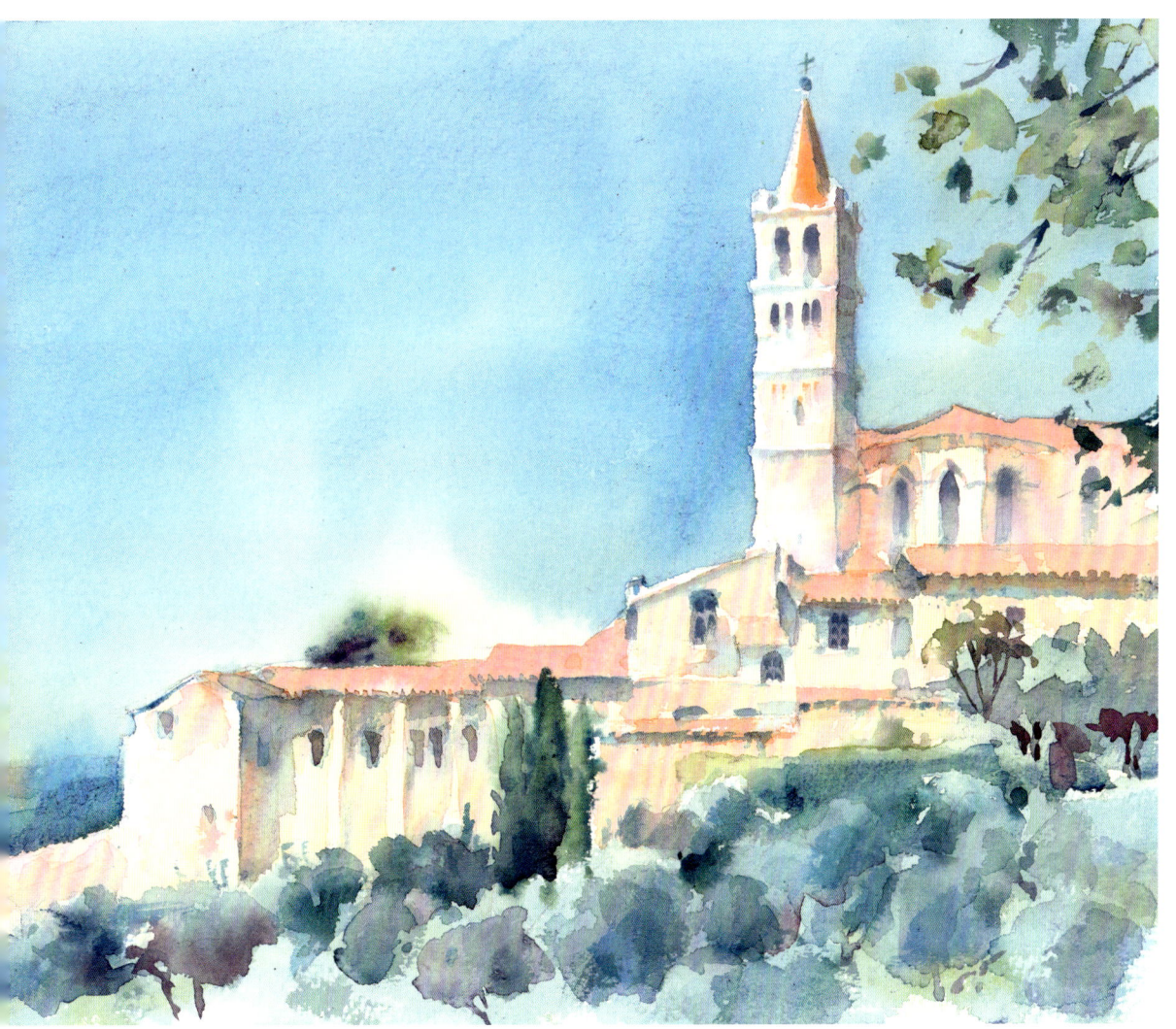

Santa Clara, Assisi
28 x 38cm (11 x 15in)

The church tower provides an obvious focal point for a painting; the landscape format makes a more serene composition, with its large area of sky, gently rising hill and tower pointing heavenward. The portrait format, opposite, emphasizes the buildings, creating a bolder, more modern design. Both work.

Light and shade

Balancing areas of light and shade is key to a good composition. Look for variety, with at least three distinct tonal values, and balance areas of light with passages of medium and dark tone. Even the most mundane of views can make an exciting composition when there is a satisfying pattern of light and shade.

▷ **Whitehall Rising**
25.5 x 35.5cm (10 x 14in)

The strength of this almost monochromatic painting is the lively pattern of light, mid- and dark tones, playing across the surface of the paper. Big Ben rises above the London traffic in a variety of neutrals, mixed from Raw Umber, Burnt Umber and Ultramarine Blue.

▽ **Dawn, Kaokoland Mountains**
15 x 56cm (6 x 22in)

The low angle of the dawn light casts an interesting pattern of shadows across the mountains. The difference between light and shade is more distinct at the beginning and end of the day, making these favourable times to paint.

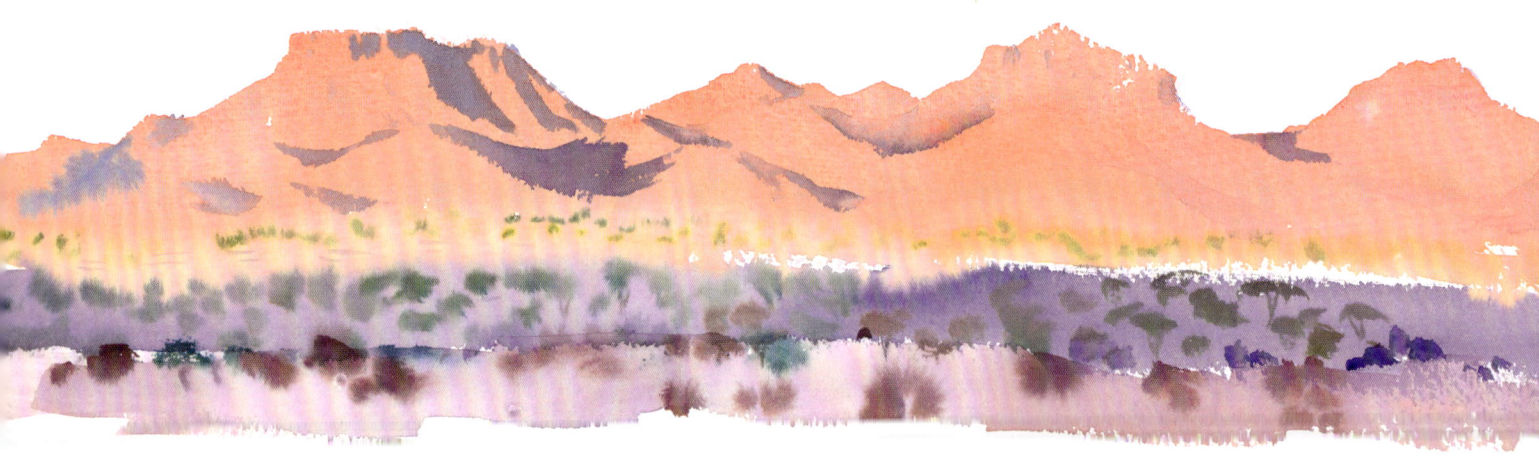

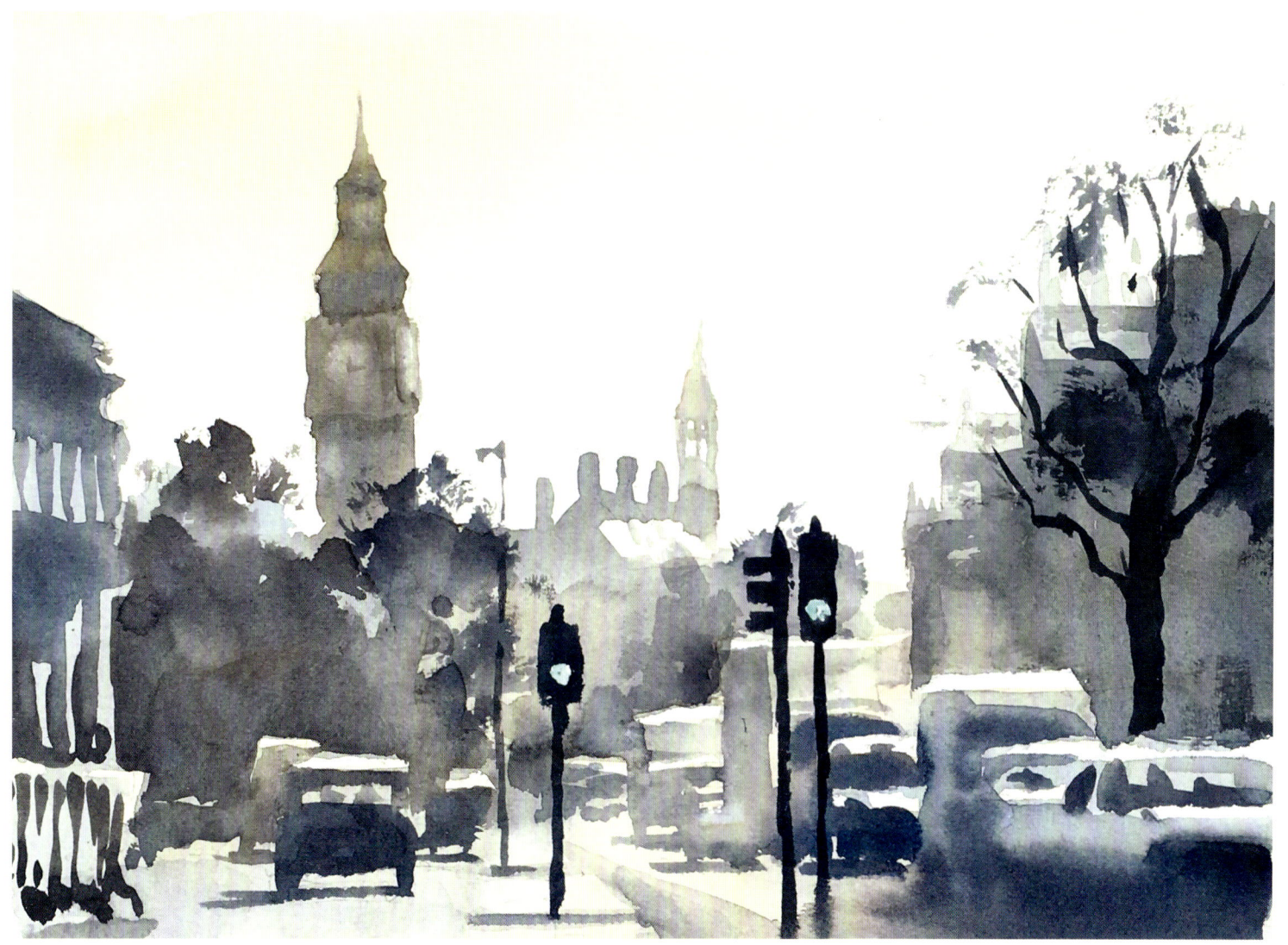

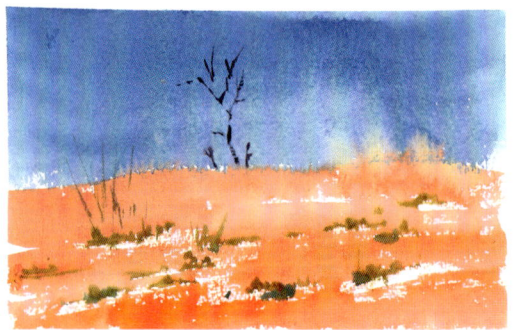
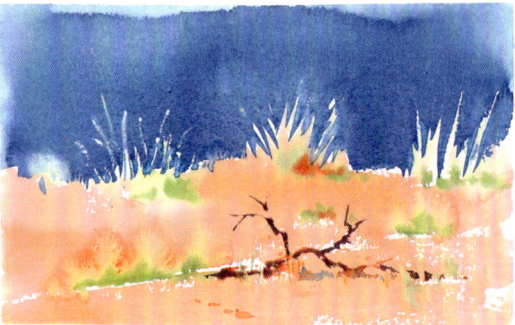

◁ Orange and blue are potent complementary (opposite) colours. In these Kalahari sketches each colour is given equal weighting to create a satisfying balance.

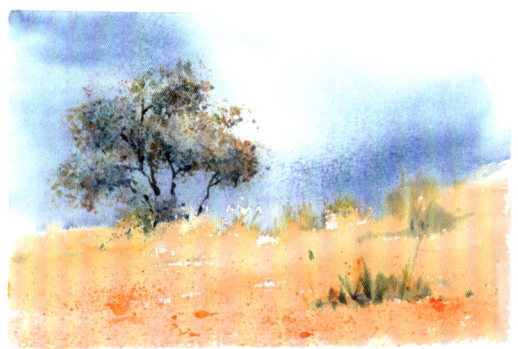
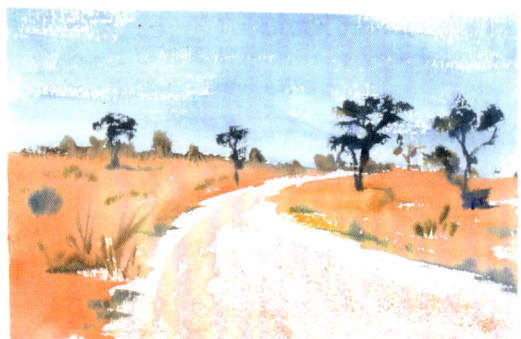

Balancing colour

Colour can make or break a composition. Balancing potent colours is as important as balancing features and tones. Broad, strong areas of colour, such as the blue of sky or sea, can be balanced by contrast with opposites (for blue this is orange), or juxtaposed harmoniously with colours closer in family (for blue this is green or violet).

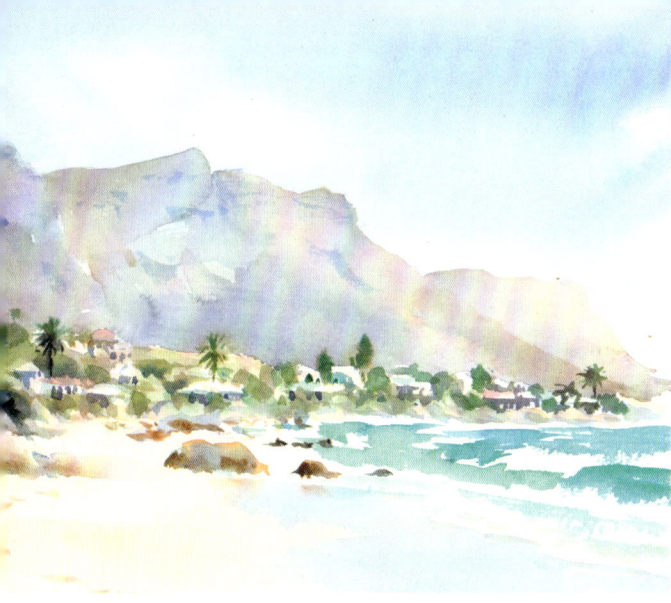

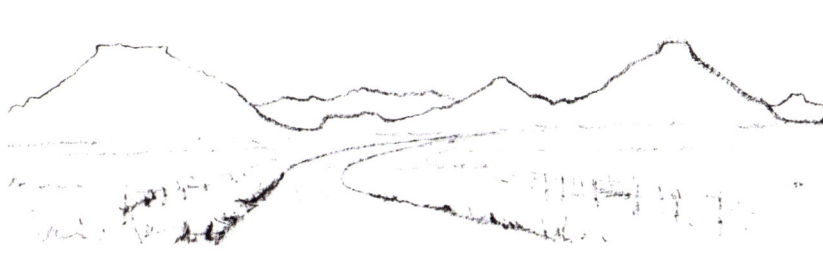

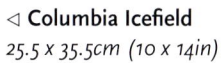 **Clifton Beach, Cape Town**
25.5 x 30.5cm (10 x 12in)
A pale line of footprints welcomes the eye across the sand and into the painting, following the leading lines of the wet beach and waves.

Leading lines

When sketched out in pencil, the initial composition uses lines to describe the contours of hills, trees, roads and buildings. Line has the power to lead the eye into and around the painting, so look for flow lines in the landscape that can help direct the eye – linear features such as lanes, rivers and fences, or lines of repetition that reinforce features, such as long reflections or linear shadows.

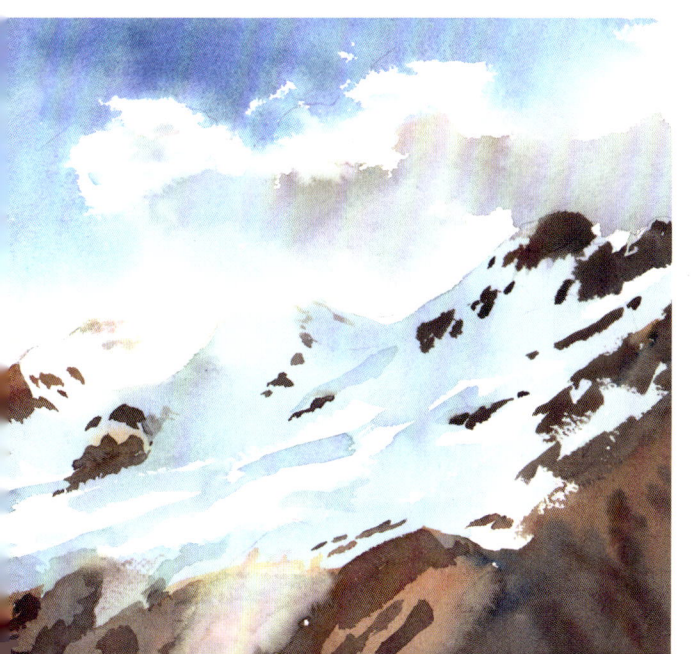

◁ **Columbia Icefield**
25.5 x 35.5cm (10 x 14in)
The leading lines are diagonal here, with the line of the clouds and lines of light on the snow directing the eye towards the summit.

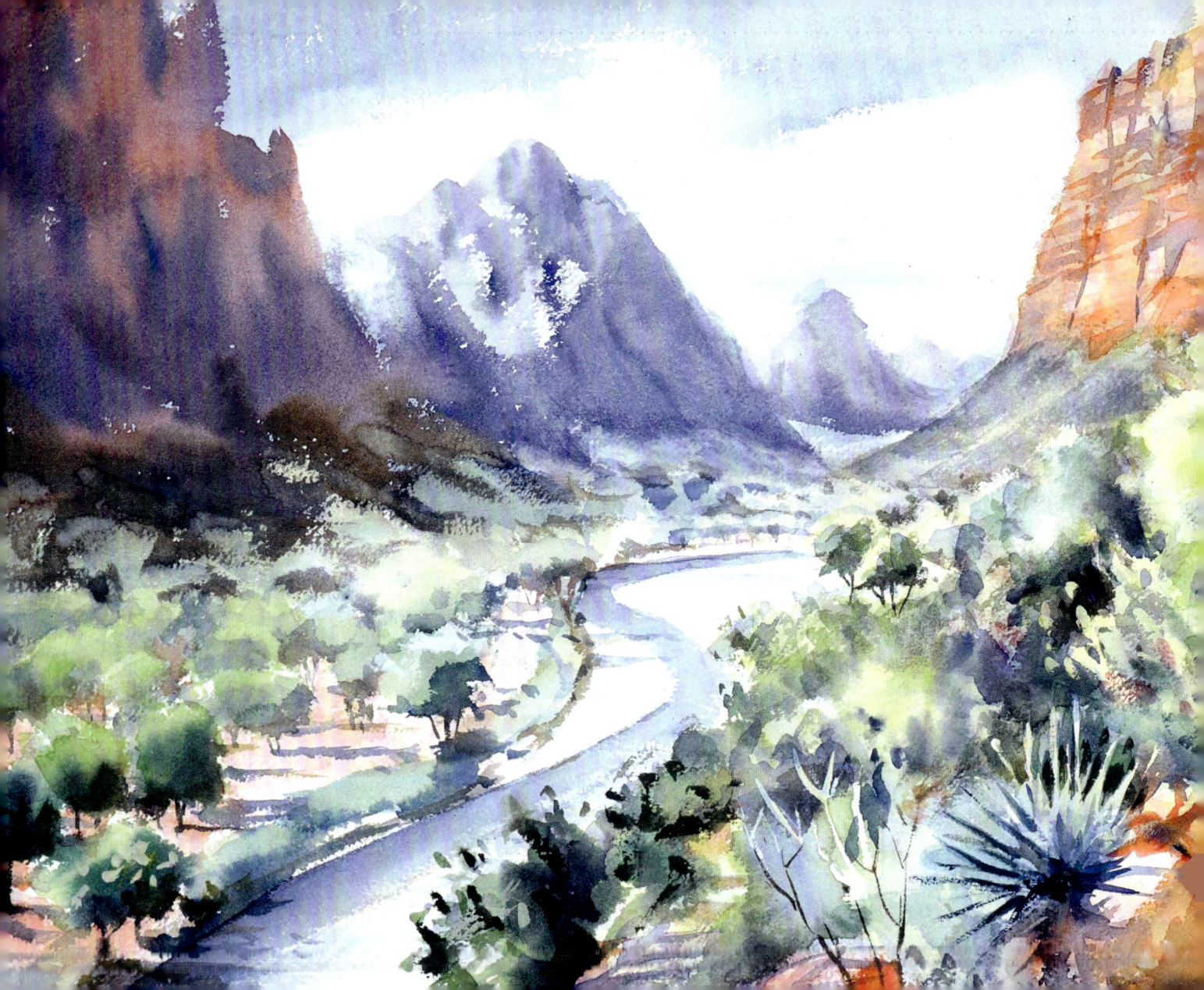

The grand view

Some landscapes appear eye-wateringly complicated at first sight. The key is to work out the underlying structure, or form. Once this is established you can add detail, but if you paint all the details first, without grasping how the landscape is constructed, the painting becomes bitty. Simplify the view into its main planes, give attention to the focus and the other elements become supportive, directing the eye to the main event. Use perspective and scale to set up the depth of field. Sidelight makes it easier to show form because it offers a change of tone on either side of objects, setting up a light/dark counterchange.

◁ **The Virgin River Bends Through Zion**
35.5 x 51cm (14 x 20in)

The magnificent Virgin River winds through the towering mountains of Utah. It is both overwhelming and irresistible to paint. There are many more lumps and bumps in the real landscape, and countless more trees, but selection of the main structures makes it possible to simplify and represent such a grand view.

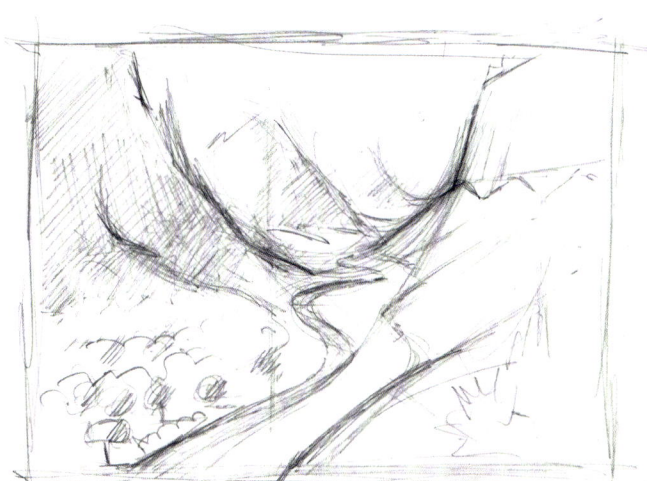

◁ A rough exploratory sketch helped me to find the main structural lines in the panorama before me, for example the V-shape of the valley and the foothills forcing the bends in the river. From these I could find flow lines to lead the eye through the composition. Details such as the trees and rocks are effectively 'decoration' on the main structure.

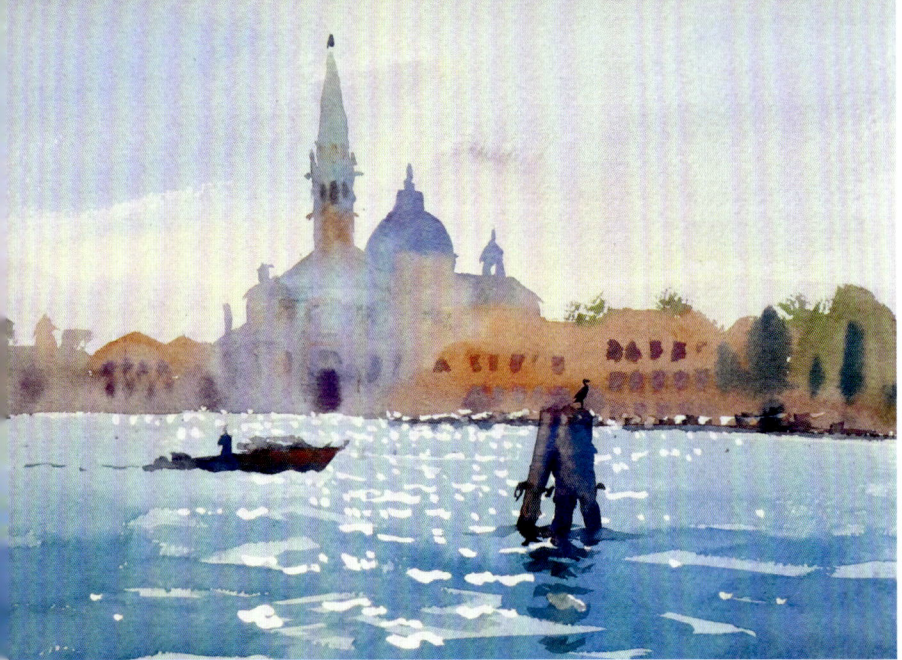

Paint from life

Watercolour landscape painting takes that which is huge, selects what matters and makes it small and flat. This involves selection and generalization. Painting from photographs may appear to make the process easier, but because the image is already small and flat, it lets the camera take away your 'job' – turning three dimensions into two dimensions – and denies you the challenge, joy and fulfilment that this creative pursuit brings. If you truly want to learn to paint, paint from life.

Once you have mastered turning large into little you can turn to photographs for reference, but if you try to learn from them you will be tempted to imitate rather than create and will find it very hard to master landscape painting to your satisfaction.

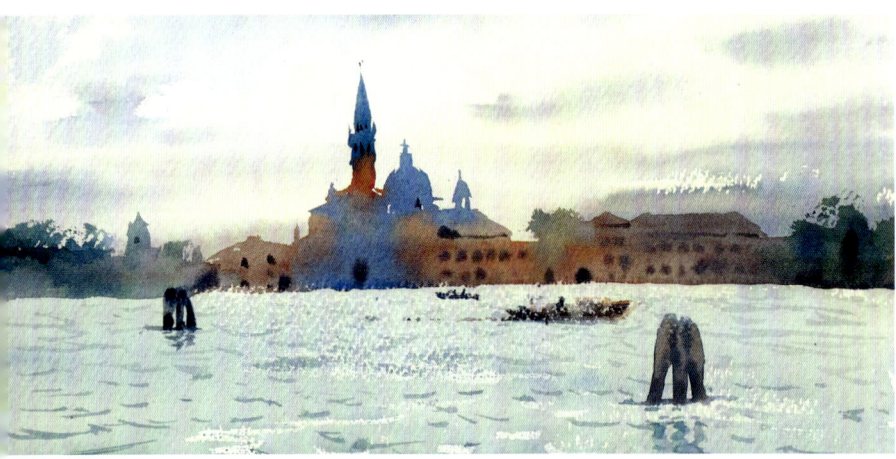

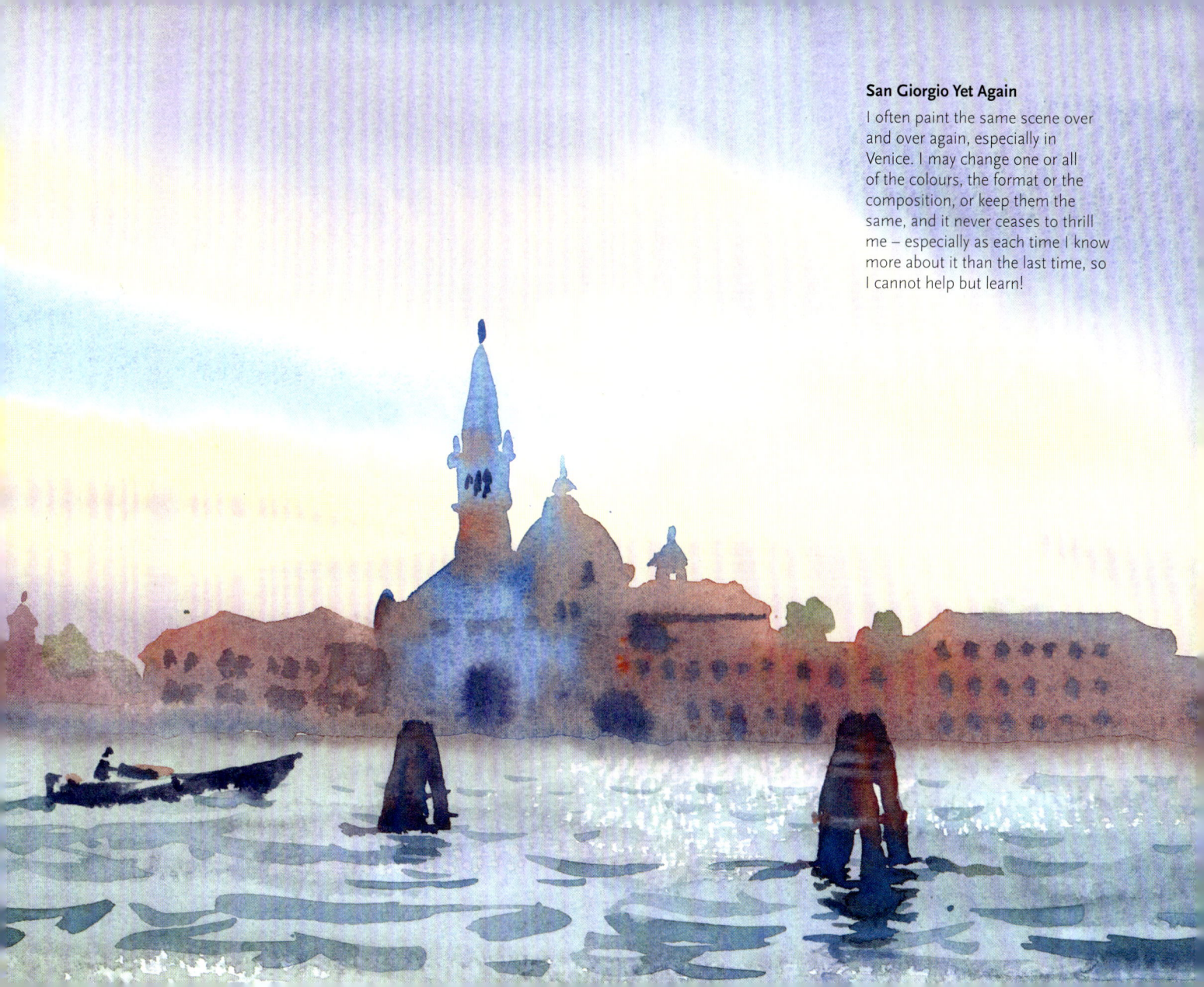

San Giorgio Yet Again

I often paint the same scene over and over again, especially in Venice. I may change one or all of the colours, the format or the composition, or keep them the same, and it never ceases to thrill me – especially as each time I know more about it than the last time, so I cannot help but learn!

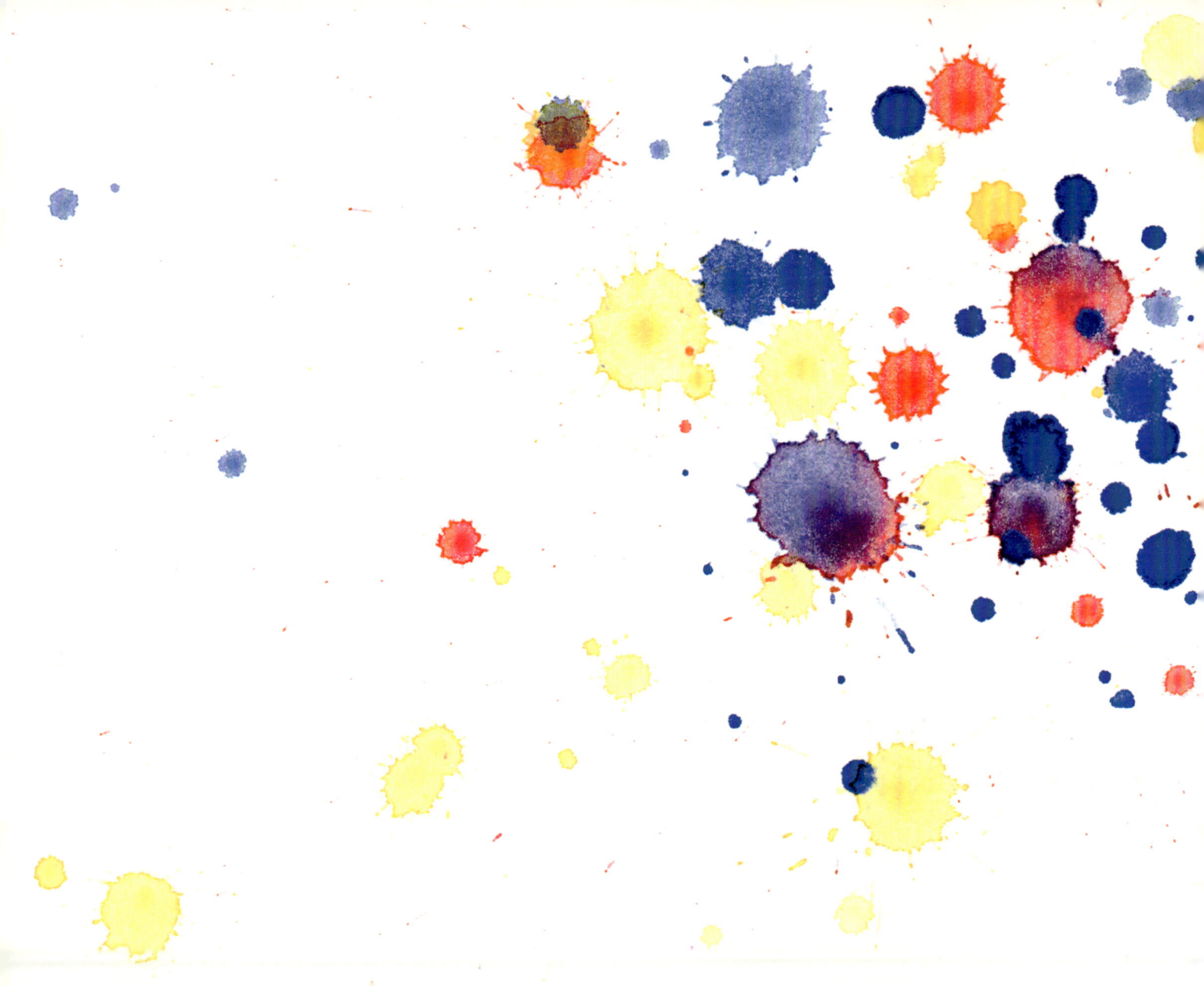

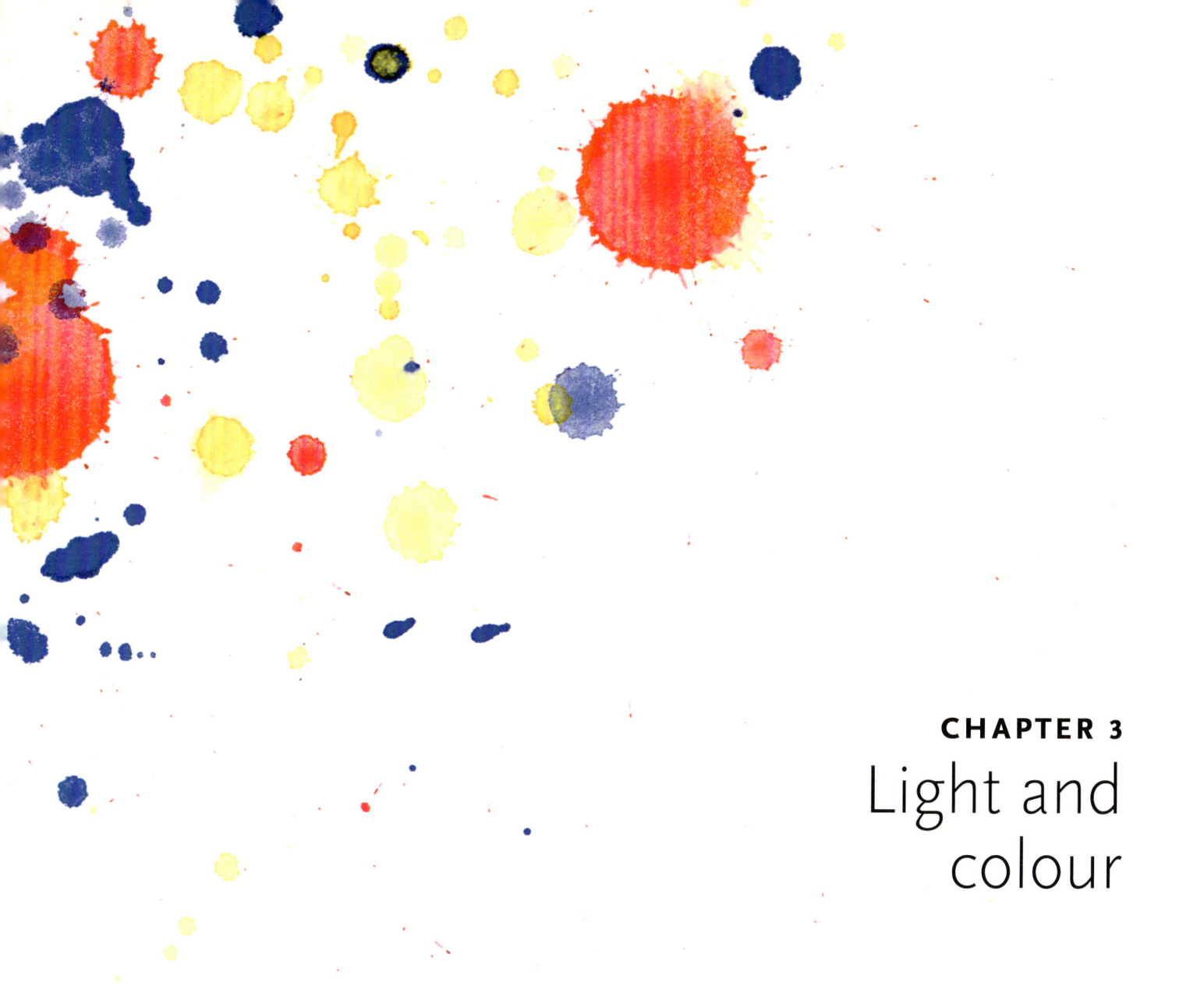

CHAPTER 3

Light and colour

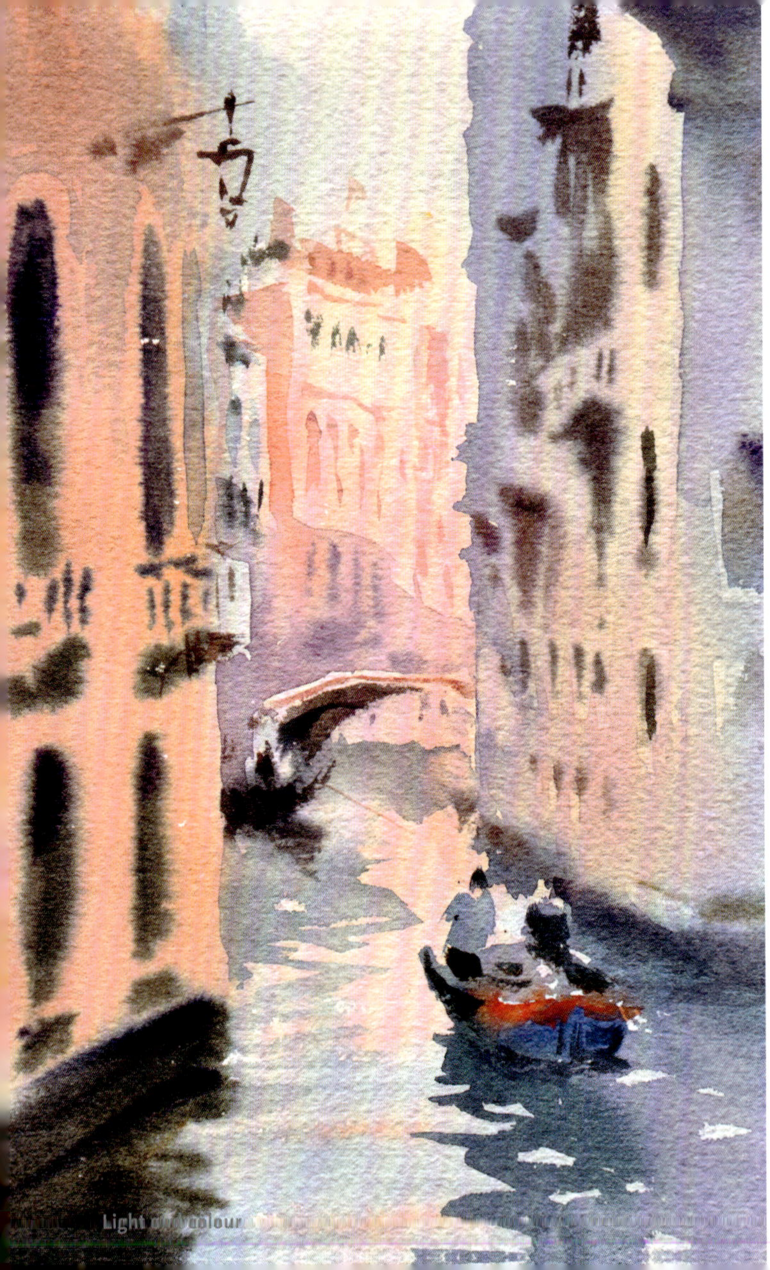

It's all about light

Light makes colours visible and in landscape painting the source of light is the sun. 'Local colour' is the term used for the individual landscape hues, but the actual colour is determined by the amount of light received; a landscape appears quite different in colouring under direct sunlight, beneath cloud or at dawn and sunset.

◁ **Hidden in Venice**
28 x 18cm (11 x 7in)

The pink of the façades is rosier when the angle of light is lower or when light is reflected from one building across to another. In shadow the reds become mauves.

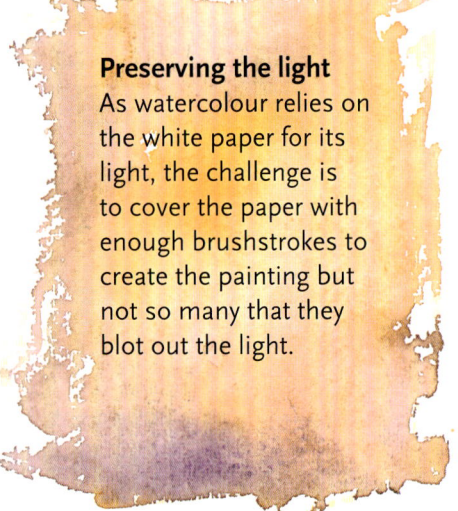

Preserving the light
As watercolour relies on the white paper for its light, the challenge is to cover the paper with enough brushstrokes to create the painting but not so many that they blot out the light.

Sunlight and shadow

As the Earth turns constantly the angle and direction of the light changes all the time, yet the light source in the painting must appear consistent. When the sun passes its zenith, the shadows of the morning will have changed sides, making it difficult to continue the same painting throughout the day. To avoid trying to rely on your memory, paint separate images morning and afternoon. Overcast days, with their cloud-filtered light from overhead, have the advantage of maintaining a steady light throughout the day, but the shadows and three-dimensional forms will be less defined.

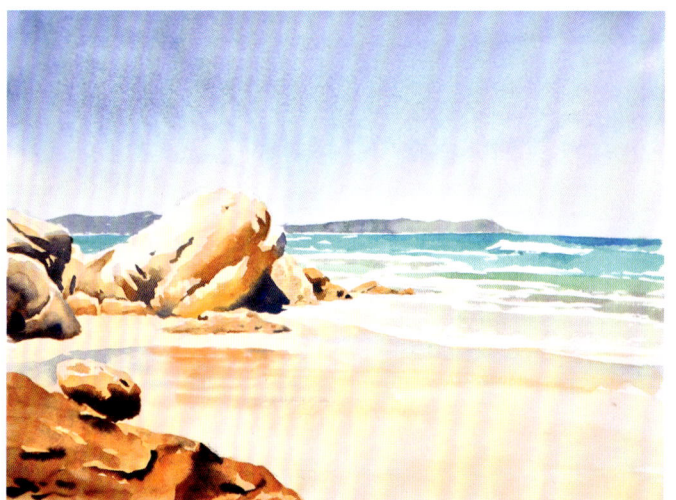

◁ In this painting the light is coming from the left and the rocks are casting their shadows to the right. Their local colour is the grey of granite, and it is warmed here by reflected light.

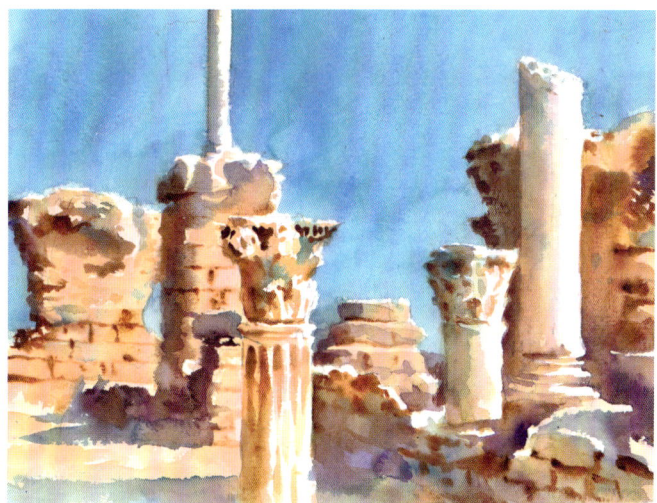

▷ **Corinth Crumbles**
28 x 38cm (11 x 15in)

Here the light is coming from my right. The local hue of the stone is yellowy-brown, but the actual colour varies around each column according to the light it receives. I laid Raw Umber first for the light mid-tones and deepened the shaded sides with Burnt Sienna and Schmincke Violet.

Paints and palette

You do not need many colours to make a watercolour painting; full-colour paintings can be achieved with just three, a red, a yellow, and a blue (see p.166). I use pans in an enamel palette and carry tubes of the same colours to give me neat paint when required. To be able to mix your colours to the right consistency, choose a palette that has sloping wells or leaves, so you can judge the mix by the way it flows down the slope (if it is too wet it runs into the gutter!). Rags or kitchen towel are essential for taking excess water out of the brush.

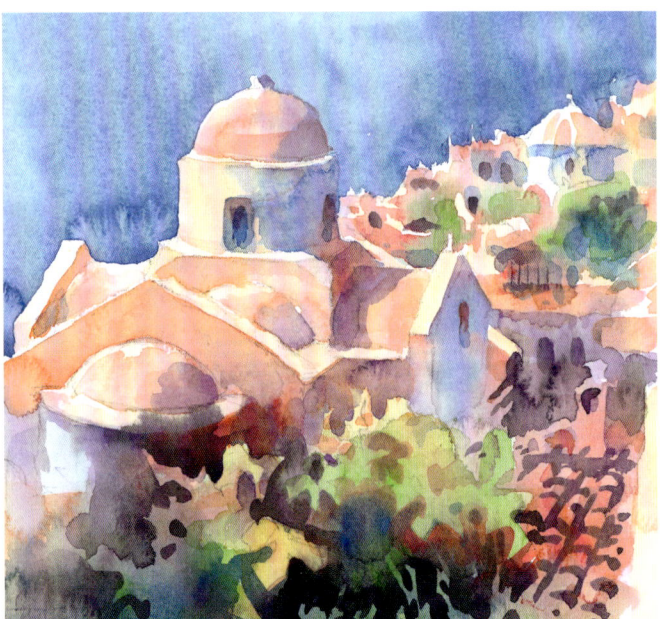

◁ **Monemvasia**
15 x 15cm (6 x 6in)

A mosaic of small washes make up the layering in this painting. Since the application of too many layers obscures light, they are best kept to a minimum, so it is vital to mix the right density and colour of your paint before you lay it on the paper.

▷ **Venetian Dusk II**
28 x 25.5cm (11 x 10in)

Few colours are needed to make an effective watercolour. This silhouette of Santa Maria della Salute employs just two, Schmincke Violet and Indian Yellow.

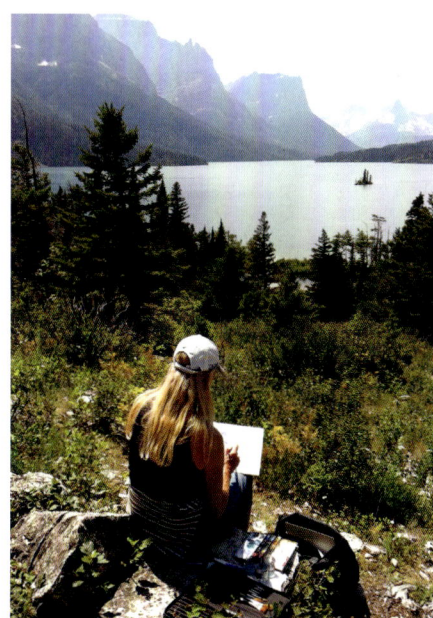

Any rock is a comfortable perch so long as I do not have to reach down too far for my paints!

Easel or not?

Many artists take portable easels and folding stools with them, which make it more comfortable to work *en plein air*. However, I have spent most of my outdoor painting life without an easel or stool, always finding some place to sit (or stand), balancing my sketchpad on my knees or simply holding it. I carry a plastic bag to sit on, in case I cannot find a rock, bench or step and the ground is damp.

Mixing colours – the limited palette

It is the interaction of colours within a painting that makes it appear colourful, not the number of different colours employed. In fact, too many can dull a painting as the mixing of numerous pigments leads to duller versions of colours, especially greens, browns and blacks. I aim to use three colours to make most of my paintings, adding more only if I cannot reach the desired colour combination with three. The limited palette does not mean you cannot use several, or even many, different colours in a painting, but a limit on the number of pigments in a mix helps to protect mixtures from becoming muddy.

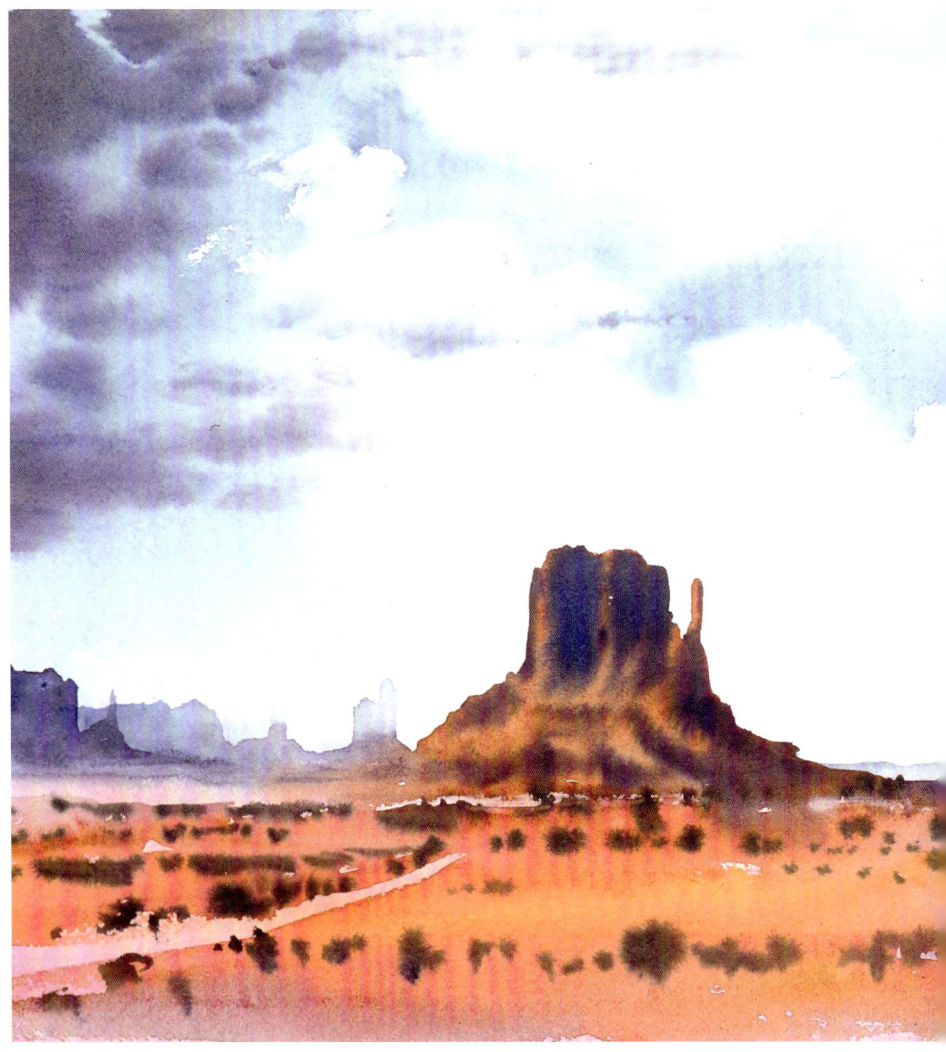

Red, yellow and blue

There are three primary colours, red, yellow and blue. Mixing two together makes the secondary colours orange, green and violet, while mixing all three gives the browns, greys and blacks, so all colours can be produced by just three. However, red/yellow/blue combinations do not necessarily mean using primary hues. Red refers to the warmest colour in the mix, and can range from purple-magenta through bright red to a reddy-orangey-brown, such as Burnt Sienna. Blue means the coolest colour, encompassing any bluey colour from Indigo to Turquoise. Yellow is usually the lightest colour, ranging from Lemon to a yellowy-brown, for example Raw Umber.

Examples of RYB combinations

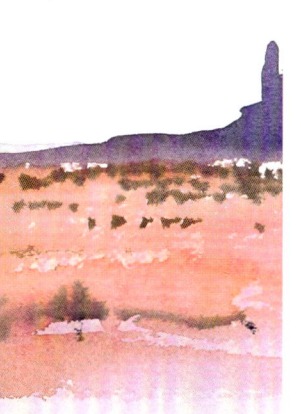

◁ **John Wayne Country, Monument Valley**

30.5 x 41cm (12 x 16in)

The three colours chosen here are Ultramarine Blue, Indian Yellow and Permanent Rose. They are used individually and together to make the blue, pink, red, mauve, orange, yellow, brown and green in this painting.

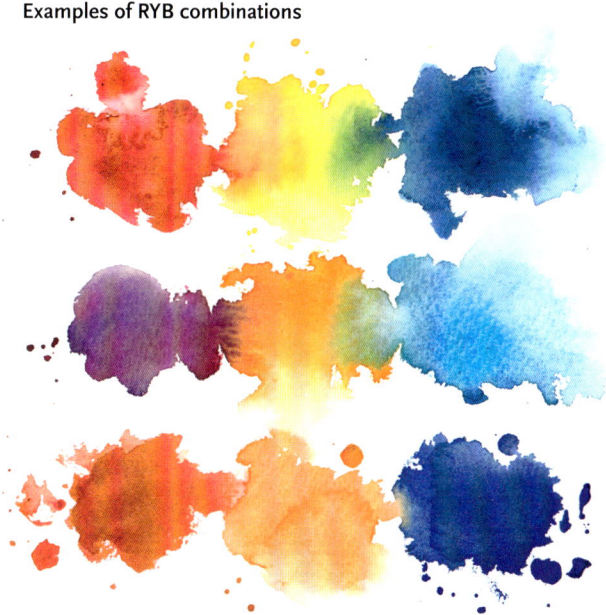

Brown Madder, Aureolin and Prussian Blue

Schmincke Violet, Indian Yellow and Cerulean Blue

Burnt Sienna, Yellow Ochre and Ultramarine Blue

Choosing colours

You might think that the hue of a colour is its most important property, but pigments have other properties – transparency, opacity, lifting, staining and granulation – which are all useful to the landscape painter. Knowing a little more about your colours makes for better choices.

Transparent colours

Watercolour is a transparent medium laid as a film over white paper. Some of the pigments are transparent like stained glass, such as the organic/carbon pigments, allowing light to pass through them and be reflected back from the paper. These pigments have extremely fine particles, moving quickly in washes, and many tend to stain the fabric of the paper, so they are ideal for layering and maintaining transparency.

Non-staining

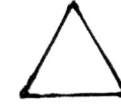

Semi-staining

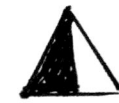

Staining

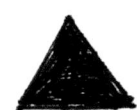

Information about pigment properties is usually given as symbols on the tubes.

Transparent

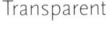

Semi-transparent

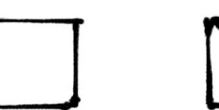

Semi-opaque

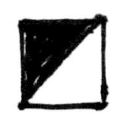

Opaque

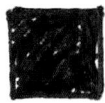

Opaque colours

Other pigments, such as the metal and mineral pigments, have larger, denser particles, which are opaque, semi-opaque or semi-transparent. When these are laid on the paper the light bounces back from between the microscopic particles, with the result that too much layering obscures light. They tend to move less rapidly in washes and some are sedimentary and granulating, settling in the tooth of the paper in attractive textures. Many of these pigments do not stain the paper and can be lifted off to varying extents even when dry. Fully opaque colours have covering power and so can be used to reintroduce highlights.

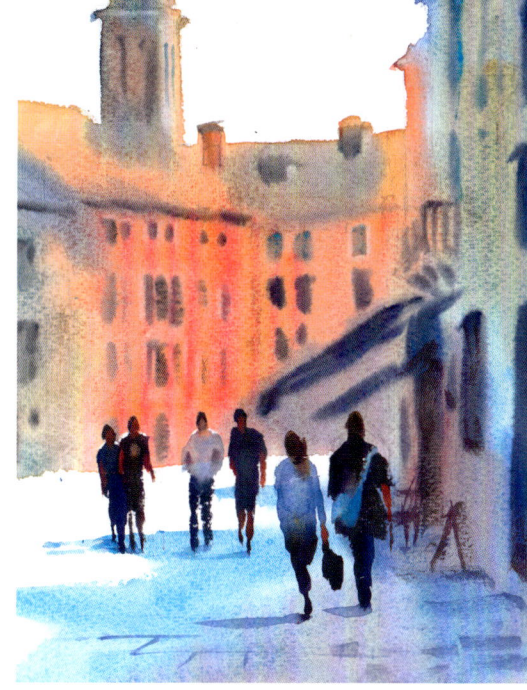

△ **Ambling in the Square, Verona**
33 x 28cm (13 x 11in)

The opaque and granulating characteristics of Cadmium Red, Cerulean Blue and Raw Umber are blended here to create the texture and colouring of the background buildings, while the transparent property of Ultramarine Blue and Burnt Sienna, that enables them to reach deep tones, is used to mix the dark colour of the foreground figures.

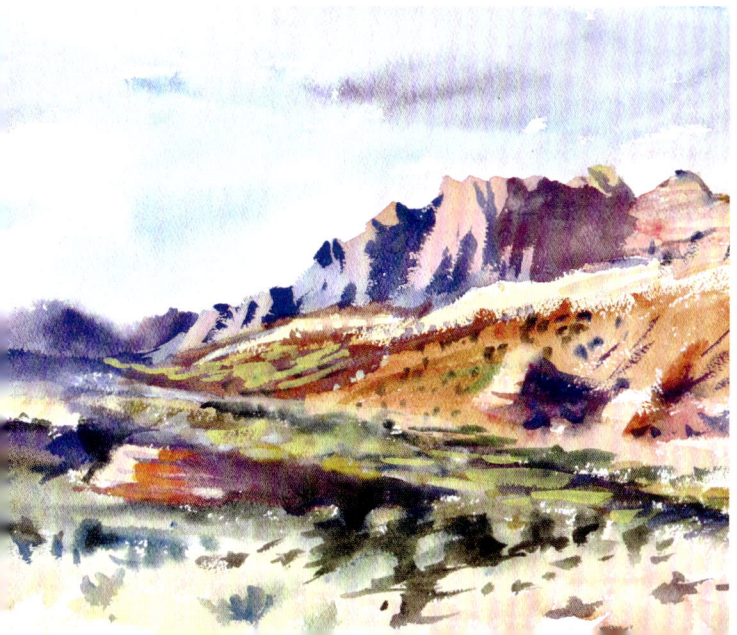

◁ **Hottentots Holland**
45.5 x 61cm
(18 x 24in)

The mountains and marginal hilly slopes are painted with transparent colours, but if you look carefully you can see strokes of opaque Cadmium Yellow, introduced to lighten the flatter surfaces.

Blue

Because it is the predominant hue of sky and water and mixes with yellow to make greens and deepens colours to make shades, blue is used more abundantly than any other colour in landscape painting. Cast shadows often exhibit blue colouring, as the opposite colour to the yellow of sunlight.

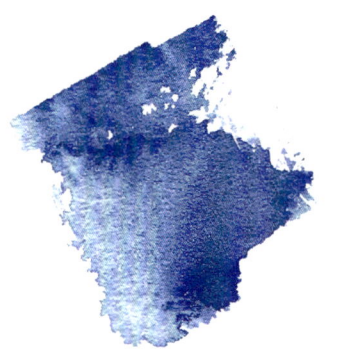

Ultramarine Blue is considered a warm blue because it veers towards red.

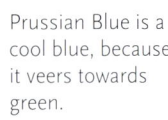

Prussian Blue is a cool blue, because it veers towards green.

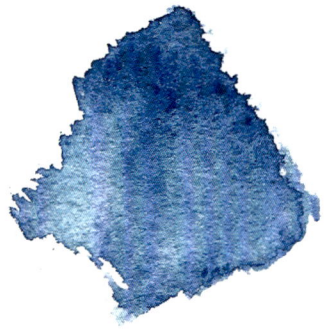

Cobalt Blue

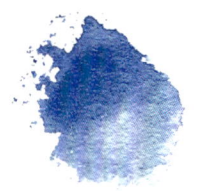

Cerulean Blue

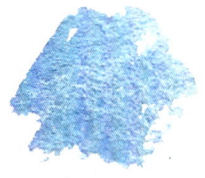

Phthalo Blue

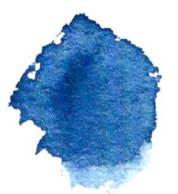

Indigo

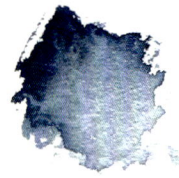

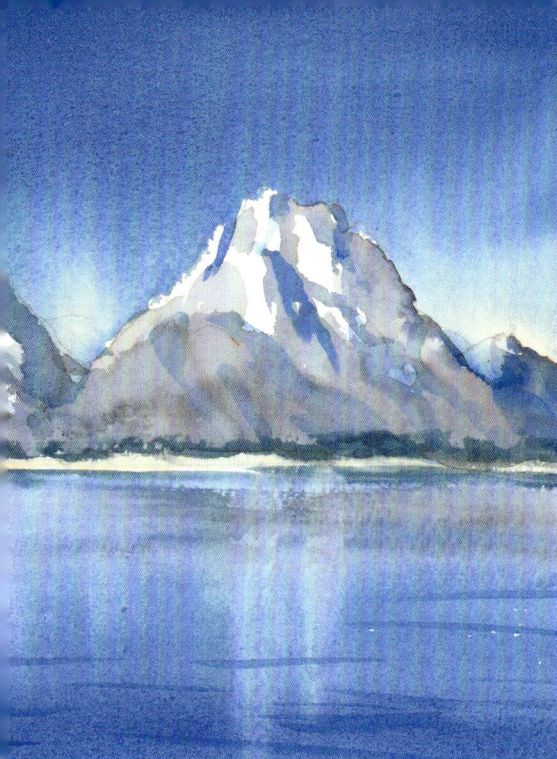

◁ The Grand Tetons
28 x 38cm (11 x 15in)

To maintain harmony, I used the same blue in the water of the lake as in the sky and the shadows of the mountains. I chose Ultramarine Blue for its lifting properties, so that I could lift out the reflected lights of the snowy slopes from the lake wash when it was dry.

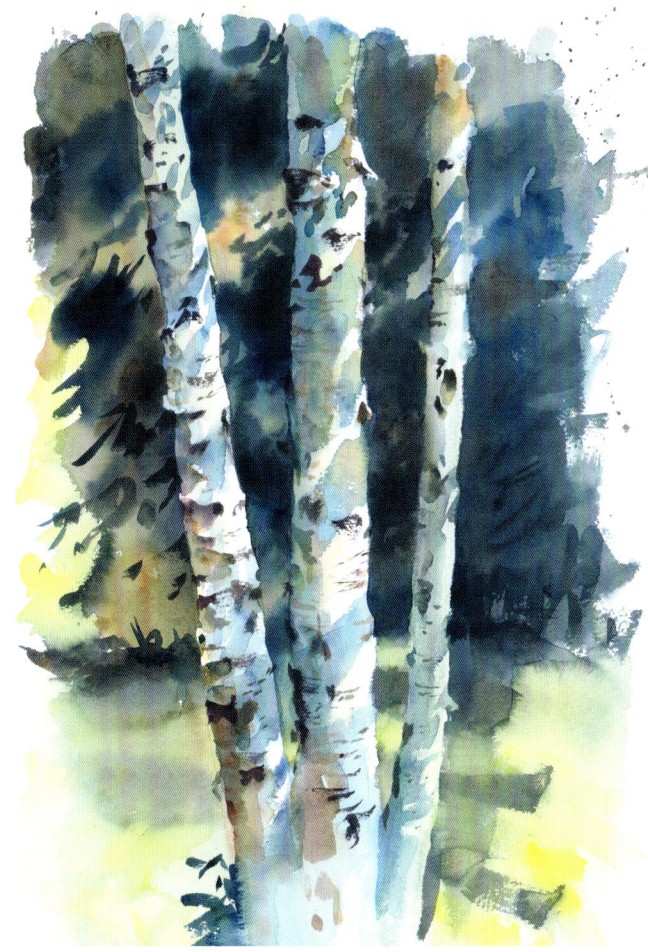

△ A blue tint over the white trunks represents the shadows cast by dappled light through foliage. I chose Prussian Blue for its cool transparency and depth of tone.

Blue is a cool colour in itself but comes in cool and warm versions. A cool blue veers towards the green side of the spectrum (turquoise), while a warm blue veers towards red (violet). Because colours interact with each other, there is no need to 'match' a blue to the blue of the sky. Any blue will work because it can be adapted by the other colours in the painting.

Green and yellow

Verdancy of foliage makes green the dominant colour in many landscapes. I prefer to mix my greens from blues and yellows as it makes it easy to alter the temperature bias and limits the number of pigments in the painting. However, there are many ready-made greens that can be used, especially if you need a large amount of green in a hurry.

Yellow is a lovely colour in the landscape, prevalent when grain is ripe or grass is dry, setting up an exciting contrast of hue and tone between sky and land. It is also often seen in the sky just above the horizon when there is dust in the air and especially as the sun is setting.

Green mixes

Ultramarine Blue and Aureolin

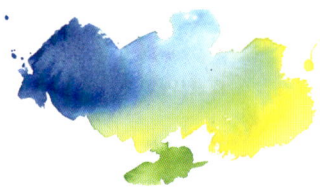

Prussian Blue and Indian Yellow

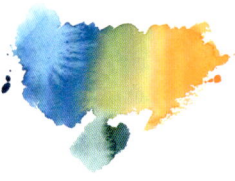

Ultramarine Blue and Raw Umber

Phthalo Blue and Yellow Ochre

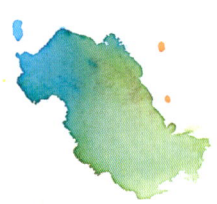

Prussian Blue and Burnt Sienna

Prussian Blue and Transparent Orange

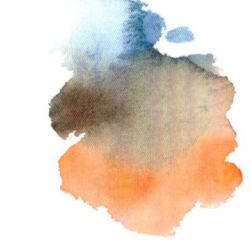

Phthalo Turquoise and Raw Sienna

Cobalt Blue and Raw Sienna

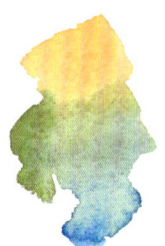

Sap Green and Burnt Sienna

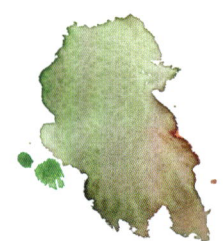

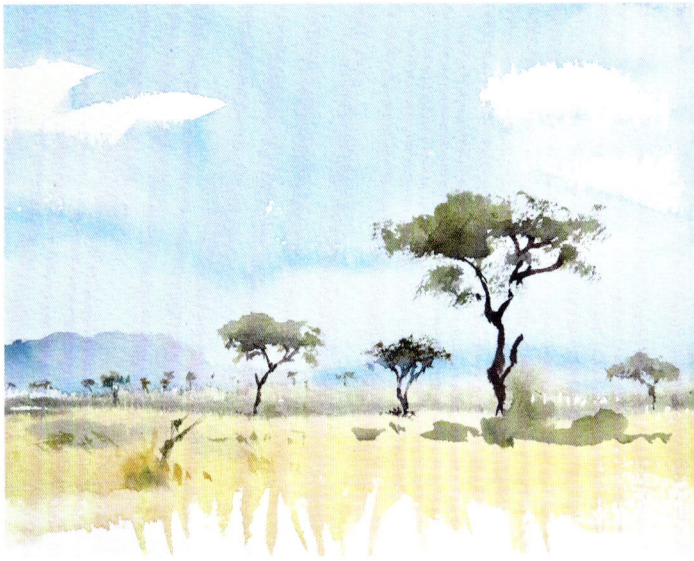

△ The Wedding Tree
18 x 28cm (7 x 11in)

In the dry season the colour of the East African savannah turns yellow. Mixing Yellow Ochre with the Ultramarine Blue used for the sky gave me the perfect dull green for the acacia trees. Schmincke Violet is the third colour here, used to tint the distant mountains and turn the tree trunks black.

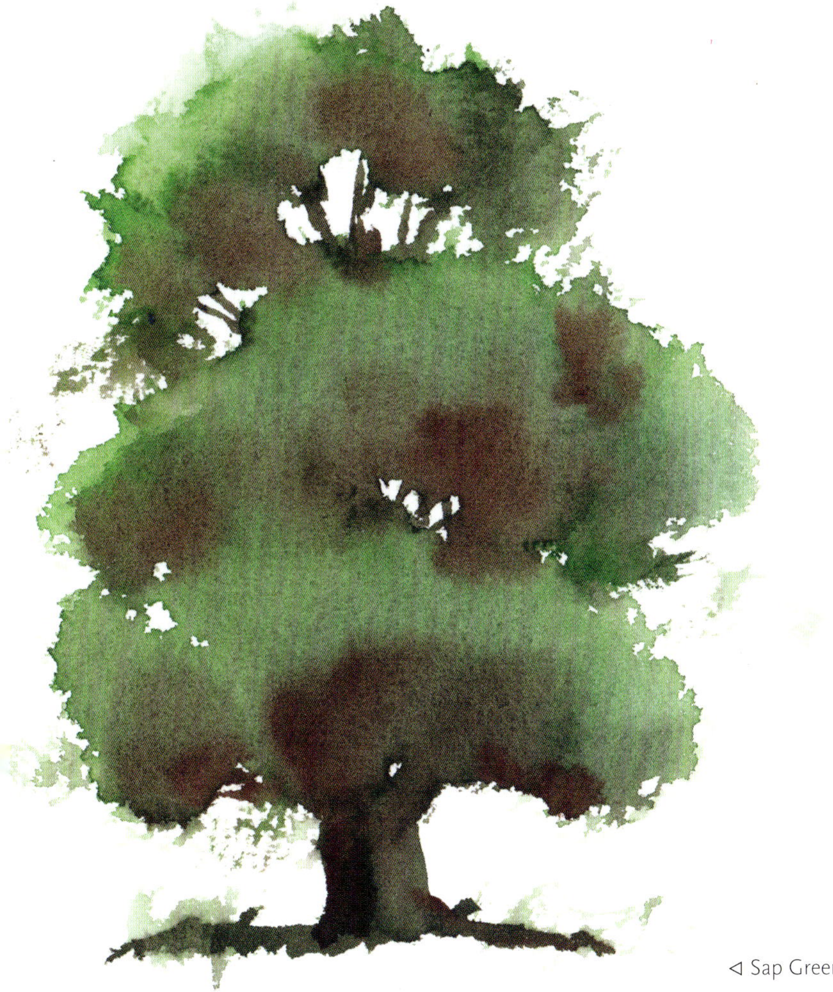

◁ Sap Green and Burnt Umber

Red and brown

The red in rocky sandstone landscapes is due to the presence of iron oxide, reddened by extreme heat such as volcanic activity. Iron oxide pigment is used to make the red earth colours in the artist's palette, which makes Burnt Sienna and Light Red natural colours to choose for hot, dry landscapes. However, these warm brown-reds are not always hot enough for the glowing reds, reflected lights and deep shadows of a red landscape lit by a setting sun. For these there are plenty of other reds to choose from, such as Brown Madder, Permanent Rose, Alizarin Crimson and Cadmium Red.

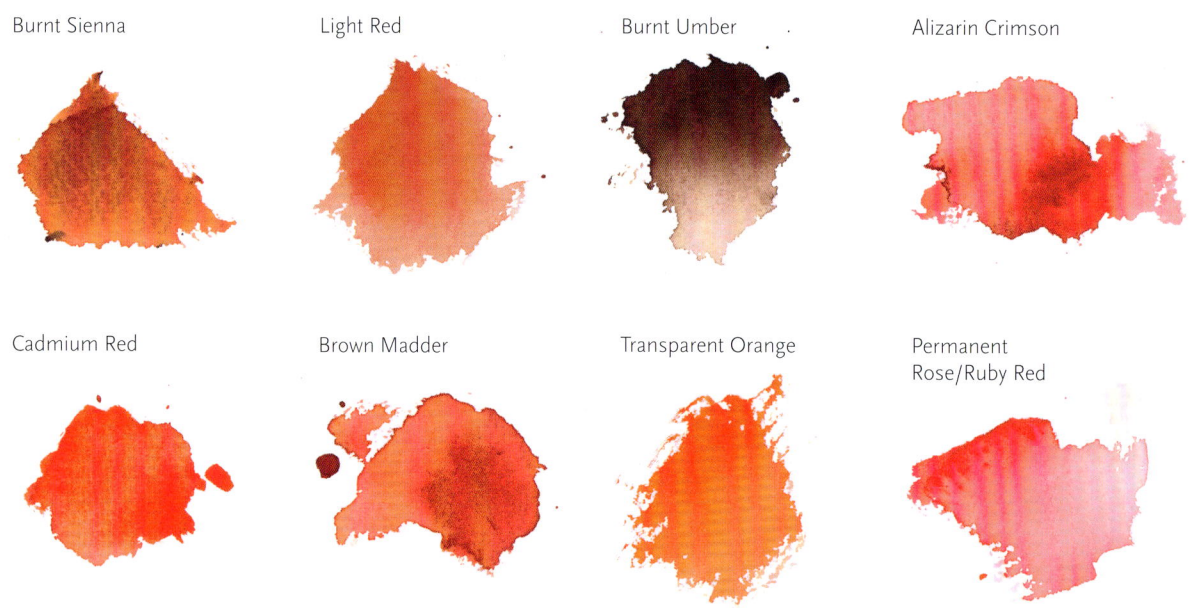

Burnt Sienna

Light Red

Burnt Umber

Alizarin Crimson

Cadmium Red

Brown Madder

Transparent Orange

Permanent Rose/Ruby Red

Light Red and
Ultramarine Blue

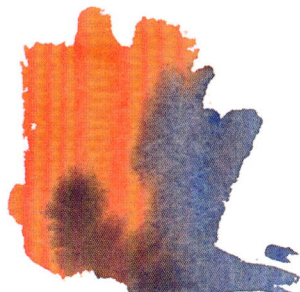

Permanent Rose
and Cadmium Red

Burnt Sienna
and Cobalt Blue

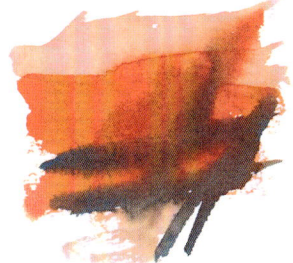

Brown Madder
and Schmincke Violet

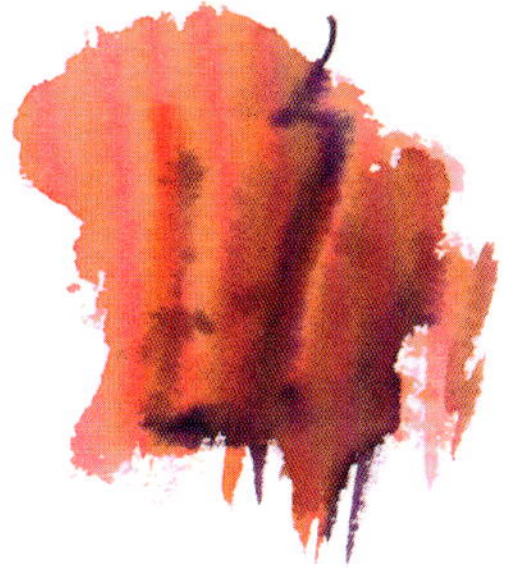

△ The colouring and form of
rocks is readily established with a
juxtaposition of light and darker
tones.

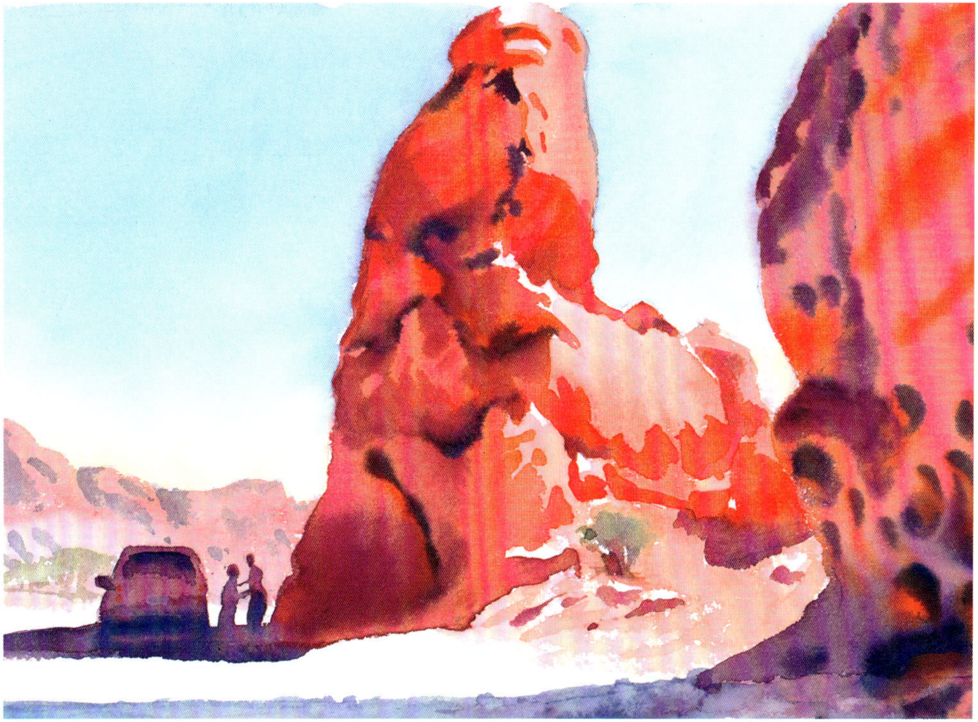

▷ **Rare Shade**
28 x 38cm (11 x 15in)

Permanent Rose and Cadmium Red
represent the intensity of the redness in
these rocks, with Alizarin Crimson and
Schmincke Violet used neat for the crevices
and striations.

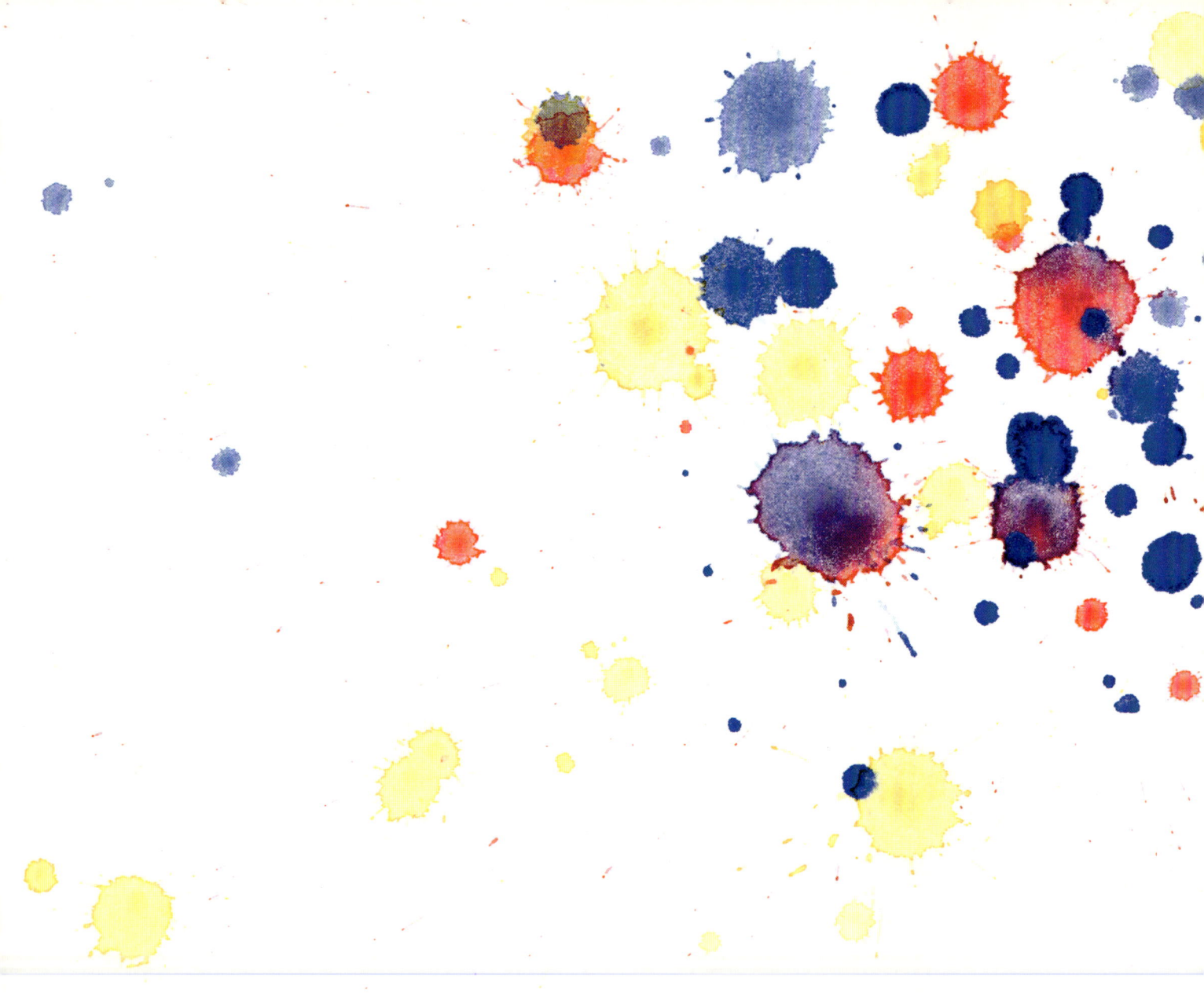

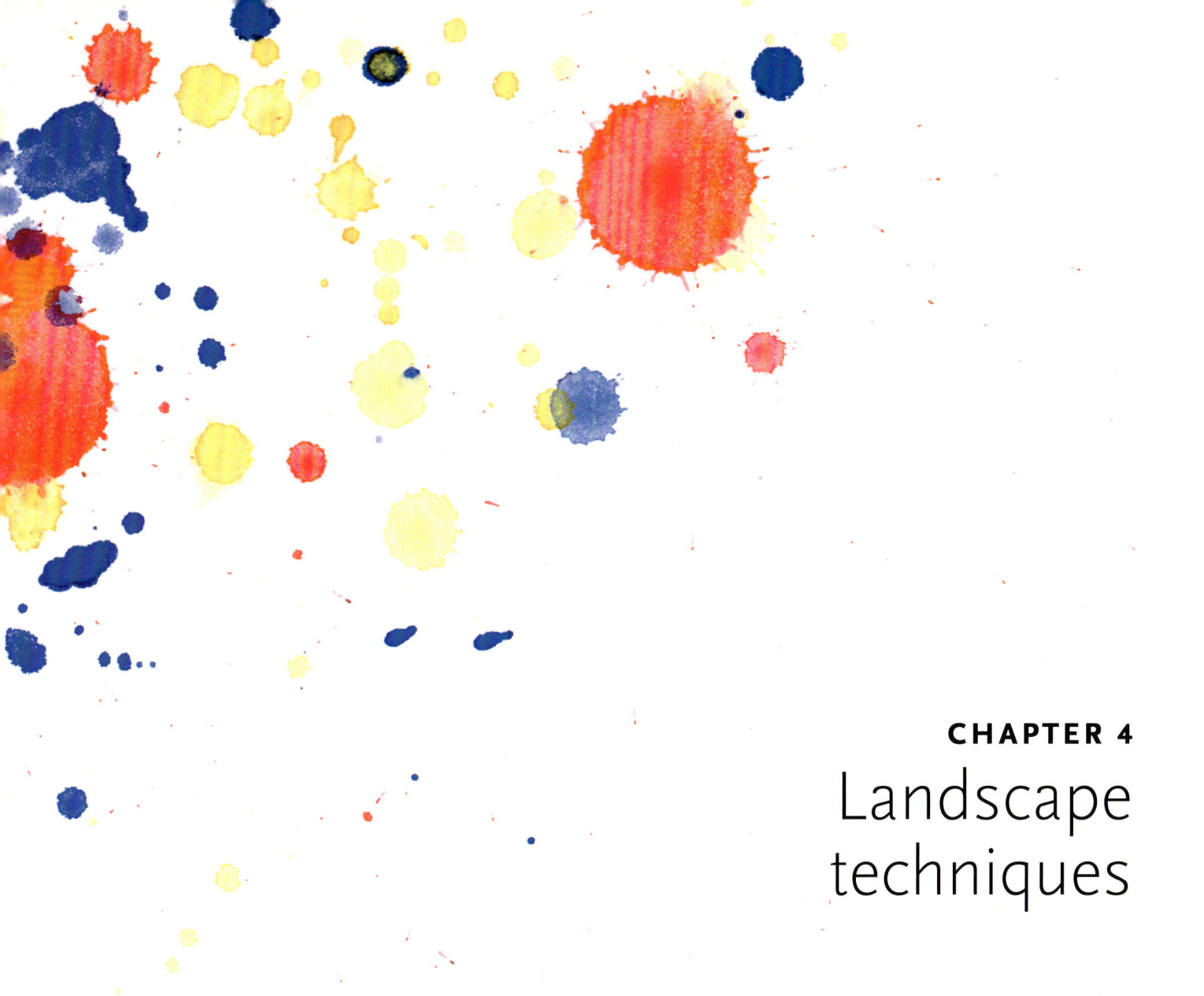

CHAPTER 4

Landscape techniques

The painting process

Watercolour is a very versatile medium, and more forgiving than many people think. It is traditionally painted from light to dark tones, but in a transparent medium you can paint in any order. This is useful on a humid day when large washes, like the sky, take a long time to dry, because you can paint small, fast-drying areas first and then overlay the more dilute washes.

Negative space
When items are lighter in tone or hue than their background, these have to be 'left out' of the background washes. These untouched paper areas are called negative spaces but they have a very positive impact on the painting.

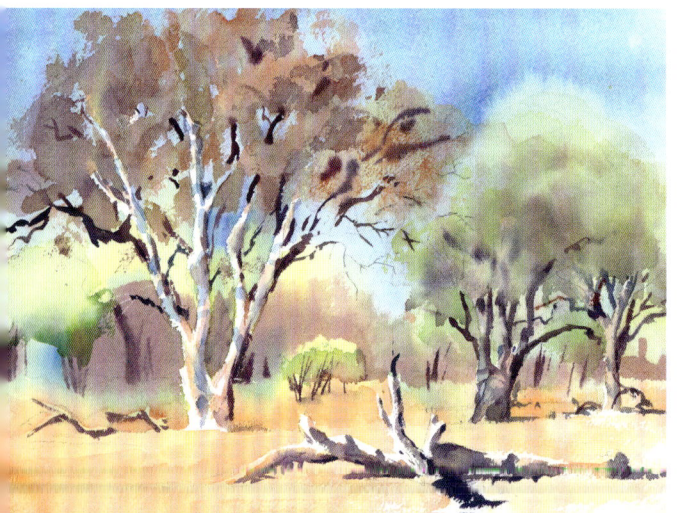

◁ The lit portions of tree trunk of the left-hand tree and the fallen log in the foreground are lighter than their backgrounds, so the white paper has to be left out of the background wash as a 'negative' space.

◁ Working from back to front

Where the background is sky and paler than the foreground it can be painted first, with additional layers on top for distant, middle and foreground features.

Multi-coloured landscapes

In a multi-coloured landscape, there may be too many different colour details to overlay washes or brushstrokes from the background to the foreground. In this case you can paint the finished details from the start, working from the middle outwards or one side to the other.

△ Positive brushstrokes

These are laid on top of previous washes, like these branches painted over the background.

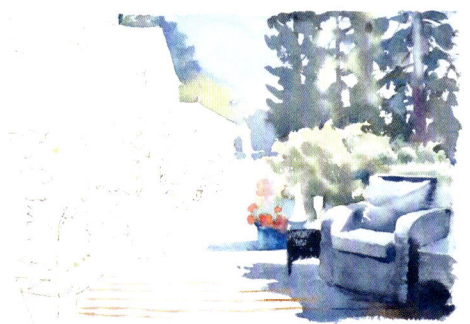
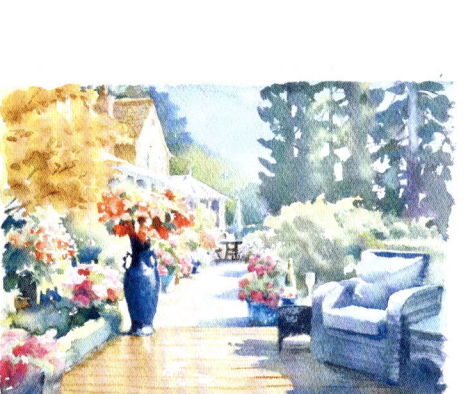

Initial stage and finished painting:

The multi-coloured flowers in the garden would have lost their vibrant hues if they had been painted over other washes. Instead, I painted the detail from the start.

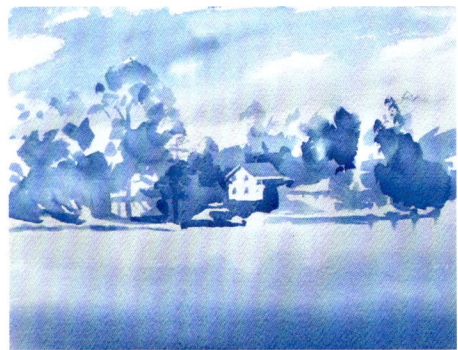

Demonstration stage 1: First I painted the sky and lake with a wash of Ultramarine Blue, leaving the highlights as blank paper. Once that was dry, I used the blue, wet on dry, to demarcate the shadow areas, showing distinct edges.

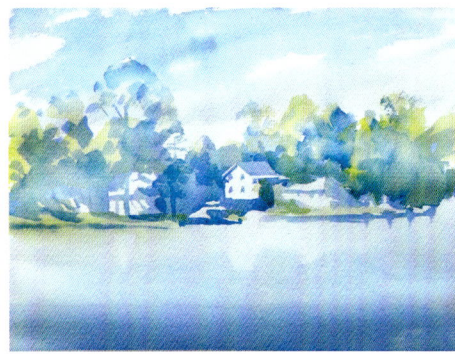

Stage 2: When the blue brushstrokes were dry, I brushed Aureolin over the tree and lawn areas, creating patches of greens where it overlaid the blue and leaving bright areas of yellow over previously untouched paper.

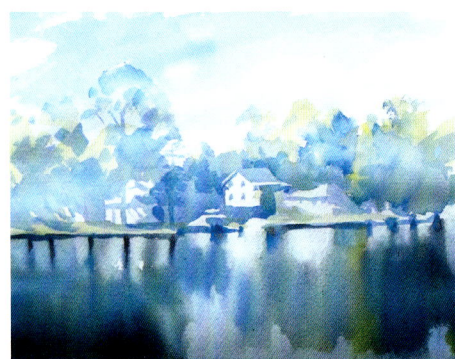

Stage 3: Next, I dampened the lake area with clean water and brushed in the reflections, wet-into-wet, with Aureolin and a dark mix of Burnt Sienna and Ultramarine Blue, creating soft blends for the reflections in the lake.

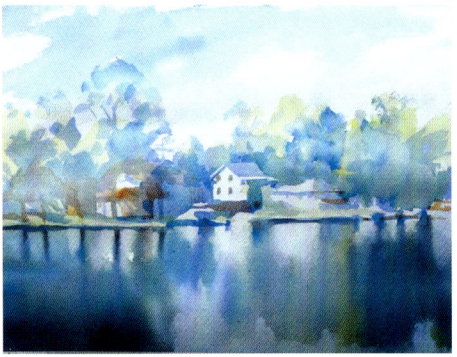

Stage 4: The next stage was to paint small patches of dilute Burnt Sienna, wet on dry, into the landscape, tinting lights and deepening darks.

Painting techniques

There are two main watercolour techniques, appropriately named 'wet on dry' and 'wet into wet'. In the wet-on-dry technique, washes and brushstrokes are only added to the painting once previous applications of paint are dry. The effect is visible edges to layers and brushmarks.

Wet into wet means that brushstrokes are added into wet watercolour washes, or onto wetted paper, causing the pigments to merge and create soft blends. In most watercolour paintings both techniques are employed.

Final Stage: For the finishing touches, I mixed Burnt Sienna with Ultramarine Blue to darken the shadows in the trees and to add small details such as windows. Some brushmarks are painted wet into wet, others wet on dry.

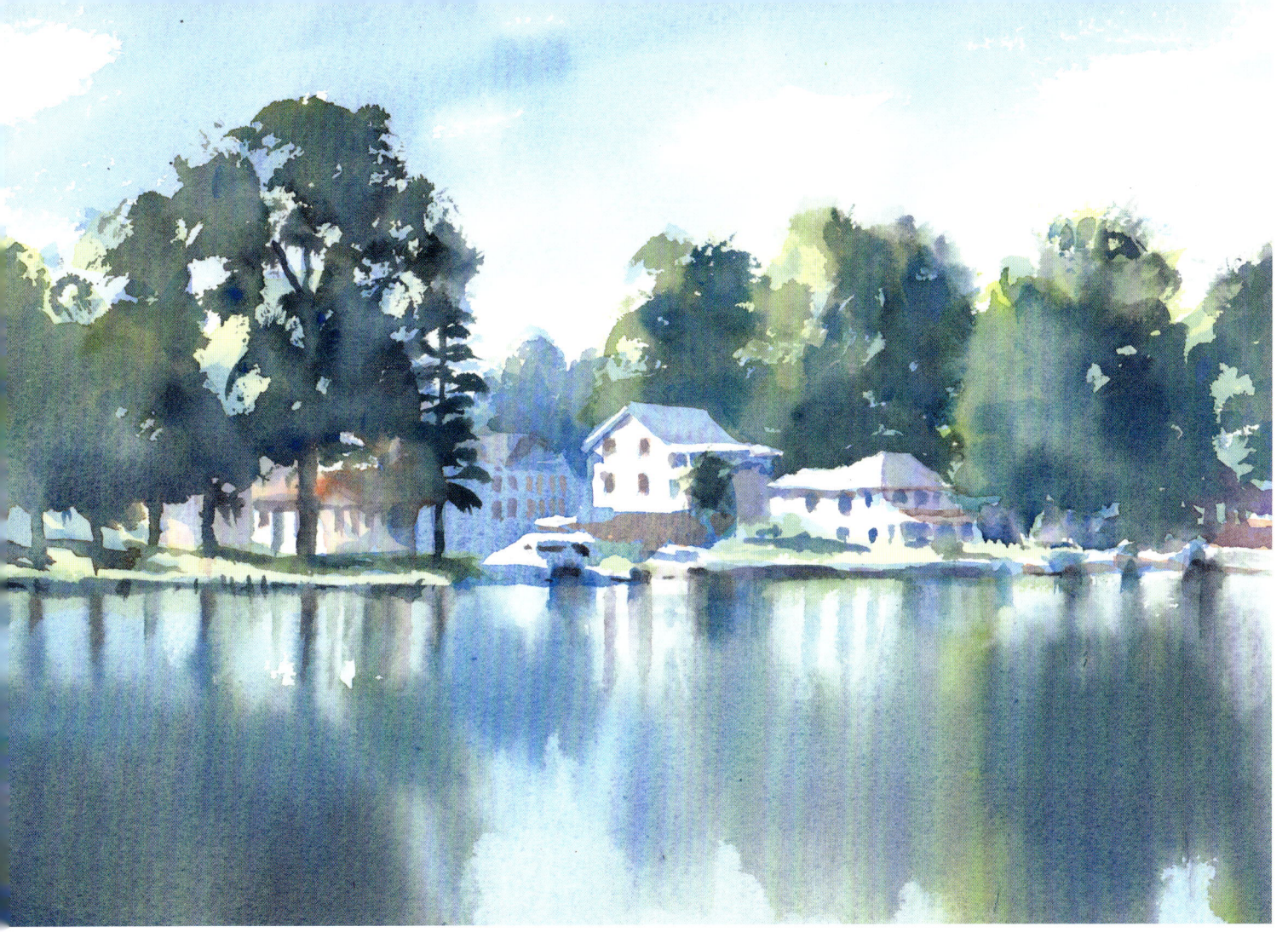

△ **In the Middle of Michigan** *28 x 38cm (11 x 15in)*

The graded wash

The clear blue sky that is a part of many landscape paintings requires a large background wash. The aim is to create a seamless blend, graded from darker at the top to lighter at the horizon. Dampen the paper all over with clean water just before you start, to encourage the pigment to blend. Use a large flat brush, which lays paint more evenly than a round brush. Lay your strokes from the top downwards, tipping the paper as necessary to gain the help of gravity. Gradually dilute the paint as you come down the paper to lighten the wash. Try not to go back and forth with the brush too much. Once it is laid, leave the wash alone! Do not touch, however tempted you may be to perfect it. The sky is in the background, a pale area compared to foreground features, and minor flaws will not be noticed.

Gravity is used to encourage the Ultramarine Blue to flow downwards. Note that wet paint becomes lighter in tone when it dries.

Tinting the horizon

The base of a clear blue sky is sometimes tinted with warmth above the horizon, particularly if there is dust or moisture in the air. Lay a pale band of yellow into the damp paper above the horizon and let this blend seamlessly with the blue in the rest of the sky.

Since blues and yellows are usually found in landscape colouring, continue the sky wash into the landscape area to help maintain harmony throughout the painting. Watch out for pooling paint, as it will back up into the wash and cause a backrun.

Here I have brushed dilute Indian Yellow across the base of the sky and the land below. I brought Ultramarine Blue down from the top, blending with the yellow to bring a warm tinge to the horizon.

Variegated washes

A variegated wash is made with a blend of several colours. Prepare them beforehand, preferably few rather than many, in order to avoid muddiness. Wet the paper all over before brushing in, and allow the colours to mix with minimum interference. If necessary, direct the flow by gently tipping the paper, using gravity to encourage the pigment particles to drift in a chosen direction. The microscopic particles of pigment disperse on the damp paper, blending in a miniature form of pointillism to create seamless and sometimes breathtaking blends. If pooling occurs, lift out the excess water without disturbing the wash.

▽ **Drifting wash**

Indian Yellow is brushed across wetted paper, then Ultramarine Blue and Burnt Sienna, increasing the concentration with each additional application. Gravity directs the drift of the damp colour.

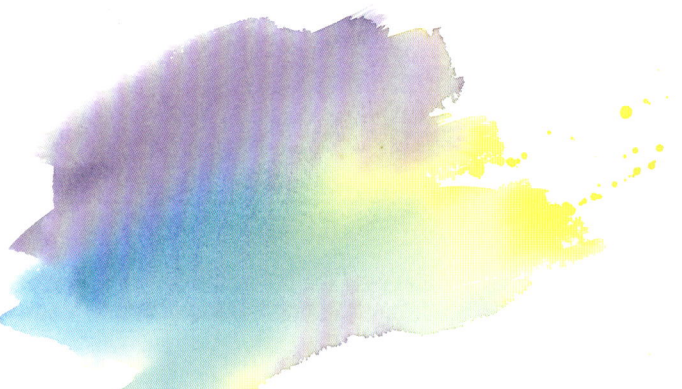

◁ **Variegated wash**

The paper is wetted all over, Aureolin, Prussian Blue and Schmincke Violet are brushed in beside each other and the paper tipped to encourage blending.

▷ **Kalahari Sunset**
18 x 28cm (7 x 11in)

Sunsets are a great excuse to use strong, bright colours. Here, three opaques, Cadmium Yellow, Cadmium Red and Cerulean Blue, were applied successively and allowed to mingle wet beside wet in a rich blend. They were then mixed together to paint the landscape silhouette.

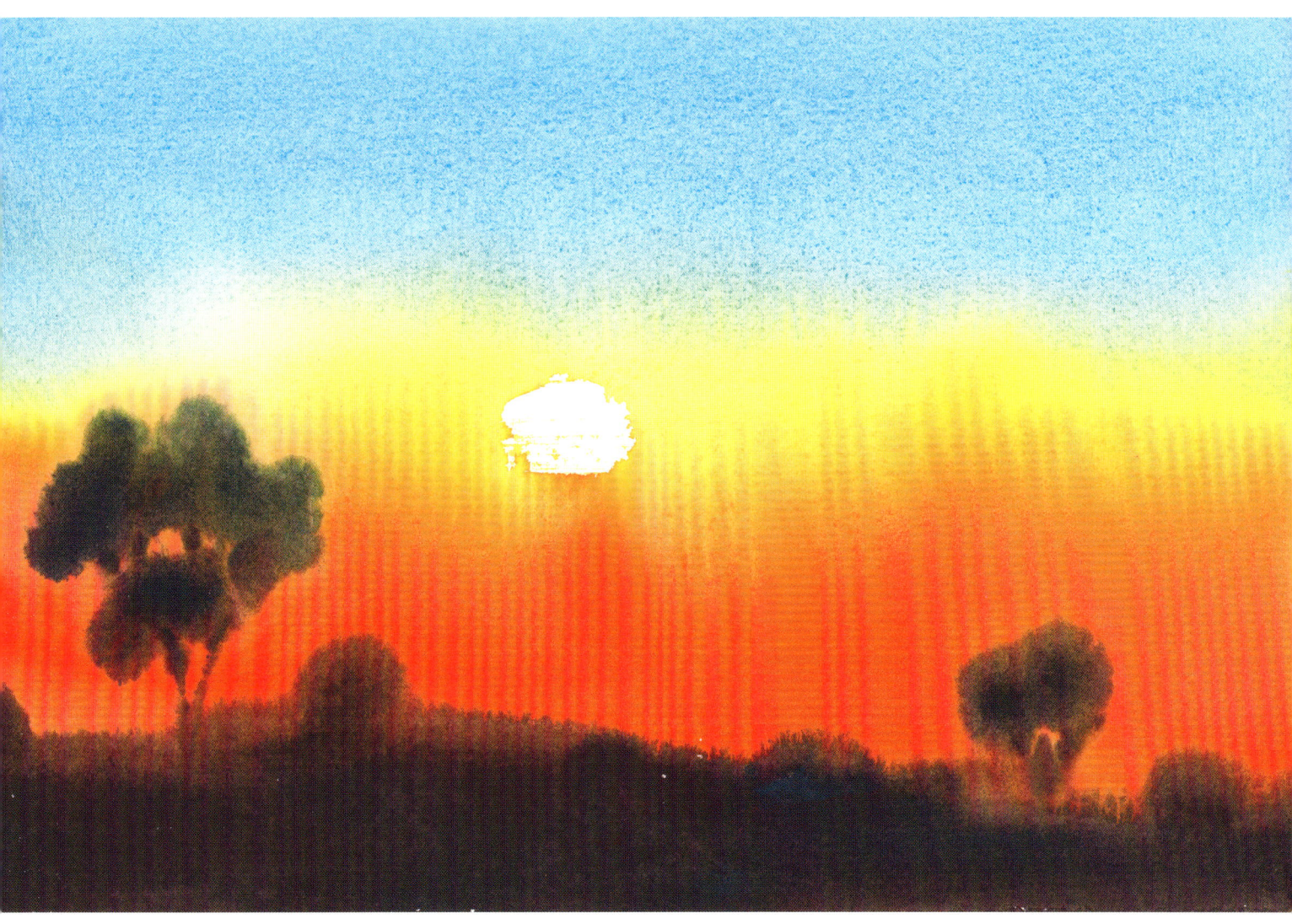

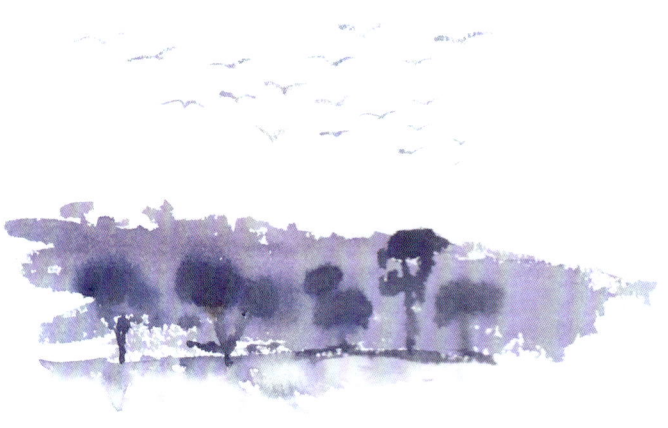

△ A brushstroke added wet into wet will have a soft appearance and blend with the background.

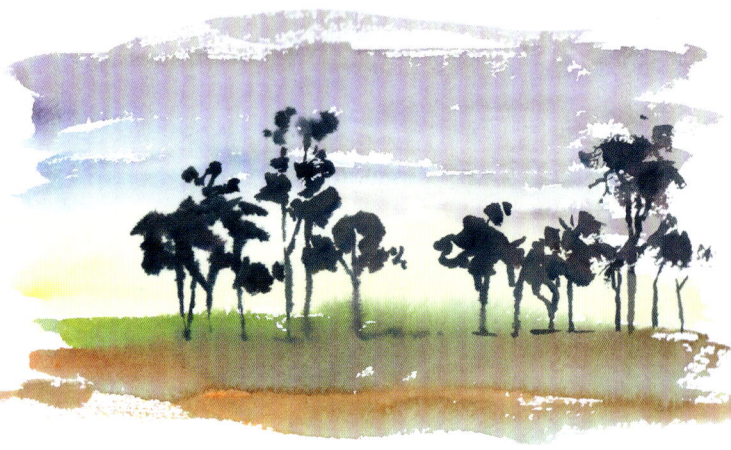

△ A brushstroke applied onto a dried wash, wet on dry, will have a crisp-edged appearance and a defined shape. Where the paper is still wet when the stroke is applied, the edges of the mark will be softened.

◁ A dry brushmark leaves flecks of untouched paper within the stroke. It can be created by lifting the pressure off the brush, by grazing the paper lightly with the side of the brush, or by using a dryish mixture. It is enhanced by the tooth of Rough paper.

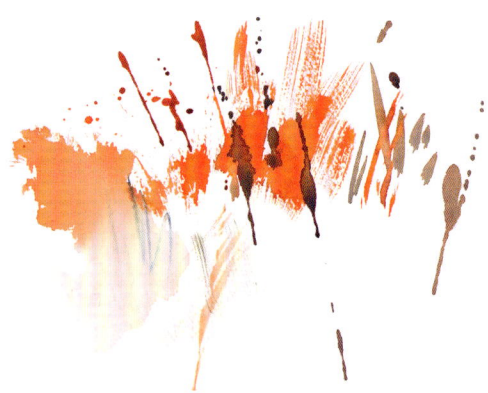

◁ Fanning the brush hairs, spattering paint from the brush and pushing paint forwards with the heel of the brush create marks that are useful in landscape painting and add variety.

Brushmarks

You need very few brushes, the bigger the better, with fine tips, so you can lay the minimum number of brushstrokes for a wash and yet still make fine lines from the point. Brushmarks benefit from being laid in a confident and lively fashion. They do not need to be accurately shaped to have credibility – in fact a looser, more expressive appearance brings life into a painting. Variety in your brushstrokes and in their mode of delivery is essential as it adds the element of surprise and entertains the eye. Take care to avoid boring the eye with unnecessary repetition; for example, in a line of trees or distant hills, seek out irregularity in height and shape.

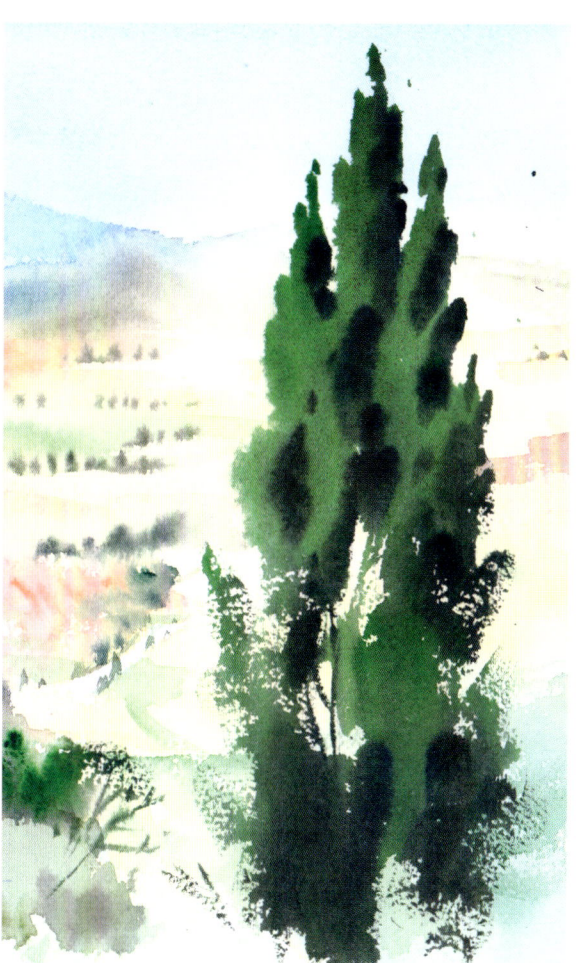

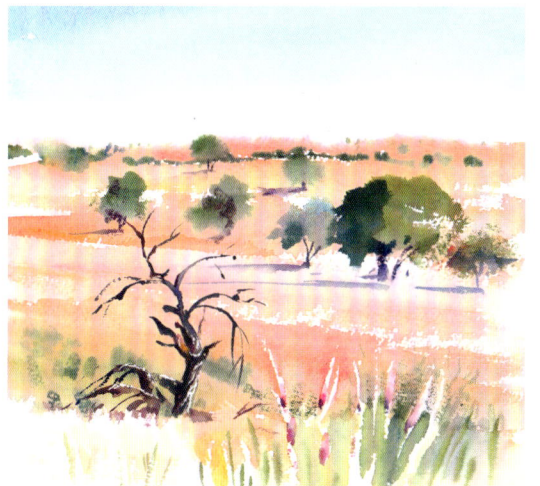

◁ In this quick sketch of the dry river in the Kalahari a variety of brushmarks are evident, delivered both from the body and the tip: wash, line, dry-brush and negative space.

△ Variety in the brushstrokes gives the cypress tree a lively appearance.

Using aids to conserve light

Protecting highlights is often the greatest challenge in watercolour landscape painting, but there are aids to help you preserve the white paper.

Masking fluid

A latex liquid used to reserve multiple highlights, masking fluid is applied to the paper before painting takes place. Once it is completely dry, watercolour paint can safely be brushed over the masked areas. When the paint is dry the masking fluid is rubbed off, leaving areas of untouched white paper that can be tinted as appropriate or left as bright highlights. Take care, though, masking fluid ruins brushes, so use old or cheap brushes or specialist applicators.

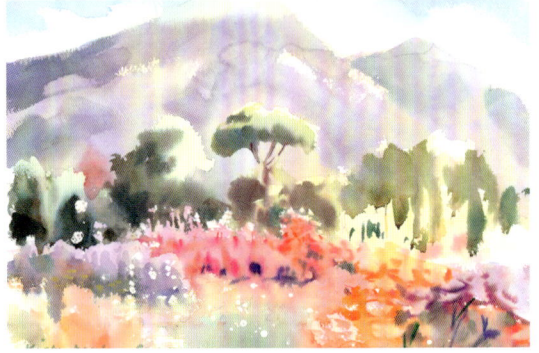

◁ Colourless masking fluid dries to a creamy colour. Even though it is hard to see when applying it, it is better to use colourless fluid, otherwise the relationship of highlights to the darker tones is hard to assess correctly while painting.

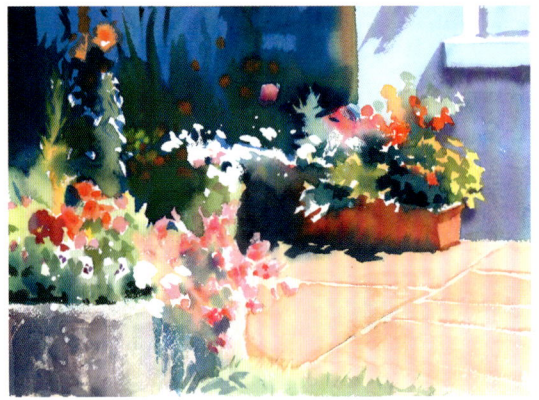

◁ Masking fluid leaves a blobby shape when it is rubbed off, so remove it before the painting is complete so that you can adjust the highlighted shapes.

◁ **Snowfall**
28 x 38cm (11 x 15in)
The flakes of snow in the sky are made by spattering the masking fluid from an old toothbrush.

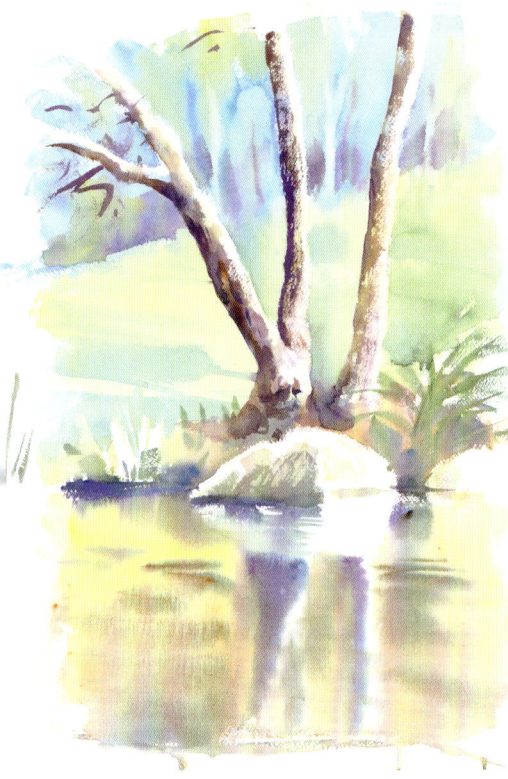

Wax resist

Wax can be used to reserve a textured light. When watercolour is painted over a smear of wax it acts as a resist, leaving flecks of white paper within a mottled wash.

◁ Reserving the light on the tree trunks with wax meant a background wash could be freely painted over the top without loss of light.

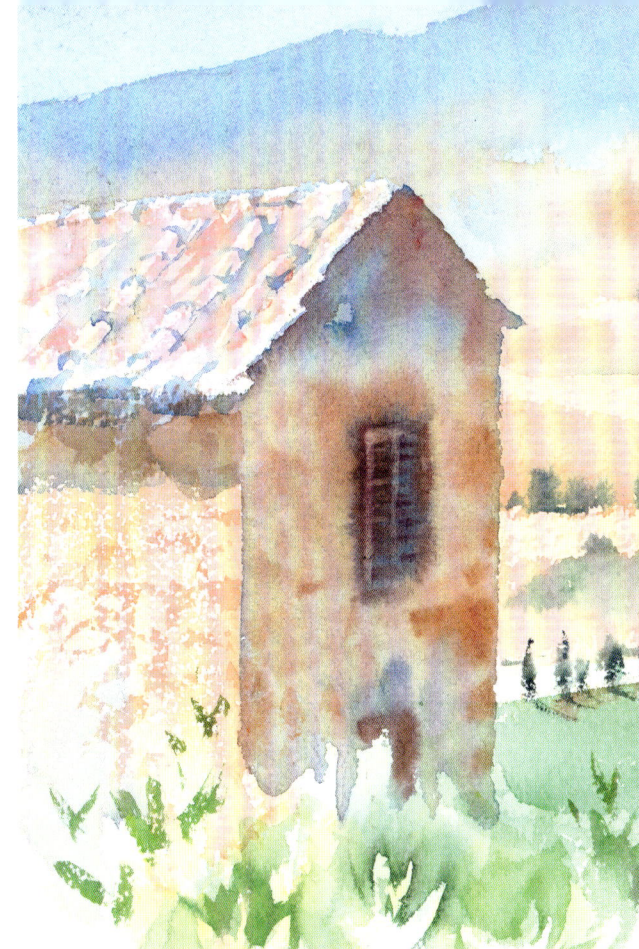

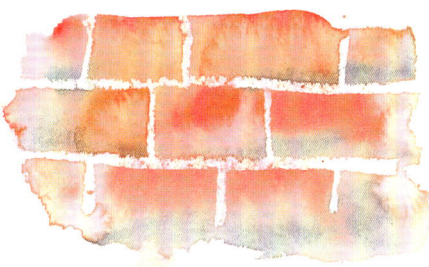

▷ Waxing the mortar lines enables a quick rendition of brickwork.

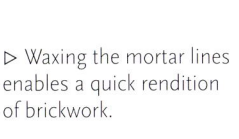

△ A white candle has been rubbed over the lit side of the outbuilding. It is then painted over with Yellow Ochre and Burnt Sienna, giving the appearance of light catching on the rough surface of stone.

Retrieving light

Watercolour has a reputation for being unforgiving, and it is true that if you overwork it or push it around too much it will refuse to reward you, which means it is often quicker to start again! However, there are several ways you can redeem lost highlights in a watercolour.

Lifting and sponging off

Watercolour pigment is bound in gum arabic, which dissolves in the water when you dilute the paint. When the paint dries after application, the gum arabic sets the pigment in place. Since the gum arabic can be dissolved again by another addition of water, any non-staining colours can be lifted, enabling the reintroduction of light. This can be done with a clean, damp brush or sponge. Useful lifting colours are Ultramarine Blue, Cobalt Blue, Burnt Sienna and most other earth colours.

The lifting nature of some pigments means they can be shifted unintentionally, so be careful not to make subsequent washes too wet when painting over these. Bleed can also occur from strong, concentrated colours, so ideally these should be painted last.

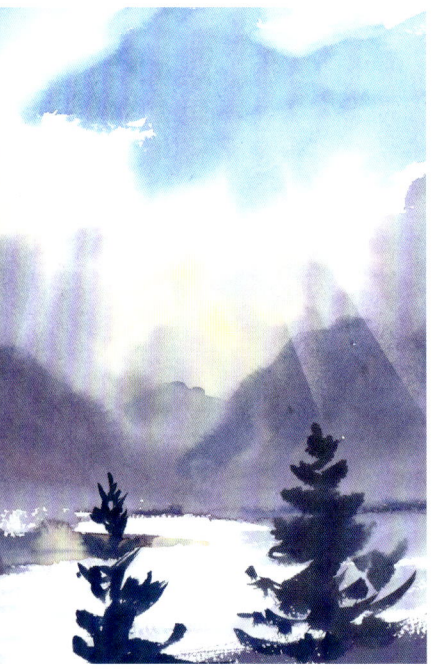

◁ The sunbeams were lifted out of the dry purple mountainside wash, which has been mixed from Ultramarine Blue and Burnt Sienna (lifting colours) and Schmincke Violet (a staining colour). A straightedge of paper was used as a stencil to position the sunbeam and a clean, slightly damp sponge was dragged along it to lift the pigment, which was dabbed off immediately.

Scratching off

When a painting is completely finished, small linear highlights can be reintroduced by scratching off the surface of the paper with a sharp blade.

White paint

While the brightest highlights in watercolour remain the white paper, small highlights can be introduced using white paint. Being a denser metal than zinc, Titanium White has more covering power than Chinese (Zinc) White and so is the better white for this purpose.

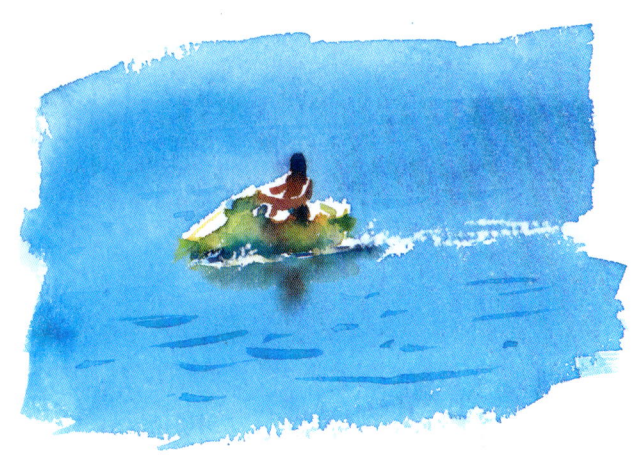

△ The wake from behind this jet-ski is scratched out of the Phthalo Blue wash to reveal white paper beneath.

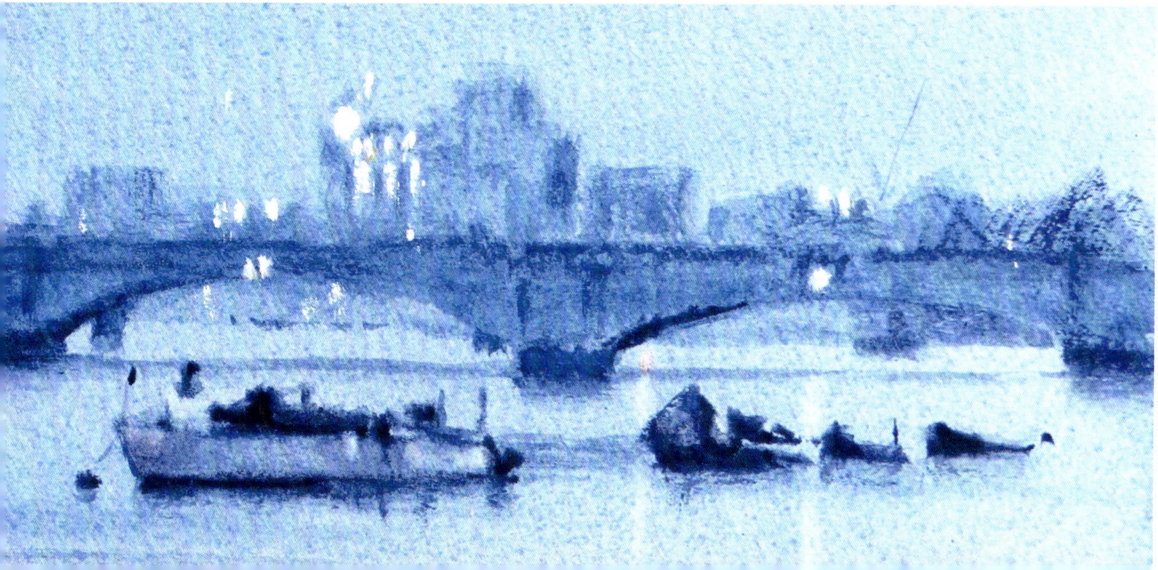

◁ In this detail from a painting the lights are touched in with neat Titanium White.

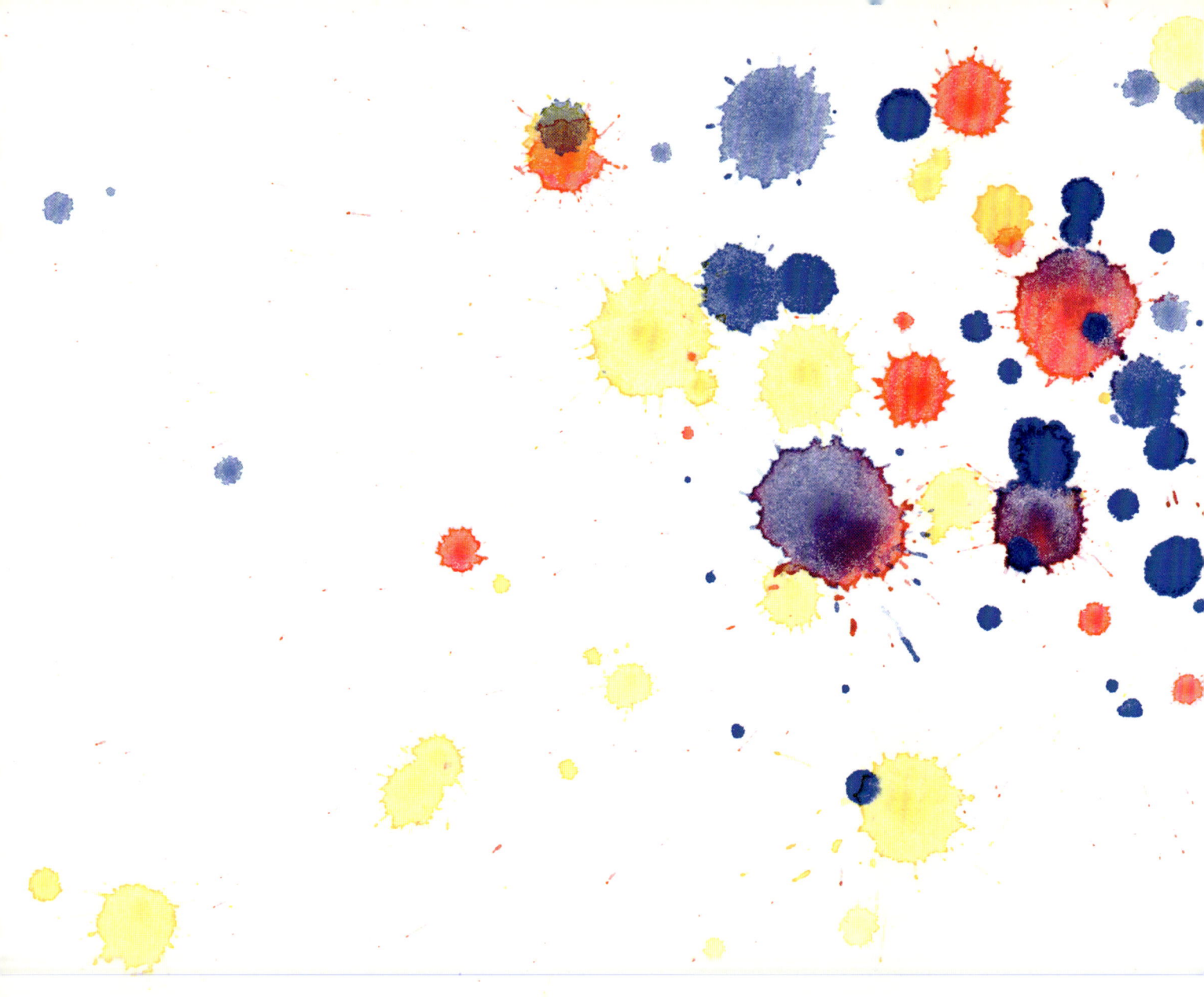

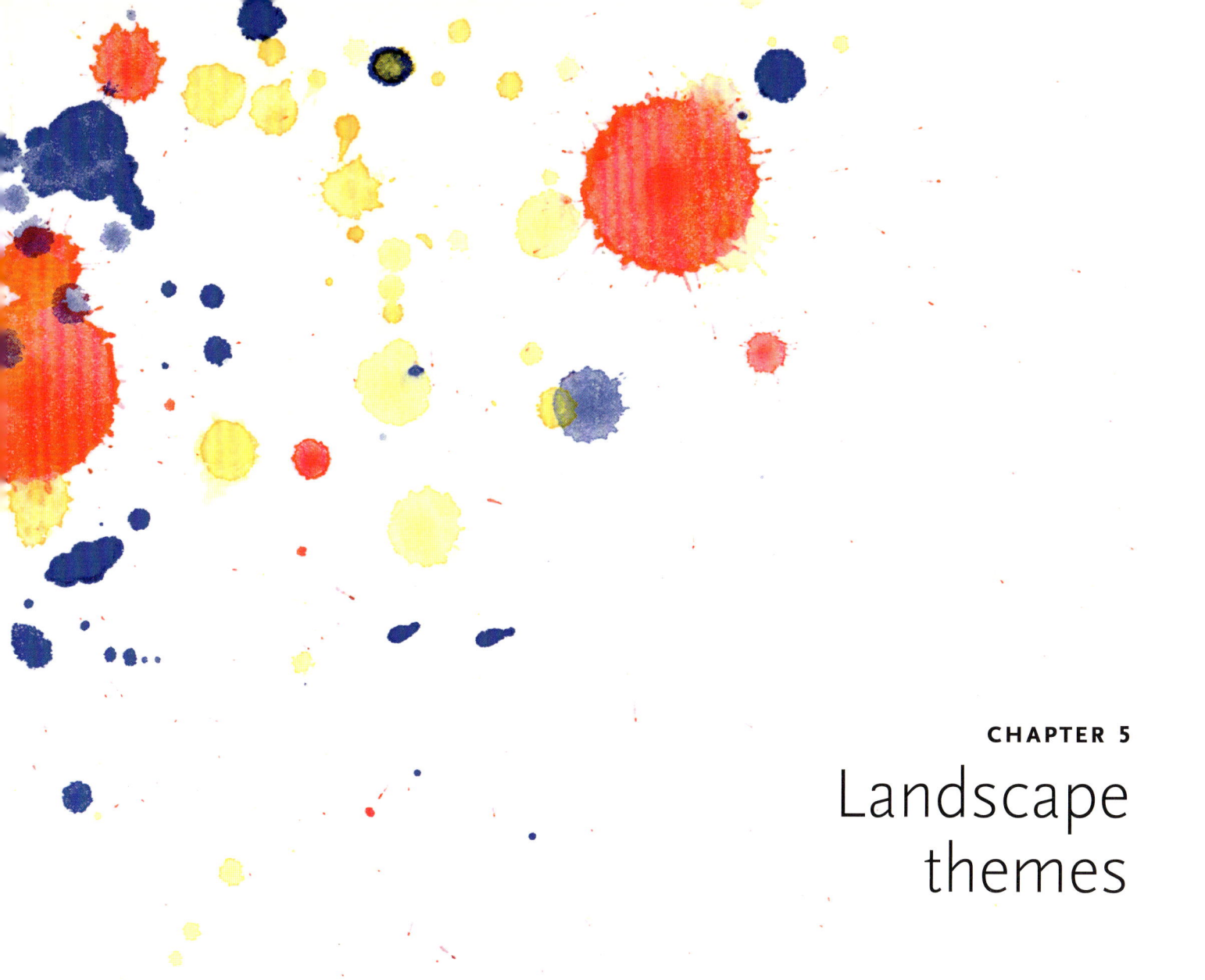

CHAPTER 5

Landscape themes

The inspiration for the painting

The previous chapters have explained the main principles of landscape painting in watercolour; this one looks at some of the landscapes you might paint and suggests ways to approach them. Even though the chapter is subject-based, remember the mantra: 'Use the landscape to paint a watercolour, not the watercolour to paint a landscape.' A worthwhile watercolour is your aim, and the landscape is your inspiration.

Additional materials

Here are some more colours that I use less often but which I would not want to be without.

Assessing tone
If you find it hard to assess depth of tone, try half-closing your eyes as this reduces the distraction of colour and makes it easier to assess tonal values.

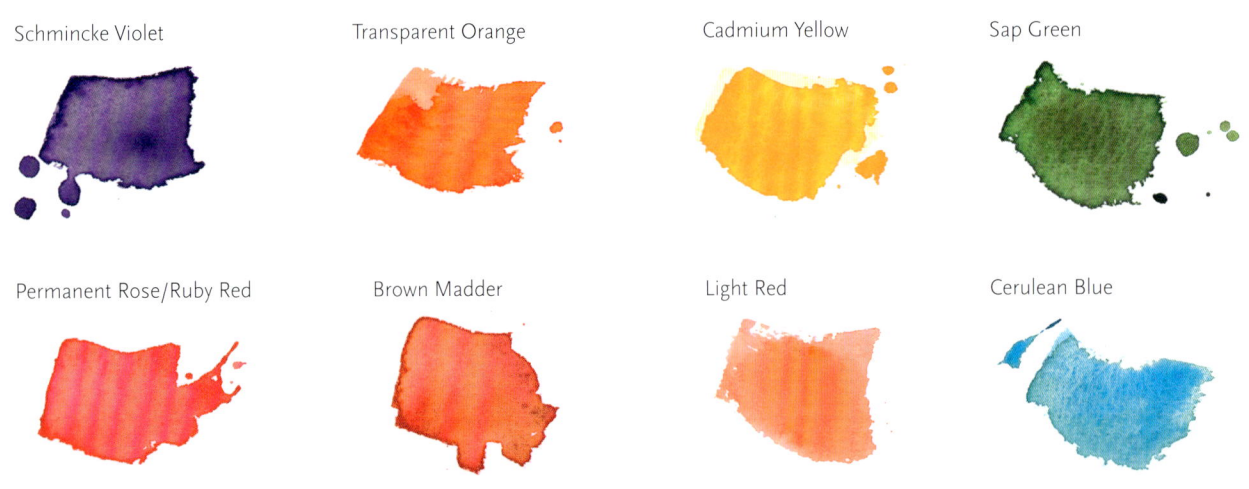

Schmincke Violet

Transparent Orange

Cadmium Yellow

Sap Green

Permanent Rose/Ruby Red

Brown Madder

Light Red

Cerulean Blue

▷ Guardian Angel

30.5 x 28cm (12 x 11in)

The rocky outcrop above Symi in Greece is adorned with a complex piece of architecture and numerous trees. By establishing structure in the painting first, through the counterchange of light and dark tones, the complexity is simplified and the representation of the view follows by default.

Cobalt Blue

Indigo

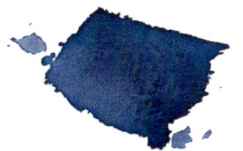

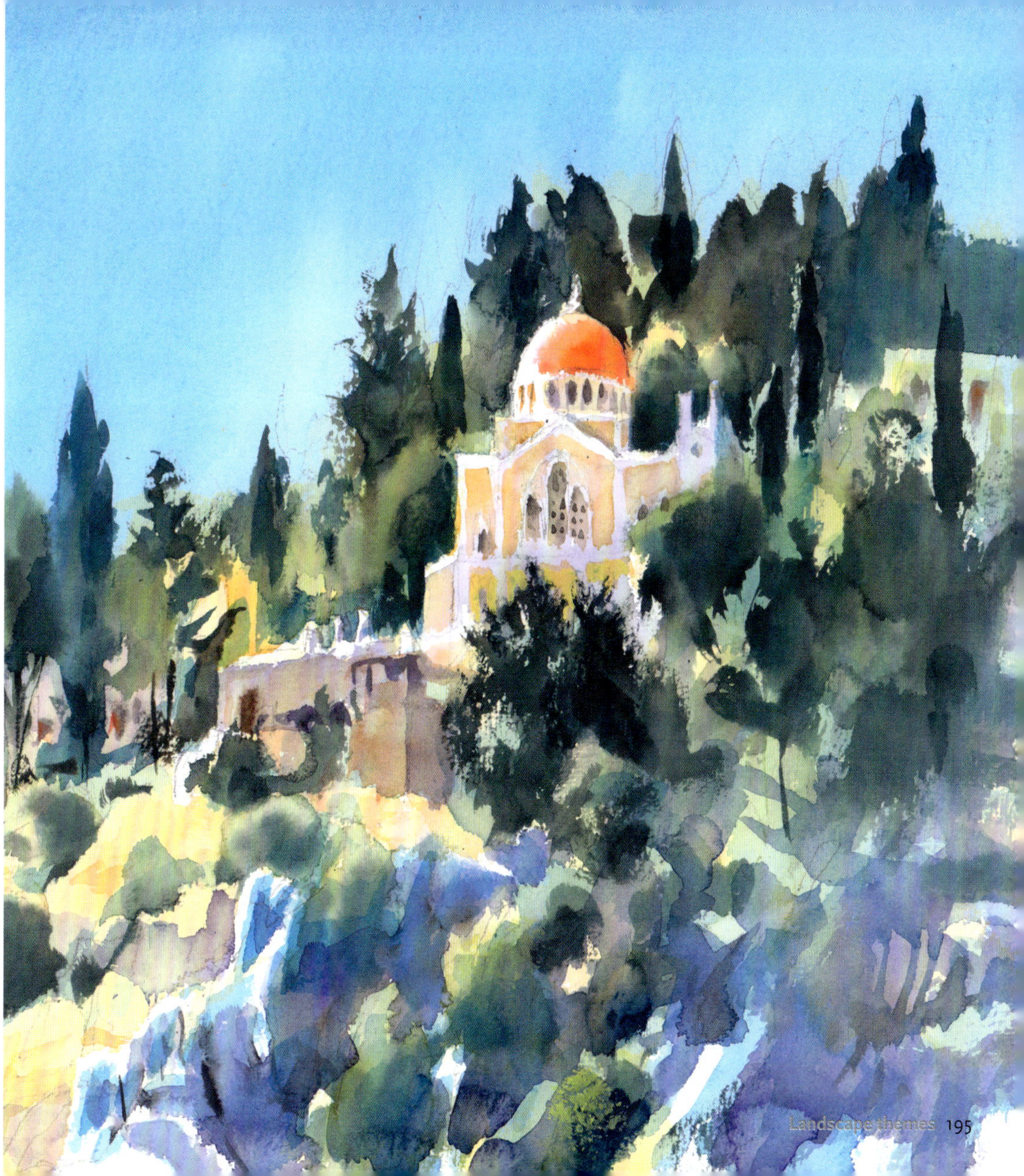

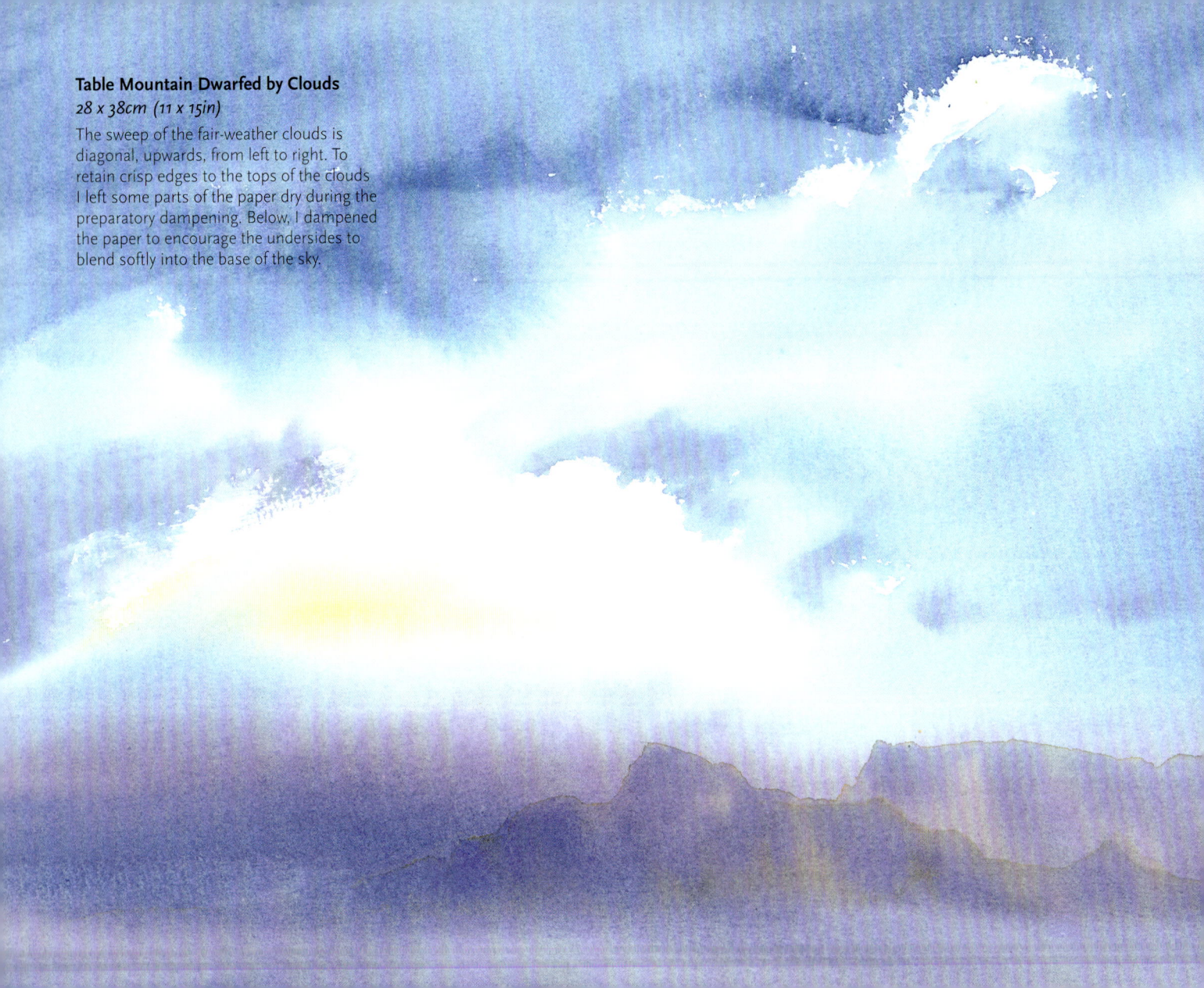

Table Mountain Dwarfed by Clouds
28 x 38cm (11 x 15in)

The sweep of the fair-weather clouds is diagonal, upwards, from left to right. To retain crisp edges to the tops of the clouds I left some parts of the paper dry during the preparatory dampening. Below, I dampened the paper to encourage the undersides to blend softly into the base of the sky.

Skies and clouds

A sky benefits from being brushed in swiftly, never laboured. Clouds move, changing the pattern of the sky constantly, so pick a section, and a moment, and having chosen the layout, stay with the pattern of clouds chosen, rather than chase the changes in the sky. Wetting the paper before laying a sky wash encourages seamless blends. A sky takes only seconds to paint – just lay the wash and trust the watercolour to blend nicely. Watch out for any backruns, then leave well alone!

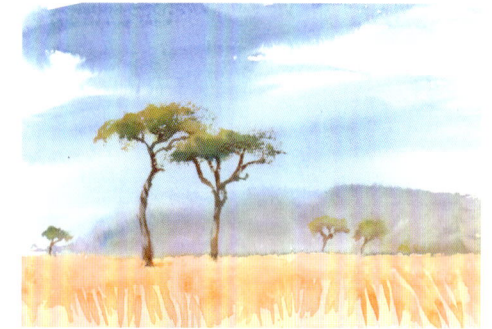

◁ The blue of the sky is applied with swift strokes and is used in the distant hills and the green of the trees to ensure harmony in the painting.

△ For soft, floating clouds, dampen the paper before brushing in the blue – in this case, Ultramarine Blue.

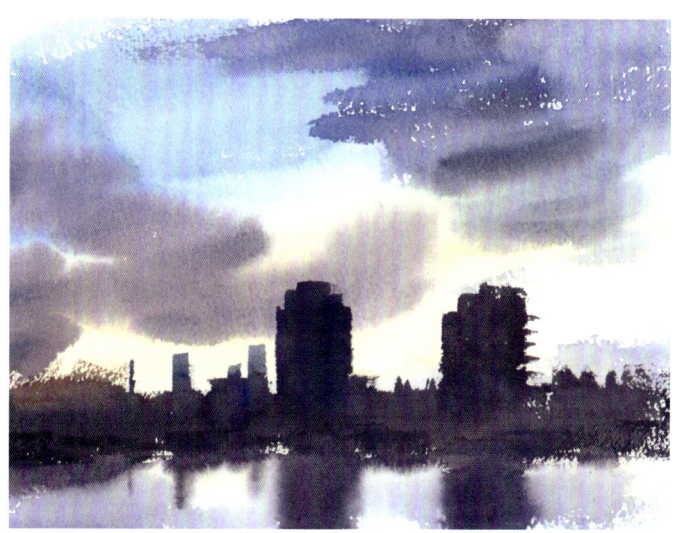

◁ Clouds darker in tone than the sky were brushed into the sky wash while it was still damp so that they blended softly. The cloud mixture must be less dilute than the initial sky wash, otherwise the excess water will cause backruns.

Inclement weather

Stormy skies are one of the most exciting subjects to paint in watercolour. The variegated wash is the perfect technique, creating stunning passages of merging colour. Choose colours that represent the light and the darkness, and use them boldly in contrasting areas. Wet paint dries lighter, so use concentrated pigment for the deepest tones, and brush in the colours with gusto to match the energy of the storm.

▷ **The Glow Before the Storm**
28 x 38cm (11 x 15in)

Here Yellow Ochre, Transparent Orange, Prussian Blue and Burnt Umber were brushed swiftly into dampened paper, in that order, from light to dark. I used a very rich mix of the blue and the brown for the darkest clouds and the landscape silhouette.

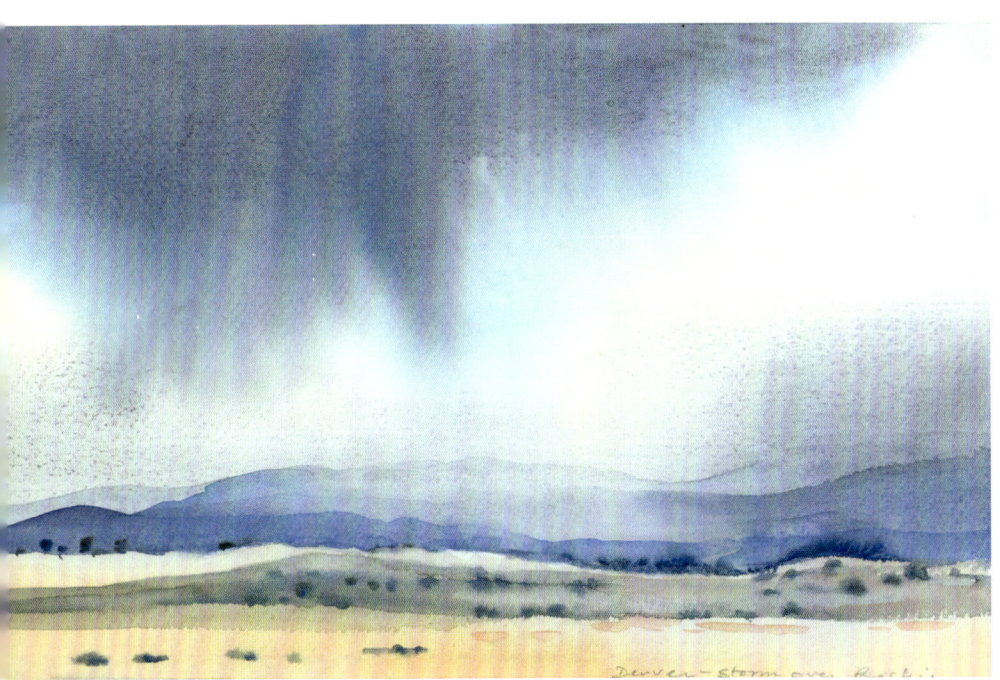

◁ **Rain Before Denver**
28 x 38cm (11 x 15in)

I tipped the paper to encourage strands of pigment to run downwards within the wet paint, suggesting the drift of rain falling from stormy clouds. The colours used were Yellow Ochre, Ultramarine Blue, Burnt Sienna and Schmincke Violet.

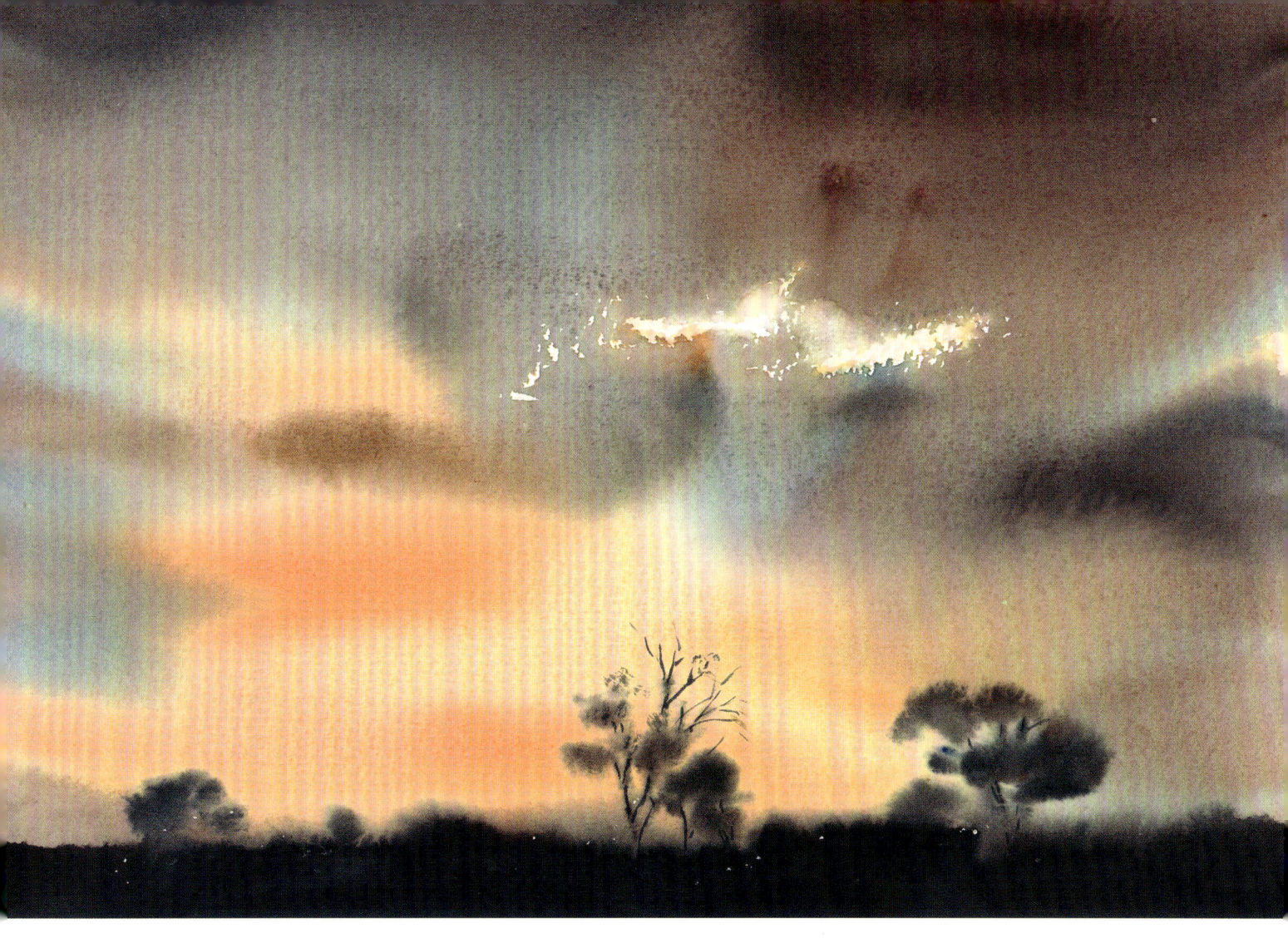

Rivers and streams

Preserving untouched white paper is the key to successfully representing moving water, because when the flow is interrupted water appears white. Masking fluid, though useful, can be blobby, so it is preferable to leave chunks of negative space (the white paper) between your brushstrokes as angular shapes better suggest the crisp, clean appearance of water. Paint ripples in the water with linear and horizontal strokes; when the surface is ruffled by a breeze, use dry-brush technique to fragment the wash to show the sparkle of light. If the water is smooth, reflections are seen on the surface, drop these down vertically below the item's position on the bank.

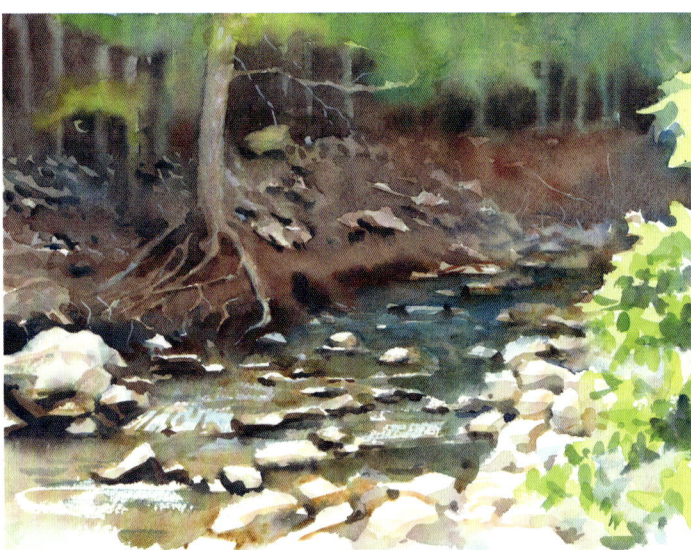

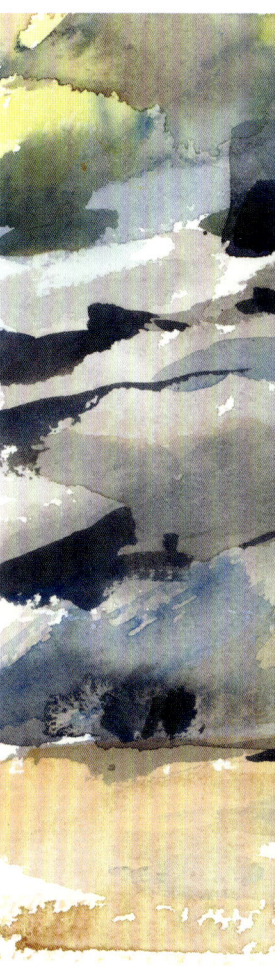

◁ **Appalachian Song**
28 x 38cm (11 x 15in)

The cold water of an Appalachian stream required a cool set of colours – Prussian Blue, Raw Umber and Aureolin, with the added warmth of Burnt Umber.

▷ **Cascade**
18 x 38cm (7 x 15in)

The patches of untouched paper left between brushstrokes of Raw Umber perfectly suggest the white water of muddy rapids and contrast with darker rocks, which are a mix of Ultramarine Blue and Burnt Sienna.

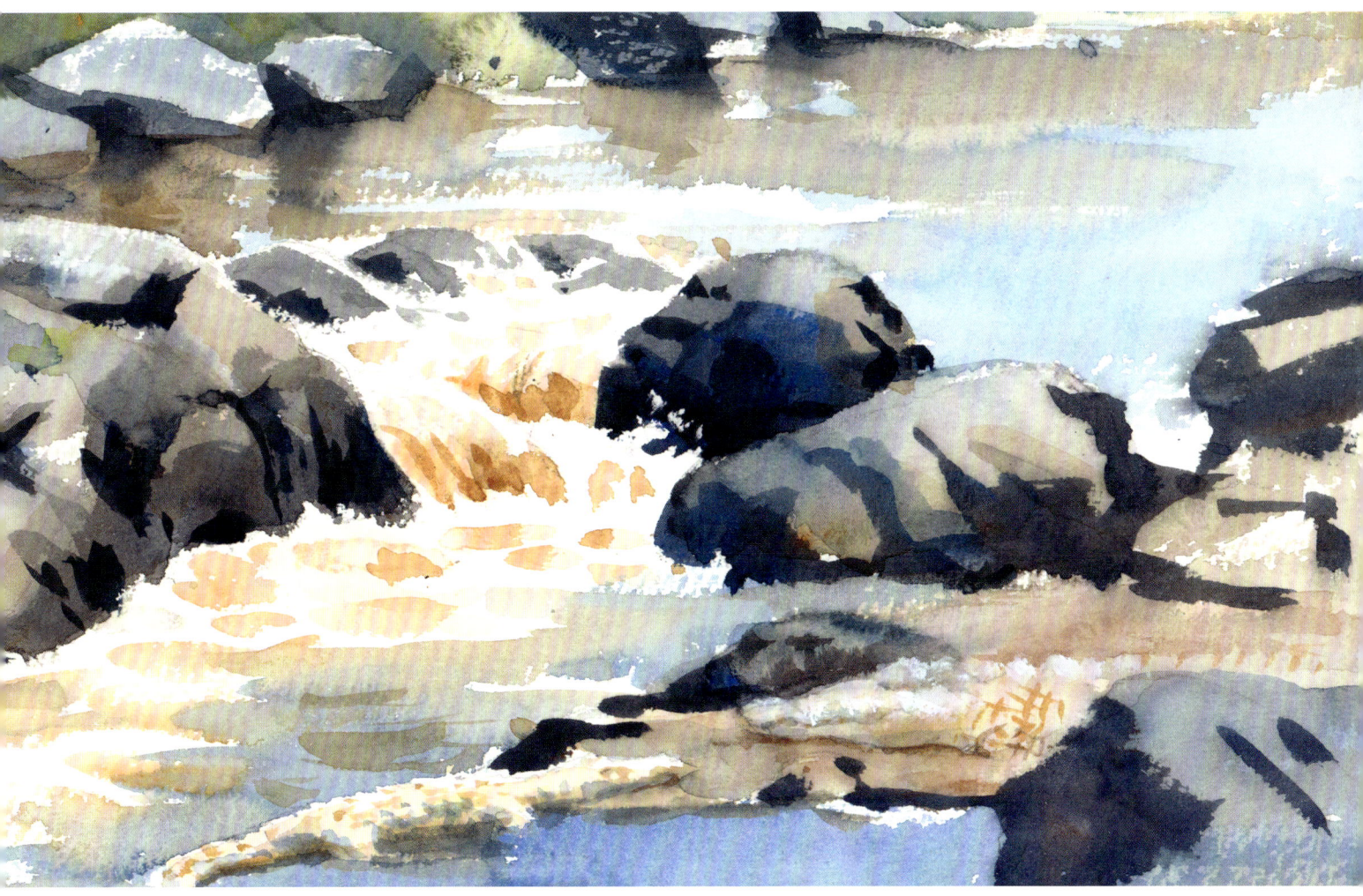

Trees

We recognize trees by their shape, so concern yourself with the overall shape of the tree rather than the foliage alone. Show the light and shade of the foliage masses and blend the trunk and branches into the shady undersides of these to affirm they are lost in shadow. Contrast definition with ambiguity.

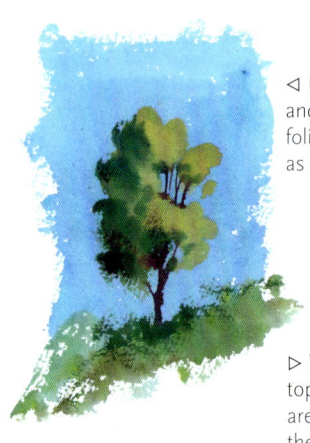

◁ Blend the trunk and branches with the foliage so they belong as one organic whole.

▷ Where the topsides of foliage are lit, as seen in the middle of this tree, separate the branches from the foliage.

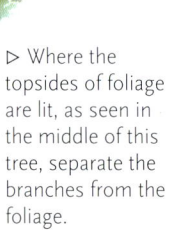

◁ Note the light and shade of the foliage masses.

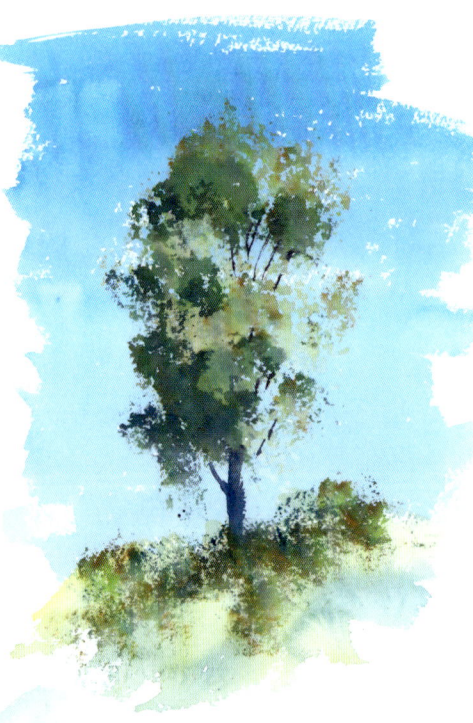

▷ Shapely brushmarks suggest the cypress and umbrella pines redolent of the Mediterranean.

△ This East African acacia is shaped by light-pressured brushstrokes delivered from the side of the brush and lines applied from the tip.

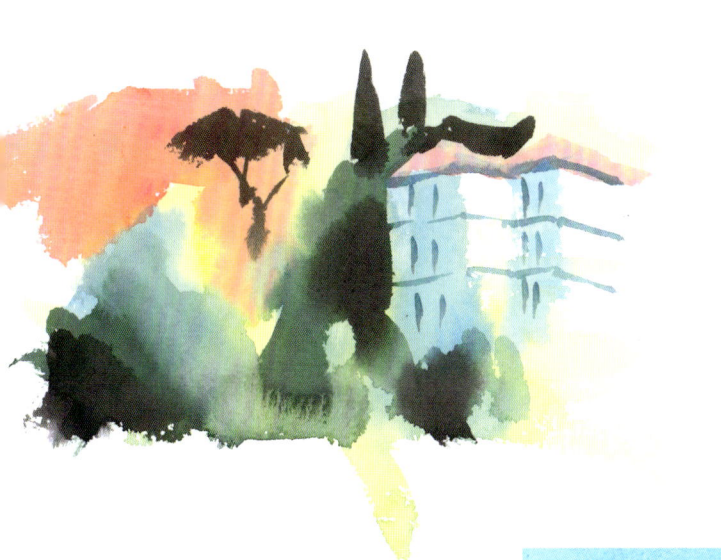

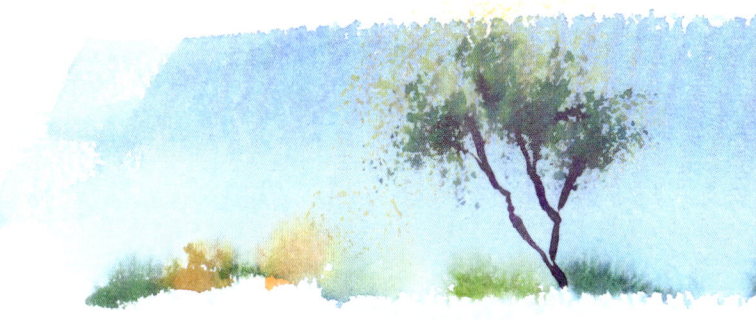

△ Use technique and brushstroke to describe the particular tree. Here, dry-brush and sponging perfectly suit the sparse, speckled foliage of the grey camelthorn.

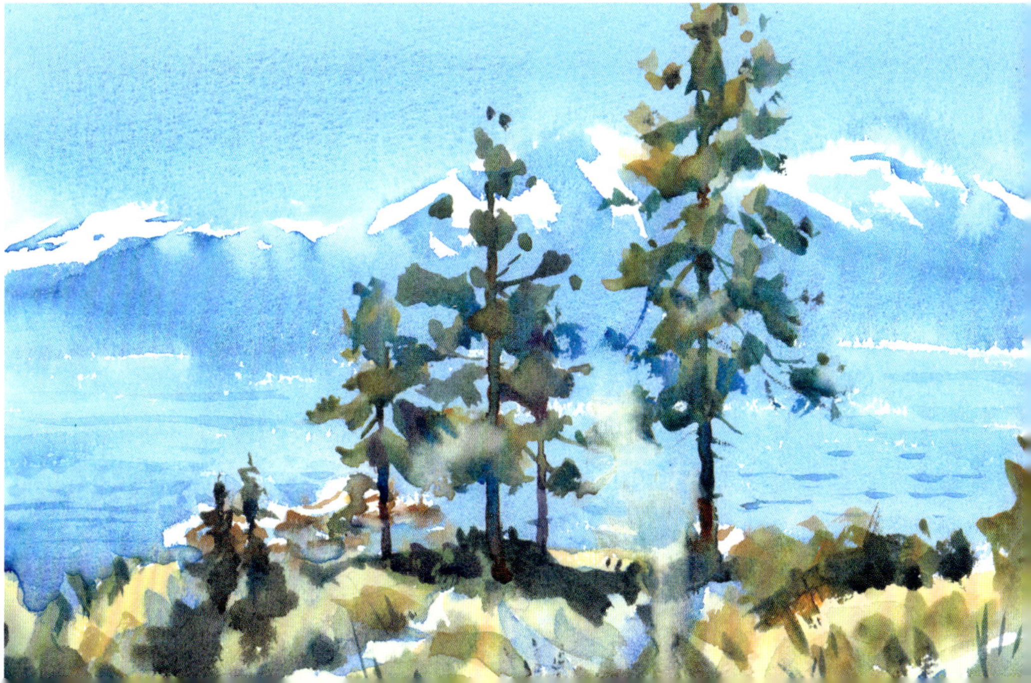

▷ **Take Me to Lake Tahoe**
18 x 28cm (7 x 11in)

Ponderosa pines, ubiquitous in the Rockies, sport multiple, often separated, foliage masses. Paint the individual shapes of the foliage masses by concentrating on the tree's overall shape, then touch in the trunk so it merges with the foliage, and add the odd branch with a fine rigger.

Fields and grasses

Field patterns and foreground grasses are a delightful subject with repetitive features. The eye is easily persuaded – all you need to do is offer a semblance of narrative in the foreground and merely suggest things in the background. Ambiguity is one of watercolour's best-loved characteristics, so show a few details and leave the rest to the viewer's imagination so that they are drawn into the painting to resolve the missing information. For example, rather than paint all the blades of grass, present a few by means of interesting brushstrokes; the viewer will guess they represent grass and enjoy the attractive marks. When grasses are sunlit, it will be the shadows behind and between the blades that you paint, not the blades themselves.

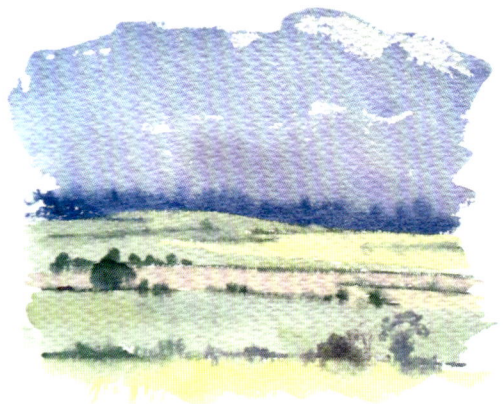

▽ ▽ Fields make marvellous patterns. Treelines and hedgerows can be touched in wet into wet, before the wash above them has dried so that the pigment spreads out in softly rounded shapes, ably representing bushes and trees.

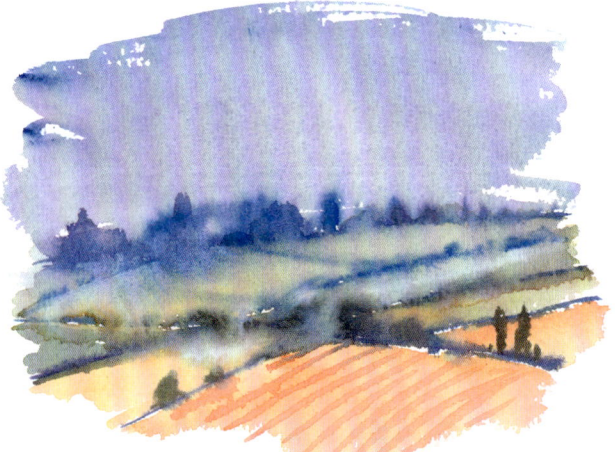

◁ Distant features can be amazingly ambiguous and still serve to describe fields and trees. Here I painted the far treeline and field patterns and then deliberately 'messed them up' by touching in dilute paint and clean water to diffuse the forms.

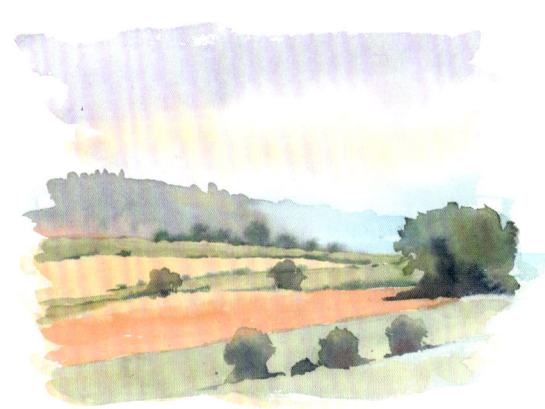

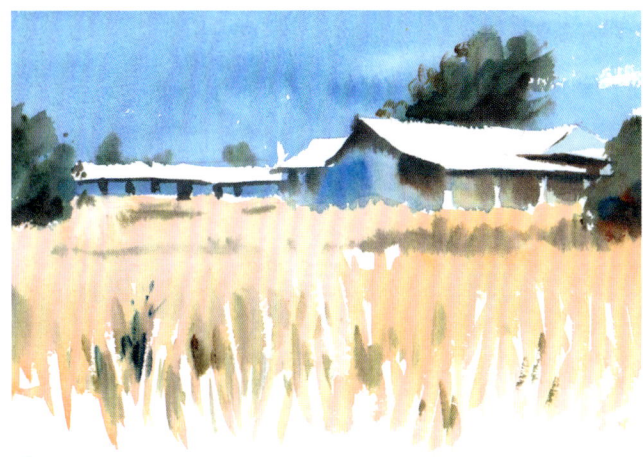

∇ For lively foreground grasses I used positive brushstrokes, negative space, wet-into-wet lines and wet paint spattered from the tip of the brush.

△ Here the foreground blades of grain are represented by the untouched white paper left at the base of the Yellow Ochre wash, setting up a pleasing lattice of contrasting tone.

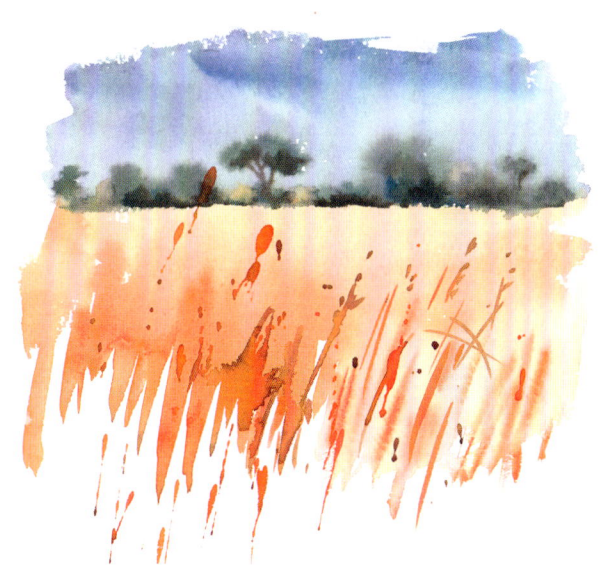

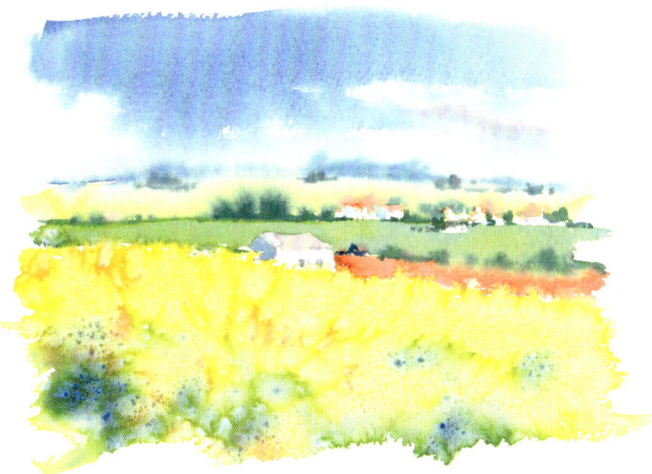

◁ A dusting of salt crystals tossed into a very wet Aureolin wash created a delightfully mottled texture as it dried, ideal for the yellow flowers of a rapeseed field in full bloom.

Sea and shoreline

The sea often plays a part in landscape painting, adding a compositional echo to the sky. Sometimes they appear to be a completely different colour, but it is usually in your interest to include the same blue in the sea's colouring to ensure harmony across the painting. Back-lit, the sea sparkles with multiple diamonds of light, which can be reserved with masking fluid or created with a dry brushstroke. For energetic ripples, use lively horizontal brushmarks delivered mainly from the tip of the brush, lifting it with a dash as it leaves the paper.

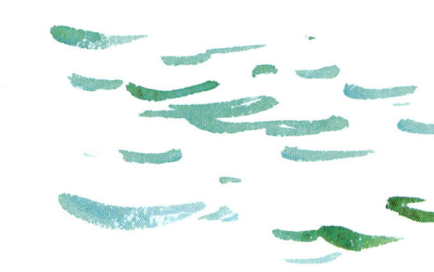

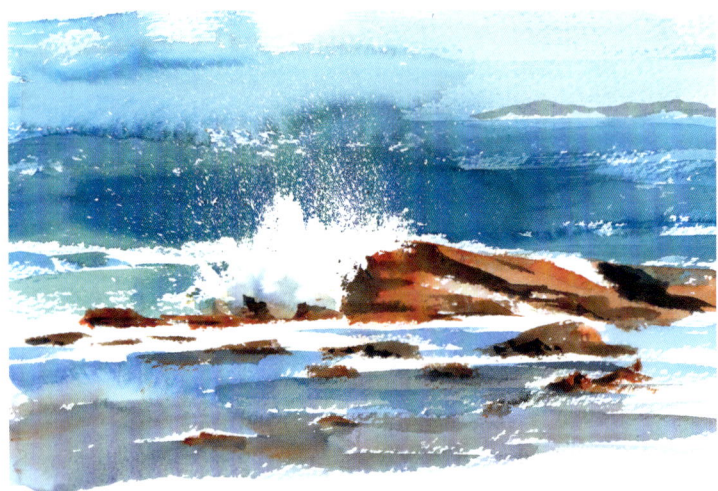

△ The fine spume of a crashing wave can be created by reserving the white paper with masking fluid spattered from a toothbrush.

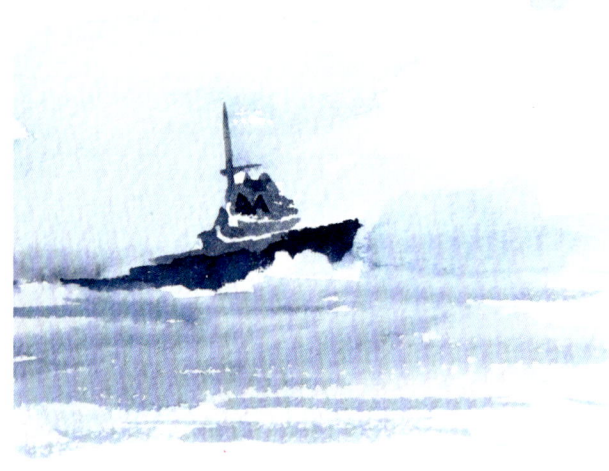

△ A boat brings interest to a sea view, not just because it adds narrative, but because the bright white of the bow wave and wake introduce contrast, always a good recipe for a watercolour.

41 x 51cm (16 x 20in)

The clear Mediterranean waters of Collioure in France offer the chance to use turquoise, deepened with bands of dry-brush, enlivened with horizontal dashes to deftly represent ripples and repeated in the landscape above. The townscape is reflected in the calm sea with a gentle tint, touched in wet into wet.

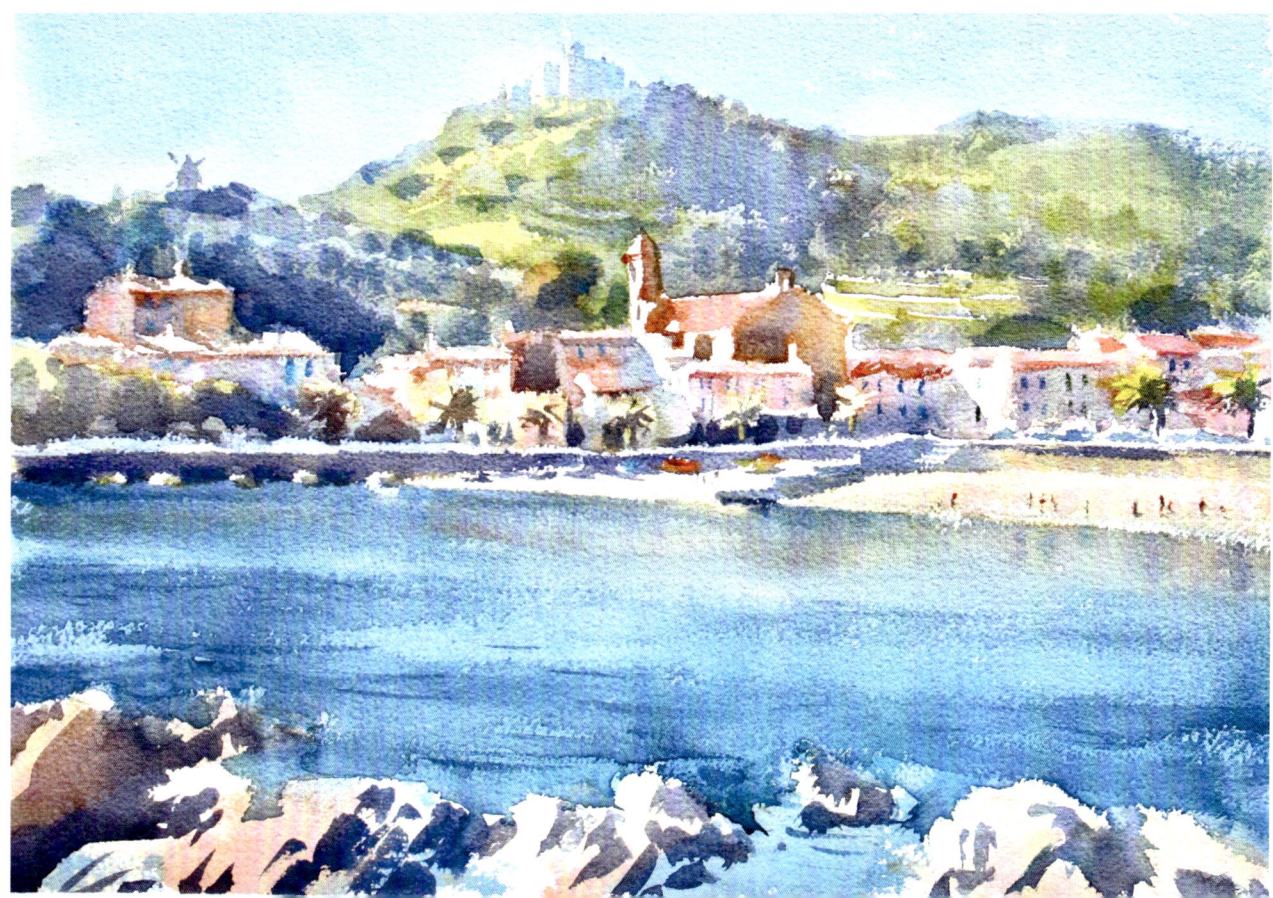

Gardens and flowers

Gardens are probably the most accessible subject for the watercolour painter, and their flowers offer a wonderful opportunity to explore colour. In the calm of a garden you can experiment to your heart's content, knowing that if the weather turns against you, shelter is close at hand! In a wider view, look for the massed shapes of flowers and shrubs rather than individual blooms. Use masking to reserve small flowerheads and narrow stems and grasses.

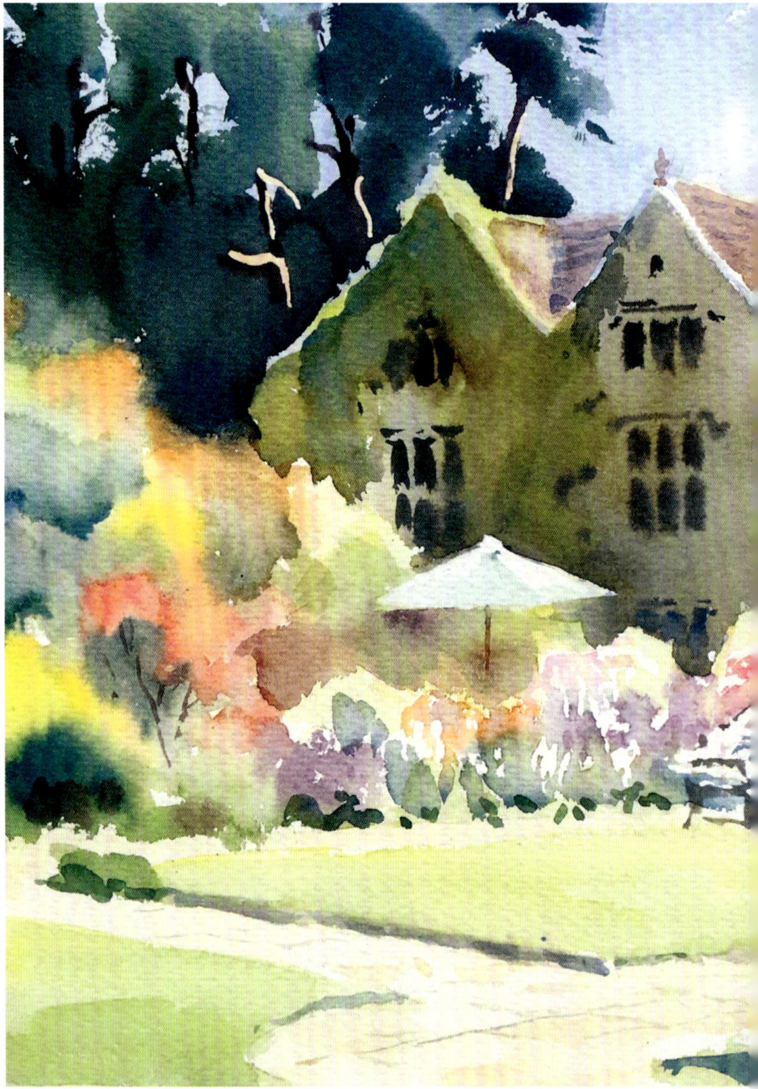

▷ **Gravetye Manor Garden**
28 x 38cm (11 x 15in)

I used masking fluid to reserve the highlights on the sundial and the middleground so that the lawn and border could be freely painted. The light of the foreground is emphasized by the dark of the background, neatly interrupted by the umbrella.

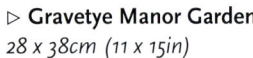

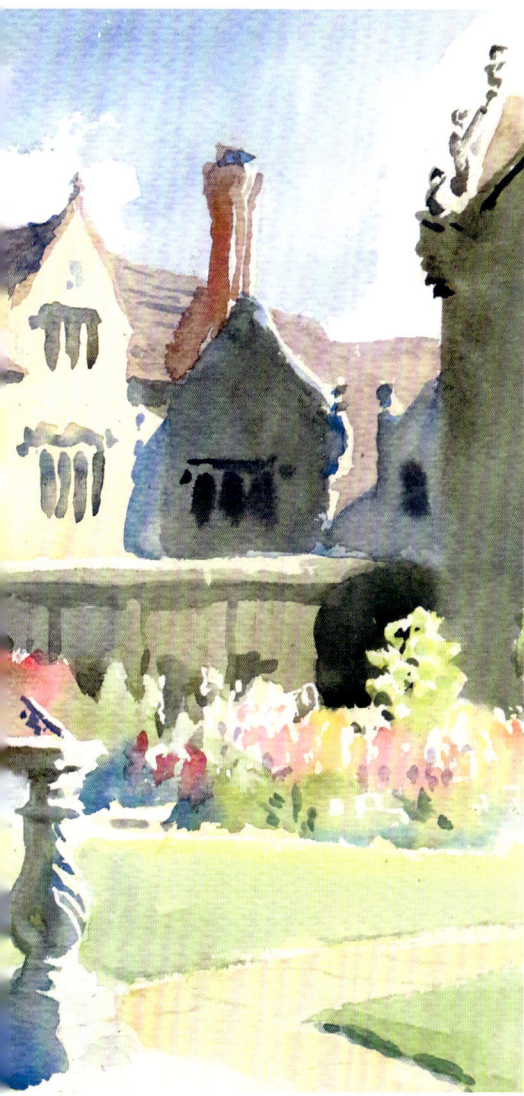

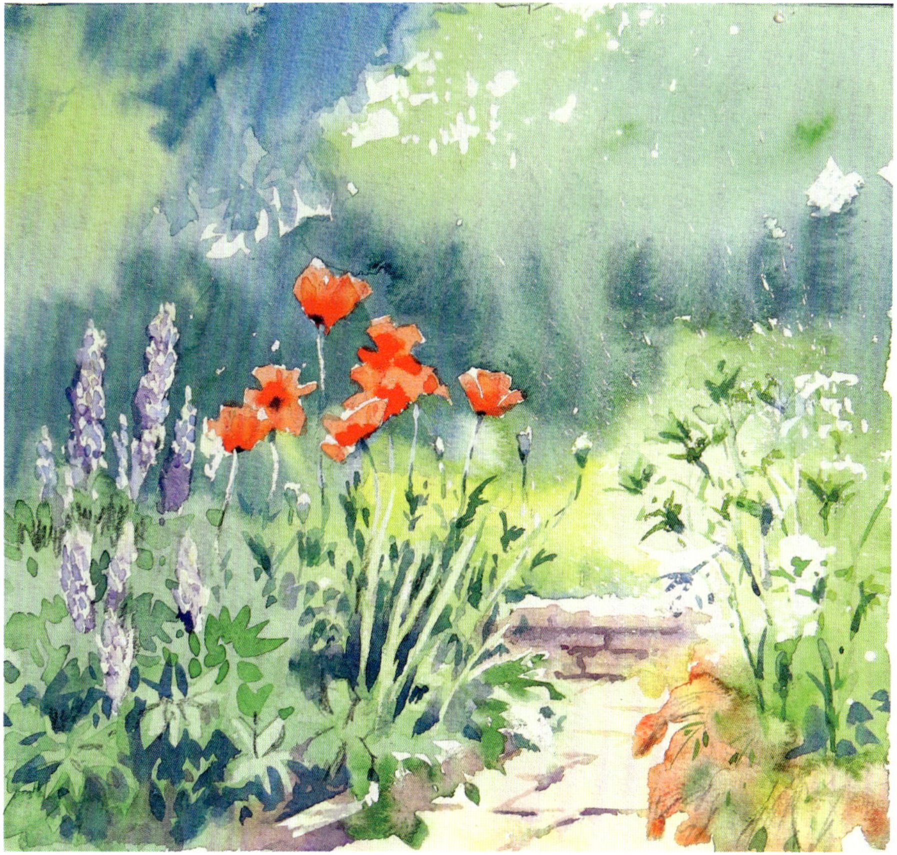

△ **Poppies**

25.5 x 28cm (10 x 11in)

Red is a great standout colour in predominantly green scenes. Here I brushed in the background wash first, leaving the shapes of the poppies as white spaces, which I tinted later with Cadmium Red. I treated the lupins in a similar fashion, tinting them with Schmincke Violet after the surrounding washes were dry.

Architecture

Architectural features make wonderful subjects for a painting. Whether as backdrops in a landscape or the main event, the straight lines, angles and tonal counterchange of architecture offer exciting elements for any composition. Try to position yourself with the light source coming from the side so that the view provides an obvious change in tone either side of adjacent elevations. Sunlight and shadow greatly enhance this counterchange. 'Light against dark, dark against light' is the mantra to have running through your head while you paint.

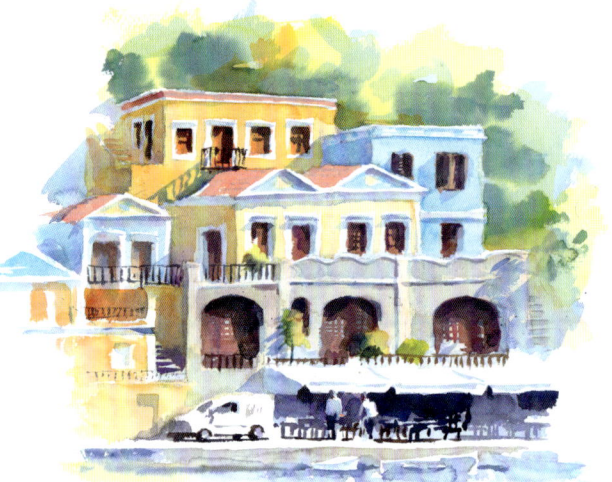

◁ **Symi**
40.5 x 51cm (16 x 20in)

When architectural subjects are viewed from a short distance away, the tricky challenges of perspective diminish. The inaccuracies of perspective in these buildings are overlooked because the eye is distracted by the dynamic tonal contrast between the colourful façades and the dark windows and doors.

▷ **City of Bells – Assisi**
51 x 51cm (20 x 20in)

The upward-facing planes of the roofs at midday receive more light than the sides of the buildings, and their eaves cast useful defining shadows. This exchange of relative tone across the picture plane enables us to read a jumbled mosaic of Yellow Ochre, Schmincke Violet and Prussian Blue as a cluster of houses.

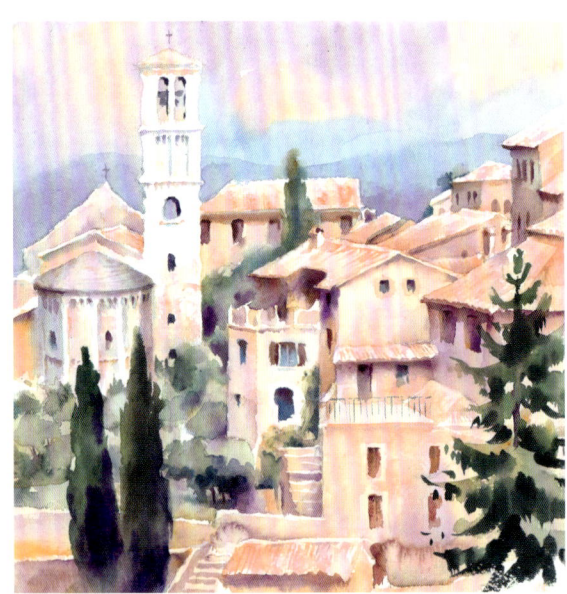

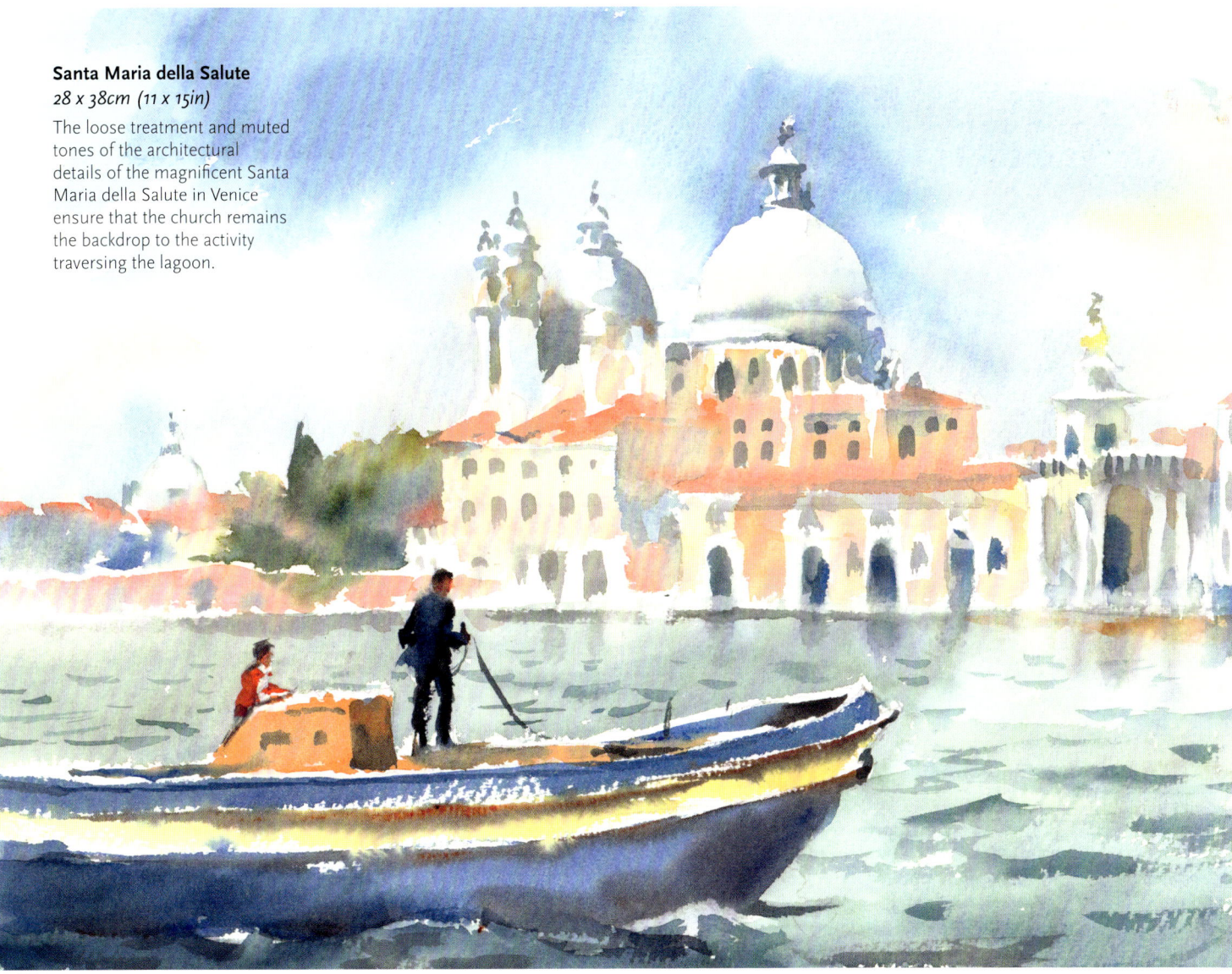

Santa Maria della Salute
28 x 38cm (11 x 15in)

The loose treatment and muted tones of the architectural details of the magnificent Santa Maria della Salute in Venice ensure that the church remains the backdrop to the activity traversing the lagoon.

The inclusion of figures (and birds!) gives narrative to a landscape subject. If you cover the people with your fingers, the view here lacks interest.

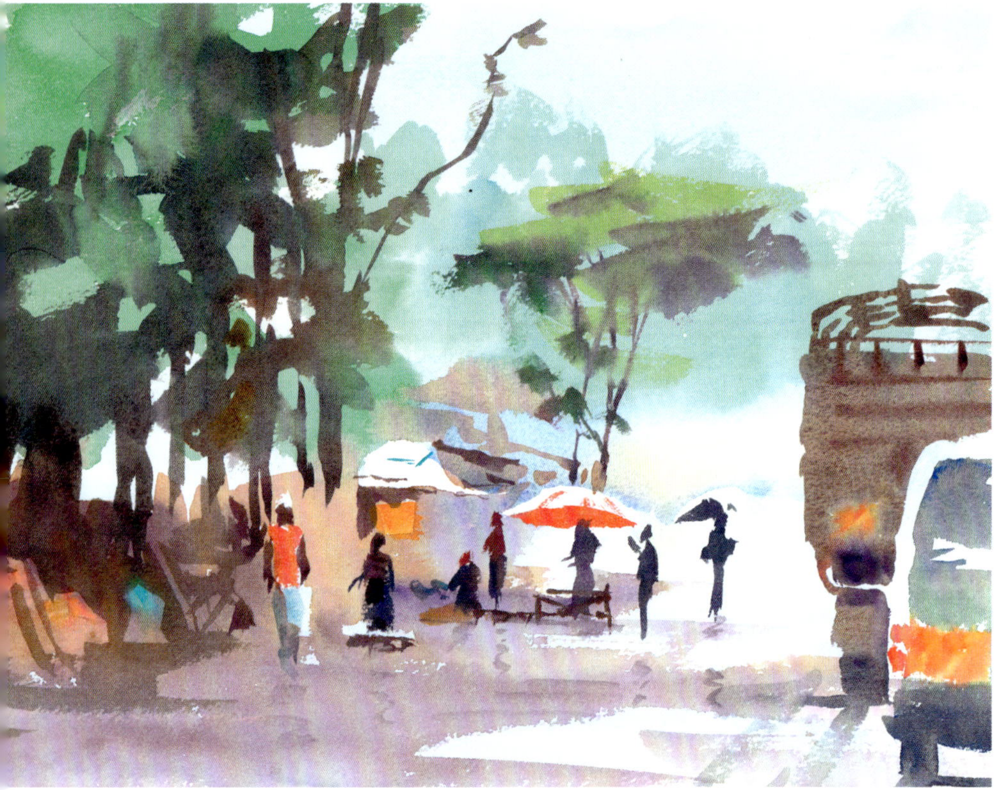

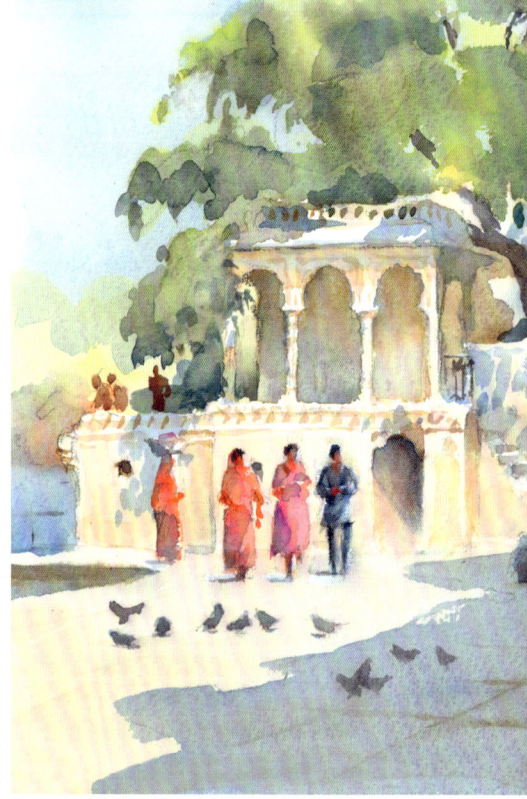

△ Nairobi
28 x 38cm (11 x 15in)

We have no problem believing that a few lively brushmarks represent people in a busy African street. The majority of the marks are painted in darker tones on top of the background washes, but the figure on the left was lit by the sun so her form was reserved out of the background wash as untouched white paper and then tinted when dry.

Figures in the landscape

Figures enliven a landscape, but whenever they appear in a painting the eye is inexplicably drawn to them (and even more so if they don't look quite right!). The trick is to make them feel active, not static, so allow the brushstroke to dance a little on the paper as it delivers the mark. Keep the head small and oval (not round) and in 1:7 approximate proportion with the height. A slight separation from the body suggests light falling on the shoulders.

Also pay attention to the head height in the composition – if you are standing to paint, the heads of standing figures are at your eye level (the horizon), or if you are sitting, slightly above. Vary the poses and merge shaded clothing and limbs; in most cases, omit the feet and simply link figures to the ground with their shadows.

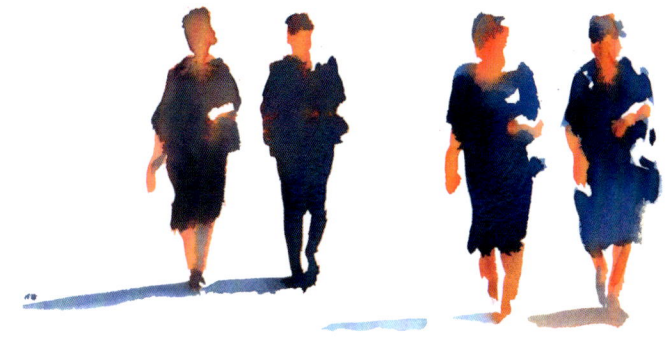

△ Forward movement is shown with one leg shorter than another.

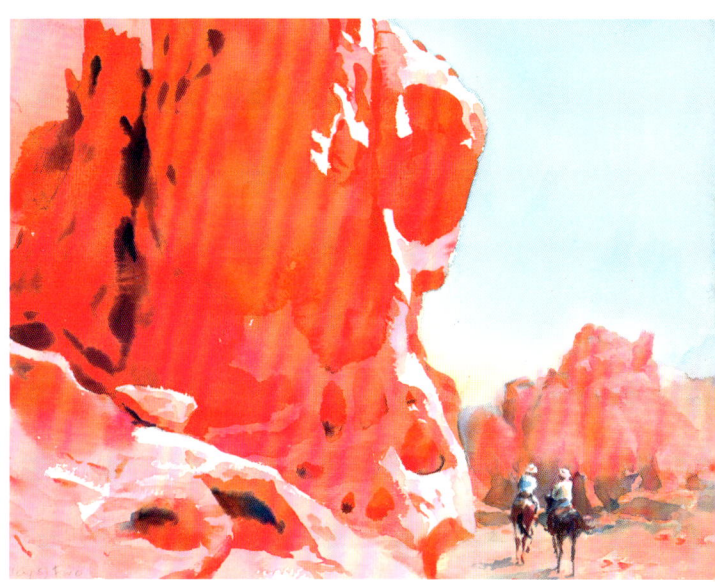

▷ **Big Red Rock, Valley of Fire, Nevada**
28 x 38cm (11 x 15in)

Because we are familiar with the height of human figures, they make excellent markers for establishing scale. Here the hugeness of the rock is understood by comparison with the diminutive riders.

Mountains

The drama of snowcapped mountains is in their size, so including elements that show scale, such as trees, buildings or figures, will help them to appear appropriately grand. Since the dazzling white of snow is best shown by the untouched white paper, it is the bare rocks and shadows cast by ridges and ravines that will actually shape the mountain. Do not overcrowd – use just a few brushmarks to describe the whole structure. Where rocks reveal bare faces, hint at their form with light and shade.

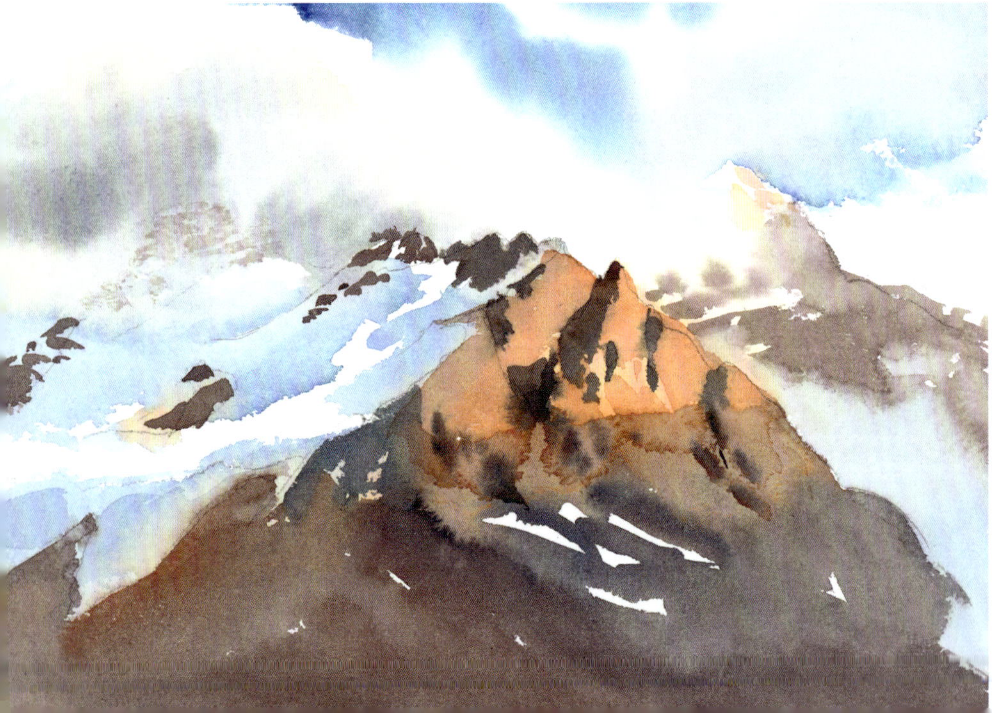

◁ **Shiver, Columbia Icefield**
23 x 30.5cm (9 x 12in)
The peak of the mountain reflects the last rays of the sinking sun. The lit and shaded sides of the rock face supply the contrast in tone, while the rest of the mountain is lost in shadow, emphasizing the glow at the centre of the painting.

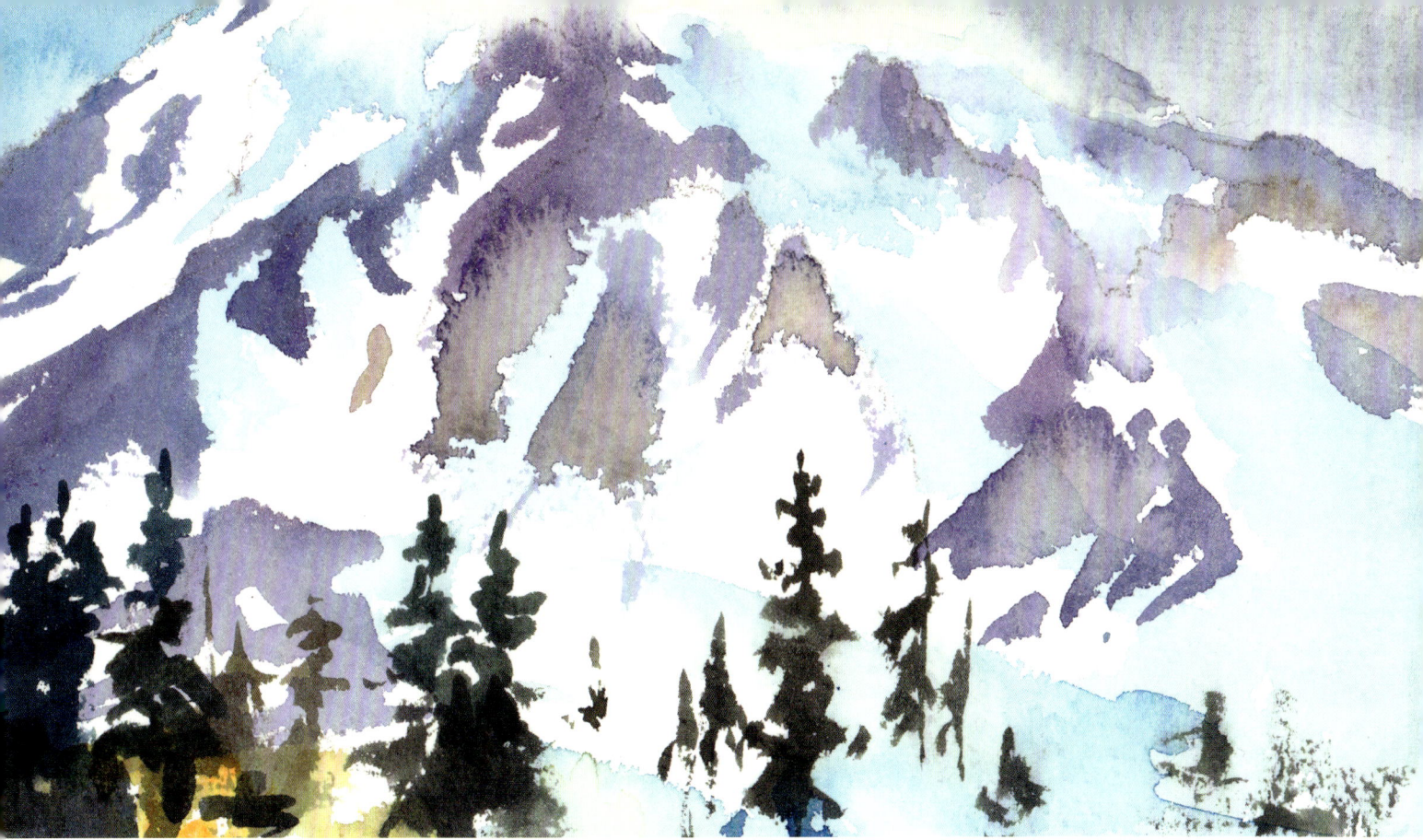

△ Slice of Mount Rainier

The shadows cast across the highlit snow
are pale blue, offset by the bare rock and
deep green trees in the foreground, providing
a pleasing tri-tone balance of light, mid- and
dark tones.

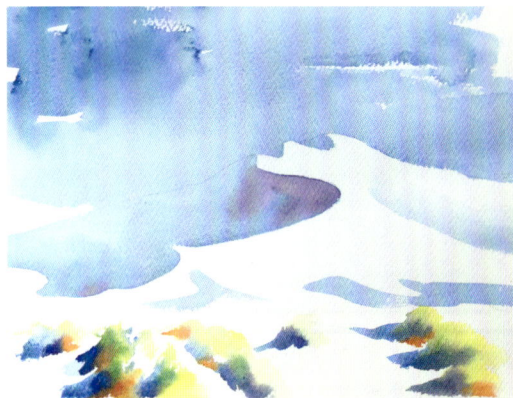

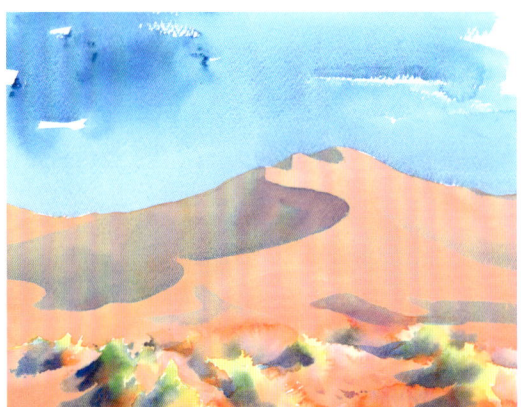

△ Sossusvlei, the Namib Desert

Striking shadows at dawn make the dunes look dramatic. I painted the shadows first with Ultramarine Blue and Permanent Rose and once they were dry I overlaid them with the local colour of the sand, using Permanent Rose and Aureolin.

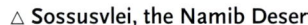

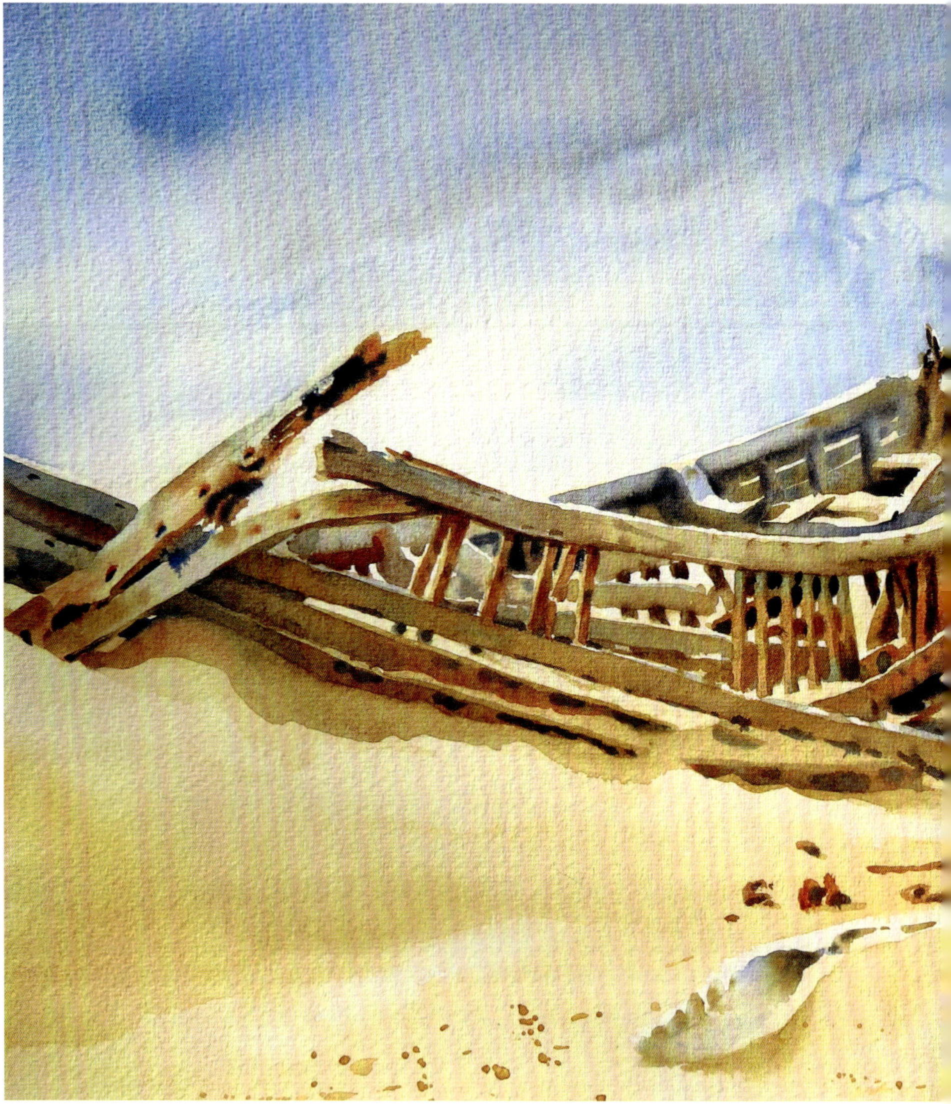

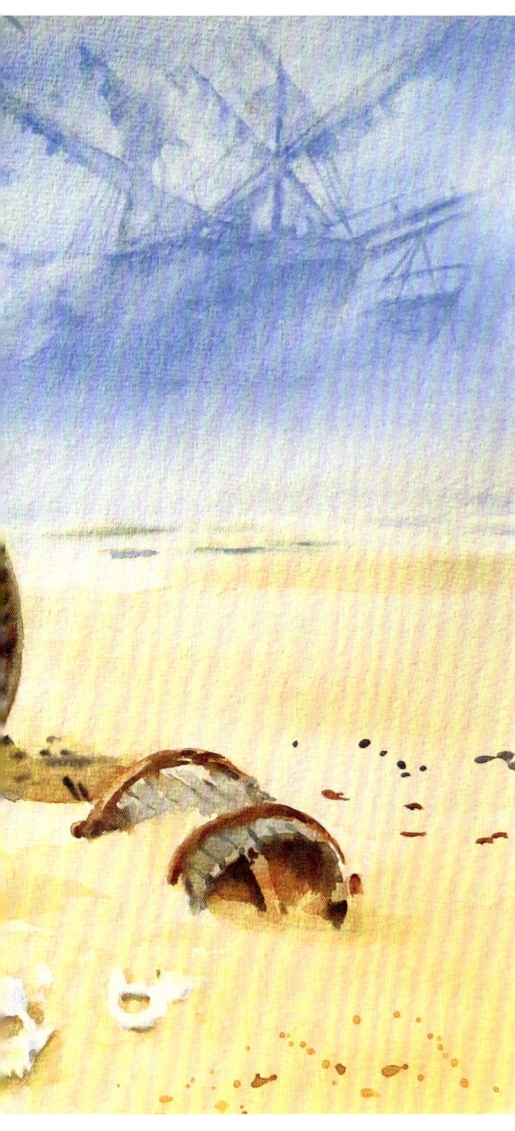

Wilderness and desert

Isolation is the mark of the wilderness and in the desert this is often marked by uncomplicated landscapes. A lone dead tree in an expanse of emptiness makes a striking composition. Vast empty spaces offer the opportunity to practice large washes, with few features and few colours. Sometimes all you need are three different bands of tone, light, medium and dark. The motto here is 'keep it simple'.

◁ **Skeleton Coast**
38 x 56cm (15 x 22in)

Watercolour painting is a serious pursuit, but don't be afraid to have a bit of fun: at first glance you see a shipwrecked vessel on a desolate beach here, but look closer at the sky!

Composition tips
Avoid positioning your main focus out on the periphery where it will get lost and fail to perform as a focus point, and, likewise, avoid large chunks of nothing in the centre of your composition.

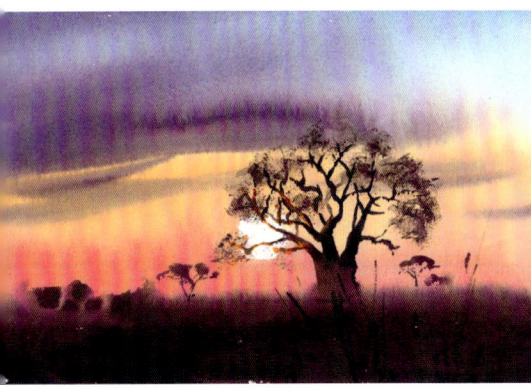

◁ As Bold as a Baobab (Tanzania)
20 x 28cm (8 x 11in)

Here the setting sun is left untinted as a circle of white paper within the blend of Indian Yellow and Permanent Rose.

▷ London Whitehall Sunset
25.5 x 25.5cm (10 x 10in)

For this cityscape I tried three colours I rarely use: Phthalo Turquoise, Quinacridone Red and Quinacridone Gold. Being highly transparent, they reach a deep black when mixed.

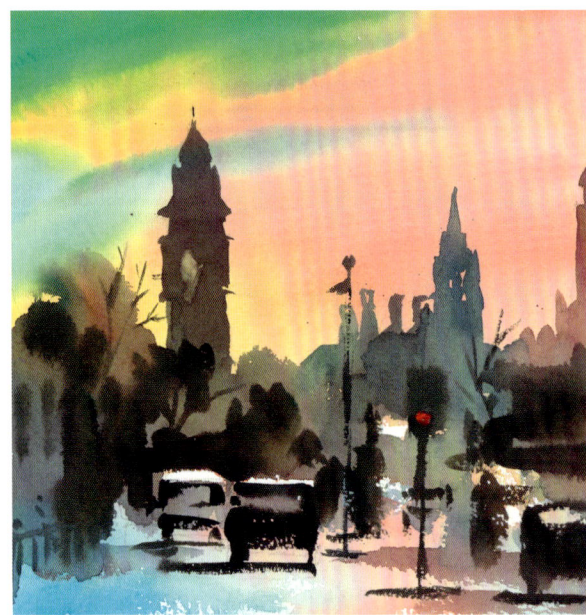

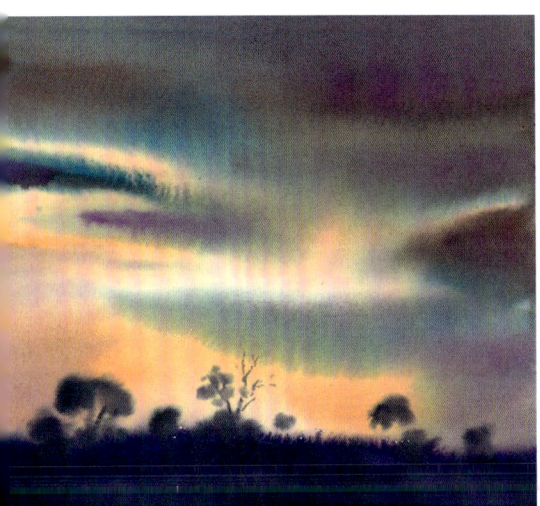

◁ Sunsets are made more dramatic by clouds across the sky. Here Transparent Orange, Prussian Blue and Burnt Umber with a dash of Schmincke Violet are blended in a variegated wash.

▷ Beyond the Horizon
28 x 38cm (11 x 15in)

The red, yellow and blue pigment mix here is all transparent: Permanent Rose, Indian Yellow and Ultramarine Blue.

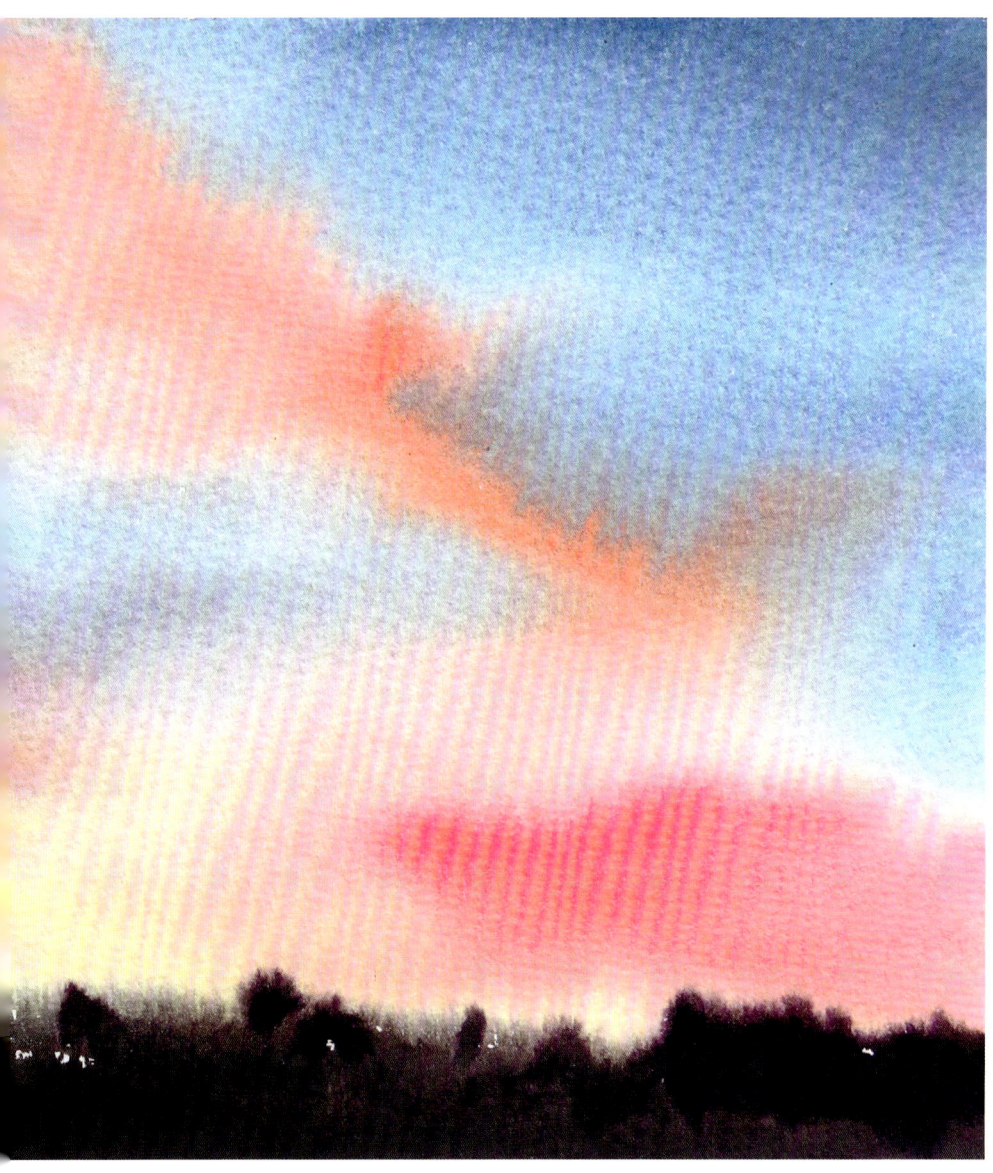

Sunsets

Sunsets sum up what colour in painting is all about: red, yellow and blue, and black. As the sun goes down in a cloudless sky the low angle scatters the light, turning the base of the sky yellow then red and transforming the landscape into a silhouette. If there are clouds these are reddened too, giving rise to spectacular colouring. The three primary colours can be laid in bands on dampened paper, blending in a variegated wash to make seamless transitions (see *Kalahari Sunset*, p.185), and the silhouette of the landscape is then mixed from the same three colours, acting as a dark foil to the colourful light. This is a subject in which it pays to be outrageously bold with colour.

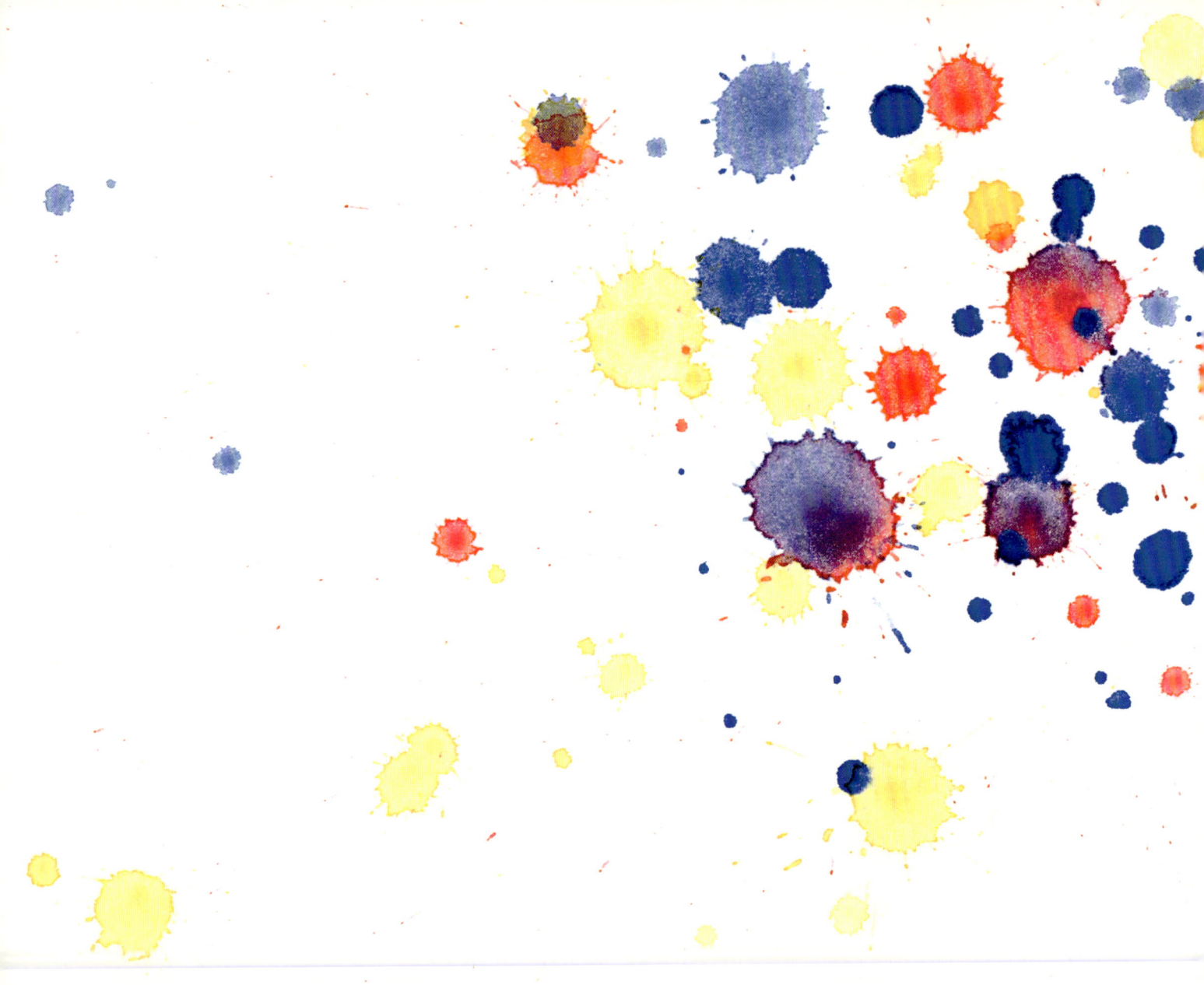

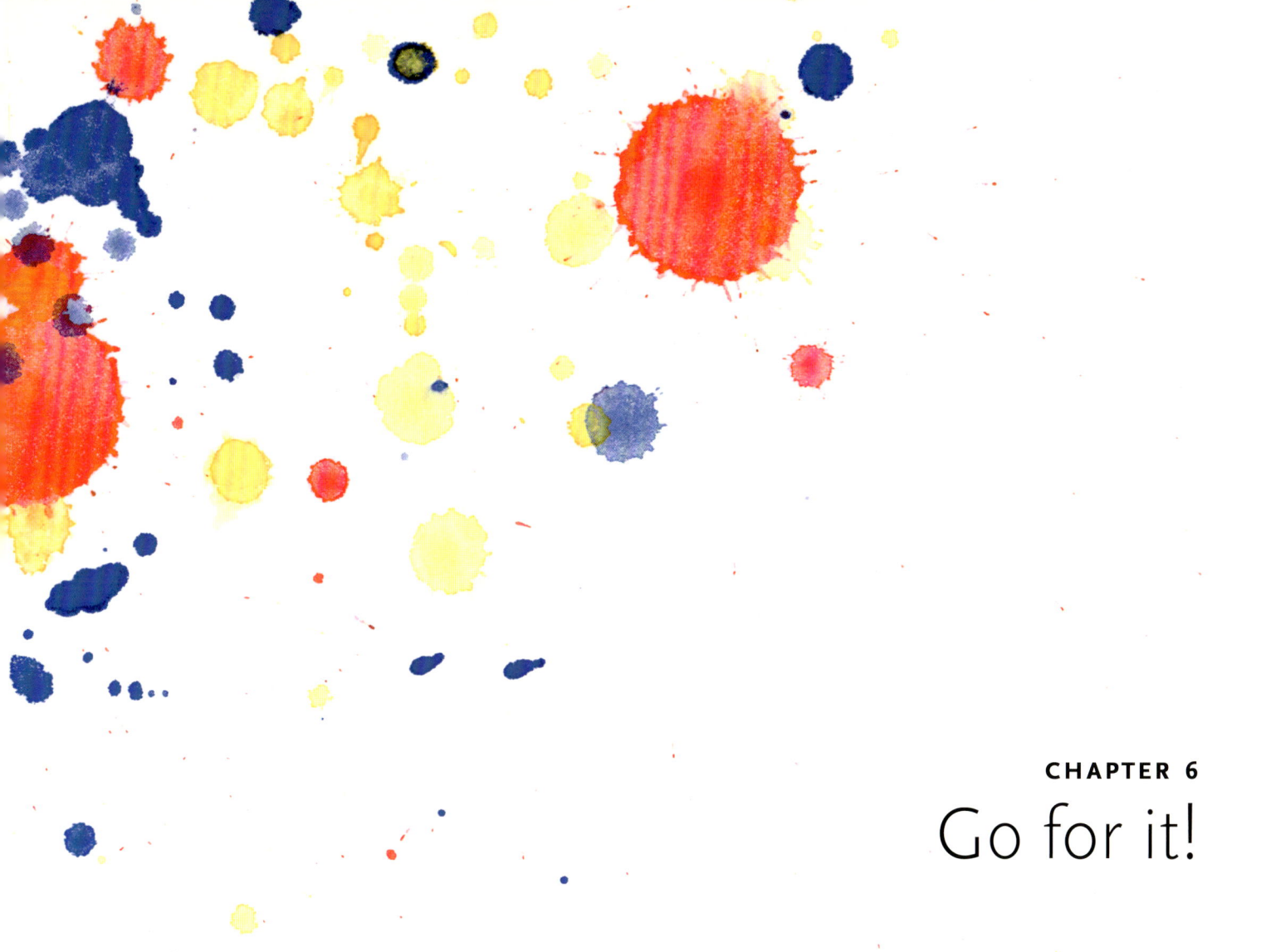

CHAPTER 6

Go for it!

Practice, practice, practice

Watercolour is a beautiful medium, and success is more about its attractive appearance than about the subject created by illusion. Painting is a process – the action is more important than admiring the finished result! Be prepared to cover a lot of paper, and remember that a failed watercolour is not a failure, it is a lesson. As with any other skill, practice is essential – no amateur golfer expects every ball to reach the hole in par, for example, and neither would a professional call a practice session a waste when a tee shot goes awry. Watercolour painters are lucky in that they can make visible 'products' quickly, but that does not mean every painting will turn out well.

Painting is a pleasure, so do not undermine your confidence by berating yourself over poor results. Just keep painting – it is an art, there is no formula. Allow the exquisite medium of watercolour to thrill you, give it some freedom to show you what it can do and do not overwork it, lest it rebel! When you feel you have mastered one aspect, get out of your comfort zone and set another challenge.

Before we introduce the subject of people, why don't you grab your art bag and go painting? The landscape awaits! You can continue reading when you get back!

▷ **Beyond Assisi**
18 x 28cm (7 x 11in)

It is only as you paint the landscape that you learn what it really looks like. The immediacy with which you can render an impression makes watercolour painting special, and very quick!

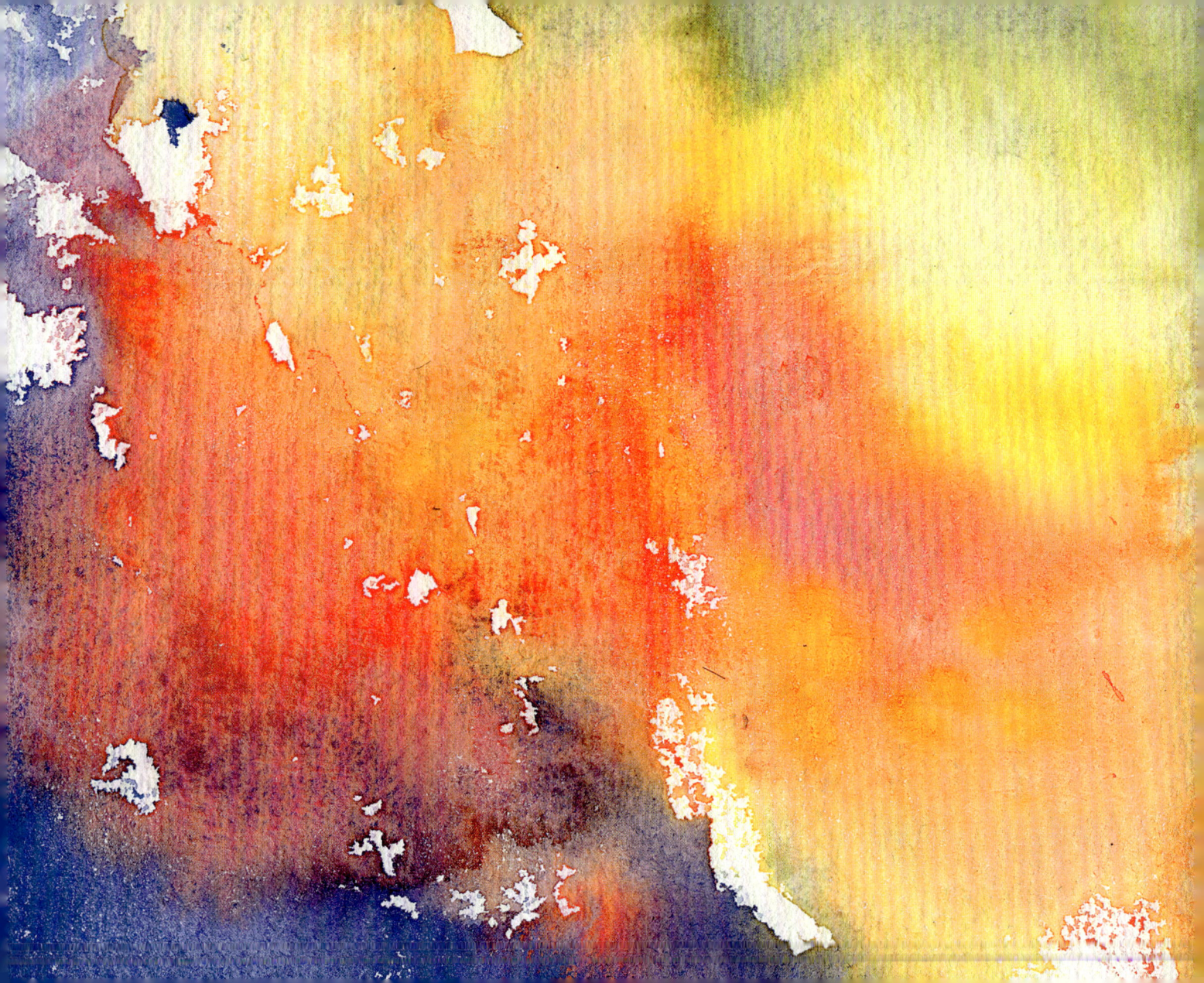

Learn to Paint
People *Quickly*

Introduction

This section concentrates on the exciting and inspiring challenge of painting people, which is less complicated than you may expect. Within these pages you will discover how readily figures can be suggested on the paper so that you can paint them on their own or include them in landscapes and other settings in a convincing and lively manner. Some of the information will be familiar, but here you will learn the value of proportion, pose and lighting; how clothing describes form and provides colour and pattern; and how a likeness is created. You may be surprised to find that gaps and spaces are as important as the figures themselves – and relieved to hear that less is often more!

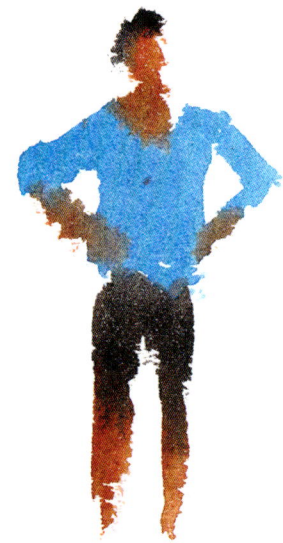

▷ **Feeling Free**
35.5 x 25.5cm (14 x 10in)
Look at how little information is actually given in regard to the figures, yet we feel their joy as their feet sink into the wet sand.

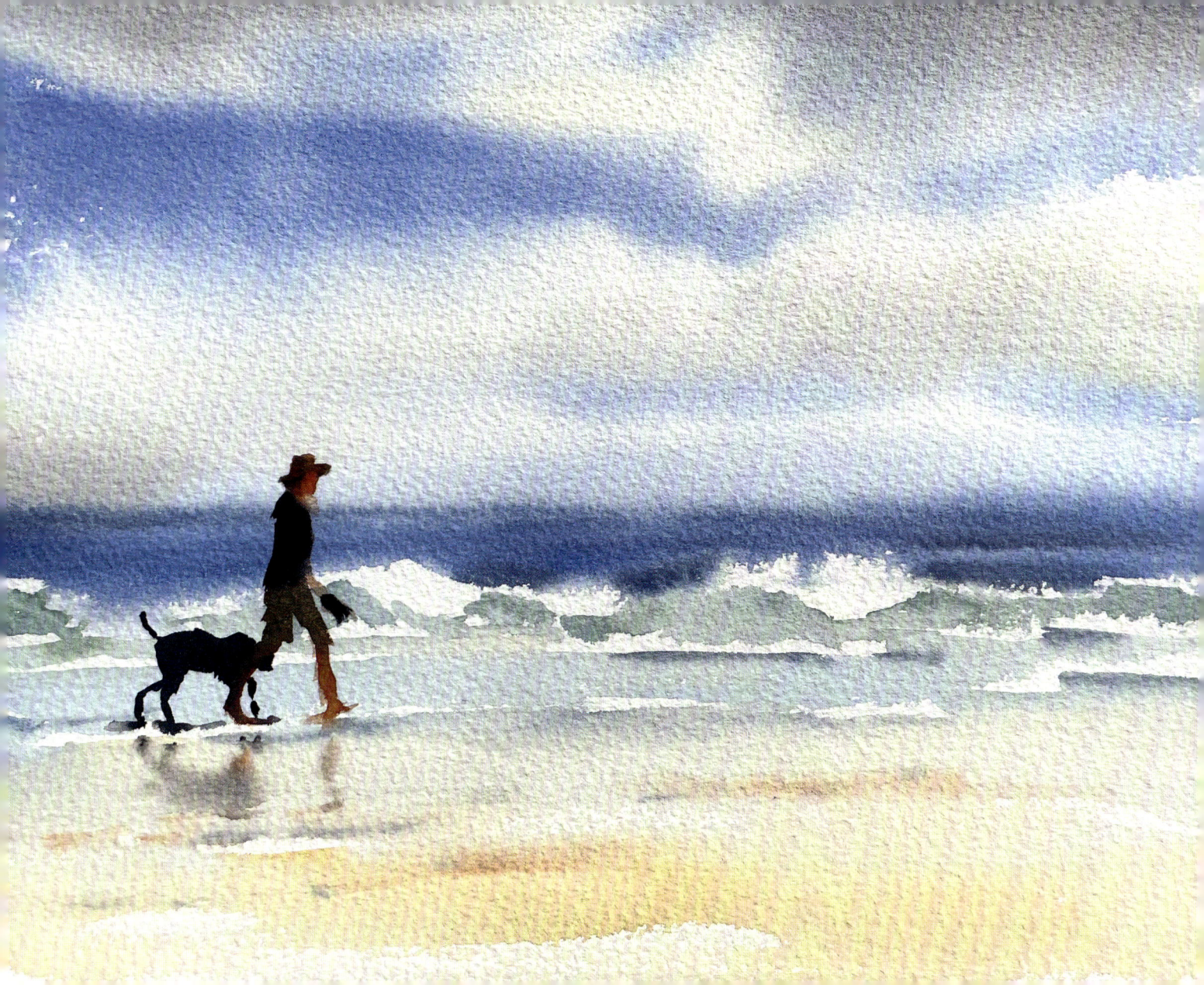

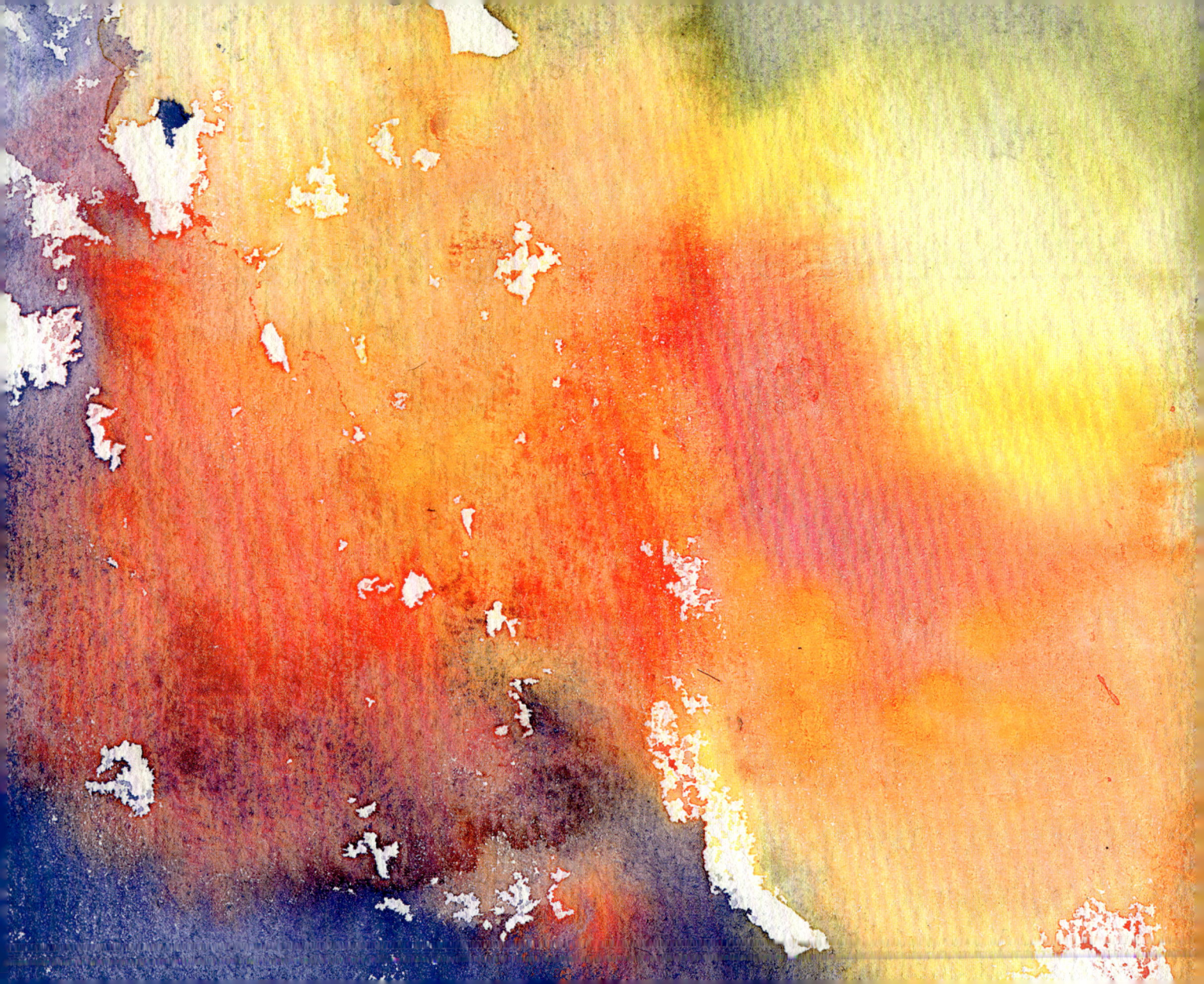

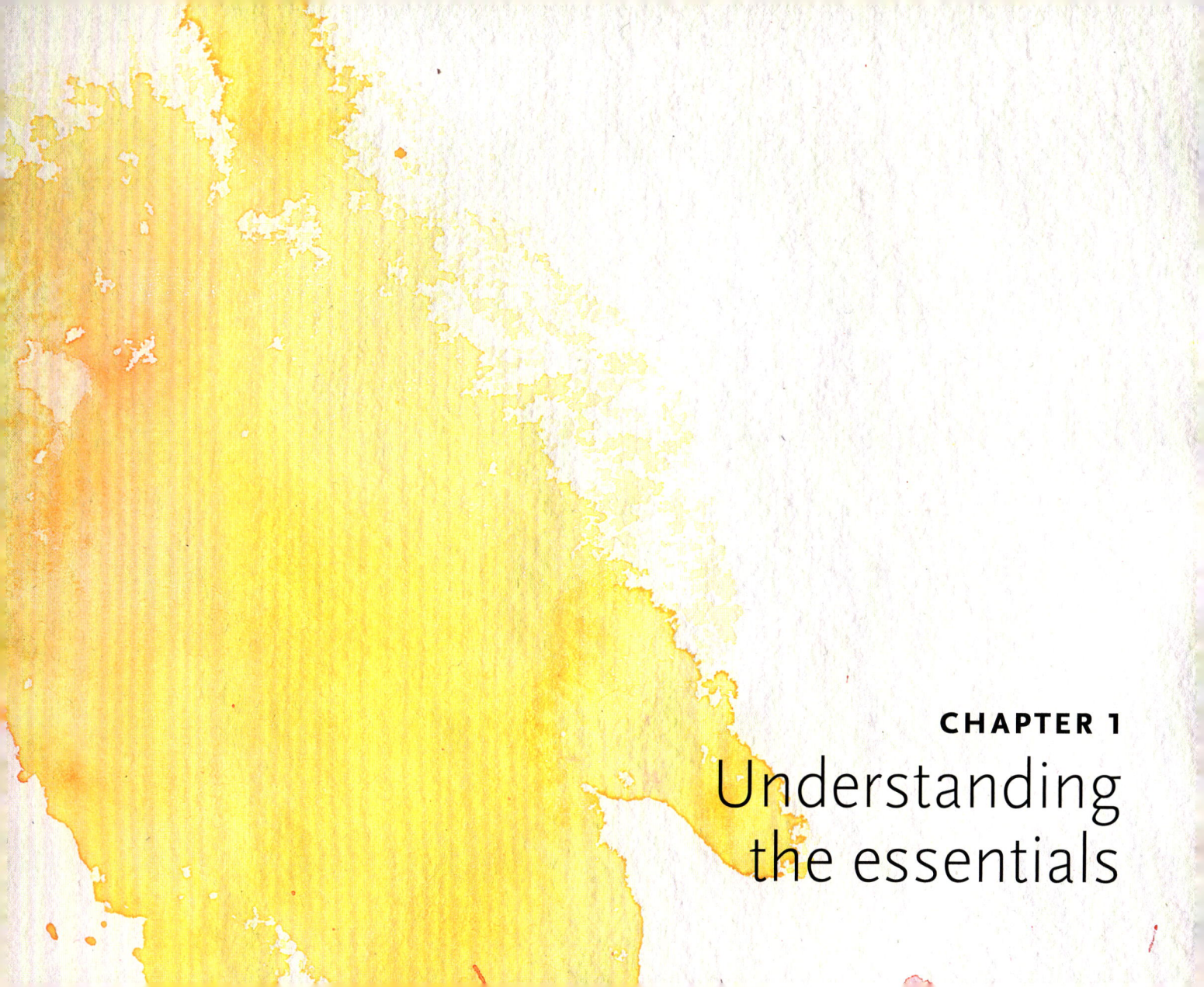

CHAPTER 1

Understanding
the essentials

The importance of people in a painting

Have you noticed that when you place a figure or a face in a painting the viewer's attention is invariably drawn to it? And that if the figure is credible it brings life to the painting, but if not, it is an irritant that cannot be ignored?

This attraction is natural with such subjective association. People bring meaning and narrative into paintings and as a result we are oddly annoyed by any misrepresentation of our own species. Consequently, the painting of people comes with rather more accountability than other subjects such as trees or buildings, and is either avoided altogether or accompanied by much anxiety. No wonder many aspiring artists find the idea of painting people scary!

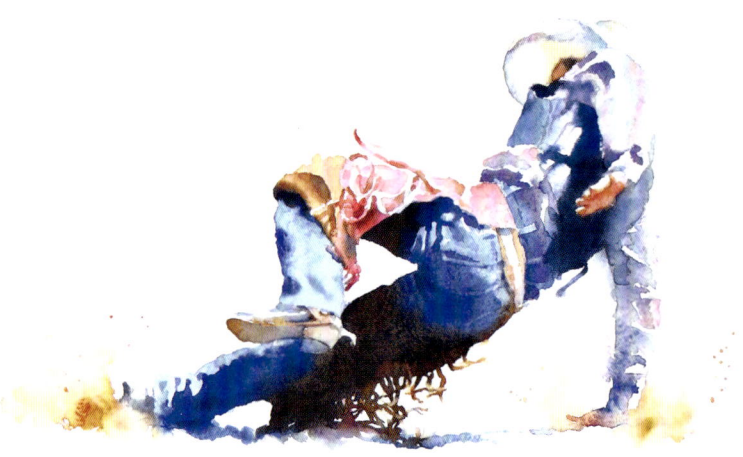

△ **Fallen Cowboy**
38 x 56cm (15 x 22in)

Painting is full of trial and error. Be like this cowboy – if it goes wrong, pick yourself up and start again! It may feel uncomfortable, but it isn't failure; it's learning.

▷ **Lincoln in Sunshine**
28 x 38cm (11 x 15in)

The inclusion of people adds significantly more context to a composition. The figures in this street bring life to the painting.

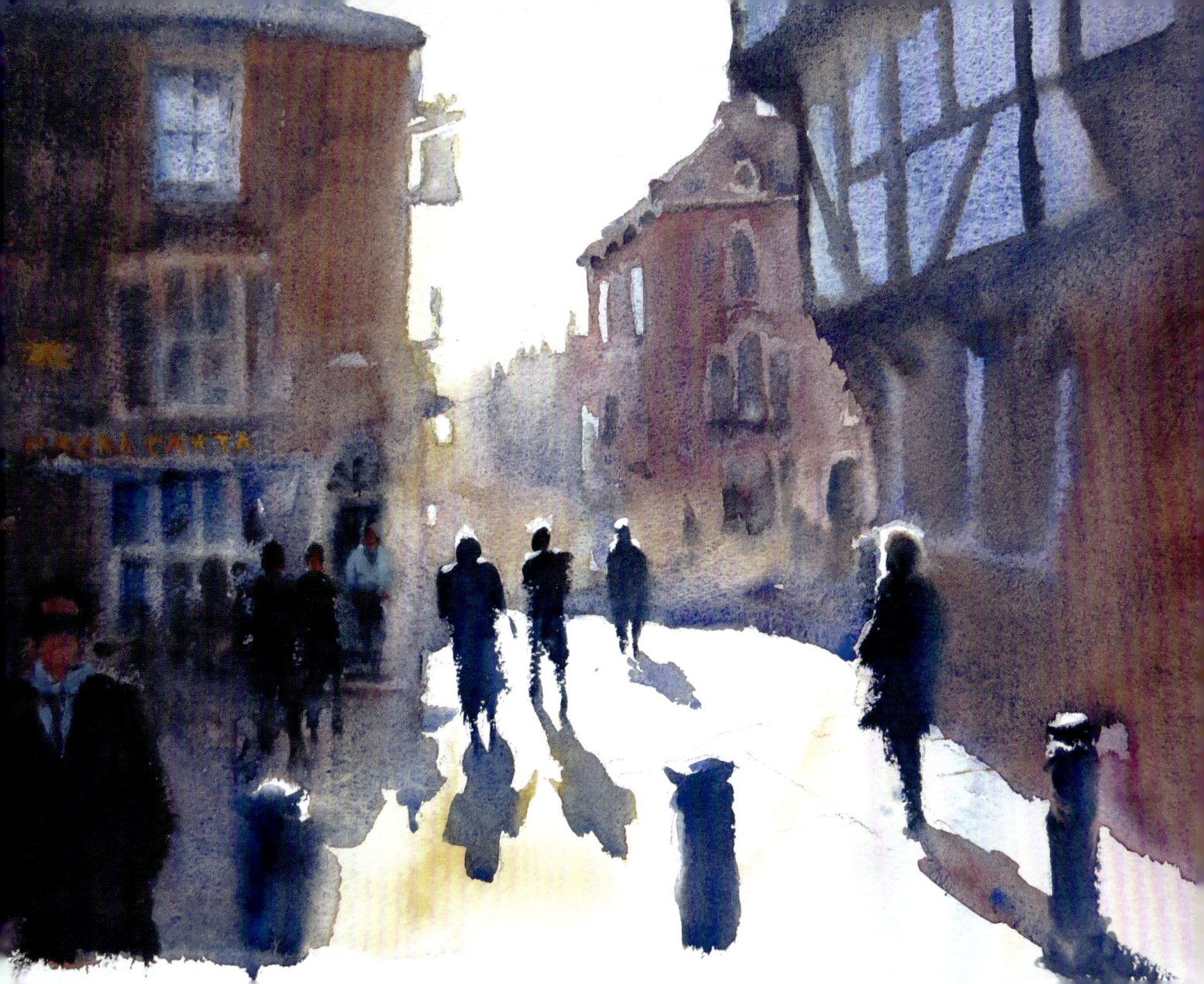

From the painting's point of view

Children have no trouble depicting people – the angst only arrives when we try to imitate reality and portray likeness. The remedy is to approach representation from the painting's point of view and 'think like a painting'. Painting is two-dimensional and therefore concerned with the elements that pertain to the flat world. These elements are line, shape, pattern, colour, light and shade. The painter looks for descriptive lines, lively shapes, exciting patterns, captivating colours and agreeable tones. With these components the three-dimensional world is brought to life by implication on the flat surface.

▽ Children paint people and faces without fear. Their figures are symbolic, using descriptive features. They do not worry about literal likeness because they are not yet concerned with suggesting the third dimension in their picture.

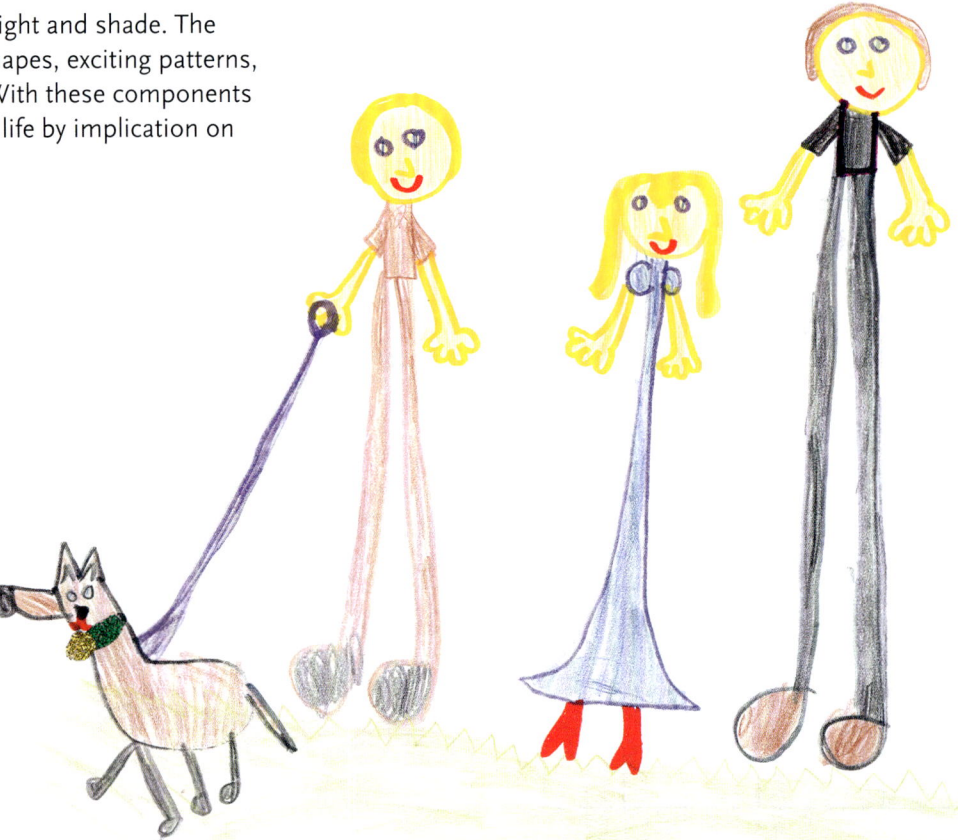

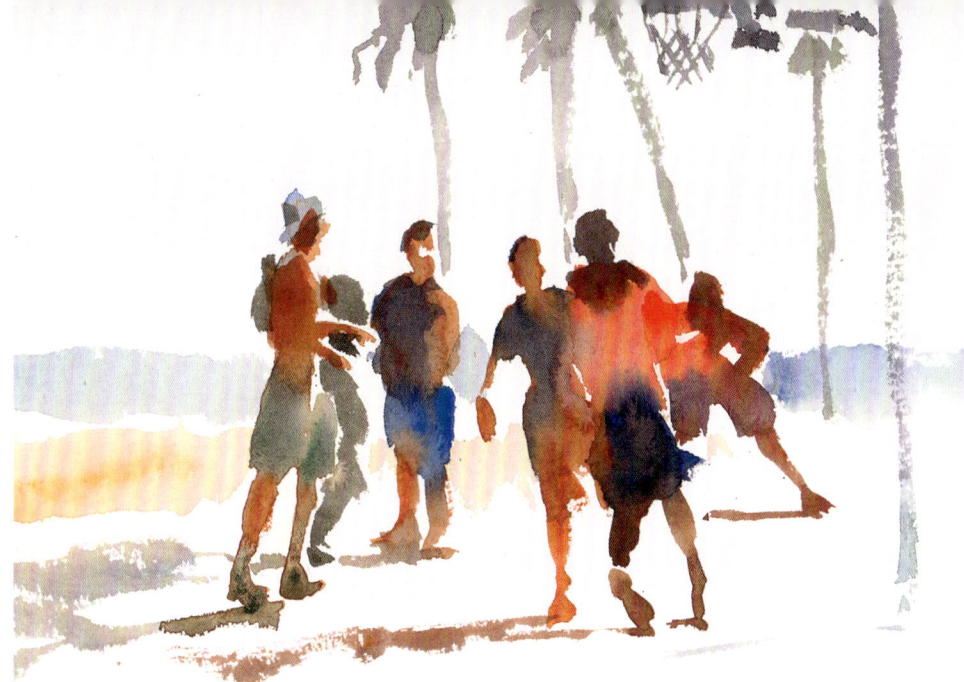

△ **Santa Monica Beach Basketball** *23 x 30.5cm (9 x 12in)*

△ From this detail you can see that the watercolour is made up of dabs, blobs and brushstrokes, yet they are laid in a fashion that presents the viewer with no problem in believing they represent a group of people playing basketball.

Dabs, blobs and brushstrokes

On the flat surface of the painting the image is made up from a series of dabs, blobs and brushstrokes in a variety of shapes and colours, orchestrated to represent an image from the three-dimensional world. To the paper or canvas, therefore, people are no different in principle from trees, flowers or rocks: all are represented by arrangements of various marks.

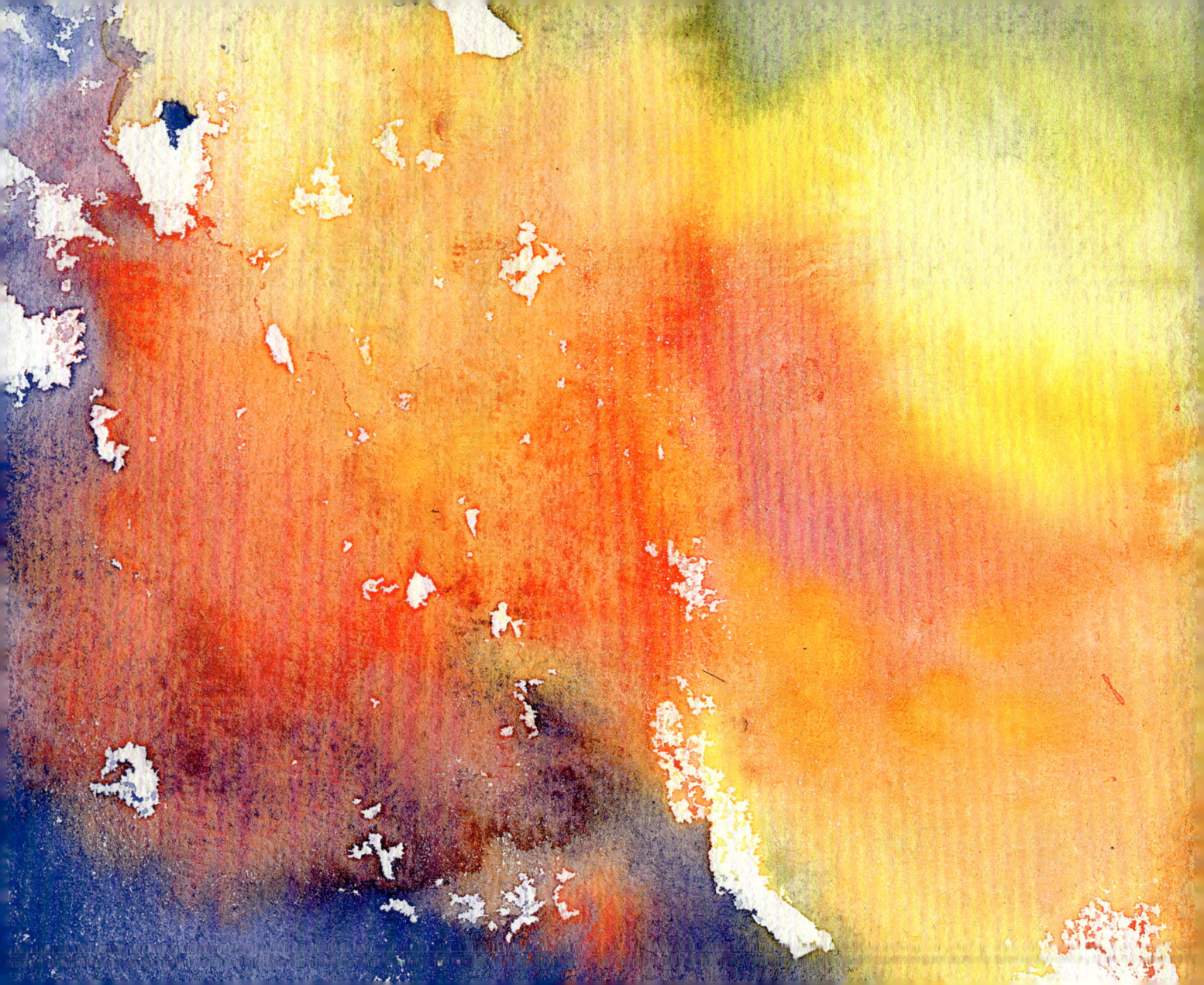

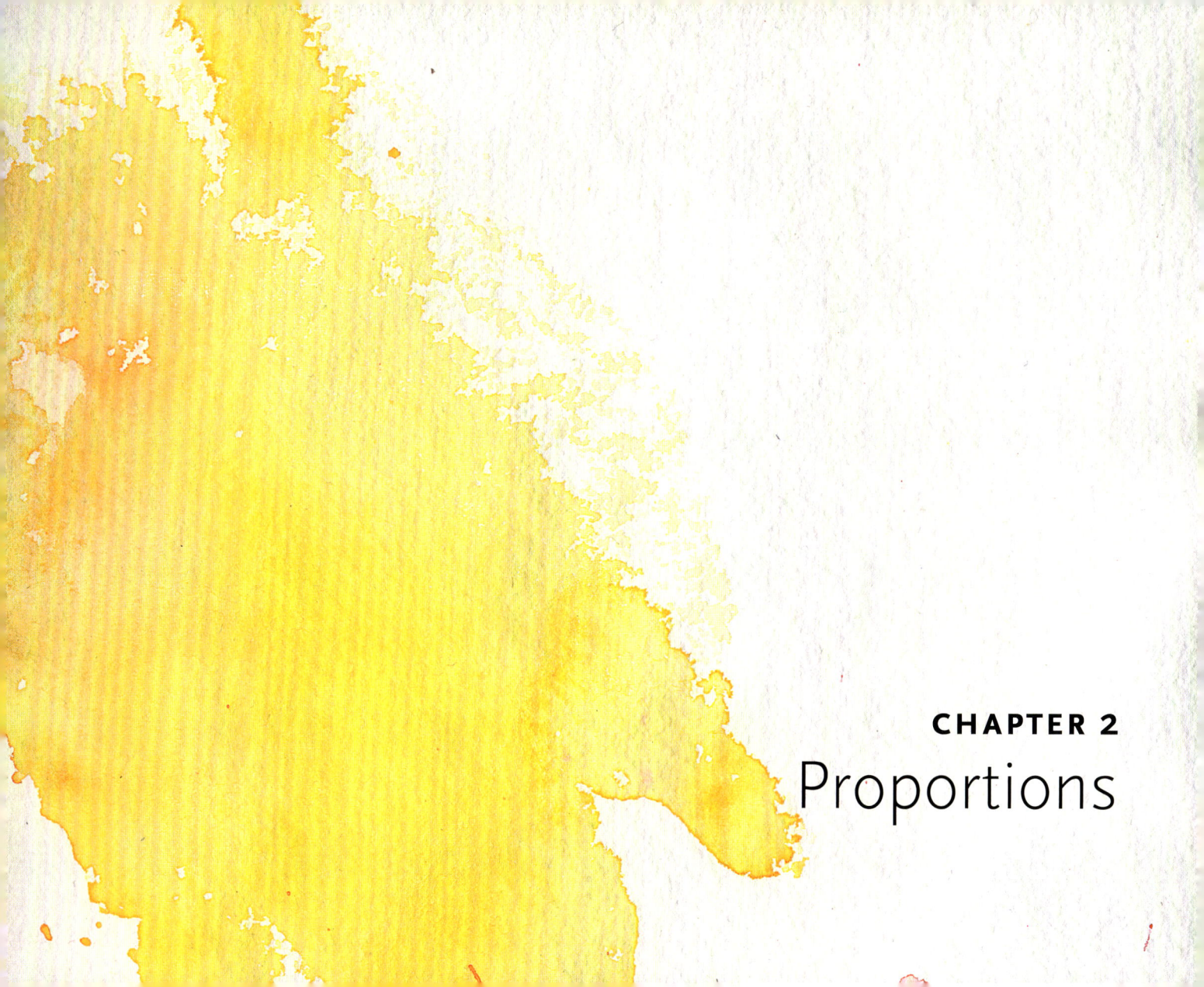

CHAPTER 2

Proportions

Getting the proportions right

Very little is needed to persuade the viewer that a person has been represented in a painting – just a small oval blob above a couple of upright lines or an elongated triangle can do the trick. However, making the figure appear credible and at home in the painting requires a few basic 'keys'. The first key is proportion.

Proportion is the relationship of one thing to another in terms of size or shape. Painting a figure in proportion means getting the head, limbs and torso in the right relationship. Thanks to our familiarity with the subject, the proportions need only be mildly convincing for a figure to be believable.

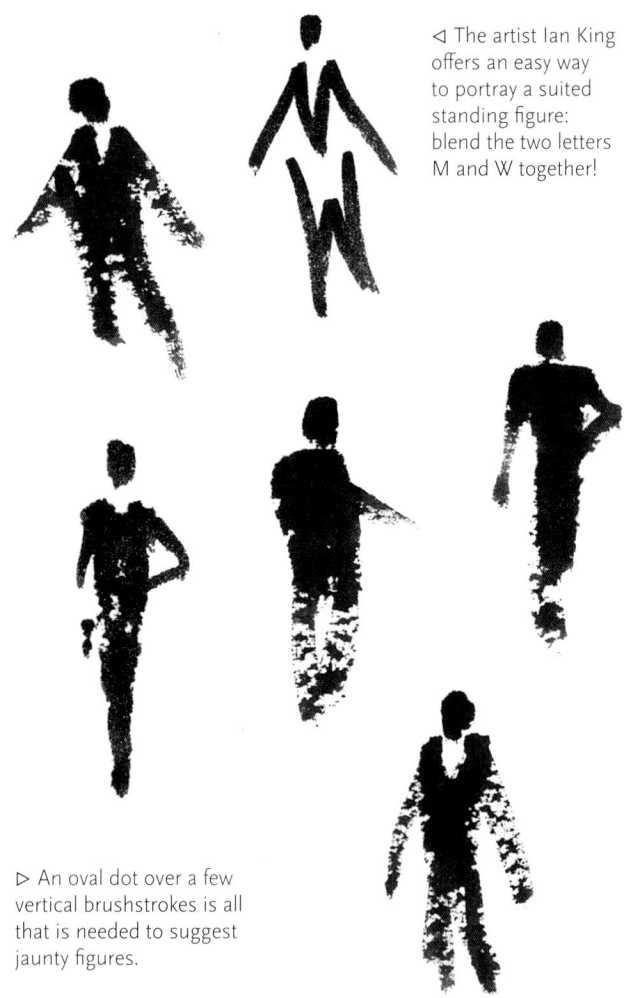

◁ The artist Ian King offers an easy way to portray a suited standing figure: blend the two letters M and W together!

▷ ▷ **Bro Code**
76 x 102cm (30 x 40in)

When figures are painted in proportion they are not only convincing but informative. Here the size and length of heads, arms, legs and bodies communicate an image of youthful camaraderie.

▷ An oval dot over a few vertical brushstrokes is all that is needed to suggest jaunty figures.

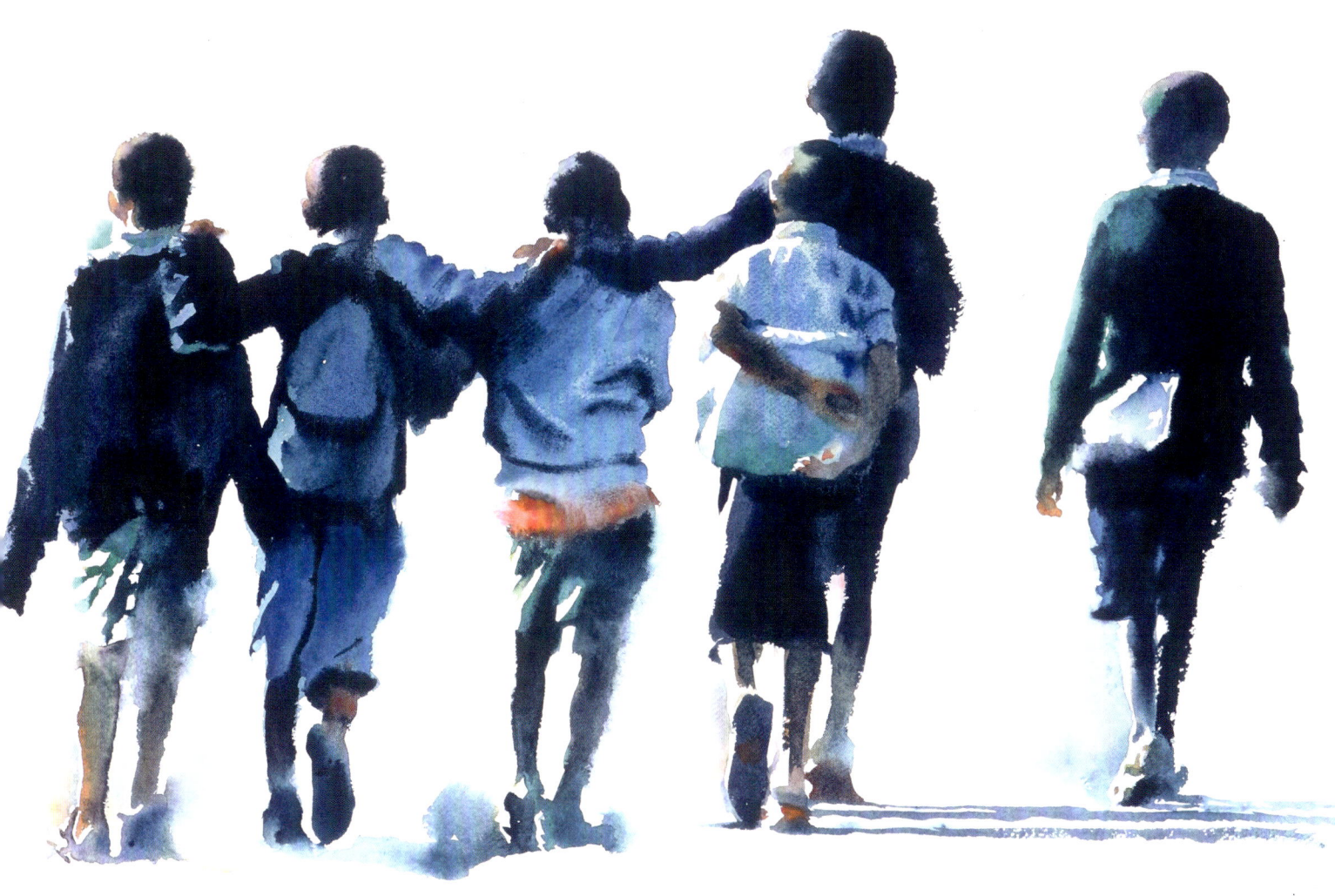

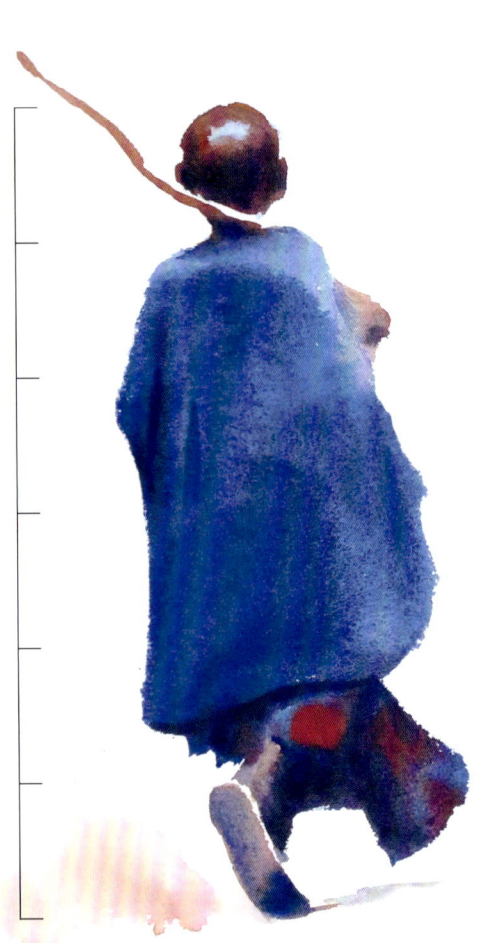

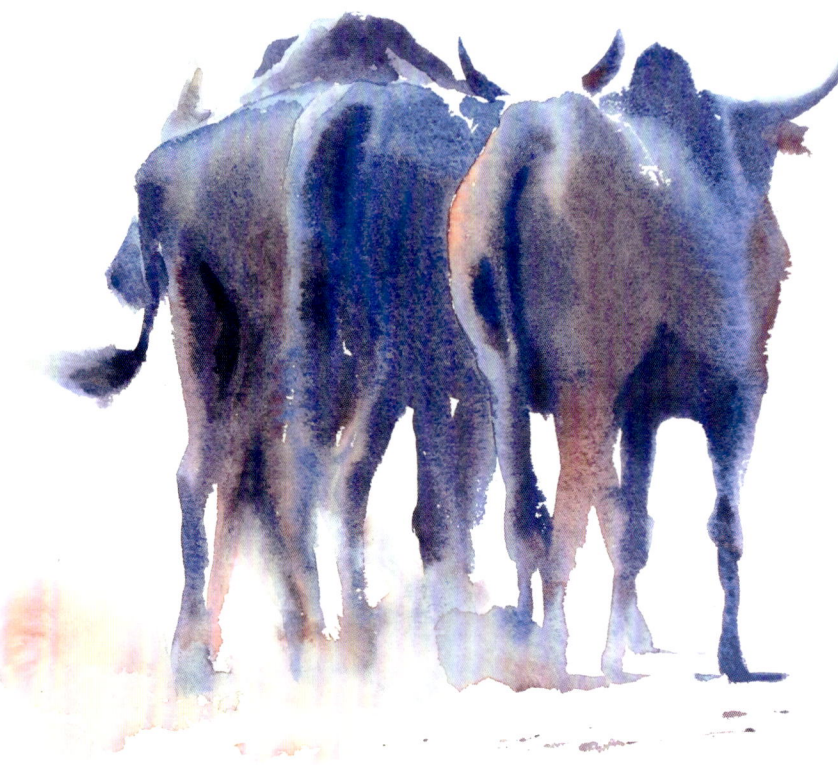

◁ **African Apprentice**

25.5 x 35.5cm (10 x 14in)

Here the boy's head goes into his height about six times. His head is rounder than that of the adult opposite and the proportion of his head to body will decrease as he grows.

Heads up: head to body proportion

The size of the head in relation to the length of the body is the first consideration. In an adult the head is oval and fits into the total length of the body seven or eight times, depending on height. In children, the head is rounder and larger in proportion to body height, which means that if you paint adult figures with heads too big or too round they will look more like children.

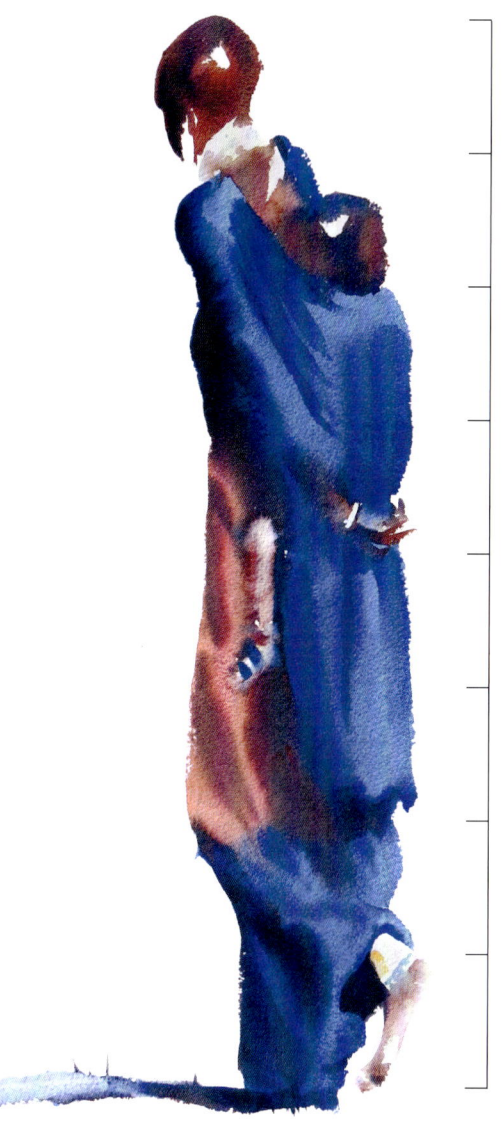

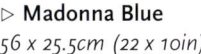 **Madonna Blue**
56 x 25.5cm (22 x 10in)
The Maasai tribe are a tall people. The mother's head fits into her body eight times, so from the proportion of her head to her body we can judge that this woman is indeed tall.

The body, arms and legs

The proportions of the limbs in relation to each other and the torso may seem obvious, but it is easy to misrepresent them in the flush of painting. Some guidelines to bear in mind: legs are longer than arms and both bend at halfway points (the knees and elbows); hands reach down to the mid-thigh and meet at the groin; arms usually fold above the waist; and the width of outstretched arms approximates to a person's height. Getting these interrelationships roughly in proportion will help you to create convincing figures.

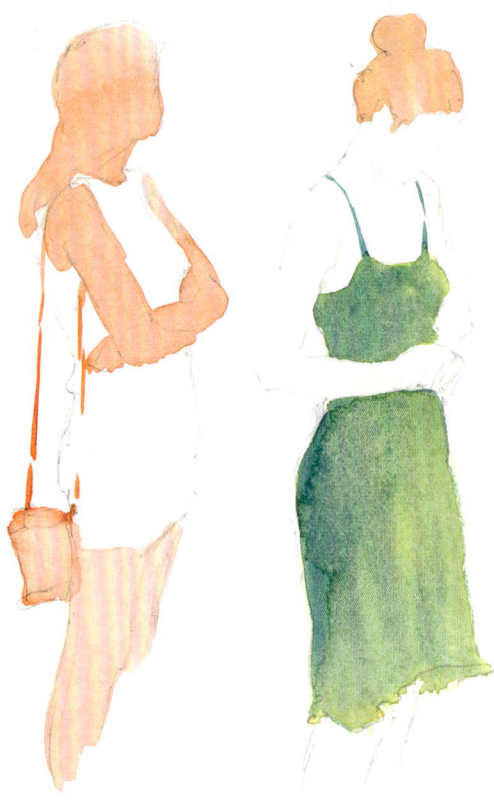

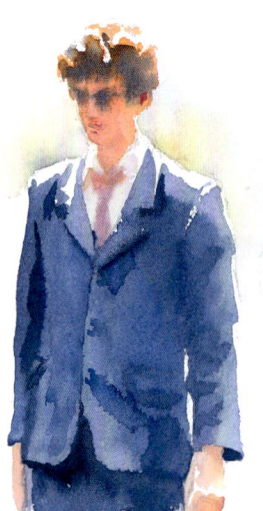

▷ The arms extend to the thigh in a standing figure.

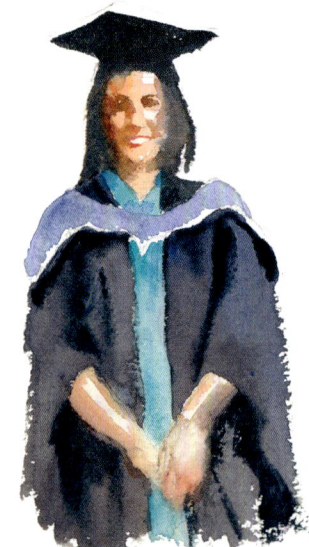

△ The arms bend and fold across the body above or at waist level, depending on the pose.

◁ Hands meet across the body at groin height. People typically take up this pose when waiting in a queue or posing for a photograph.

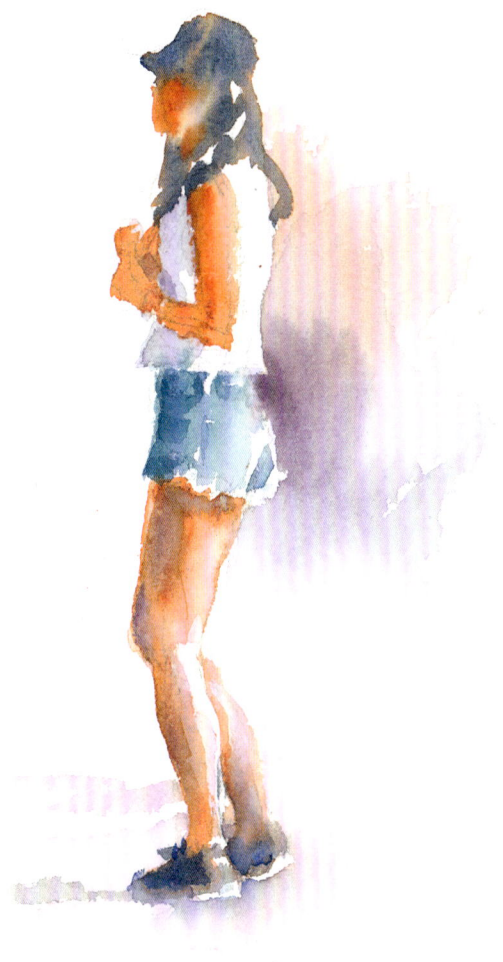

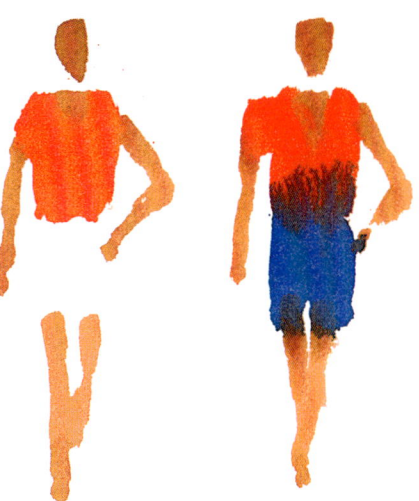

△ You can paint convincing distant figures in watercolour by blending the colours wet into wet: indicate the head and limbs first, add in the body while the paint is still damp and let all components blend together.

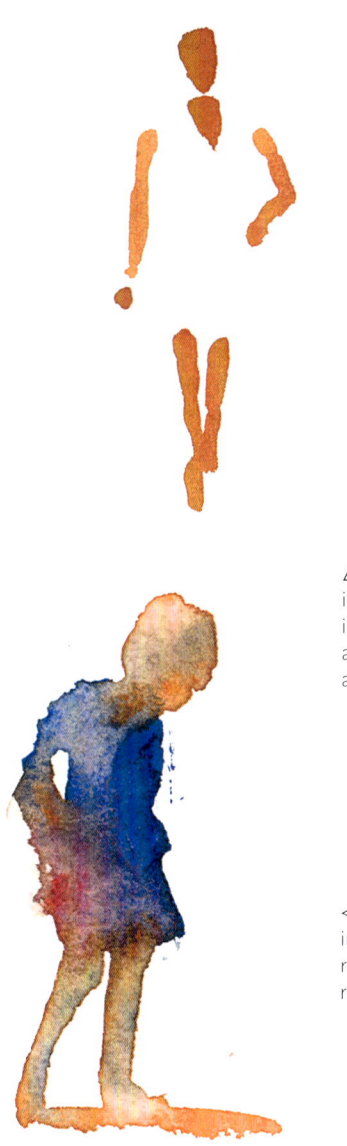

◁ A child's limbs are proportionately shorter in length. Avoid painting children too small in relation to adults – it is estimated that a child reaches half their adult height by the age of two.

△ Arms and legs bend roughly in half, at elbow and knee, which means the upper and lower part of the limbs are approximately the same length.

Face: the facts

The human face has a set of relative proportions that are easily implied. Unless the person is in close-up you need only indicate these relationships sketchily to create convincing faces on your figures. The shadows cast by the features are often more useful for suggesting the face than the features themselves. Likeness to a specific person requires more particular positioning of the features and is covered more fully in the chapter on portraits (see page 272).

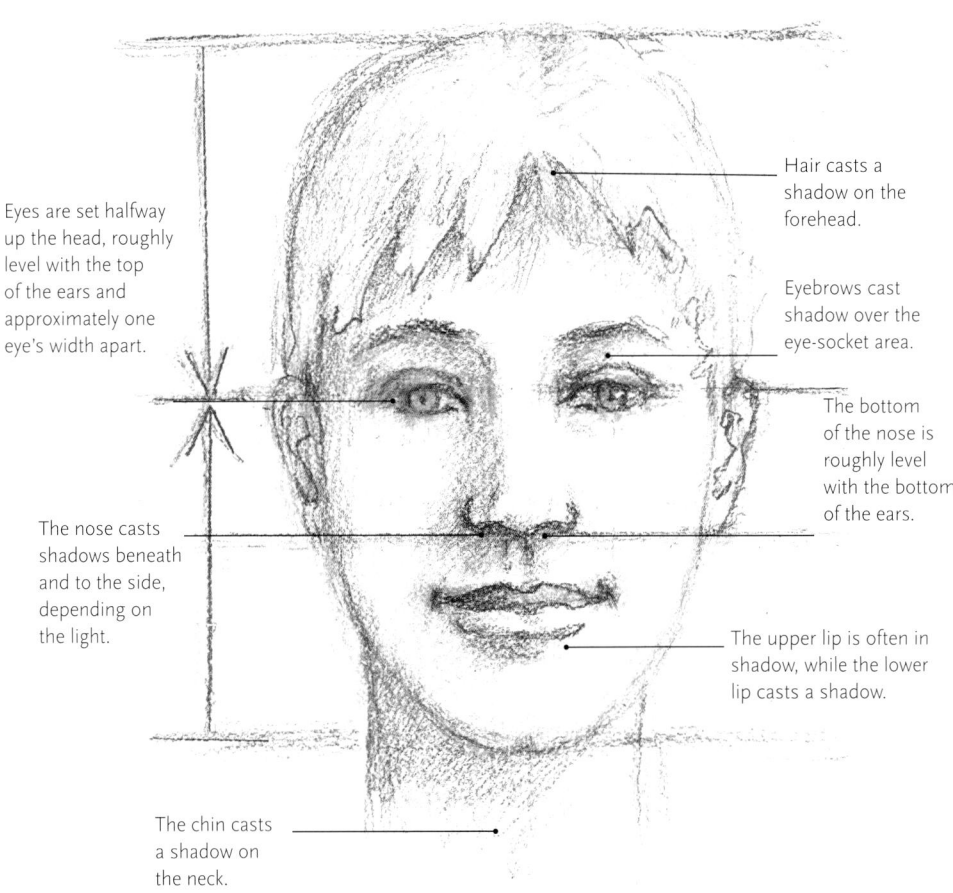

The adult head is not round but oval and egg-shaped.

Eyes are set halfway up the head, roughly level with the top of the ears and approximately one eye's width apart.

The nose casts shadows beneath and to the side, depending on the light.

The chin casts a shadow on the neck.

Hair casts a shadow on the forehead.

Eyebrows cast shadow over the eye-socket area.

The bottom of the nose is roughly level with the bottom of the ears.

The upper lip is often in shadow, while the lower lip casts a shadow.

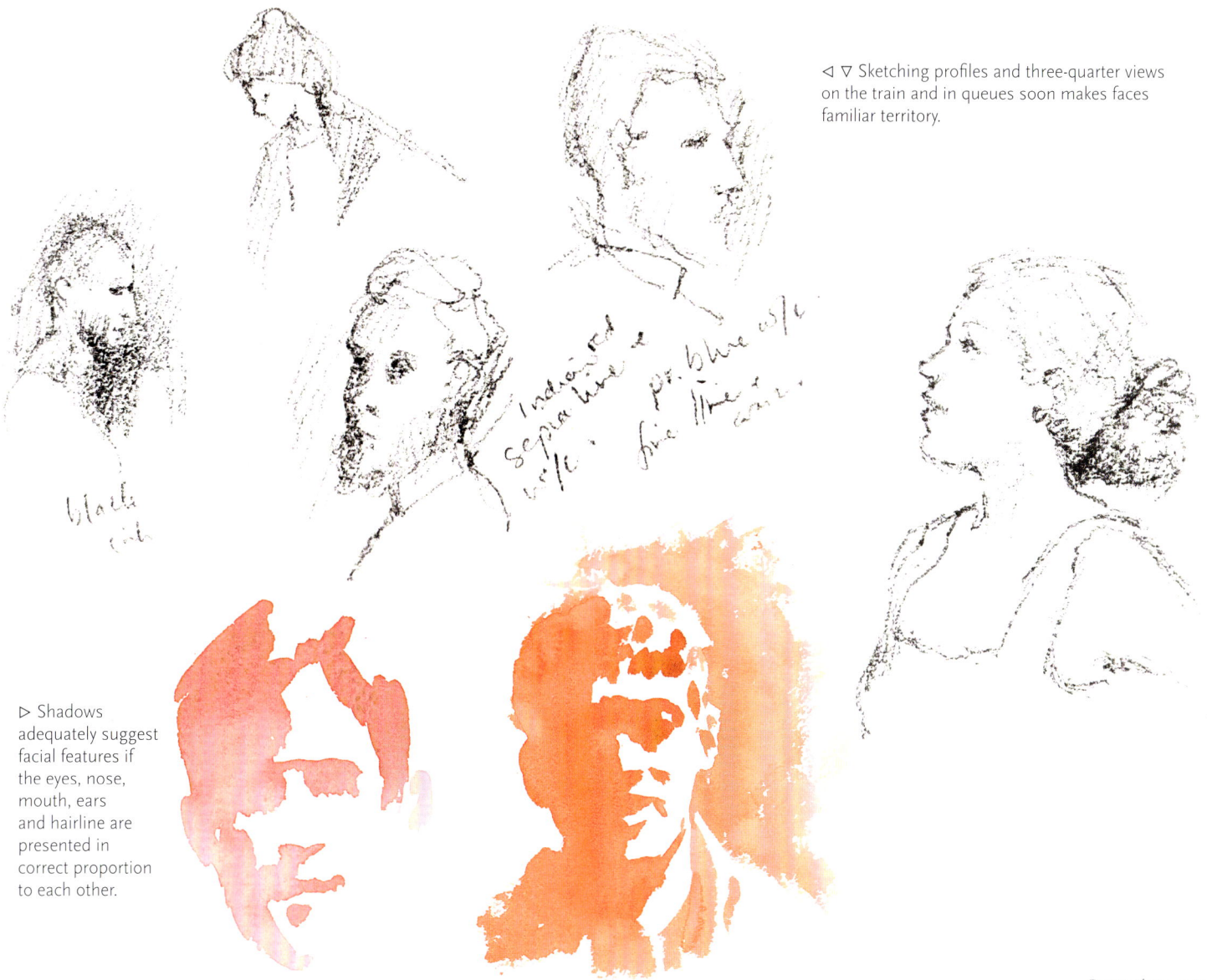

△ ▽ Sketching profiles and three-quarter views on the train and in queues soon makes faces familiar territory.

▷ Shadows adequately suggest facial features if the eyes, nose, mouth, ears and hairline are presented in correct proportion to each other.

Symmetry

For a figure to be convincing, the right and left sides must be in similar proportion. It is easy to forget to address this simple and obvious relationship when concentrating on other parts of the body, so a loose initial sketch encompassing the whole figure is often advisable to check everything is at least roughly in proportion before proceeding with paint or detail.

 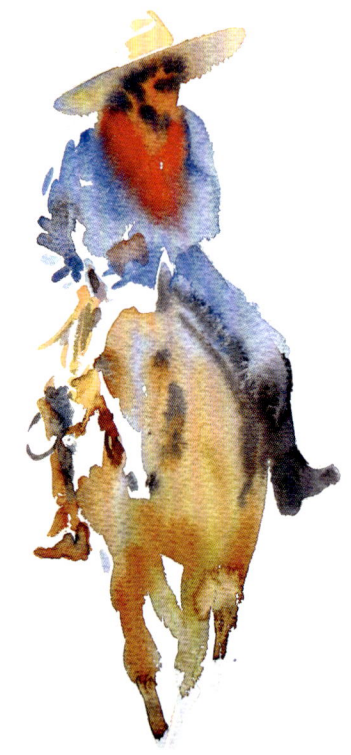

△ **The Mexican**
38 x 18cm (15 x 7in)

Here the man's body is painted quite loosely but the proportions are still maintained and correlate right and left: the legs and arms bend at the halfway mark, and the elbows, knees and feet run parallel with the tilt of the head and shoulders.

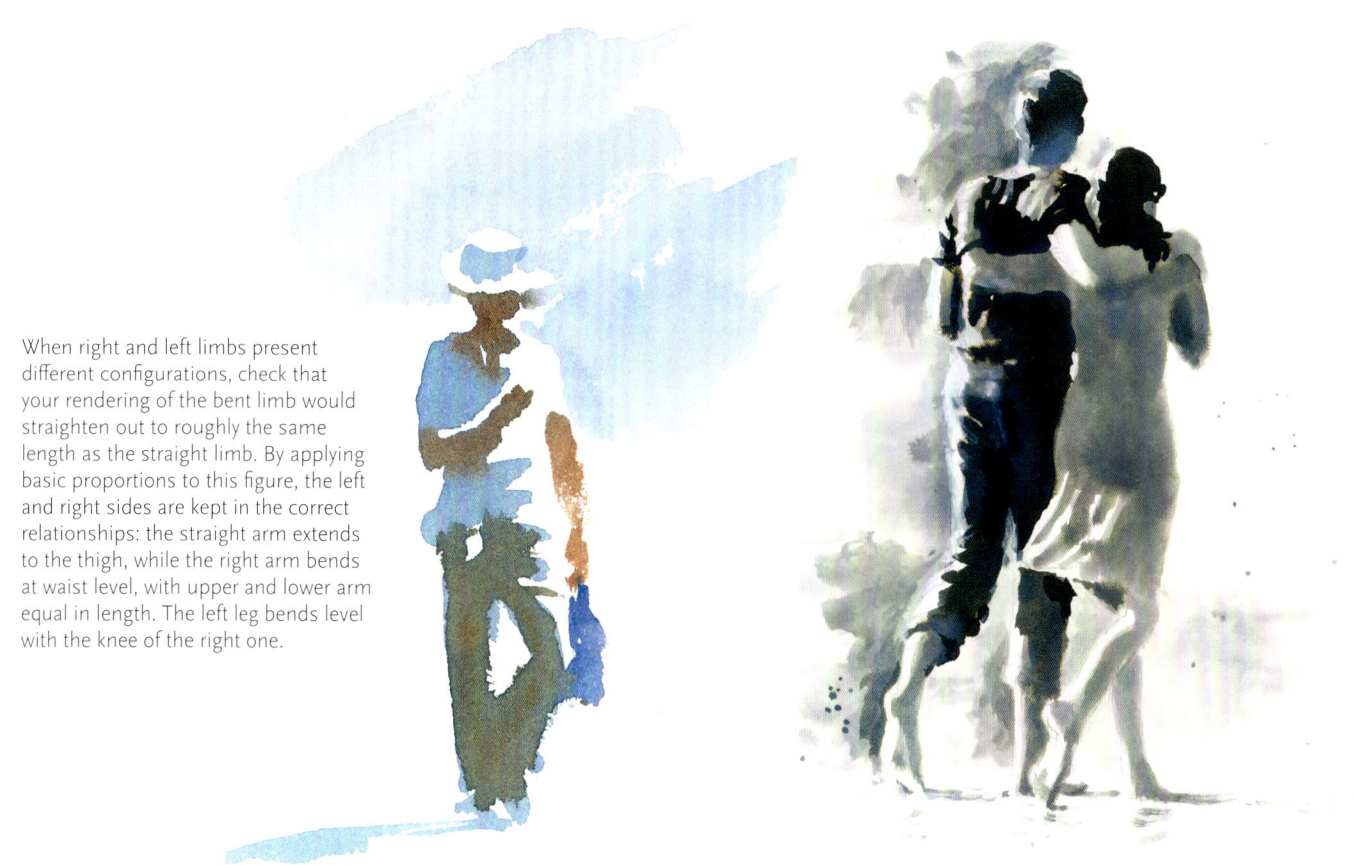

When right and left limbs present different configurations, check that your rendering of the bent limb would straighten out to roughly the same length as the straight limb. By applying basic proportions to this figure, the left and right sides are kept in the correct relationships: the straight arm extends to the thigh, while the right arm bends at waist level, with upper and lower arm equal in length. The left leg bends level with the knee of the right one.

△ **Strolling the Strand**
30.5 x 25.5cm (12 x 10in)

When more than one figure is involved, ensure that they relate to each other. The man here is taller than the woman but they are both painted in the same relative proportion. Note where the toes and feet touch the ground: these levels must match in order for the figures to link.

Perspective

Proportion in relation to other people or features in the foreground or background of a painting needs to be taken into account for the space depicted between them to appear feasible. Here the rules of perspective come into action and enable the painter to show figures in convincing relationship with each other.

The use of perspective implies distance by means of a reduction in scale towards the horizon: people nearby are painted larger in scale than people in the background. The horizon is always at eye level, so whether you stand or sit to paint determines whether your figures 'shrink' in scale from the feet up, from the head down or in both directions.

Moments Like These
35.5 x 41cm (14 x 16in)

Look how large the foreground waitress figure is in relation to the background figures. And we can tell that the standing lady behind the right-hand diners is coming down some steps because her head is higher than it could be if she were on the same ground level as the waitress.

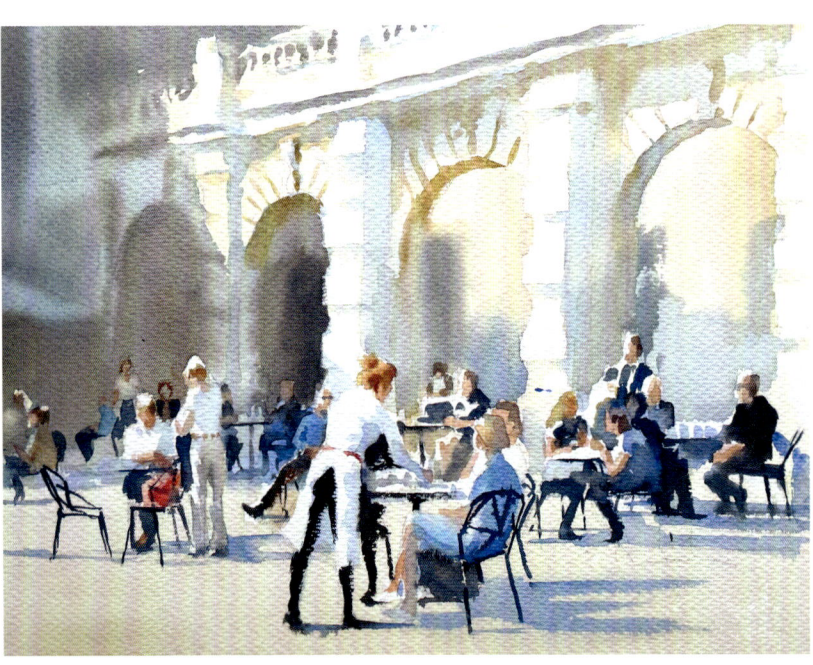

Foreshortening

Perspective also comes into play within the form of the figure, causing foreshortening whenever a part of the body juts into the foreground or recedes into the background. The distance is short – maximum 2m (6½ft) – but the results of foreshortening can be unnerving to paint because normal proportions appear all messed up. An obvious example is someone lying feet first towards you.

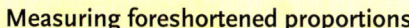

Measuring foreshortened proportions

Hold a pencil vertically at arm's length in front of you (yes, the classic artist's pose) and use it as a measuring rod to compare different parts of the body, for example the size of the head to the foot, the thigh to the calf. Keep the pencil in an upright plane, as if pressed against a window pane.

△ **Chilled**
56 x 76cm (22 x 30in)

At this angle, the feet become large in relation to the head: measure the length of the boy's left foot with your thumb and you will see that astonishingly it is the same length on the picture plane as the distance from the top of his head to his waist.

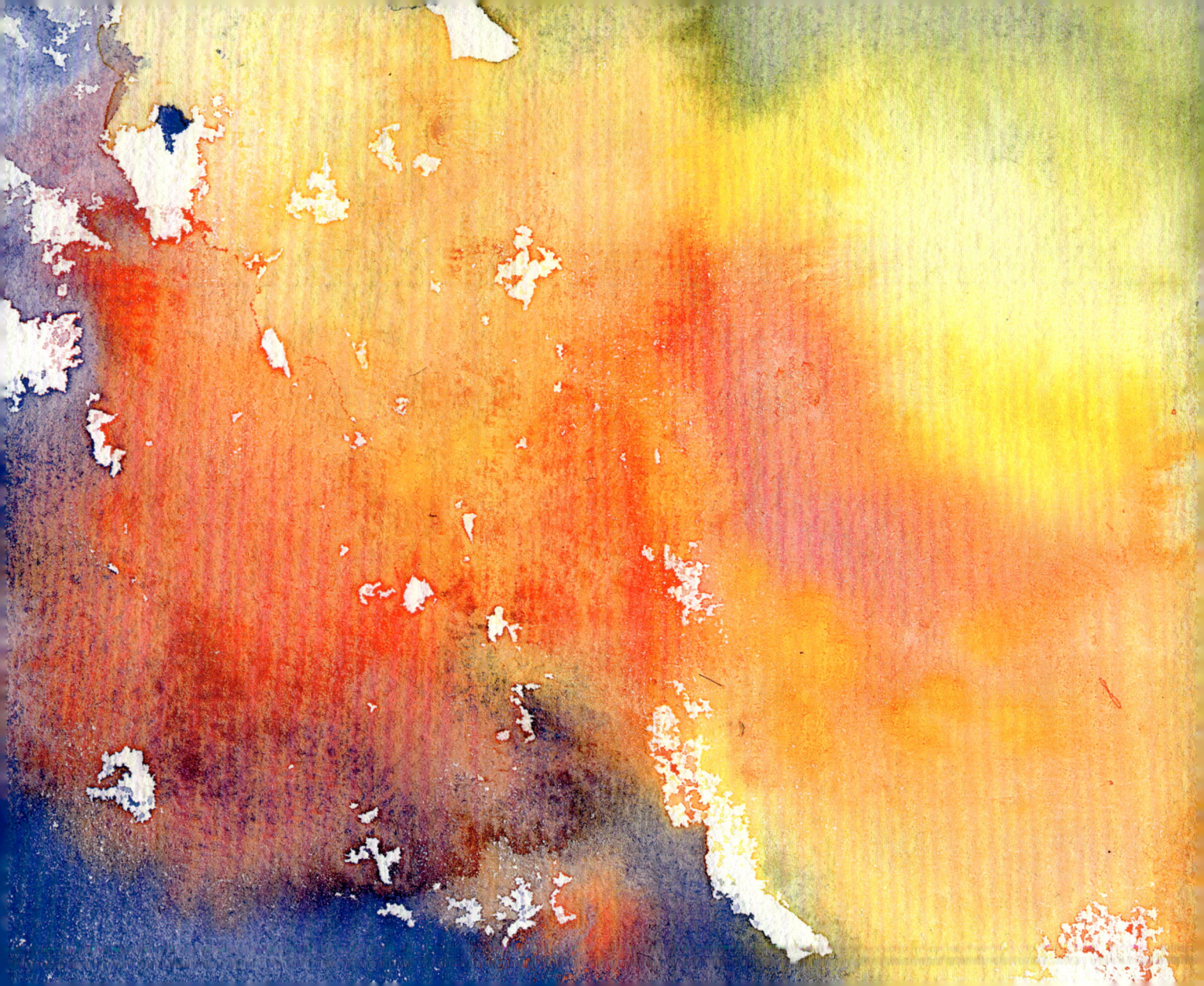

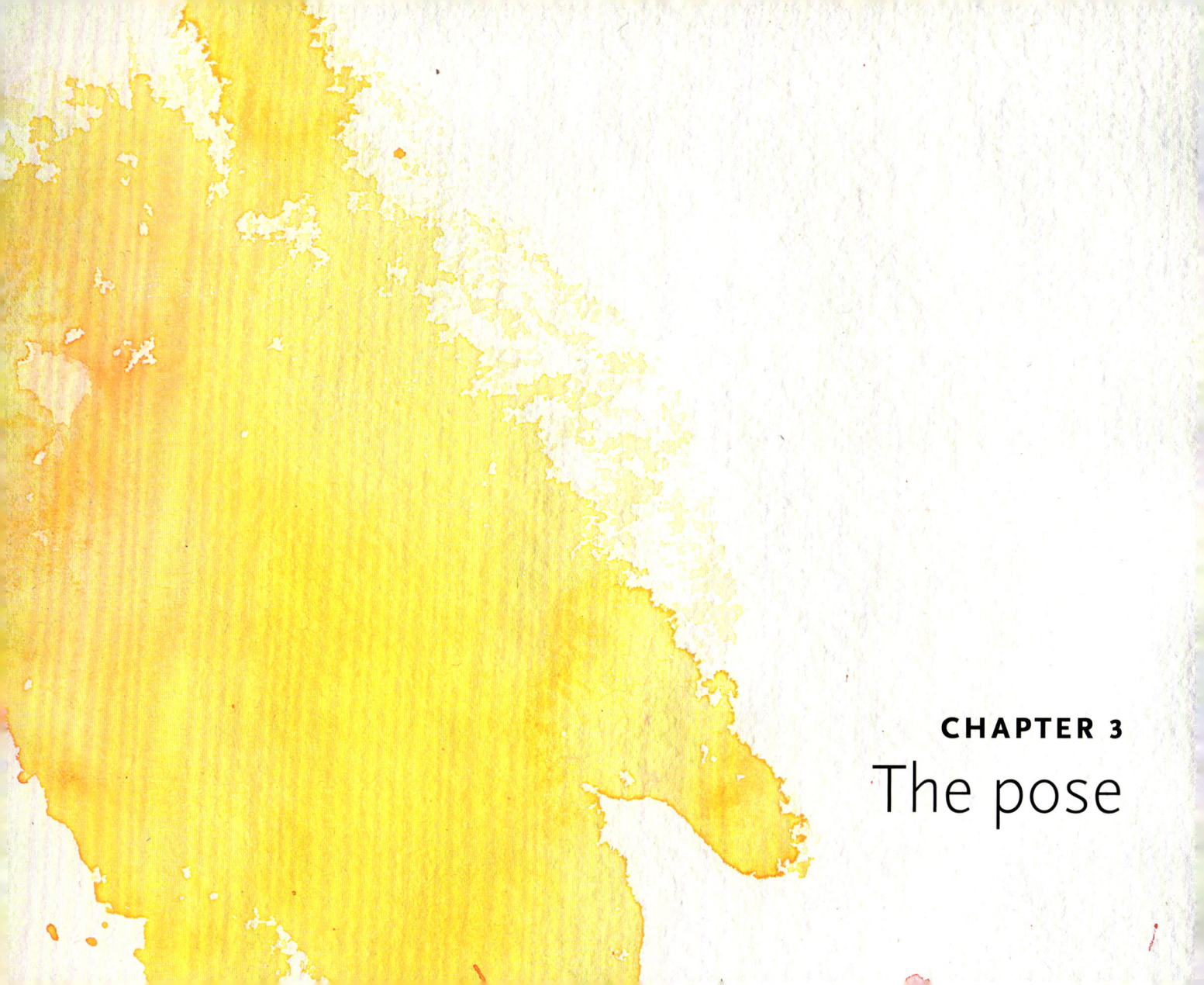

CHAPTER 3

The pose

Plausible poses

Portraying figures in natural and lively poses is a must if you want them to look credible in the painting. An active posture is generally more interesting than a static pose, and offers a storyline. The aim is to present poses that are anatomically possible and circumstantially probable. Happily, as with proportions, poses do not have to be highly accurate to be effective.

A pose needs to appear balanced, which means checking where the weight is placed. The balance can be assessed and adjusted with the use of an imaginary plumb line dropped from the nape of the neck to the feet.

If a figure is standing straight with the weight evenly distributed, the line touches down between both feet. When the weight is taken by one foot or the other, the ankle taking the weight lies directly below the nape of the neck.

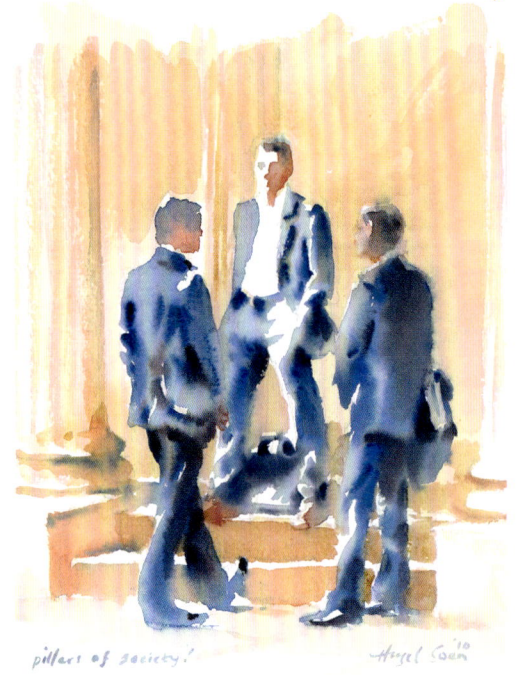

pillars of society!

△ **Pillars of Society**
35.5 x 28cm (14 x 11in)

The men here are all standing still but there is variety in their poses: from left, the first man's weight is mainly taken by the back foot, the man in the middle balances evenly between both feet, and the man on the right leans all his weight on the right foot.

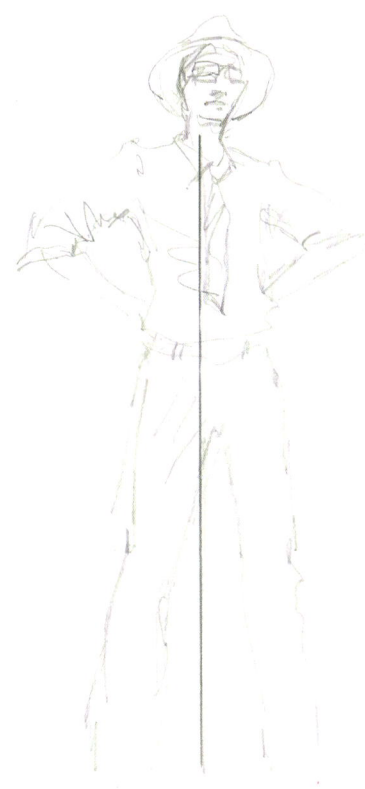

△ A vertical line dropped from the nape of the neck shows that the weight in this pose is distributed evenly between both feet.

▷ When the figure leans, his weight is taken by one leg. An imaginary plumb line from the nape of neck meets the ankle taking the weight.

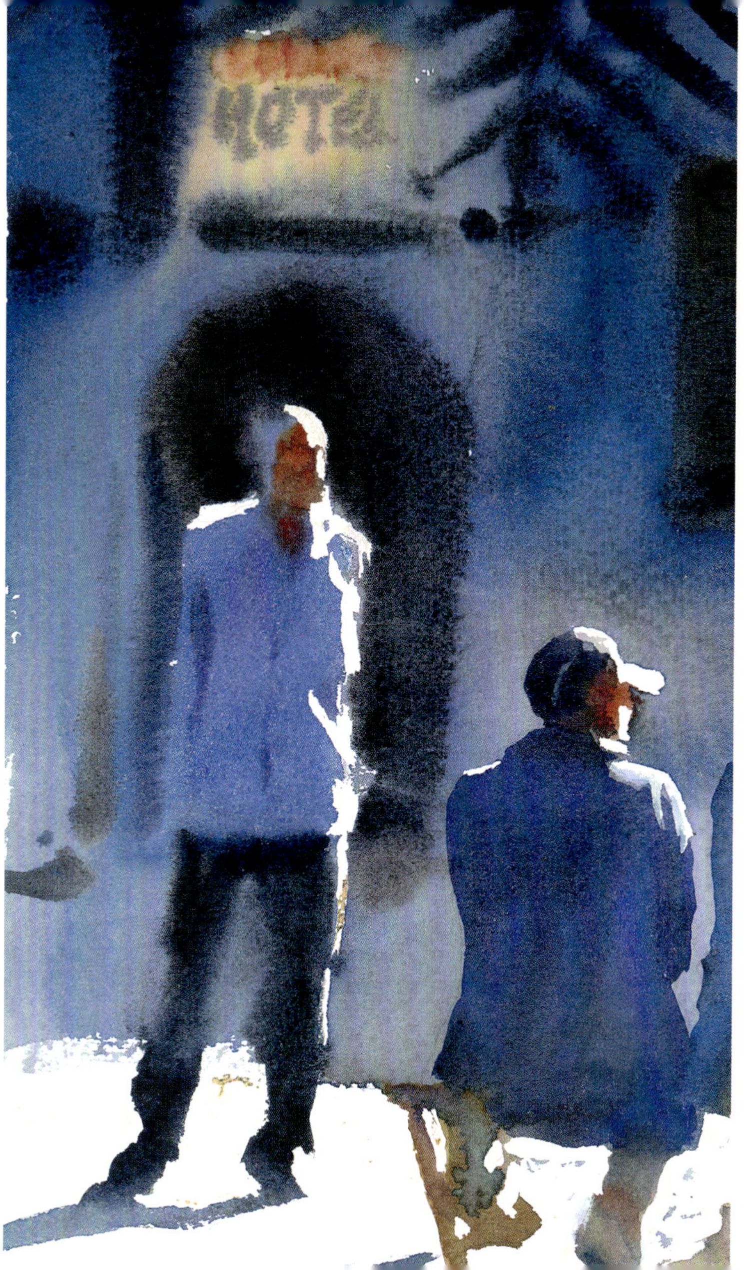

Sitting and leaning

When weight is taken by something other than the person – a wall, chair or table – the pose is dependent on the support. The task is to show the connection between figure and prop in order to convince the viewer that the person is linked inextricably to the prop and cannot hold the pose without it.

Sitting and leaning poses come with benefits – the prop can be usefully employed to obscure 'difficult' parts of the body, such as hands.

▷ **Lunchbreak**
35.5 x 20cm (14 x 8in)

Very little actual information is given here, but it is enough to suggest two seated figures enjoying a conversation.

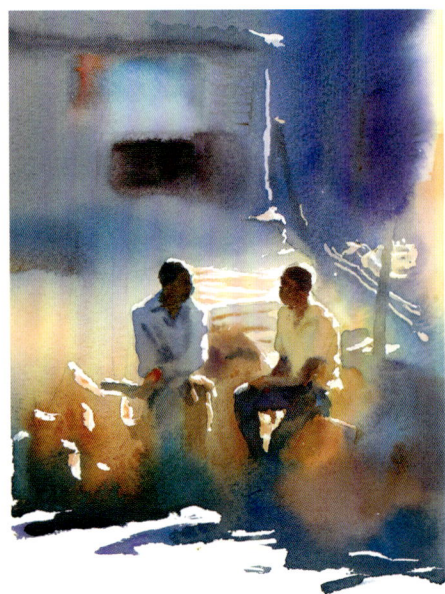

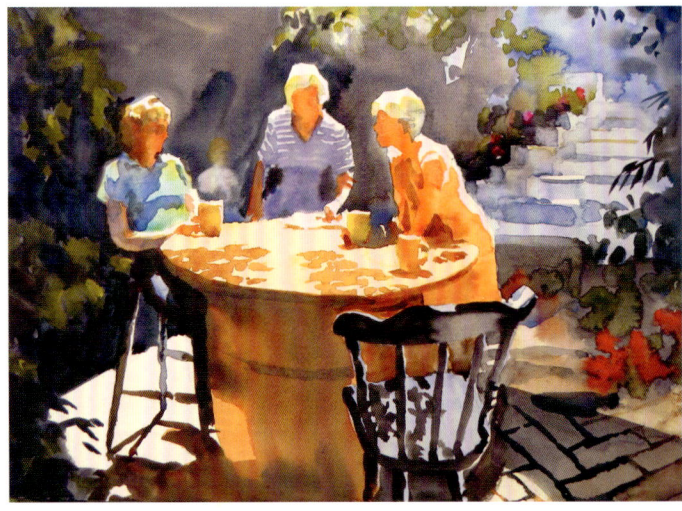

△ **Conversations in a Courtyard**
25.5 x 35.5cm (10 x 14in)

In this painting the women are connected to the table and objects by means of small, warm shadows.

Indicating the movement

Simply by painting one foot higher than the other, you can suggest a person is walking towards or away from the viewer. The foot taking the weight falls directly below the nape of the neck.

From the side view, the triangular gap made between the legs is indicative of where the person is in their stride. A big triangle is made between the legs when the stride is fully extended, while a small triangle is made below the knees when the back leg is bent at the knee (shown below right).

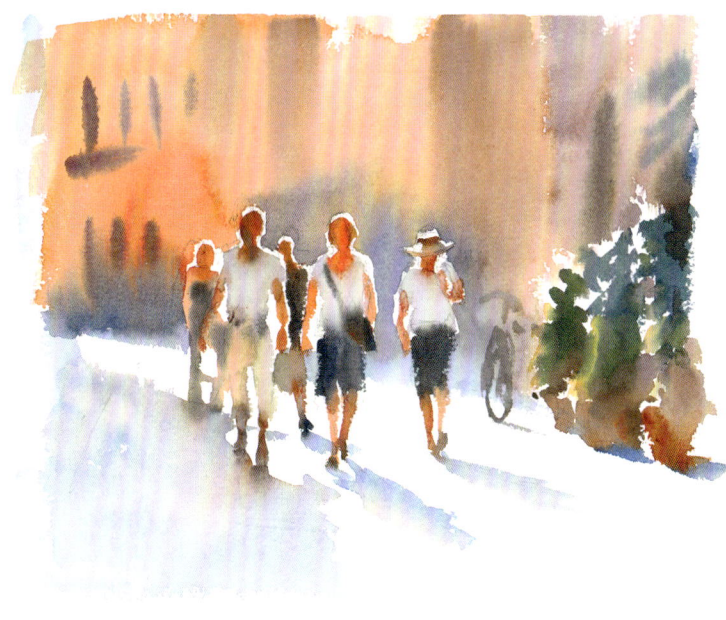

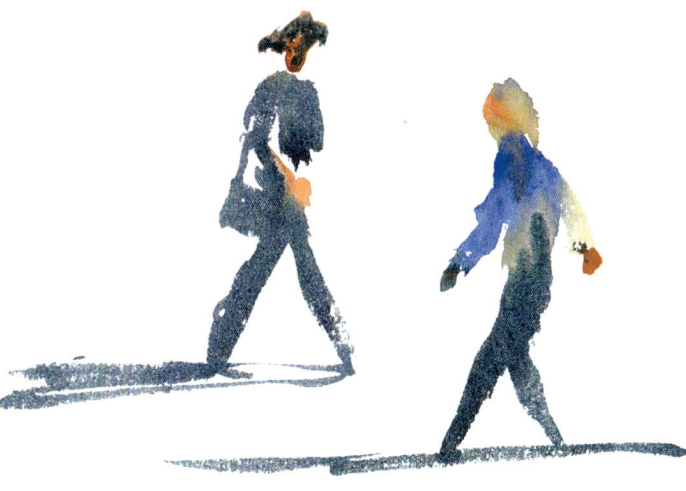

◁ We can tell the figures are not static but walking towards us because one foot is shown higher than the other.

Proximity shadows

Where the figure meets and touches the support, deeper shadow is cast. This is called a proximity shadow, and it is very useful because it establishes a point in the painting where you can show the viewer that two surfaces meet and interact. Think of the prop as a continuation of the figure, rather than a separate item, and you will imply this sense of mutual belonging.

Making contact

Proximity shadows are not only important where contact occurs with props or supports but also where contact occurs between people and other surfaces, or within the figure itself. The connection point is shown in the painting by a proximity shadow. Quantum physicists explain that we never really touch things – our atoms literally float in very close proximity to each other. Seen this way, the proximity shadow signifies this space in between. The proximity shadow is a place where light is blocked and may therefore be the darkest point in a painting.

▷ **Beach Girls**
25.5 x 25.5cm (10 x 10in)
Darker tone in the long blue shadows cast across the ground denotes the proximity shadows where the girls' bodies make contact with the sand. The angle of the shadows serves to describe the flatness of the support on which the girls sit.

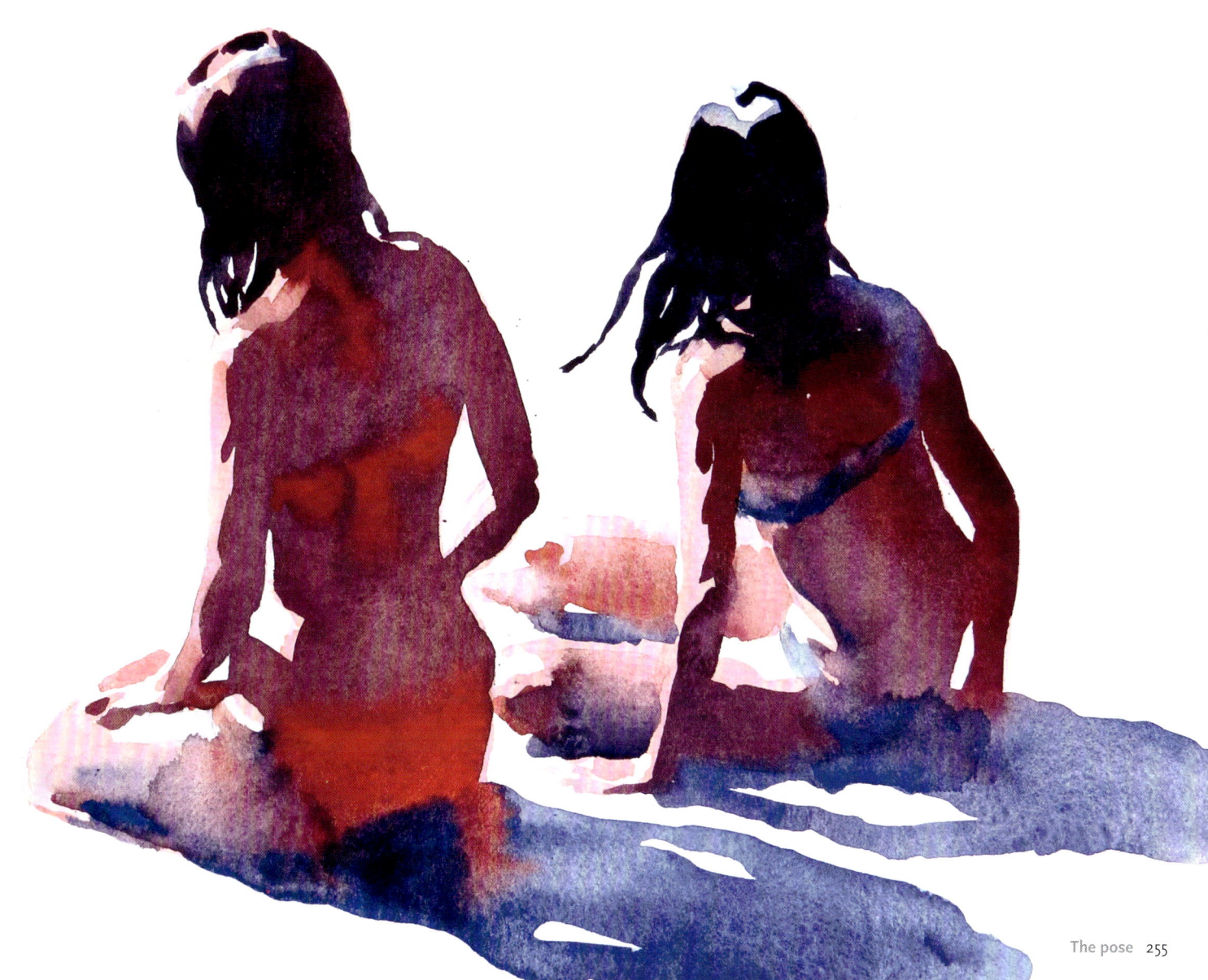

Gaps and spaces

In a painting, figures do not need to be touching for a connection to occur. On the picture plane the spaces between figures are as vital to the pose, stance and composition as the figures themselves. Getting spacing 'right' between people and things is key in order to link them. Go through the pictures in this book, and instead of looking at the figures, study the spaces between them and the gaps visible between limbs and body. In artspeak these areas are called negative spaces, and they should be factored into the composition.

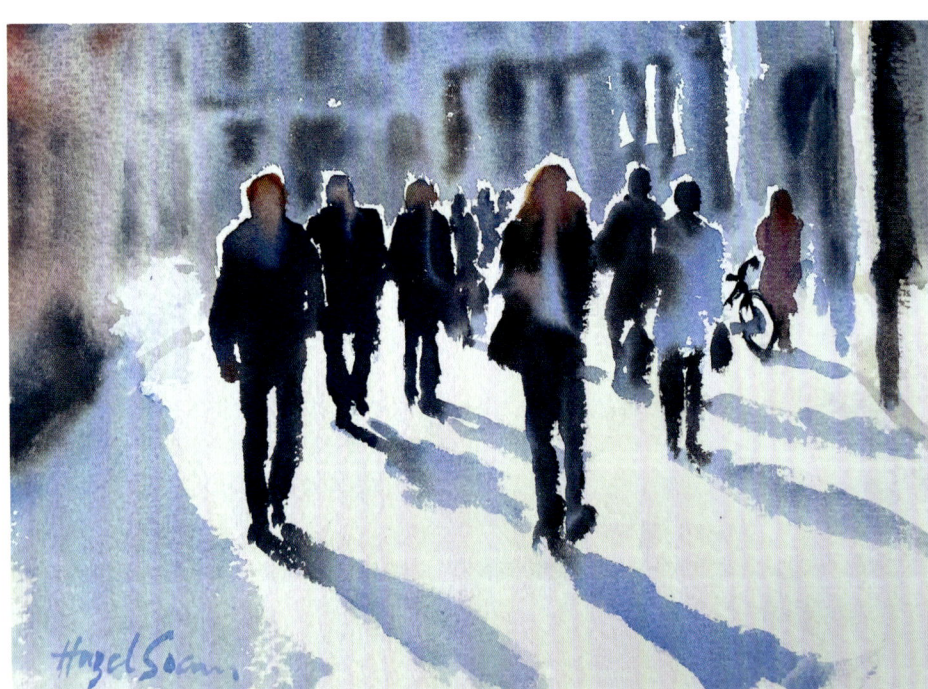

◁ **London Rising**
23 x 30.5cm (9 x 12in)

The gaps between the people's legs and the spacing between the shadows may be called negative shapes in art terms, but as you can see they exert a positive effect on the painting and are just as important to the flat pattern of the surface of the paper as the darker-toned positive figure and shadow shapes.

The shapes in between

The shapes of negative space are called negative shapes. Although intangible in the three-dimensional world, on the two-dimensional painted surface these shapes are very real and as important to paint as the brushstrokes that depict the solid forms. Negative shapes help to describe the person's pose from the outside and enable the artist to determine the contour line around the body. Within poses, bent limbs often create negative shapes that are triangular in character, for example between an arm on the waist and the torso or between striding legs.

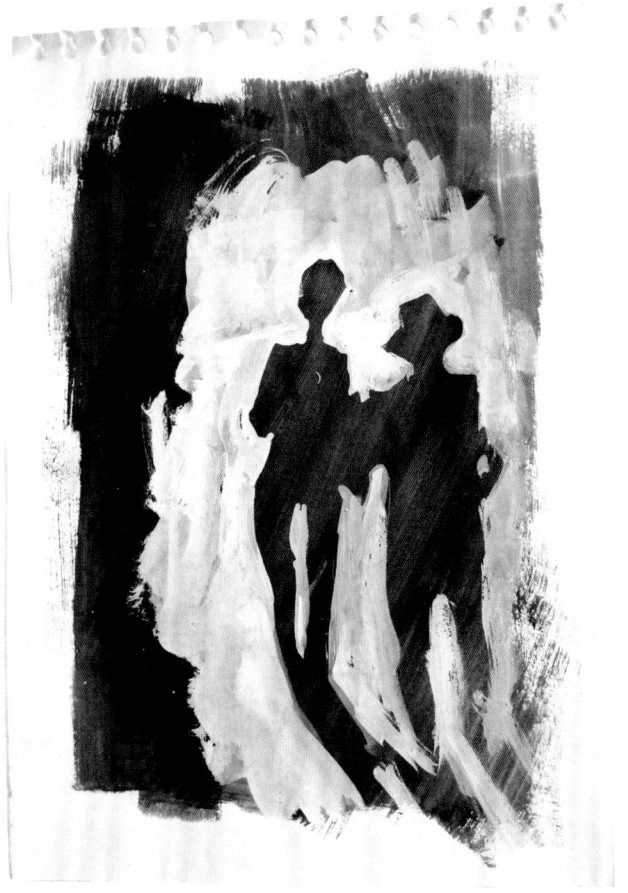

△ Negative shapes are made by the spaces around and between solid things.

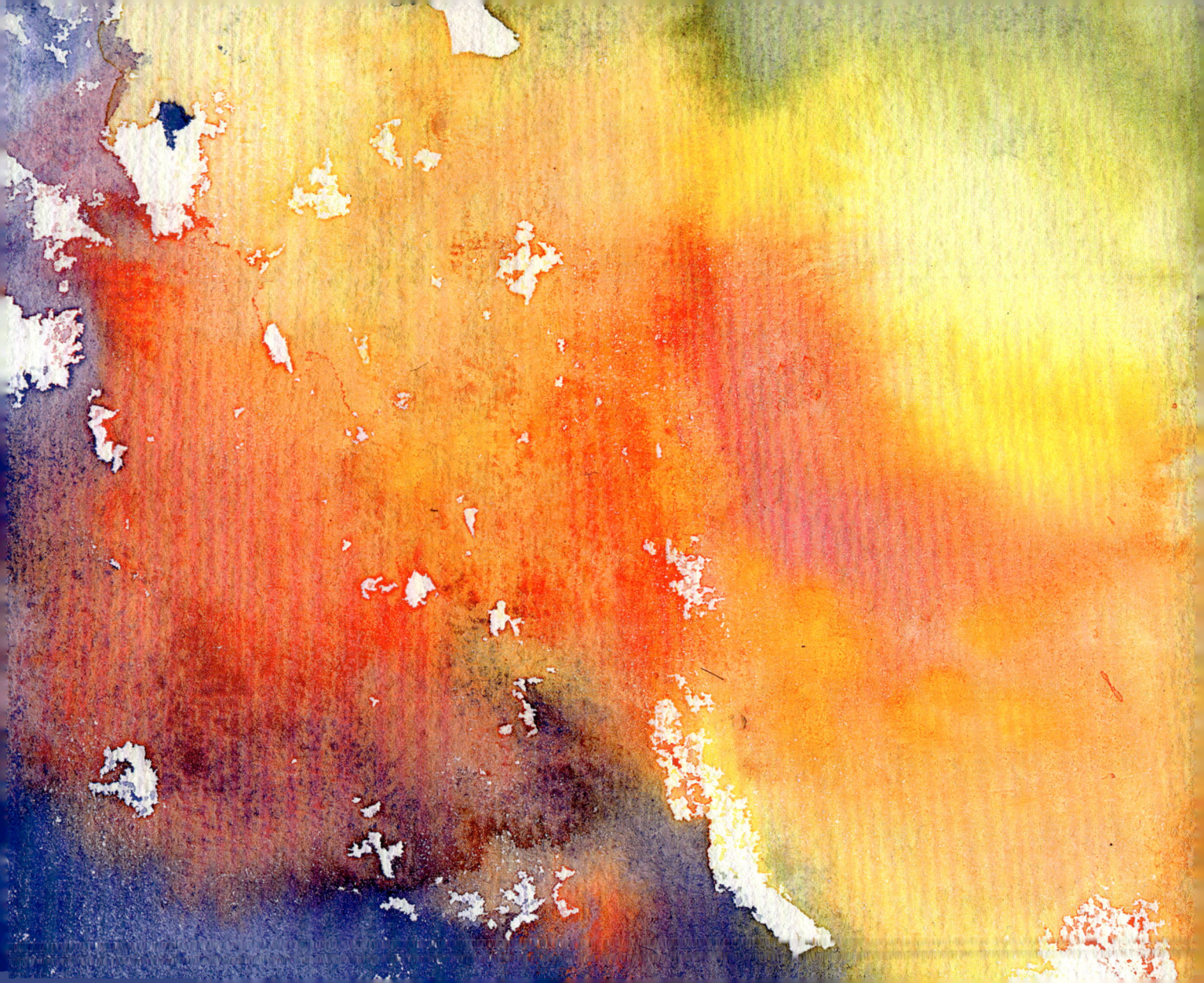

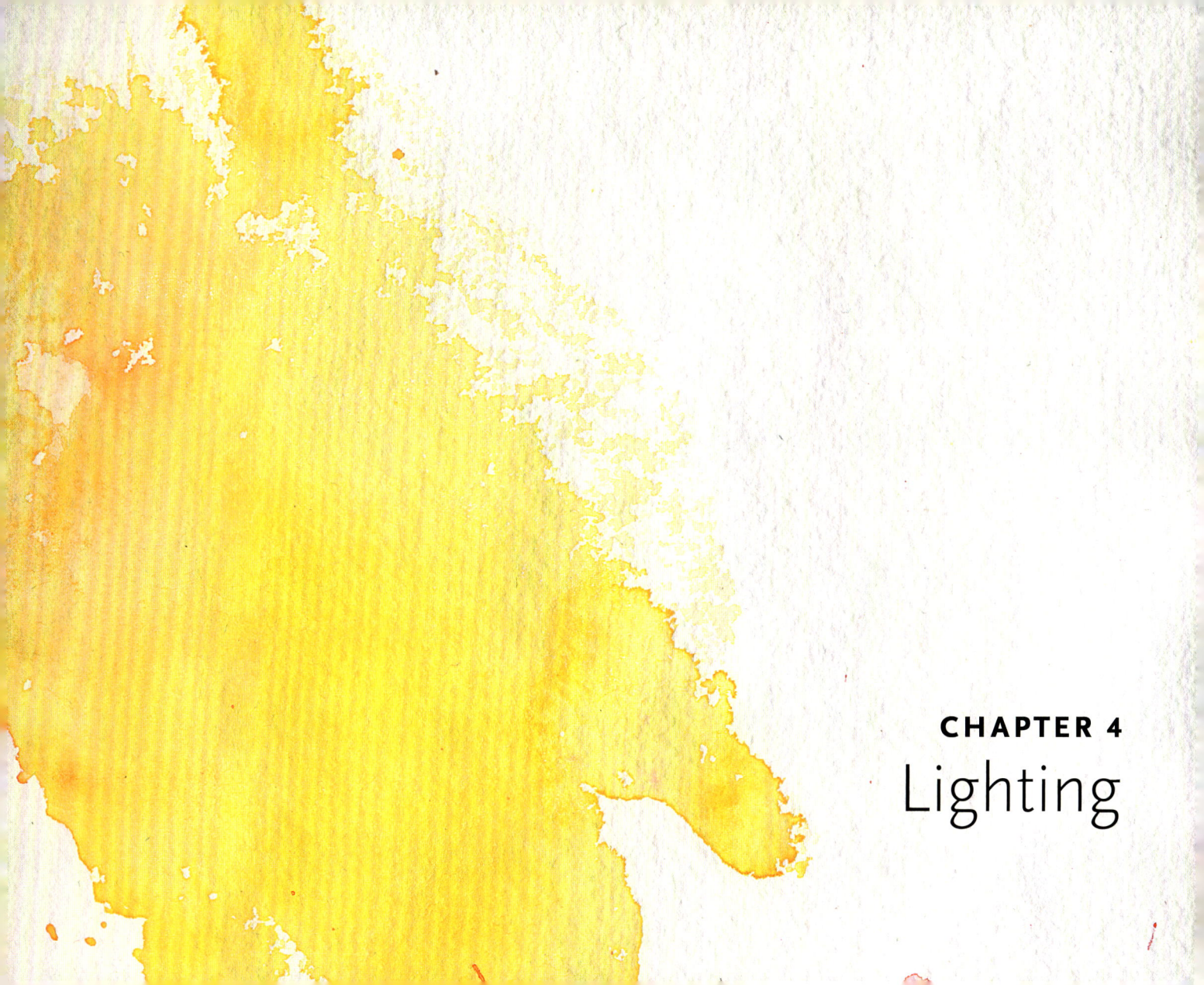

CHAPTER 4

Lighting

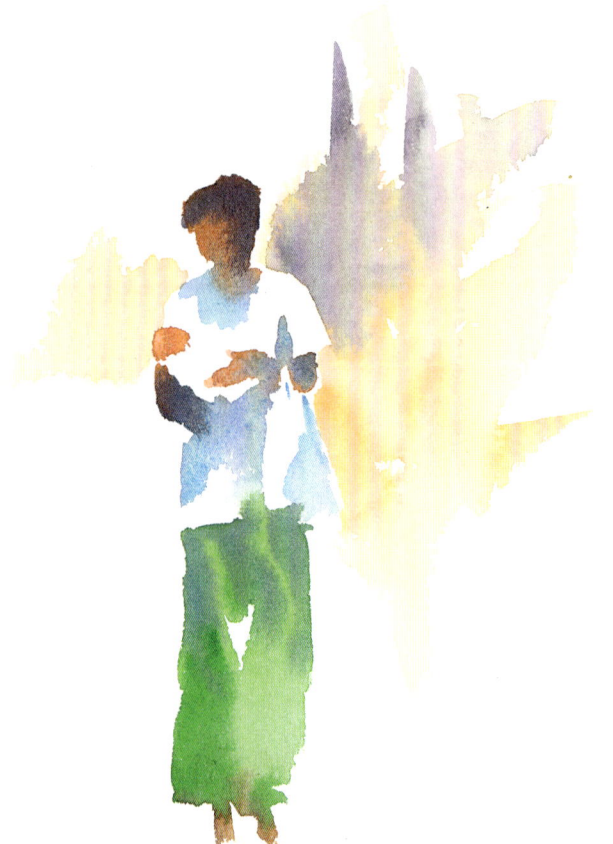

Light and shade

There is one more vital ingredient to add to proportion and pose before the figure can fully inhabit the painting. This is light, or rather light and shade. Light emanates from a single source, such as the sun, the sky or a lamp, or from multiple sources, such as streetlights or combined interior lighting. The direction and angle from which the light comes and its strength are crucial considerations for an artist, because creating interesting counterchanges between light and shade is the substance of representational painting.

△ The three ingredients that are important to making a lively, convincing figure are clear in this watercolour sketch: the woman is in proportion, her pose looks plausible, and the light and shade on her clothing offer a lively and descriptive pattern.

▷ **The Portal, Kairouan**
28 x 38cm (11 x 15in)

In this painting we can believe sunlight is shining on a Tunisian market scene from a top-right direction because the figures, ramparts, stalls, etc., with their lighter sides facing to the right of the picture plane, are all shown lit from the same source.

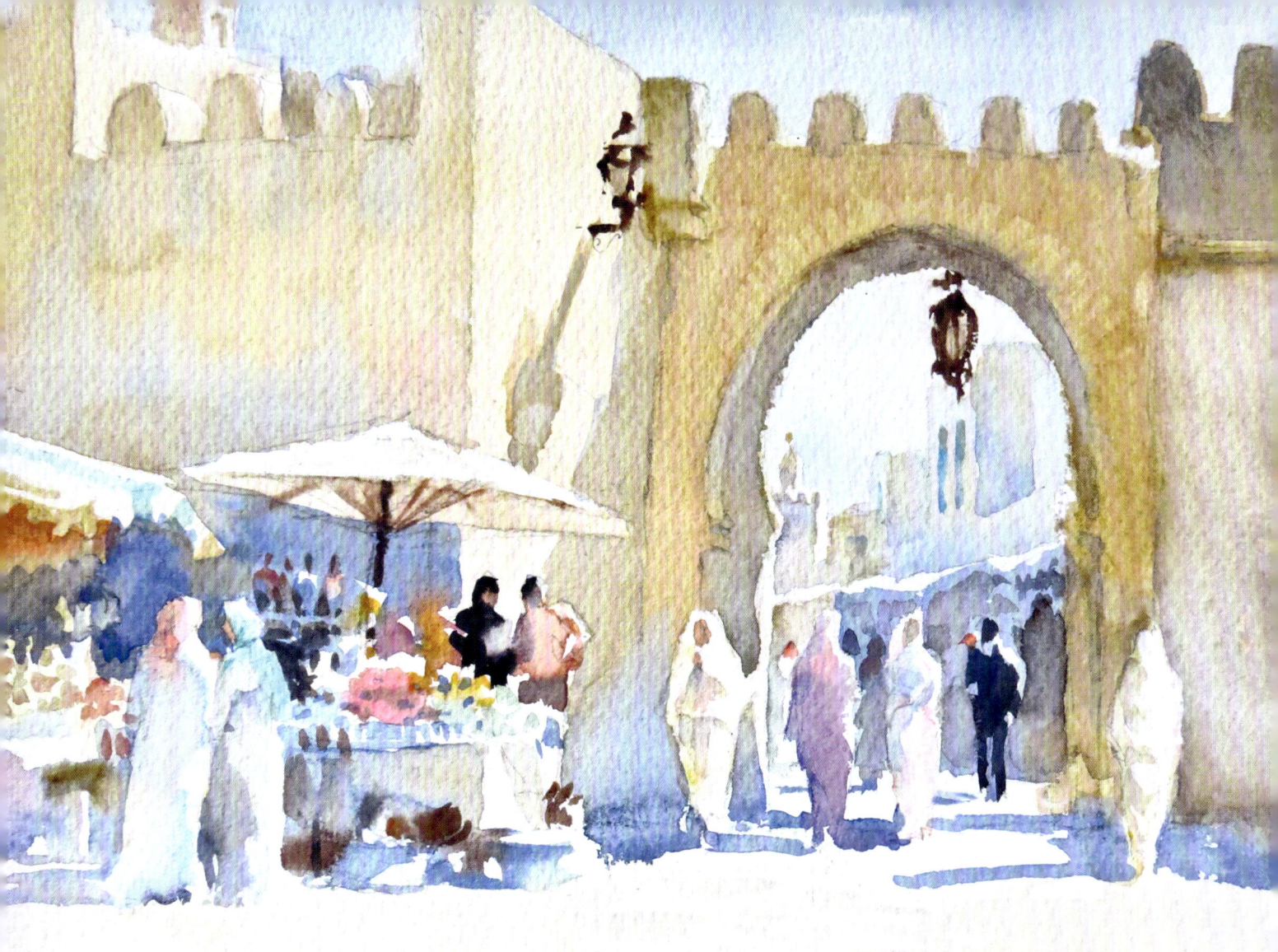

Porte de Tunis Kairouan

Tone

The gradations between light and shade are collectively termed tones or values, and three-dimensional form is implied on the painted surface by their interrelationship and counterchange – darker against lighter and lighter against darker. Confusion in seeing and painting tonal variation often causes weakness or mismatch in paintings, especially if the light indicated on the figures does not marry with the light implied in the rest of the painting. Tonal values are always relative and only have to be convincing in terms of the painting, rather than a replica of their strength in real life or photographs.

▷ To enhance contrast, show a lit feature against a darker background (here the face) and a shaded feature (back of the neck) against a lighter background. Think of phrases such as 'darker than' or 'lighter than' to determine the strength of individual tones in relation to each other.

Light sources

As the Earth moves around the sun there is a change in the direction and angle of light, which alters tones and colours. The sun reaches its highest point in the middle of the day, after which light and shade 'swap places'. A painting will not make sense to the viewer if it appears to display multiple angles of light. Once the direction is determined, stay consistent. The following pages demonstrate the effects of light from different angles.

A sunlit scene begins the day lit from the east, by late morning front-lit, at midday top-lit, during the afternoon side-lit from the west, and by evening back-lit.

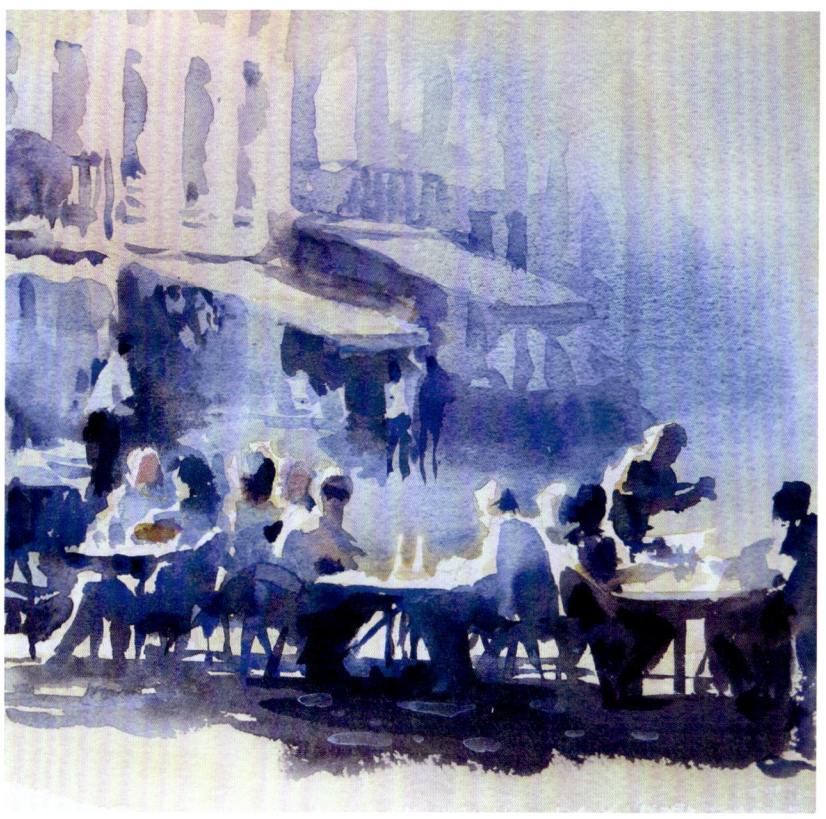

△ **The Light of Collioure**
25.5 x 25.5cm (10 x 10in)

Three main tones are needed to imply the three dimensions – light, dark and mid-tone. Here the sunlight on the figures is the light tone, the shadows under the tables and awnings are the dark tone, and the background is mid-tone.

Top lighting

In the middle of the day, and under overcast skies, light comes from overhead. This top light manifests itself in slivers of light on upward-facing features. The tops of heads, shoulders and folded arms, the lap of a seated figure, the instep of a foot and a bent-over back are all areas where lighter tonal values will be displayed on a figure lit from above.

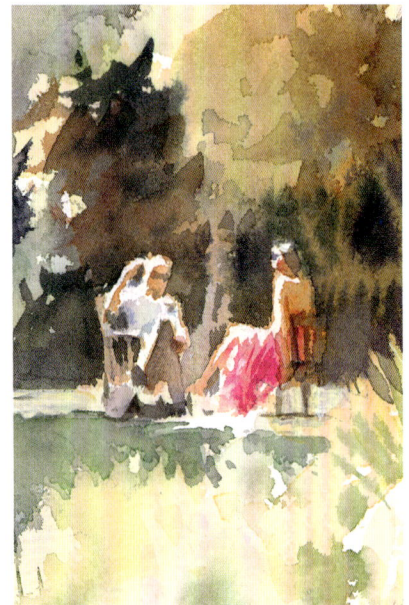

▷ Against a dark background, the highlights from a top light stand out vividly.

▷ ▷ **Sarong**
51 x 28cm (20 x 11in)
In equatorial regions the midday sun is directly overhead. The light catches the top of this woman's head and highlights the sarong at the base of her back and on her calf as she walks.

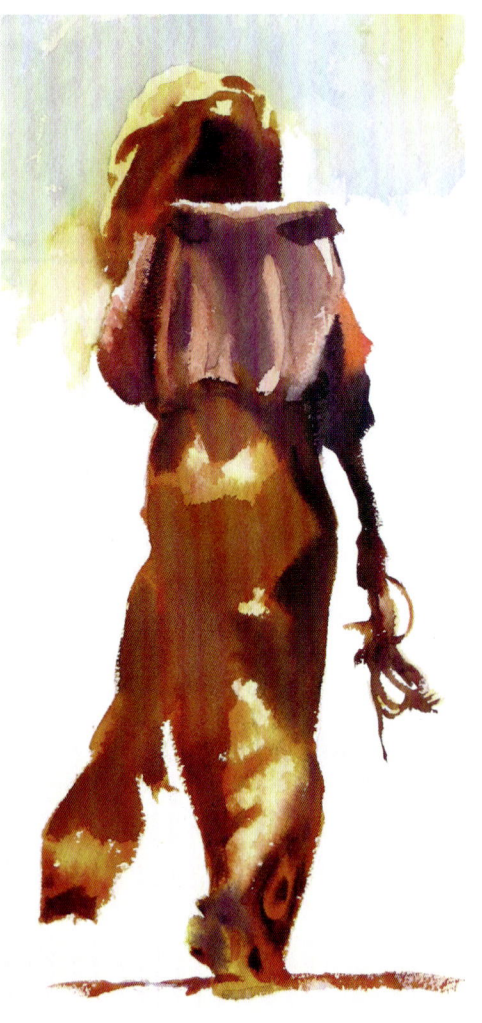

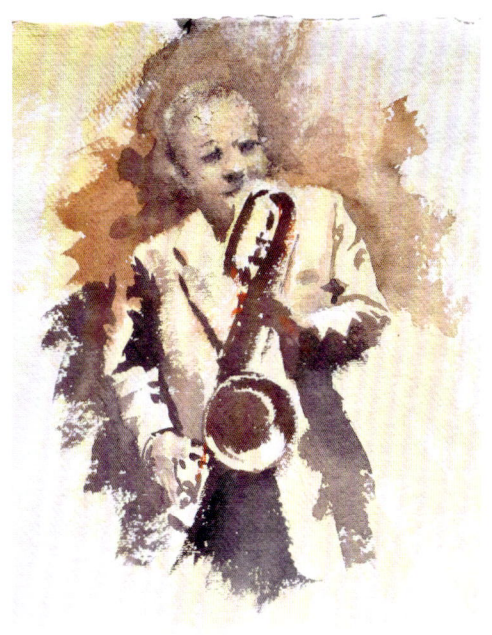

Front lighting

While this angle works well in photography, light mainly from the front is not easy pickings for a painter, especially in watercolour. The features are clearly visible but there is little useful tonal variation playing over the surface to suggest the third dimension. With few shadows evident in full light the painting can appear flat. Shadows made by folds in clothing or from projecting features are precious under this light source.

△ The background, the shadows created by the creases in the sleeves and the cast shadow under the arm enable this front-lit jazz musician to come alive on paper.

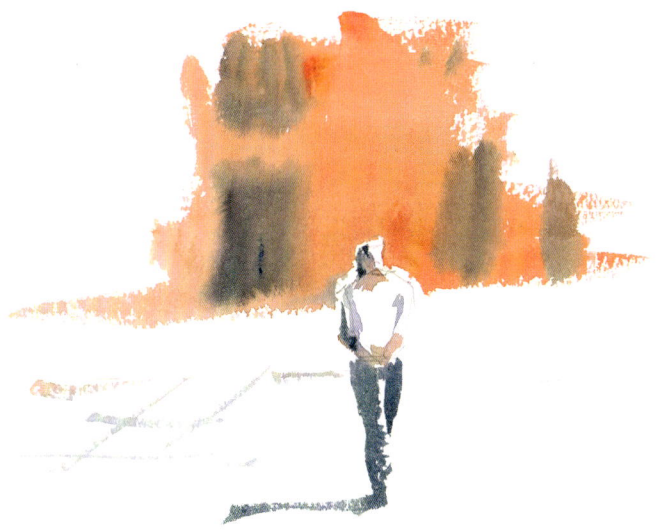

◁ In watercolour a figure lit from the front is created with the surrounding background. Here a space left in the background allows this front-lit figure to emerge. Placing the man's shadow to the left helps root him to the ground.

Three-quarter lighting

When a figure is lit mostly from the front, but with enough shade on one side to make modelling possible, the light and shade create an attractive asymmetrical exchange of tones across the body and three-dimensional form is easy to imply.

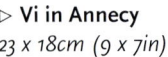

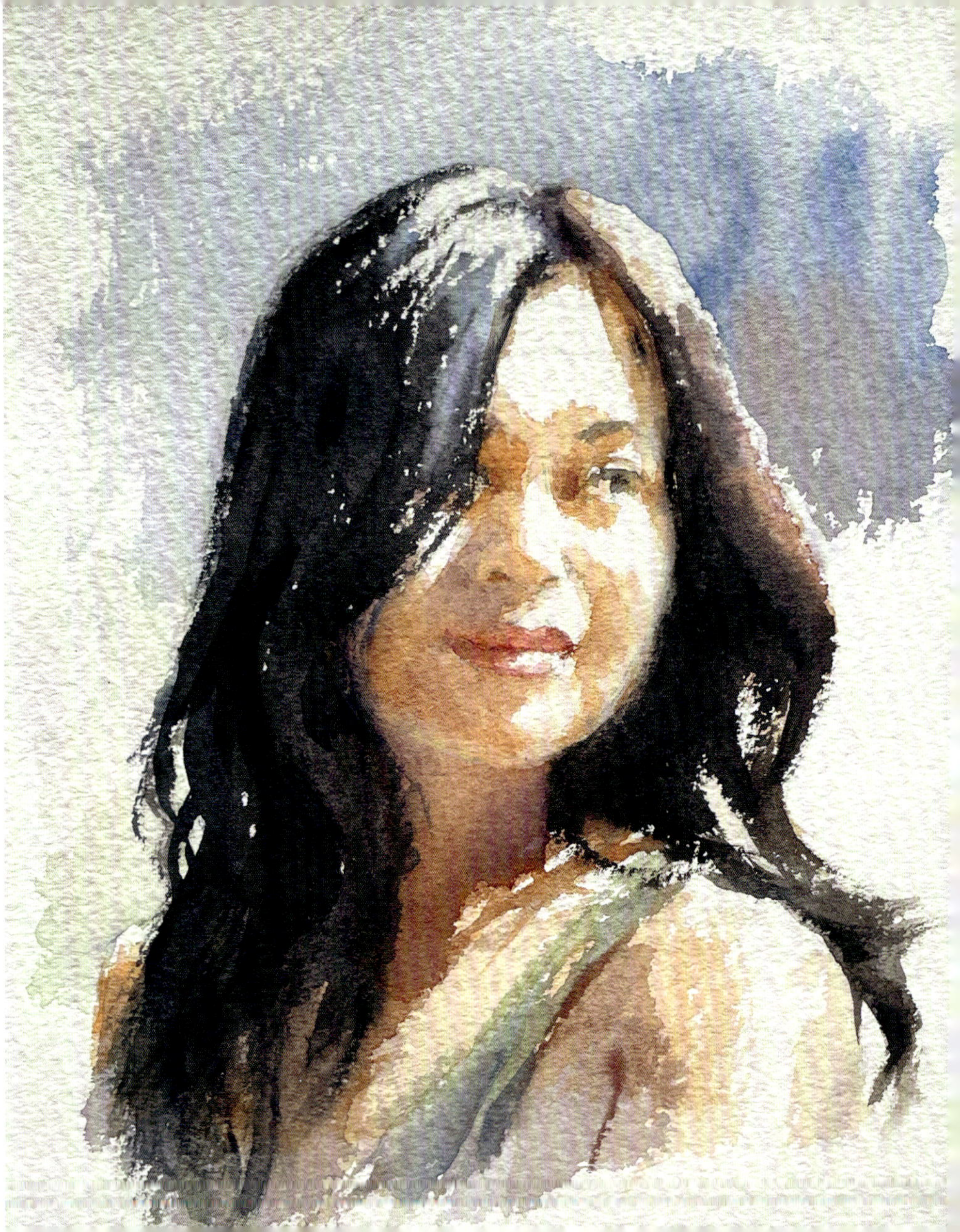

▷ Vi in Annecy
23 x 18cm (9 x 7in)

Sunlight falling on the face from a slight angle causes shadows to form between the facial features. These are tinged with reflected light from the brightly lit surfaces and take on warm, luminescent tints.

Side lighting

With this angle of light, one half of the figure is bathed in light and the other half is in shadow, offering a pleasing balance of tonal interchange on the painted surface. Side lighting is fun to paint, as both the right and left side are often entertainingly broken up by zigzag patterns of alternating light and shadow from folds in clothing. For maximum effect, contrast the darker, shadier side of the figure against a background lighter in tone and place the lighter side of the figure adjacent to darker tone.

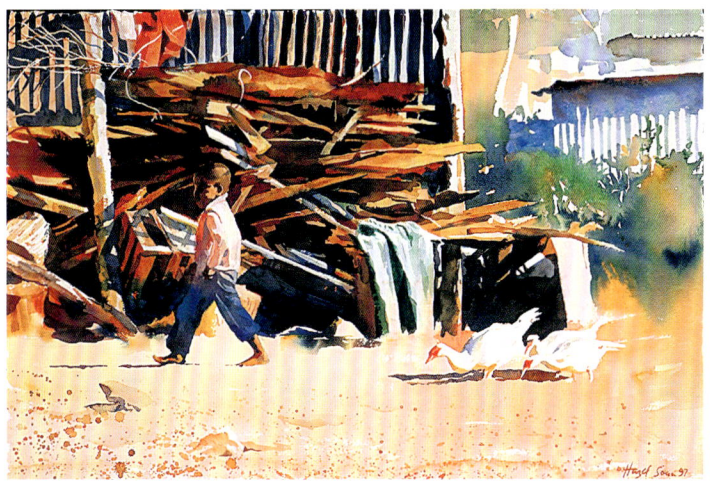

◁ **This is My Town**
43 x 56cm (17 x 22in)

Here you can see the light on the back of the boy is contrasted against dark shadows within the woodpile, and the shaded chest is set against lit planks.

Quarter lighting

An interesting counterchange in light and shade is set up when a figure is lit by light coming from above and behind. Under this quarter-lit angle the figure is predominantly suffused in shade with just a splash of light on one side. Set amid darker tones, the glimpses of light appear more vivid and create exciting tonal counterchange.

Large Glass II

76 x 102cm (30 x 40in)

In this watercolour the light is coming from the left above and beyond the figures. The lit features are made visible only where they come up against a darker tone, and are imagined in the 'missing' pieces of a head or limb.

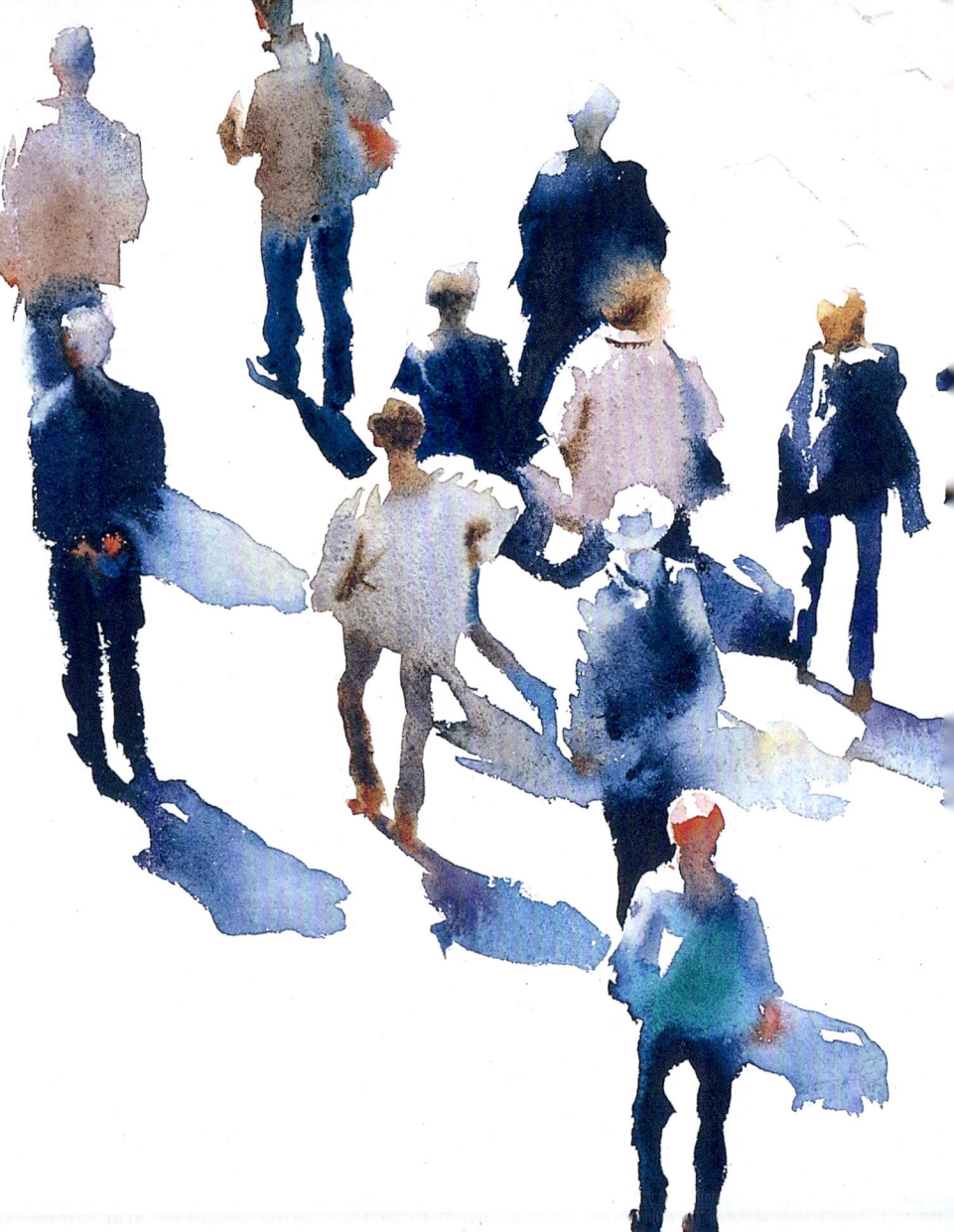

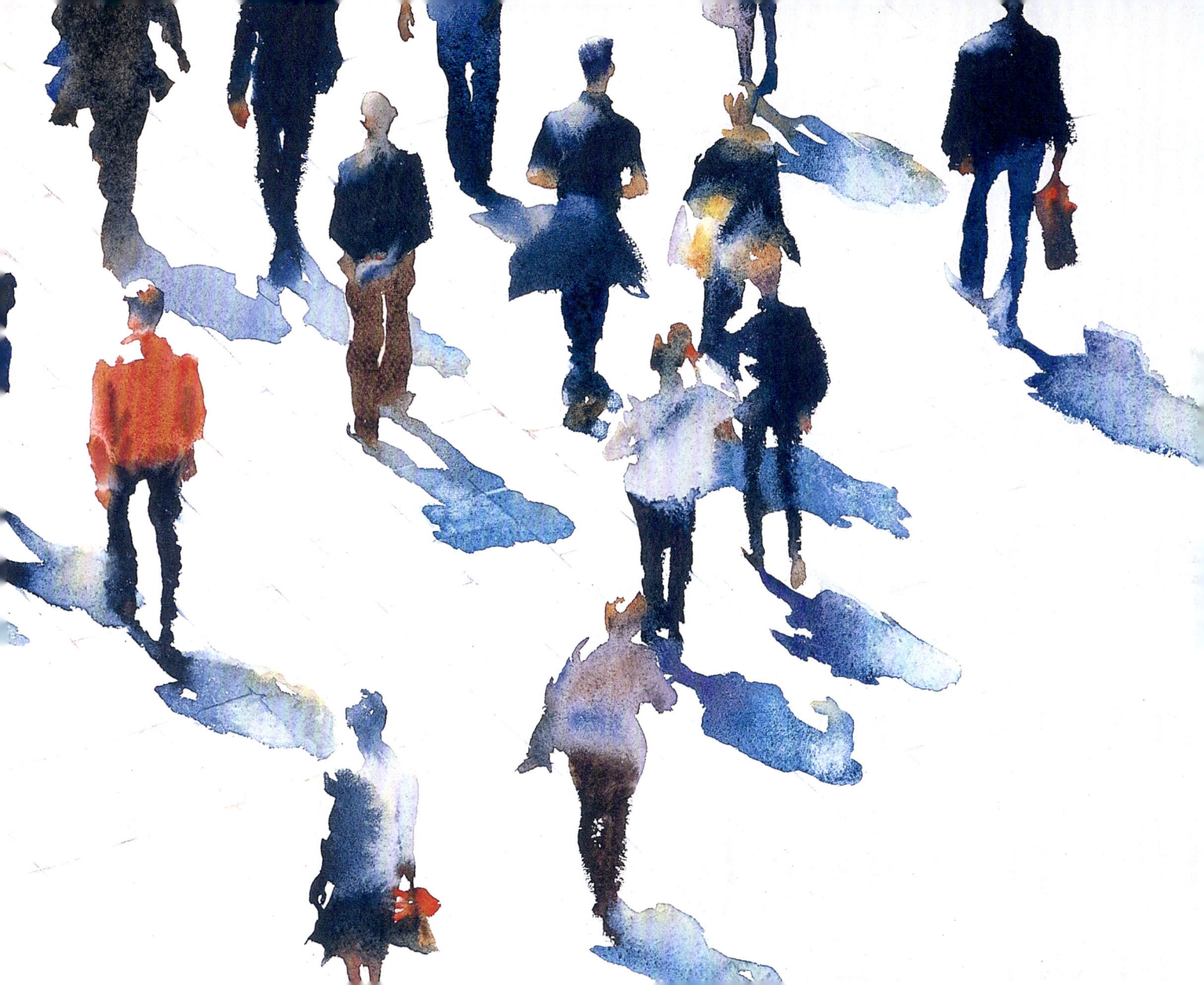

Back lighting

A figure is thrown into silhouette by backlighting. This light, known in visual art as *contre-jour* (meaning 'against the day'), creates dramatic contrast between light and shade. Dark figures become flat shapes since there is no modelling. Mid- or dark tone backgrounds bring out exciting halos of light around heads, and rims of light balance on shoulders or slither down sides that catch the light.

◁ **Taking the Weight**
33 x 30.5cm (13 x 12in)
Exiting the dark interior of the stable, the cowboy is thrown into silhouette against the bright light outside. Carrying his riding paraphernalia, he makes a rugged and fascinating shape.

▷ **Streetlight**
28 x 38cm (11 x 15in)
The sunlight shining down the street creates backlighting for the figures, casting them into silhouette. Against the mid- and dark tones of the buildings, the sunlight catching on the top of heads and shoulders is left as untouched white paper to show the dazzling effect of the light.

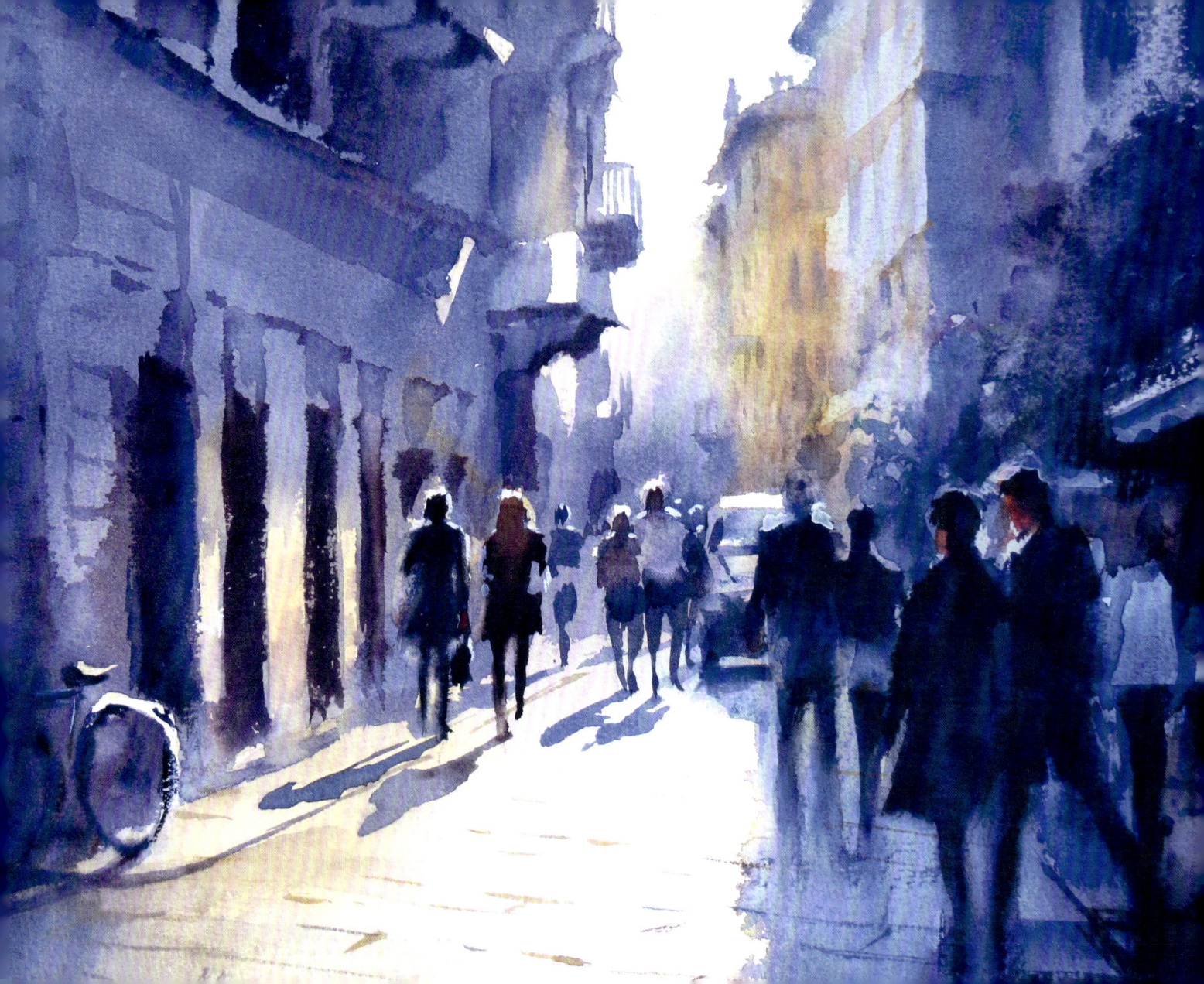

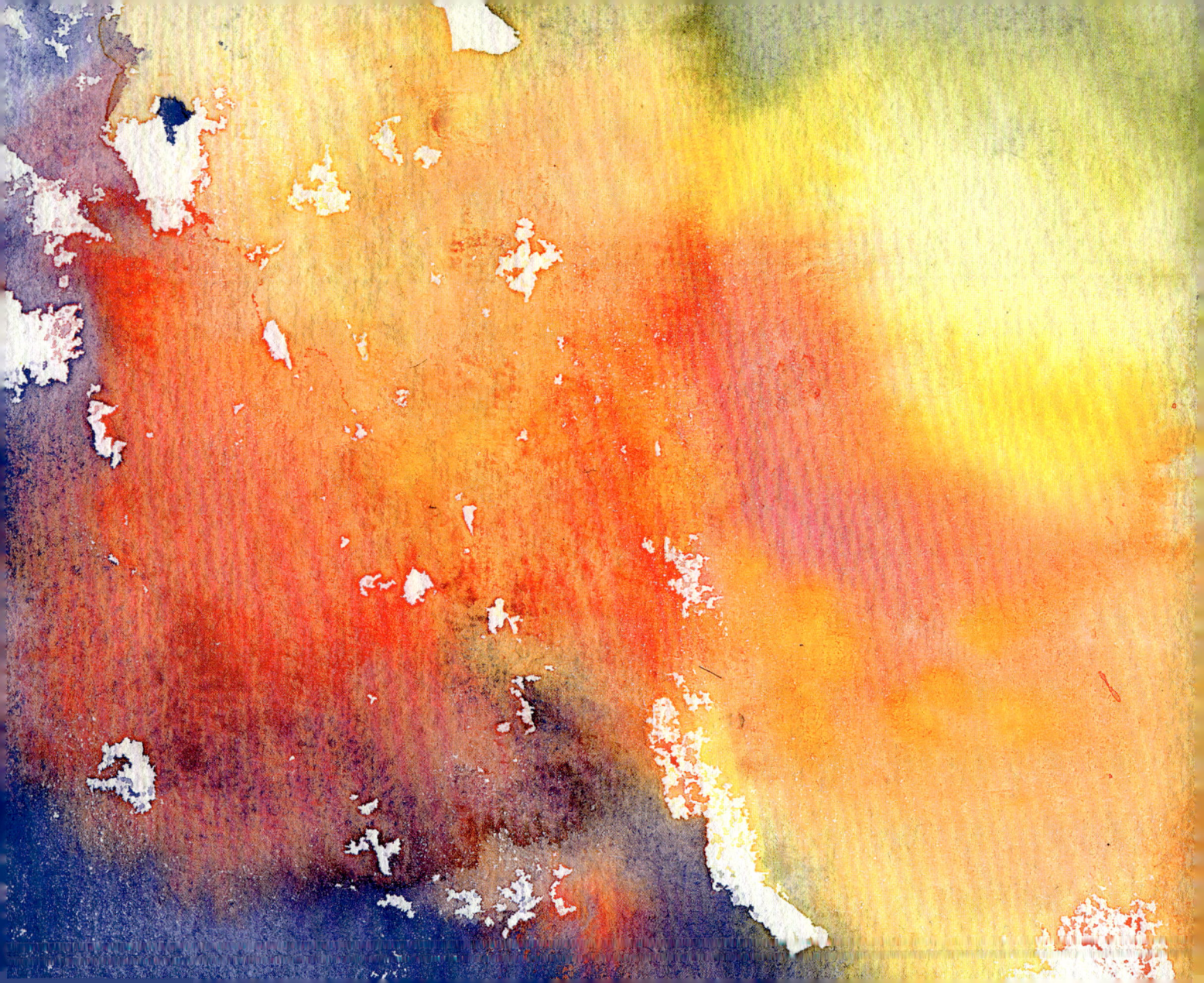

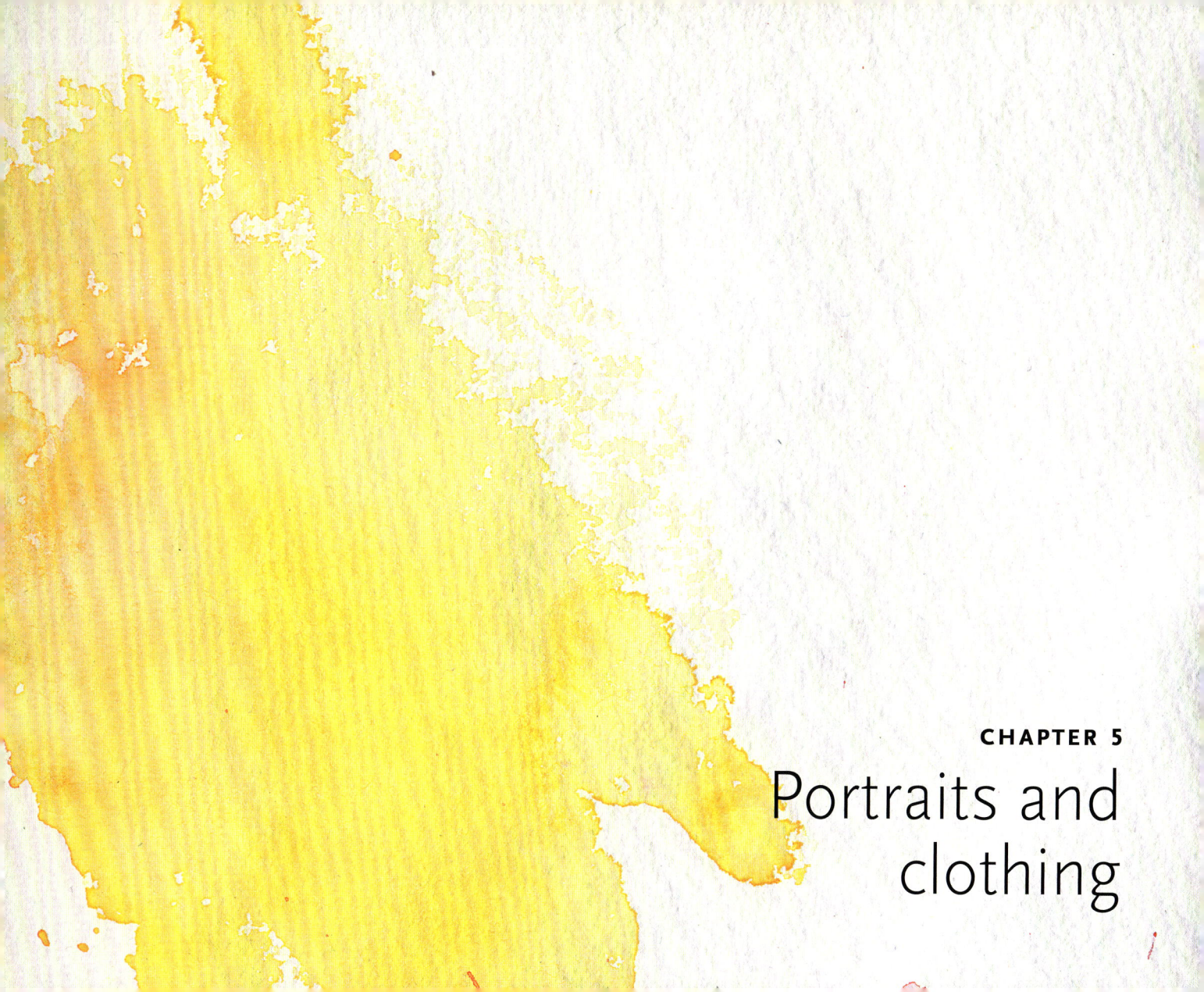

CHAPTER 5

Portraits and clothing

Catching a likeness

When the intention is to represent a particular person, the painting is called a portrait. Catching a recognizable likeness and character requires careful observation, especially of the face. Faces are not flat and features cannot just be pasted into position; the eyes, nose, mouth, chin, eyebrows and hairline must be seen in relation to each other and integrated to construct the whole form of the head. The distances and spaces between facial features are just as important as the features themselves.

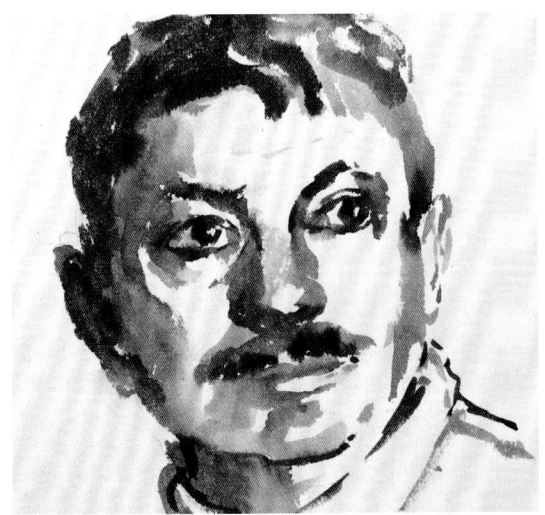 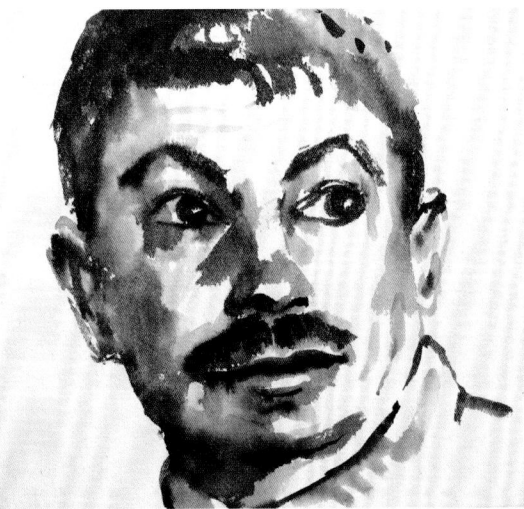

◁ **Philippe**
28 x 35.5cm (11 x 14in)

Portraiture requires study. Here the left-hand picture was my first attempt and while it works as a face it does not look like Philippe. On the right is the second attempt, where I paid more attention to the shape of his face, eyes and eyebrows, and thus found his likeness.

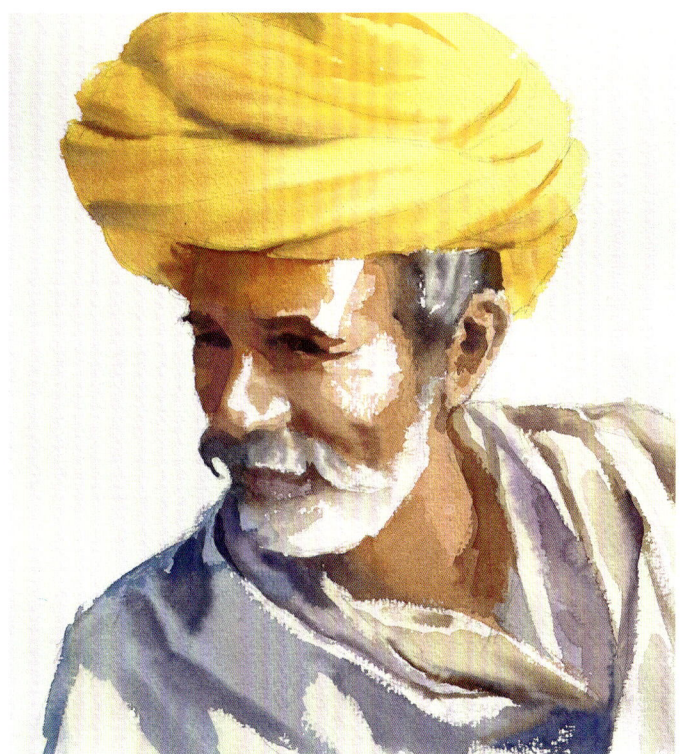

Skin tones and colouring

To help sculpt the head, position your sitter so that more light falls on one side of the face than the other. Use warm colours such as Burnt Sienna, Brown Madder and Crimson for skin tones glowing with warmth. For the facial features that project – nose, mouth, cheeks and ears – use warm colours to bring them forward. Cooler colours, such as blues and greens, help to sink back the side planes and lower face.

Dark accents, such as the lip line, nostrils, corners of the mouth and eyes and the inner ear, can be shown warm and dark with deep crimsons and violets.

△ **The Yellow Turban**
38 x 33cm (15 x 13in)
Burnt Sienna is a wonderful colour for skin tone. Here it is mixed with Schmincke Violet in the shadows and tinged with Indian Yellow on the forehead where colour reflects from the underside of the turban.

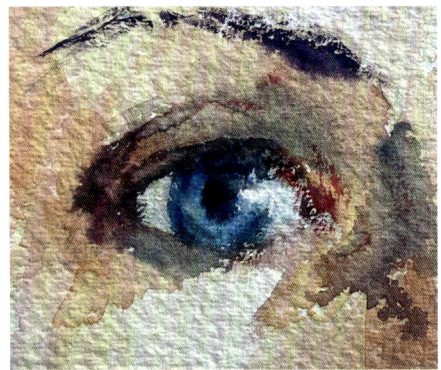

The eyes

Start work on the facial details by putting in the eyes. They are set back in the face, under the shadow of the brow. Paint the curve of the upper lid of one eye first, then bring in the iris and pupil, leaving a highlight in the eye. Next, paint the shadow of the socket and the fold of skin above the eye, and then lightly mark in the lower lid. Go across the bridge of the nose and mark up the other eye in the same way. Once established, the eyes become a measure and guide for the other features.

△ Points to note: the upper eyelid overlaps the top of the iris; the bottom of the iris sits on the lower lid; the top lid is darker than the lower lid; the inside lid gets lost as it merges with the socket cavity next to the nose. Crimson is used here for the darks.

▽ The distance between the eyes is approximately the width of an eye. The second eye here is on the lighter side of the face so, though the shapes may be similar, the treatment is not a repeat of the first eye.

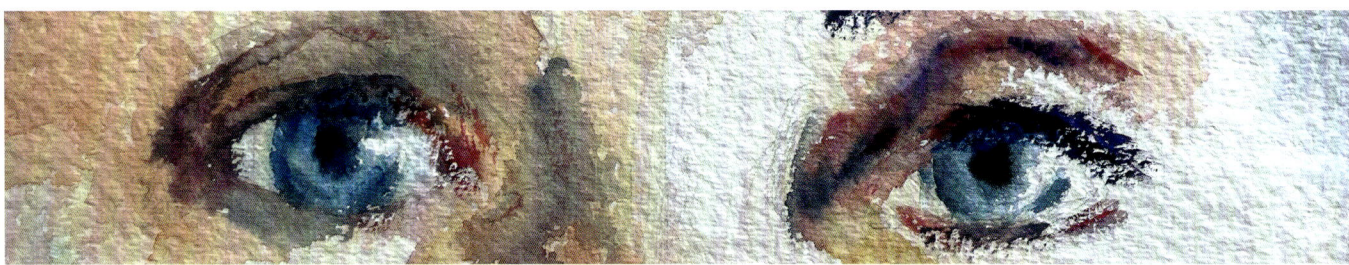

The nose

To measure the length of the nose, compare it with the width of the eyes. From the front, the nose is created with shadow and highlight; only as it turns toward the profile does its outline become distinct. The nostrils point towards each other and can be painted quite dark, set softly in the shadow under the tip of the nose, which is usually the lightest part.

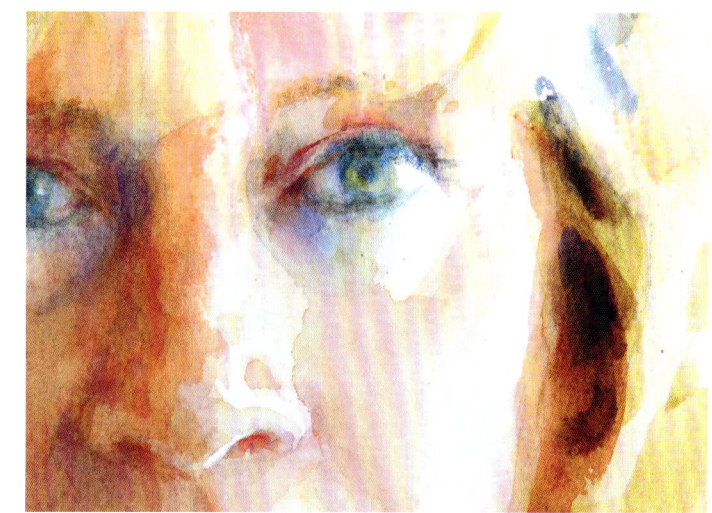

▷ △ A difference between the amount of light and shade on each side of the face makes it easier to use tone to sculpt the shape of the nose.

▷ In this three-quarter view, the line of the nose becomes more apparent.

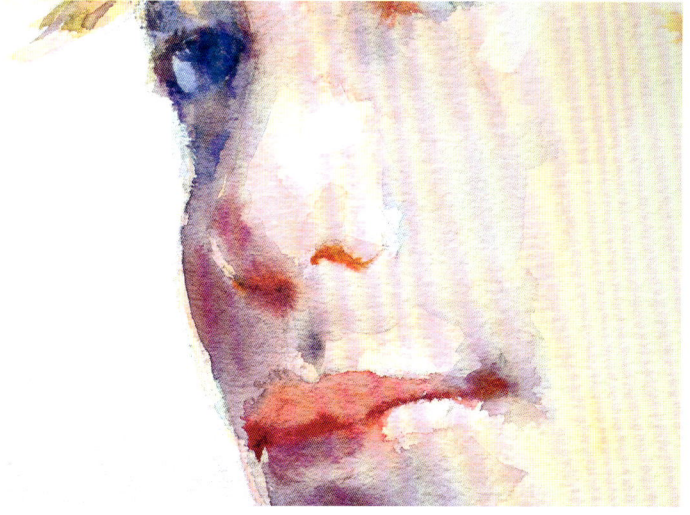

The mouth

It is easier to paint the mouth closed, with a relaxed expression. The lips follow a curve and are rounded, not flat. Begin with the contour line between the lips for both positioning and expression – tilting up the corners hints at a smile – then add the upper and lower lips. The form of the mouth is created with light and shade.

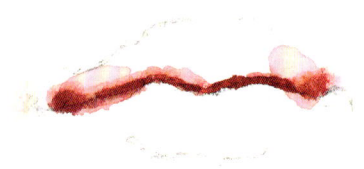

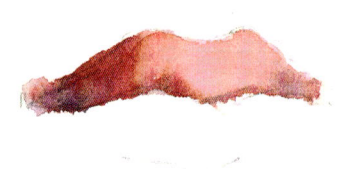

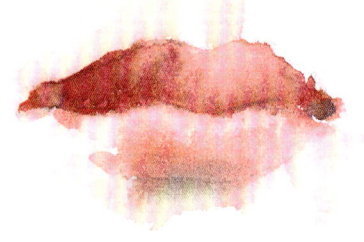

△ Mark the line where the two lips meet and end the corners of the mouth in soft indented shadows beneath the cheeks.

△ Shape the top lip, which is usually shaded, and will be darker on the non-lit side.

△ Shape the rounded lower lip, lighter in tone than the upper lip. The cleft above the lips is indented – the dip can be shown with light and shade.

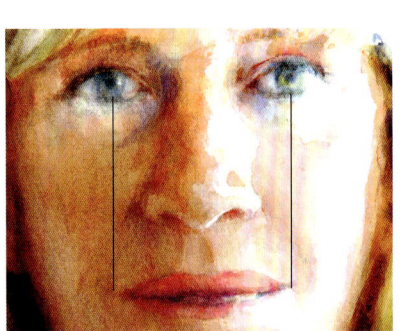

◁ To establish the exact position of the corners of the mouth, drop imaginary lines down from the middle of each eye.

The hair

The hair should look as if it belongs to the head, not added like a wig. While it consists of myriad fine strands, overall the hair is three-dimensional. Rather than paint individual hairs, look for sections, main clusters of strands, overlaps and the shadows between. Show where hair and face meet in a 'lost and found' fashion, varying between lights and darks and hard and soft edges: in some places there will be no contrast, in others the contrast will be stark. Half-close your eyes to limit yourself to the important lights and darks.

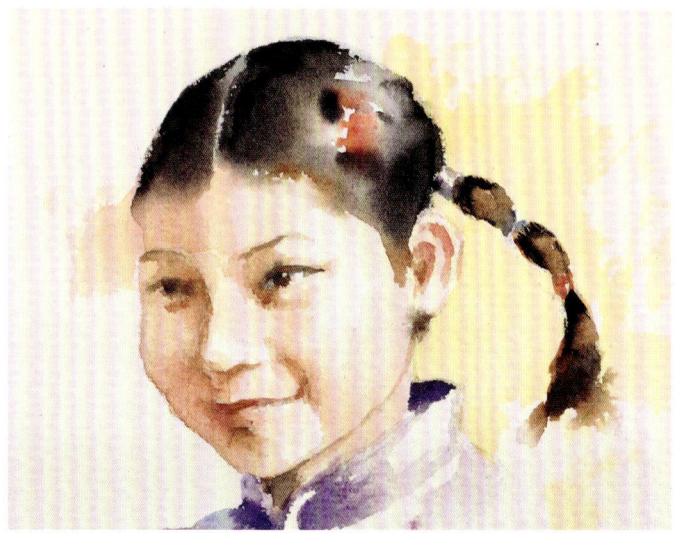

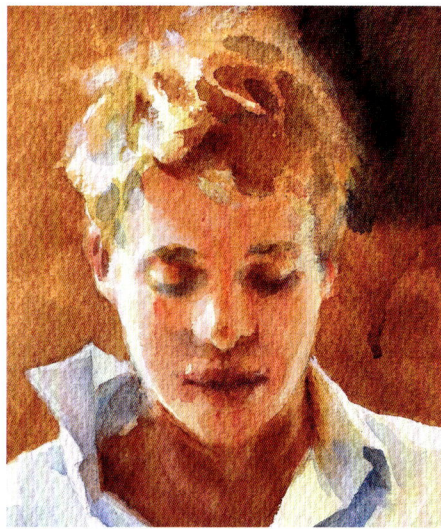

◁ Rather than overcrowd the hair with a lot of detail, the main contrasts of light and shade build the form.

△ Even though the girl's hair colour is much darker than her skin tone, the connection is not abrupt. The hair is darkest where it meets highlit parts of the face and transitions gently in shadow.

Demonstration: Portrait of Ulene

In order to focus, do not fret about catching a likeness. Instead, concentrate on rendering lines, shapes, light and shadow by measuring and comparing as carefully as possible, then a likeness should result by default. Stop, step back from your work and check it against your sitter. Resist the temptation to correct or tidy up the portrait unnecessarily. When you catch the likeness it may register as a visual jolt or a moment of recognition.

Colours

Alizarin Crimson

Burnt Sienna

Permanent Rose

Sap Green

Sepia

Ultramarine Blue

Violet

Yellow Ochre

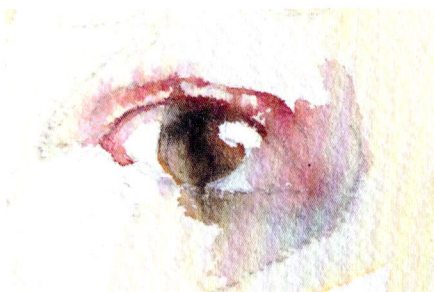

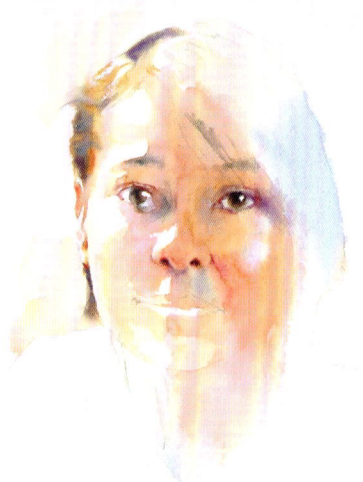

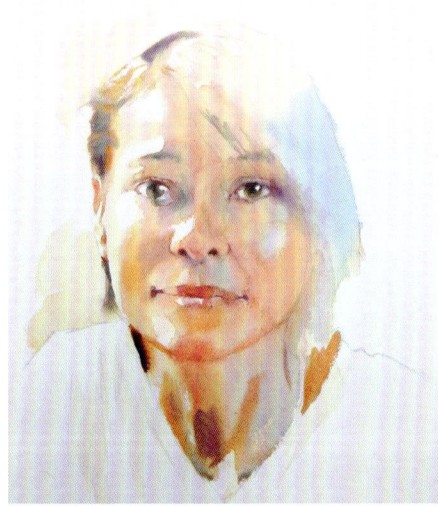

Stage 1: Over a pencil drawing and pale Yellow Ochre undertone, I began detail with the eyes, using Alizarin Crimson to mark in the eyelids and Sepia for the iris.

Stage 2: I used Burnt Sienna as the primary skin tone, building to a darker tone on the shadier side of the face. Then I introduced more warmth with Alizarin Crimson.

Stage 3: I painted the upper and lower lips with Alizarin Crimson, paying close attention to the change of tone from side to side and on the top and bottom lip.

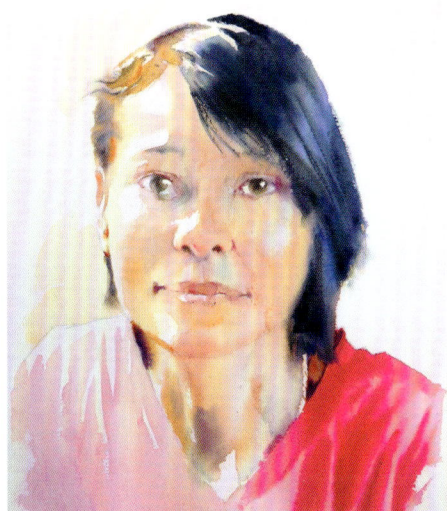

Stage 4: The next step was to introduce the vibrant colours and deep tones of the hair and T-shirt wet in wet, with concentrated colour added into dilute washes. I mixed Ultramarine Blue and Sepia for the black of the hair and used Permanent Rose neat for the shirt.

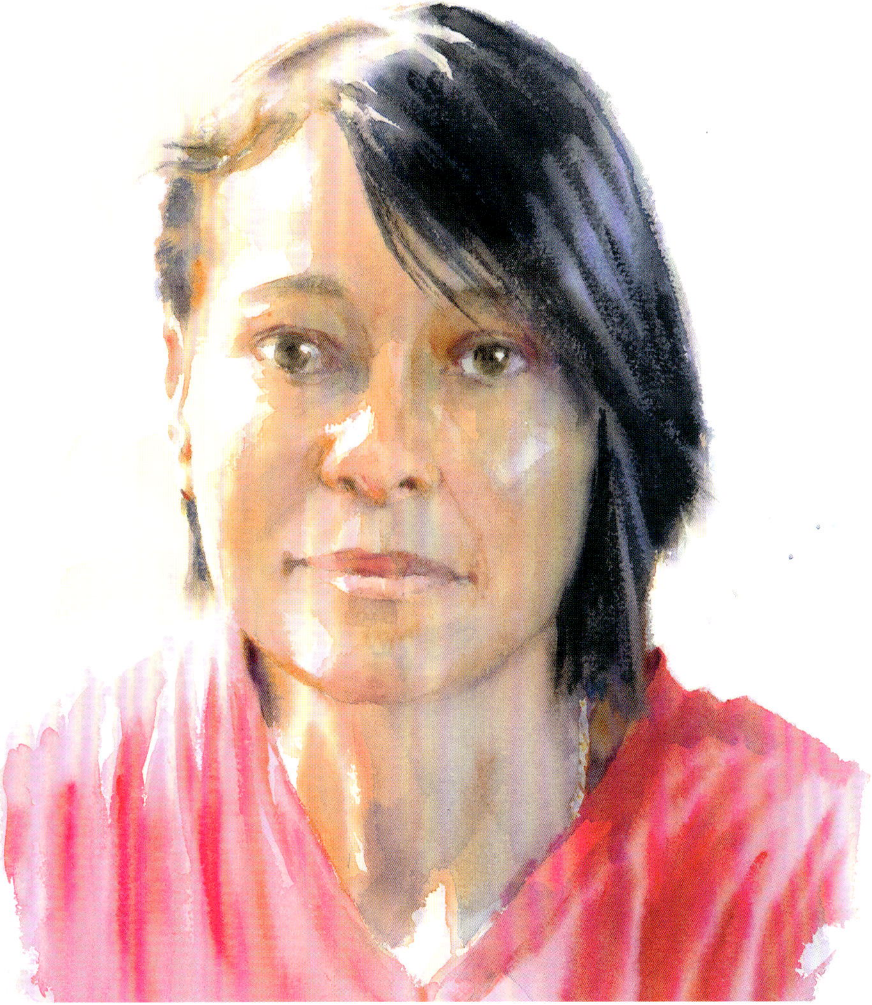

Ulene *51 x 41cm (20 x 16in)*

Final Stage: I brushed a pale blue wash gently over the shaded side of the head, neck and shirt and deepened the eye sockets. As I evened out the pink on the lower lip the 'hello' moment happened and knew I had caught Ulene's likeness.

Folds and creases

There is no doubt that folds and creases in fabric are two of the chief delights of painting clothes. The reason is simple: they create patterns of alternating light and shade, and this tonal variation is very satisfying to behold and to paint.

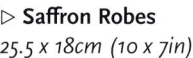

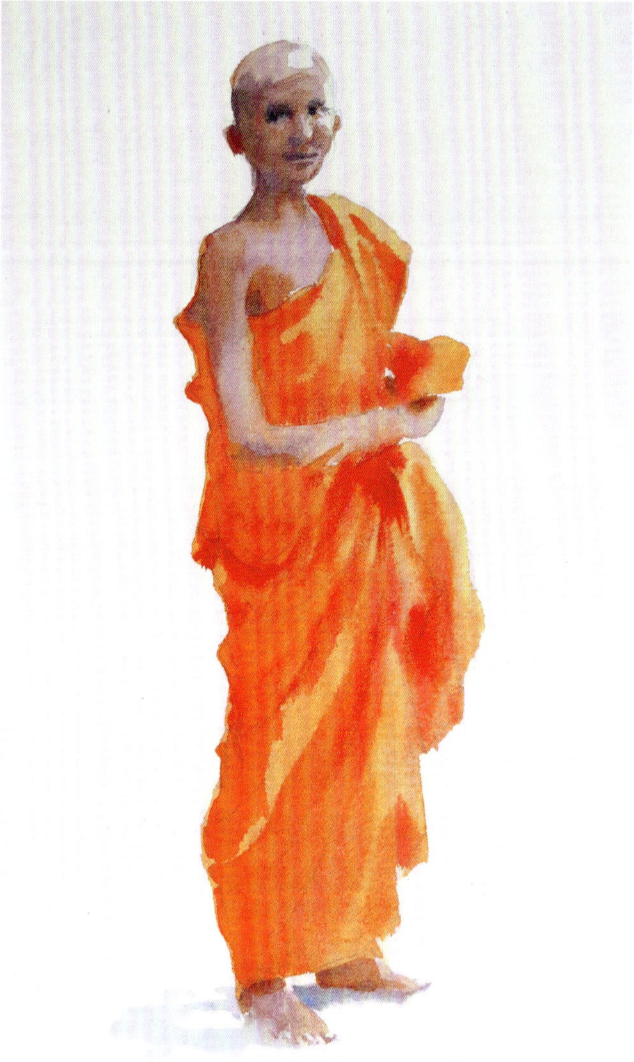

▷ **Saffron Robes**
25.5 x 18cm (10 x 7in)
The wet-into-wet technique of watercolour makes representing folds a quick process. I painted the robe with pale orange and then, along the line of the fold shadows, added more concentrated pigment into the damp wash. The paint spread out gently, creating effortless gradations in tone.

Patterns and logos

Unless it is the detail of a pattern that excites you, pattern may seem like too much intricacy to manage. However, patterns do bring richness and texture to a painting and are fun to paint. The secret lies in 'less is more'. You do not have to imitate the pattern – including a fragment is enough for the viewer to imagine the existence of much more. Just place a dab here, a touch there, to show some of the arrangement, ensuring that the pattern follows the folding of the fabric so that it plays its part in creating form. Let it lose itself in the shadow, be revealed in the mid-tones and fade in the light. The same applies to logos – limit your marks to mere suggestions and the viewer's eye will fill in the rest.

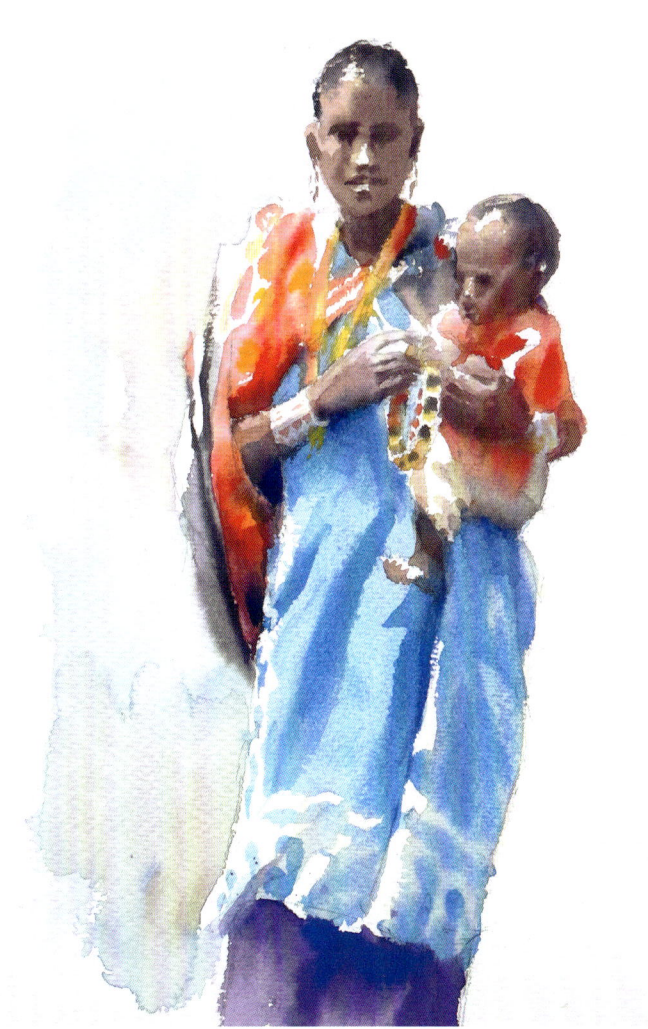

▷ **Maasai Mother and Child**

38 x 28cm (15 x 11in)

Maasai fabrics are highly patterned, but I was more interested in the movement of the fabric than the precise pattern, so it is generalized and simplified in order to paint it quickly.

Using stripes

Striped fabric is really useful to the artist. With just an indication of direction, stripes can deftly describe the form of a limb or torso and the angle of a pose. Like pattern, stripes are subservient to the rolling folds and creases. Allow them to get lost and found in the undulating landscape of the fabric.

◁ **Learning the Ropes** *56 x 76cm (22 x 30in)*

◁ The mere indication of pink stripes on the cowboy's shirt is enough to describe the form and position of the arms and body and allows the rest of the figure to be rendered loosely to enhance the sense of action.

A few stripes are enough to show their general width and direction. There is no need to show every stripe – too much information will stifle liveliness.

Blending, blur and separation

While clothing is enjoyable to paint, it can become overcomplicated by details, patterns and folds. The best way to find the information that matters to the painting is to observe the subject through half-closed eyes; you will find that the meaningful tones remain distinct while the minor variants vanish.

Colours lose distinction when a figure is in motion. By blurring detail and encouraging ambiguity, you can impart a sense of energy and movement to the figure. Paradoxically, lessening definition usually makes clothing appear more life-like than showing every detail. In general, aim for definition in the lighter mid-tones and softening in the shadows.

▷ The man's red jacket and dark trousers blend completely together in the shade covering his back.

▷ ▷ In these back- and side-lit figures the definition between different colours and the keen difference in tone between faces and clothing is softened by blending.

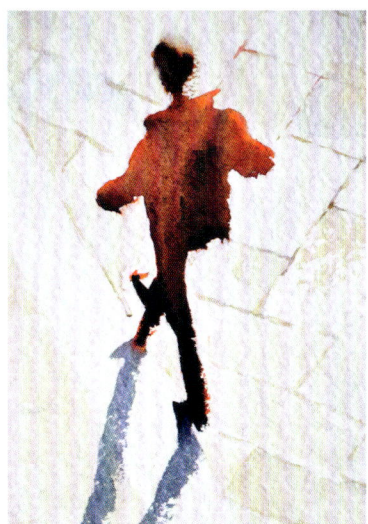
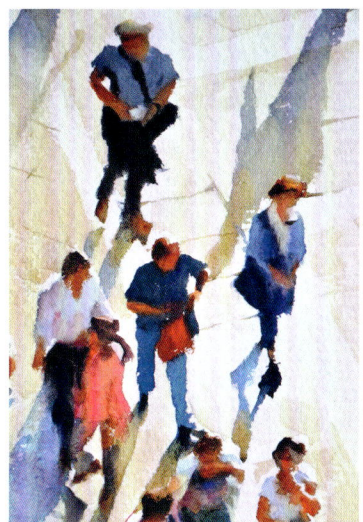
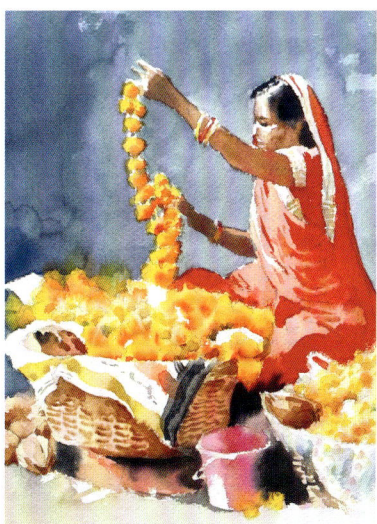

Accessories

Giving a figure something to hold adds interest to the shape and gives narrative to the pose. Bags, umbrellas, books and so forth are helpful accessories, so take advantage of them whenever you can.

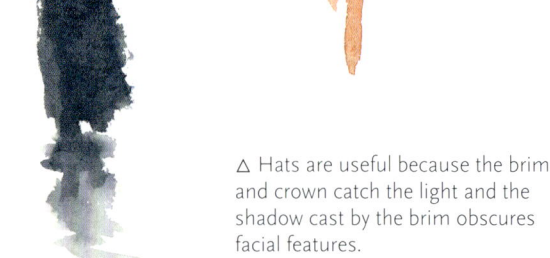

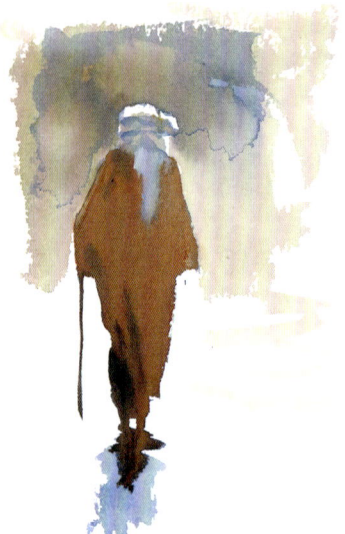

△ The addition of the stick adds a story to the old man's pose.

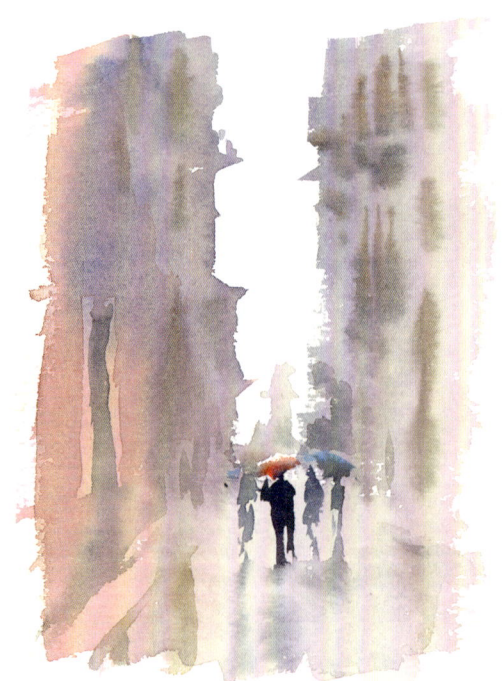

△ Hats are useful because the brim and crown catch the light and the shadow cast by the brim obscures facial features.

◁ △ Umbrellas bring colour and tonal contrast. They are lit on top and cast shade underneath.

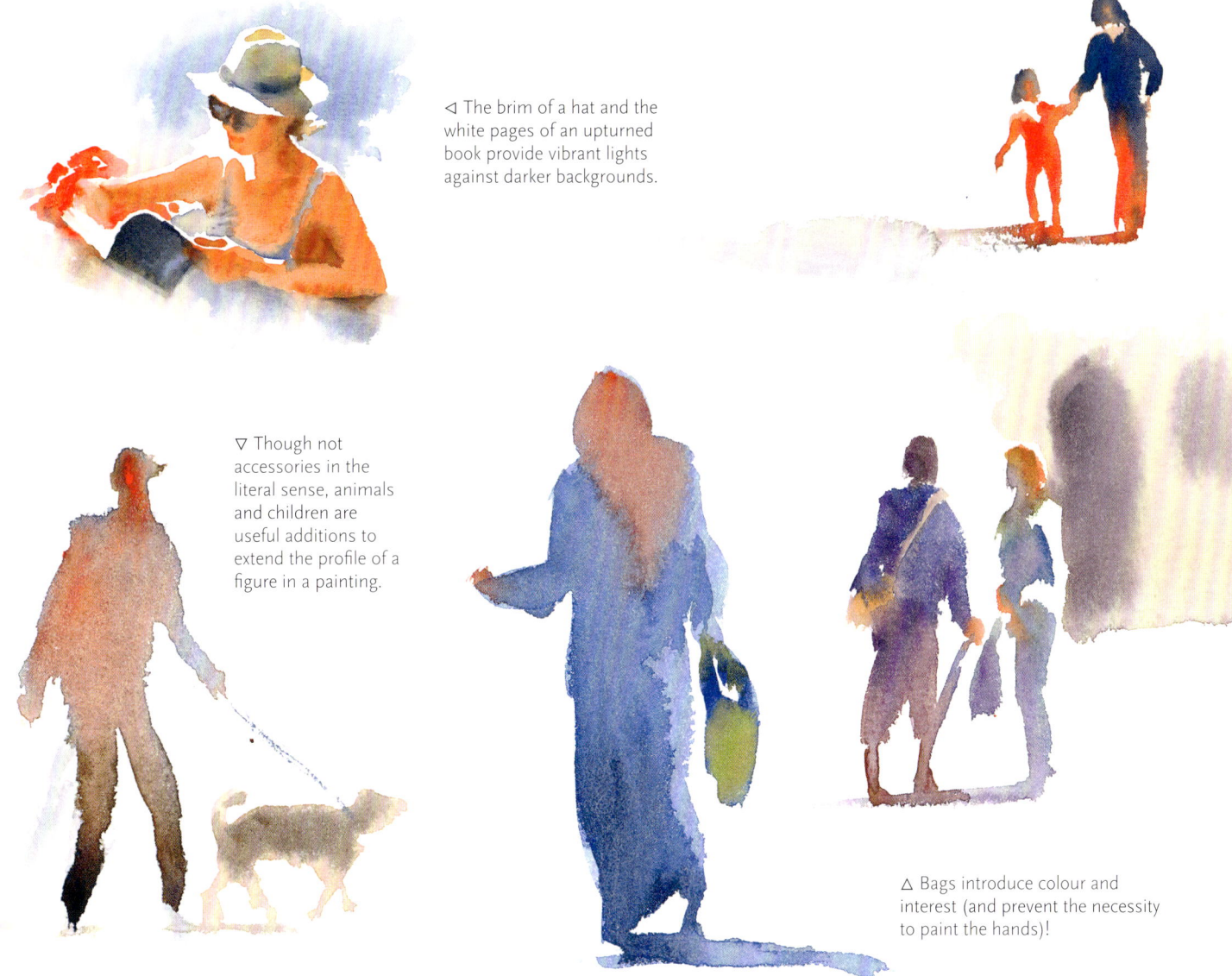

◁ The brim of a hat and the white pages of an upturned book provide vibrant lights against darker backgrounds.

▽ Though not accessories in the literal sense, animals and children are useful additions to extend the profile of a figure in a painting.

△ Bags introduce colour and interest (and prevent the necessity to paint the hands)!

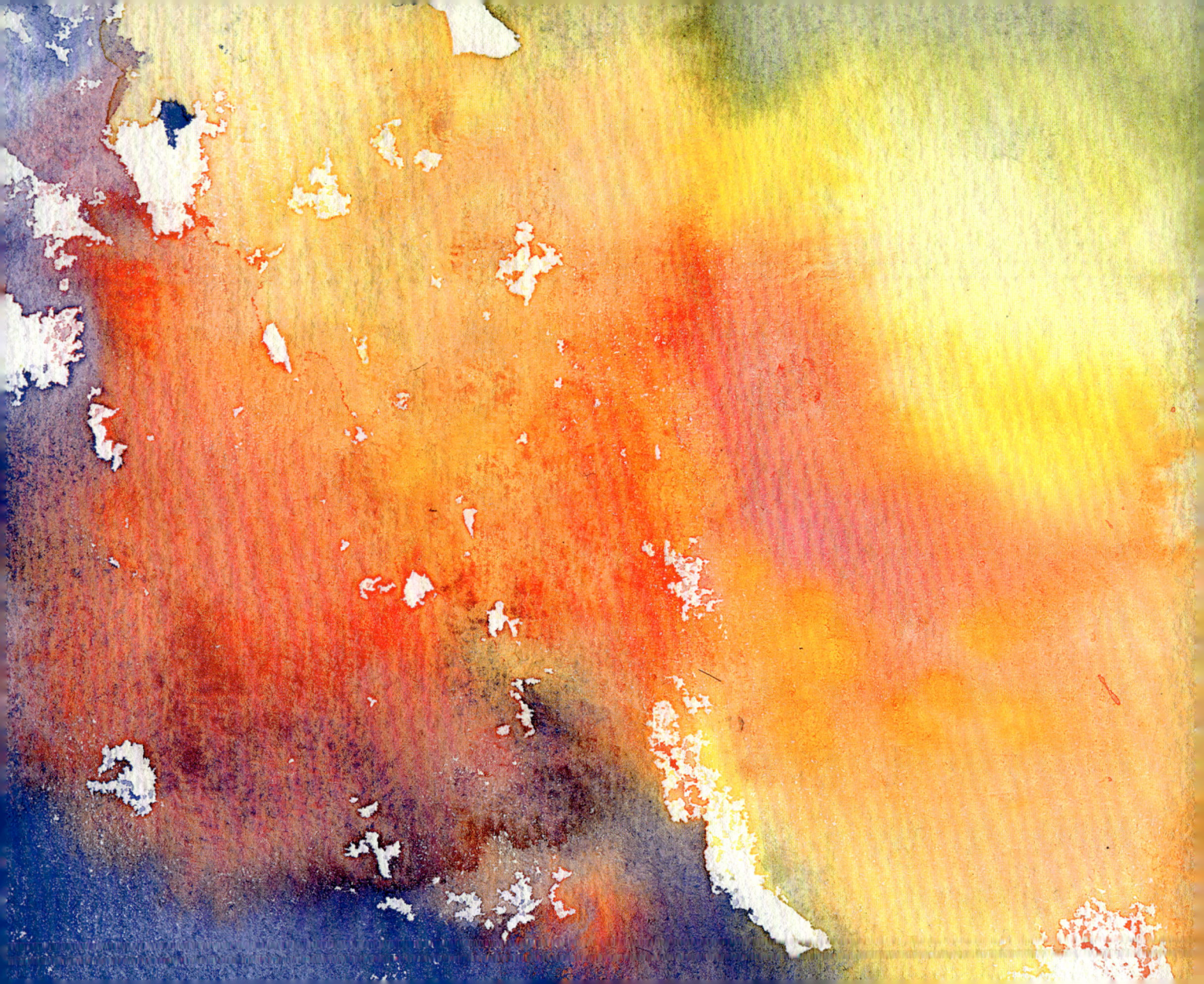

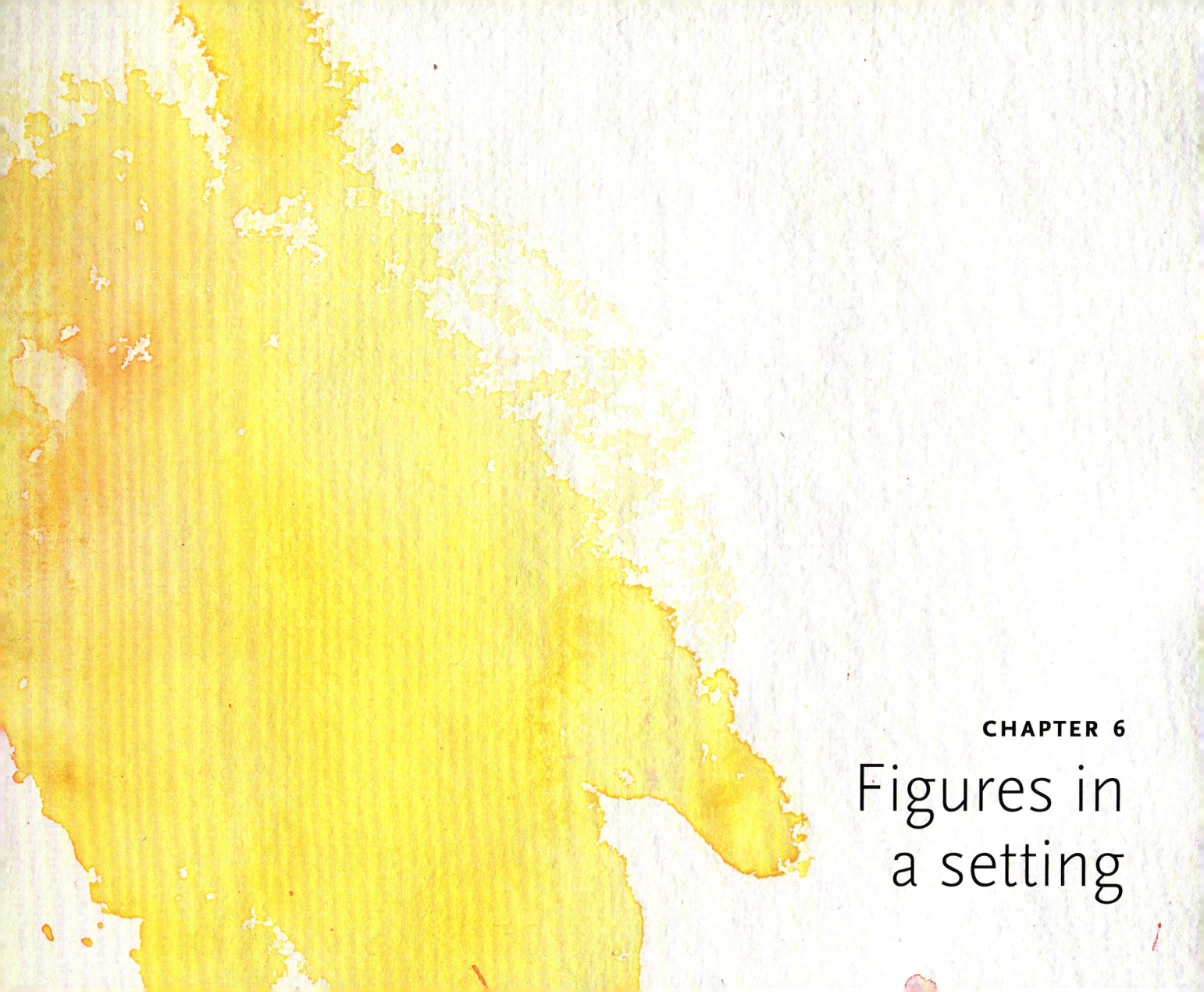

CHAPTER 6

Figures in a setting

Figures in the landscape

This chapter looks at placing figures in settings in lively, meaningful and accomplished ways more comprehensively than we touched on in the landscape section. Although the figures may be fairly small within the whole composition, and detail limited, it is crucial to keep in mind proportion, pose, lighting and colouring.

▷ **Passage of Time**
20 x 28cm (8 x 11in)

In this watercolour the figures, being darker than their background, could be painted on top to provide meaning and narrative to a simple setting.

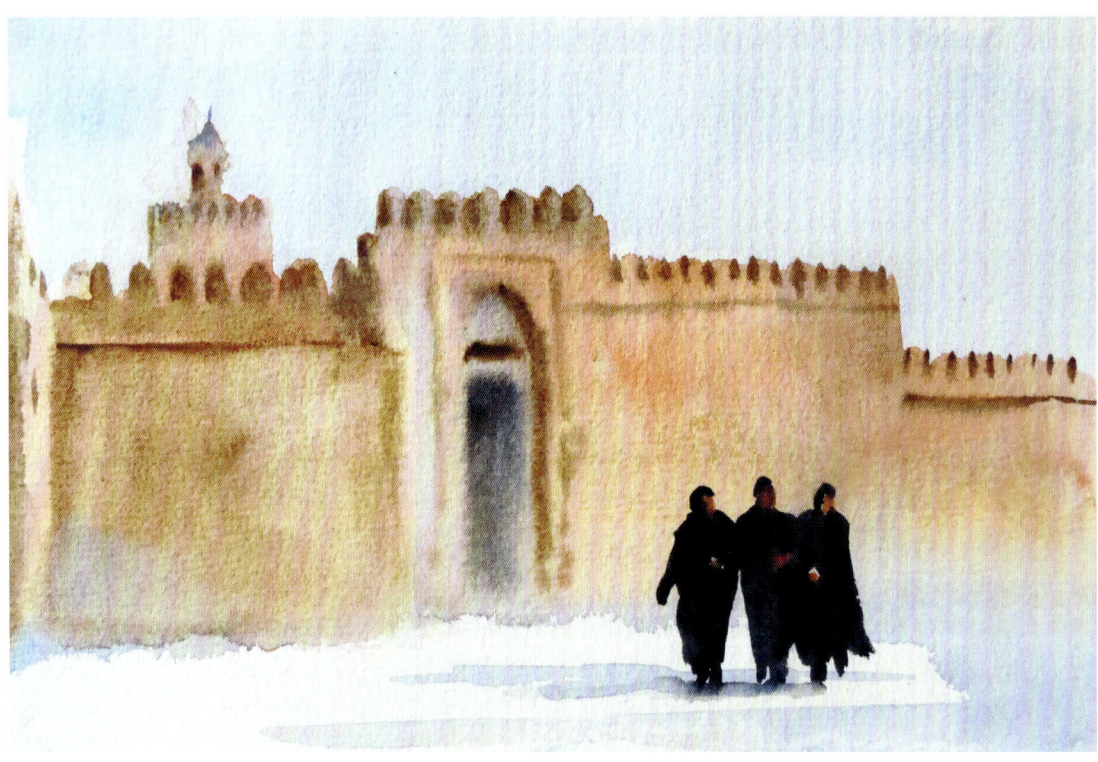

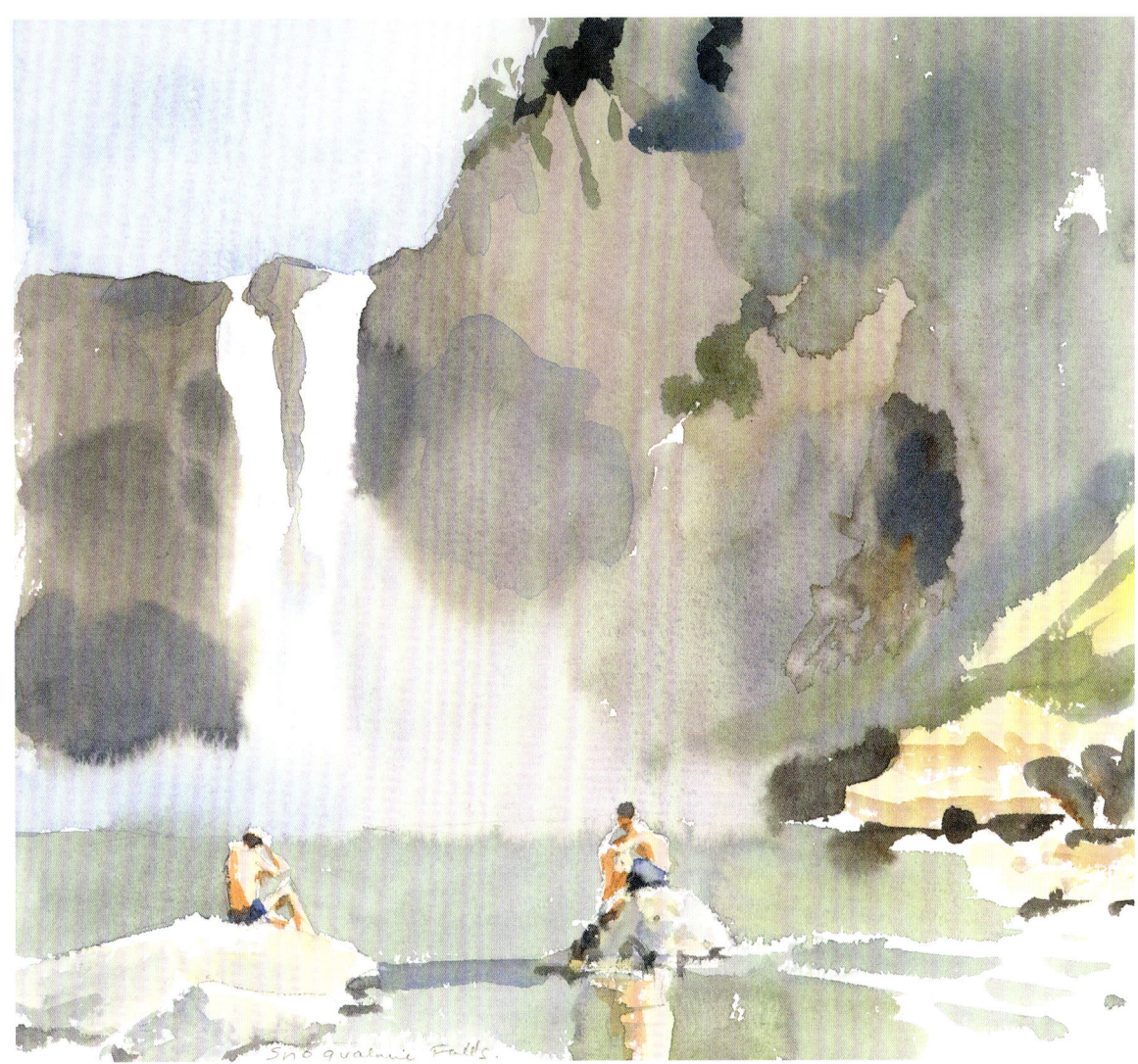

▷ **Beneath Snoqualmie Falls**
25.5 x 28cm (10 x 11in)

The figures here provide the scale that shows the height of the waterfall. As the sunlit bodies are paler than the background pool, I sketched them in pencil first to guide the wash of green around them.

Snoqualmie Falls.

At the beach

Some of the best figure-painting opportunities can be found at the beach, as people relax into poses unencumbered by heavy clothing. The presence of a figure brings paintings of wide open or empty shorelines instantly to life.

▽ ▷ All you need are a few well-placed brushstrokes to indicate people in action and give a storyline to a simple scene, as can be seen in these three watercolours painted by the sea.

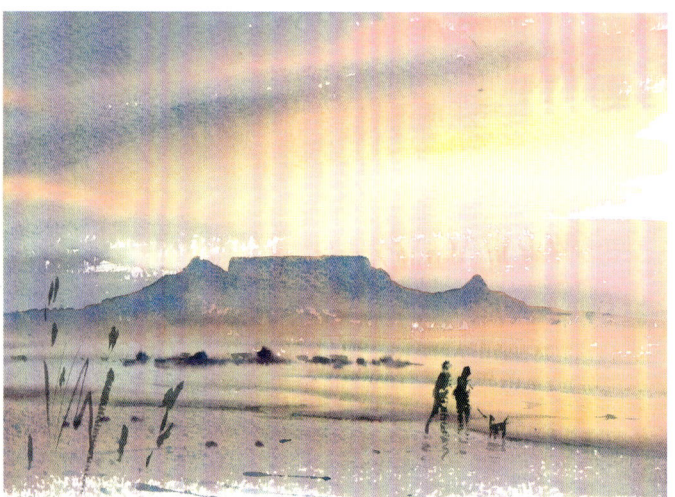

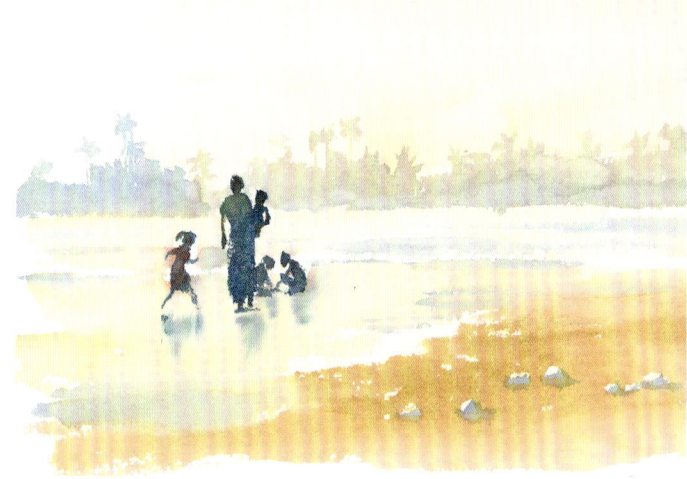

Street life

Manmade landscapes benefit hugely from the inclusion of people: streets come alive when they are populated and comparison reinforces the scale of buildings. The more figures you include in the scene the less you have to worry about the definition of each one, so there is definitely safety in numbers! Place dark figures against lighter backgrounds and vice versa. Be aware of perspective and the correlation in diminishing size between the figures and the buildings, cars and other things.

▷ In this painting a crowd is readily understood, even though little definition is offered in the sparsely indicated distant figures.

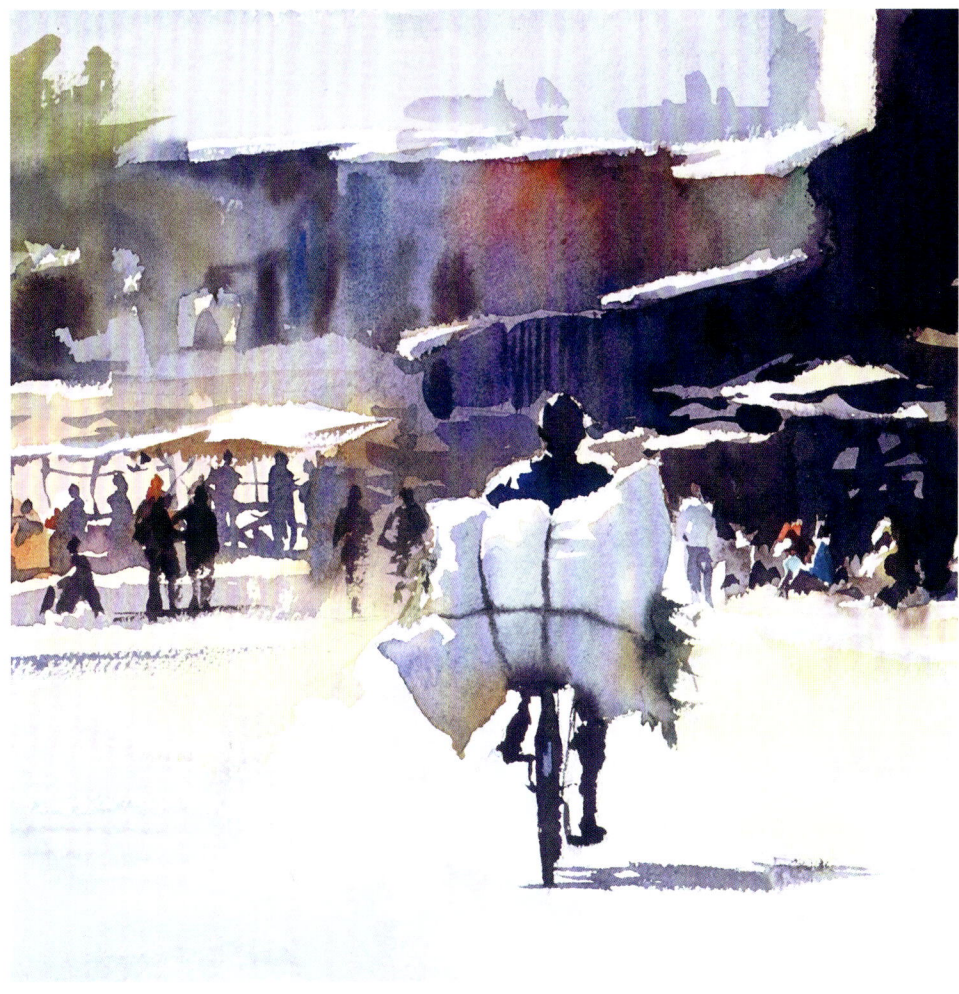

Pedal Power *20 x 20cm (8 x 8in)*

Café scenes

Figures in cafés and restaurants make popular painting subjects. Not only do they provide interactive sitting and standing poses, but the tops of tables are often lit and the chair legs beneath are in shadow, offering the painter both variety of stance and lively exchanges between light and shade.

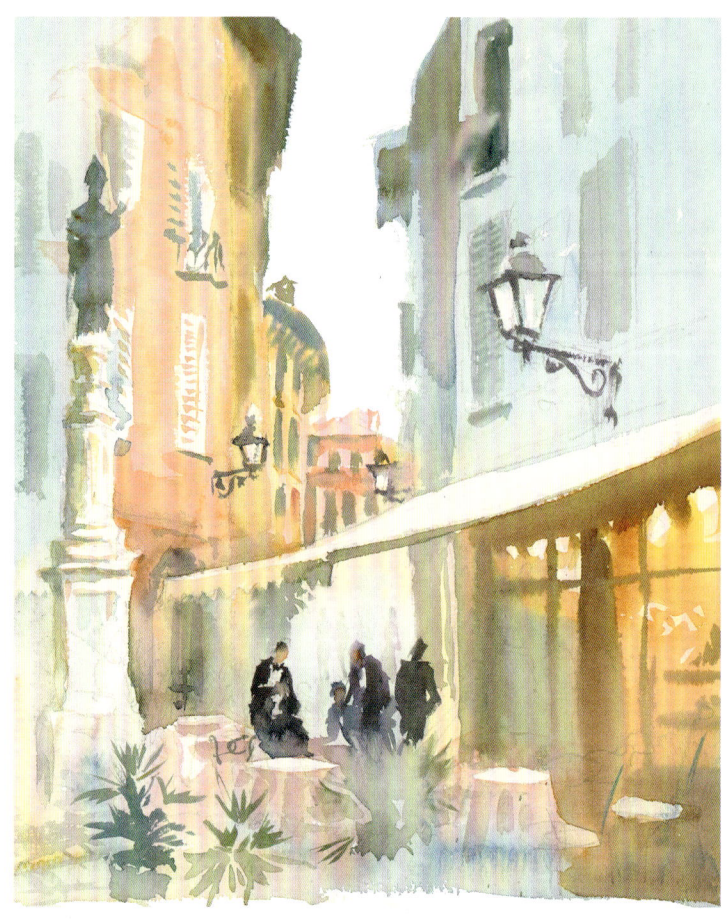

◁ △ In these details you can see how the looseness of the brushmarks makes the figures appear lively, whether they are seated or serving at tables.

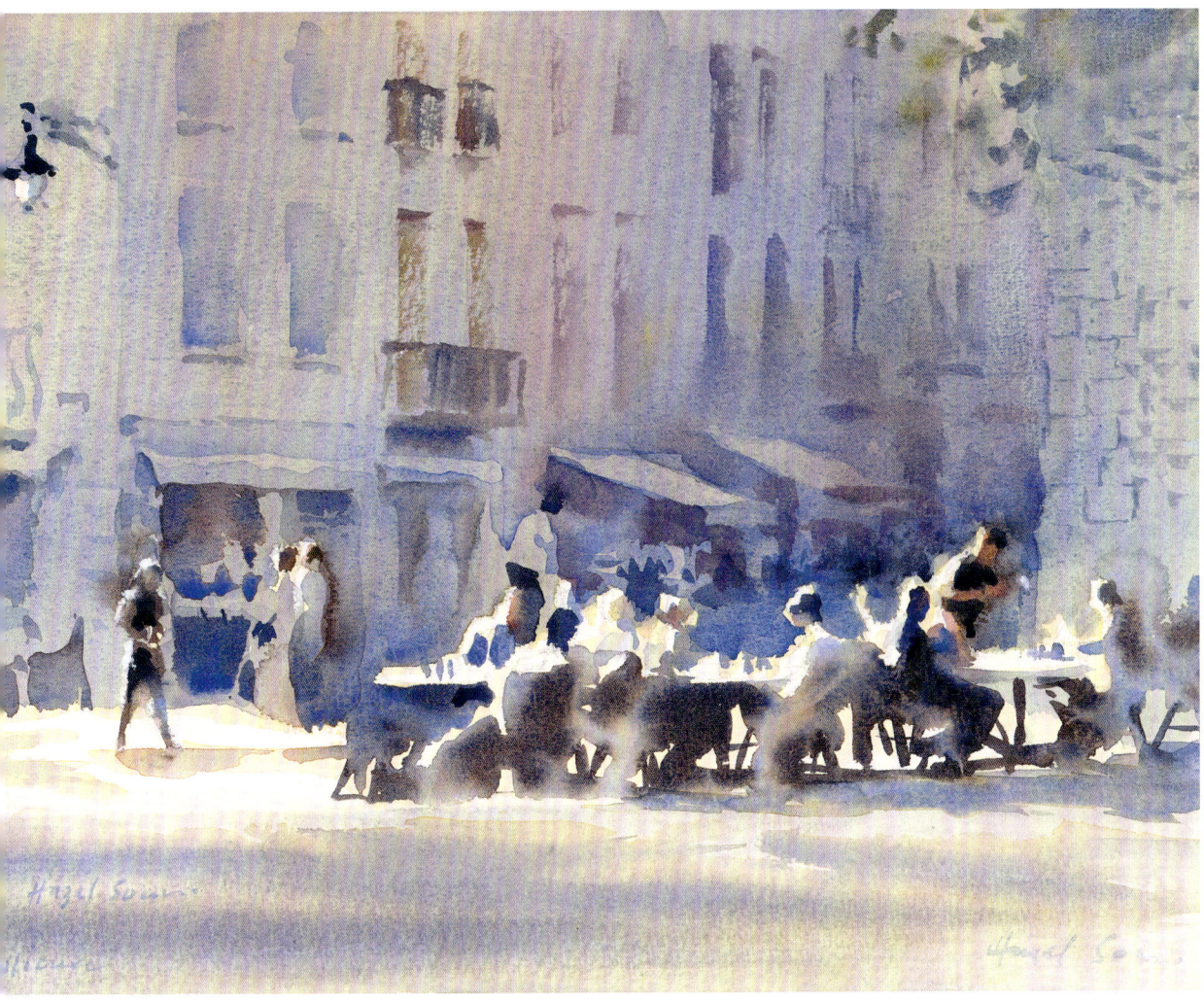

◁ **Al Fresco**
25.5 x 35.5cm
(10 x 14in)
With only a few colours
the semblance of a
busy street café is
created with blobs
and brushstrokes in a
range of tones, from
untouched white paper
highlights through
mid-tones to the dark
undersides of tables
and chairs.

Demonstration: An interior scene

A restored diner on Route 66 provides a perfect setting for a painting inspired by Edward Hopper. The bright light outside casts the diner into warm, dark shadow and highlights the solitary woman in the window.

Colours

Burnt Umber

Cadmium Red

Light Red

Ultramarine Blue

Yellow Ochre

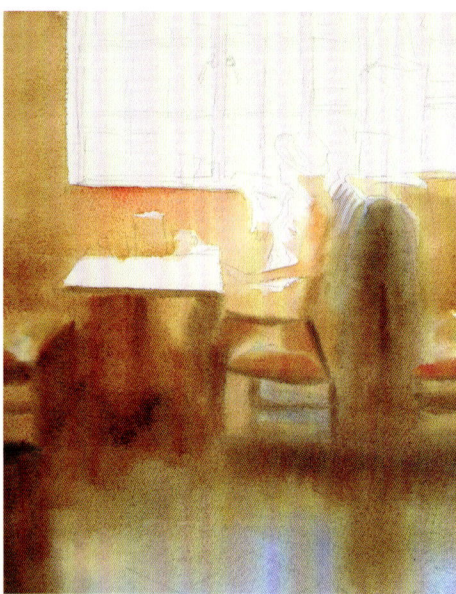

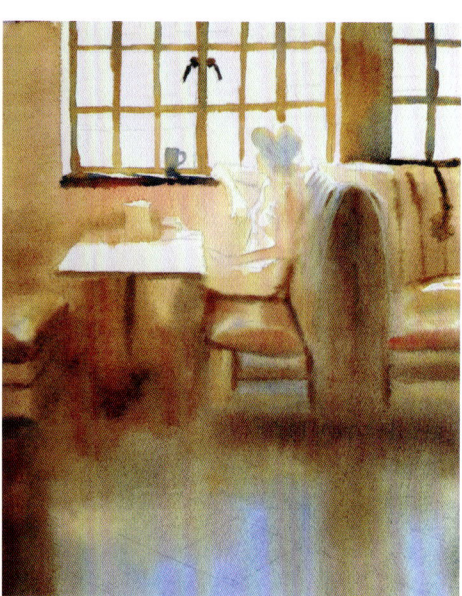

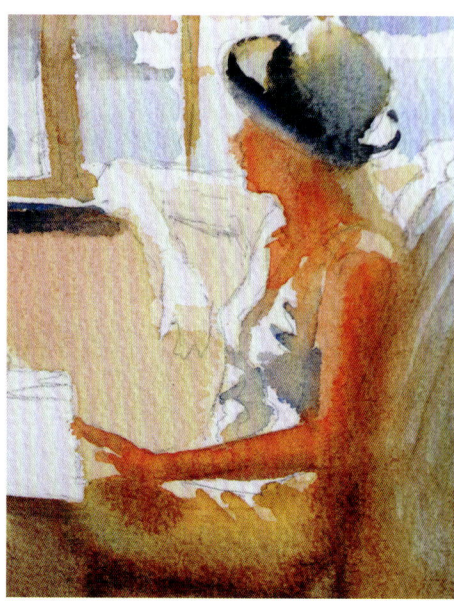

Stage 1: After mapping out the composition with a pale Yellow Ochre and Ultramarine Blue undertone, I deepened the shadowed interior with a more concentrated Yellow Ochre and Burnt Umber wash.

Stage 2: The criss-cross of the window frames and the pattern of light and shade on the figure complete the tonal pattern of the composition.

Stage 3 (detail): I strengthened the skin tones in shadow with concentrated Light Red. The limbs are blended with the bench cushions while darker proximity shadows show where the body makes contact.

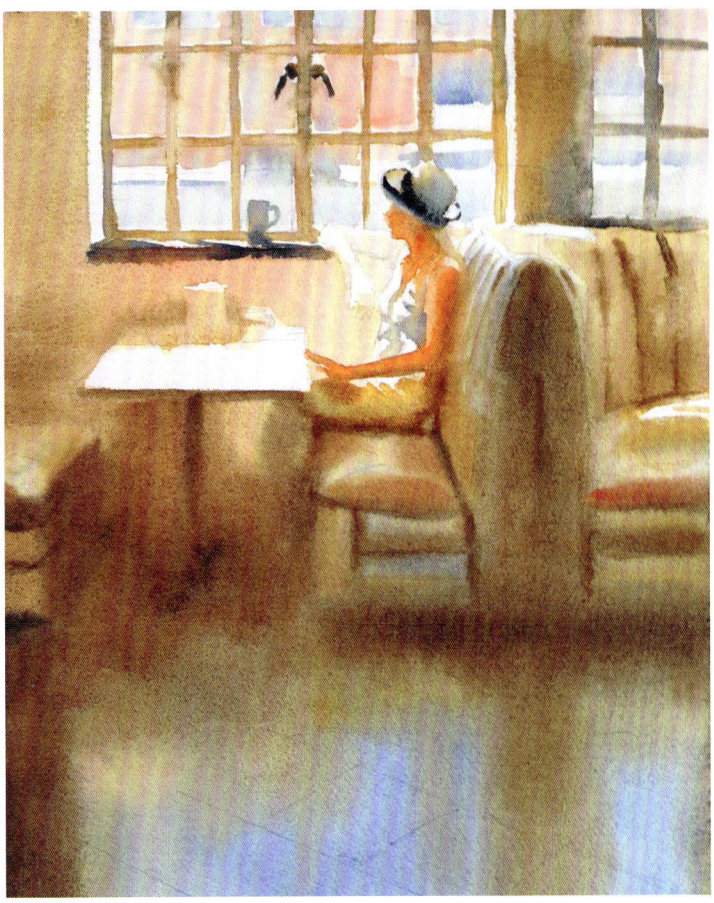

Stage 4: The introduction of the mid-tone buildings seen through the window helps to bring out the main focus, which is the light on the figure, and introduces warmth.

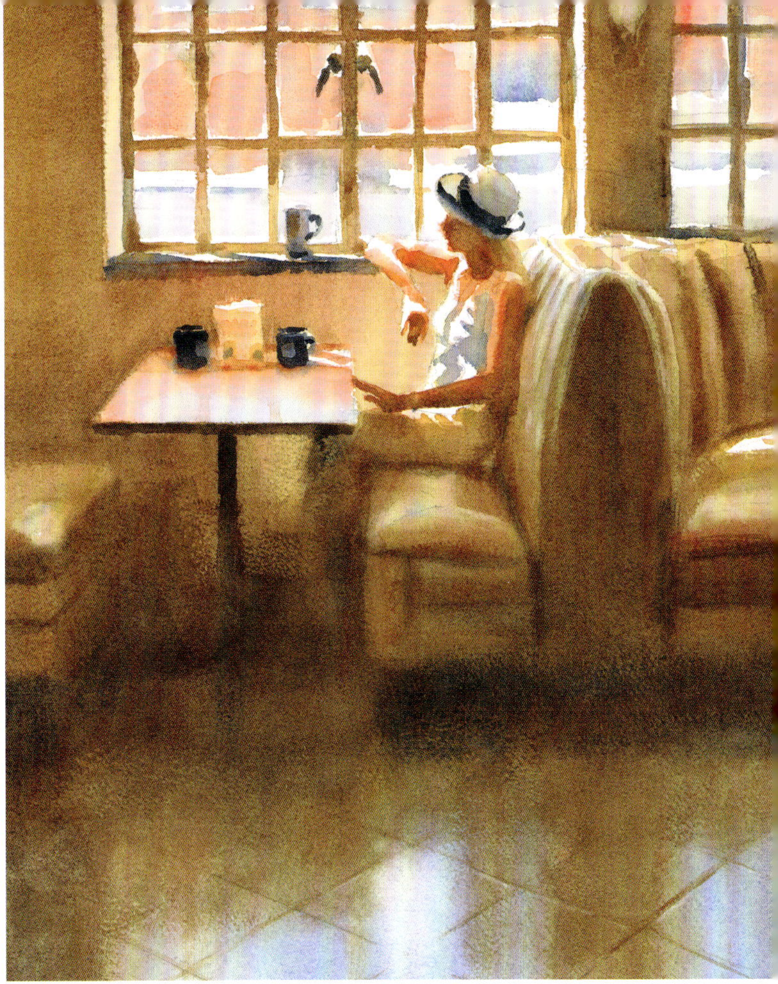

Diner

30.5 x 41cm (12 x 16in)

Final Stage: I strengthened all the shadows with Burnt Umber and a little Ultramarine Blue to enhance the light on the woman by greater contrast of tone. The chequerboard tile lines complete the picture.

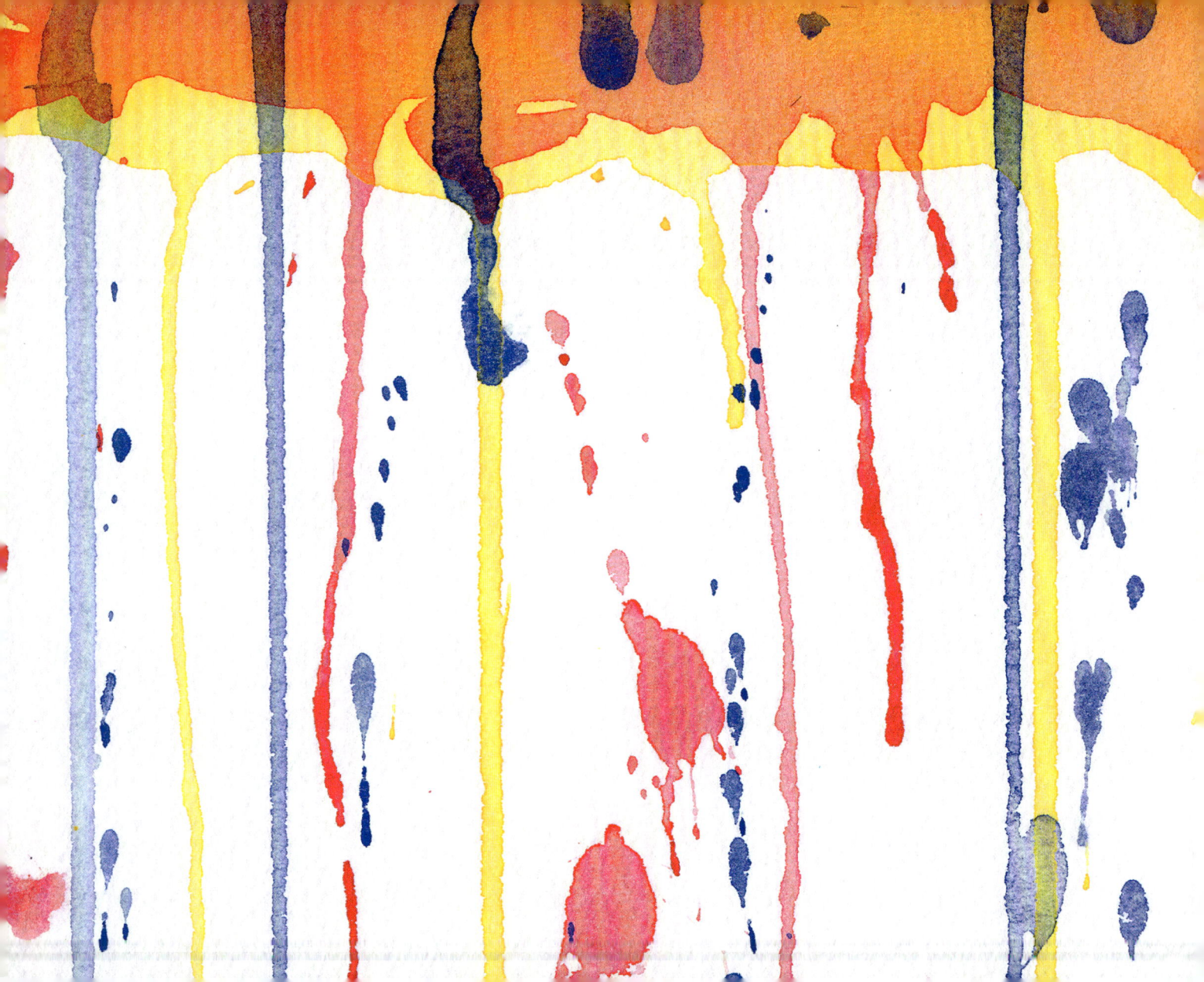

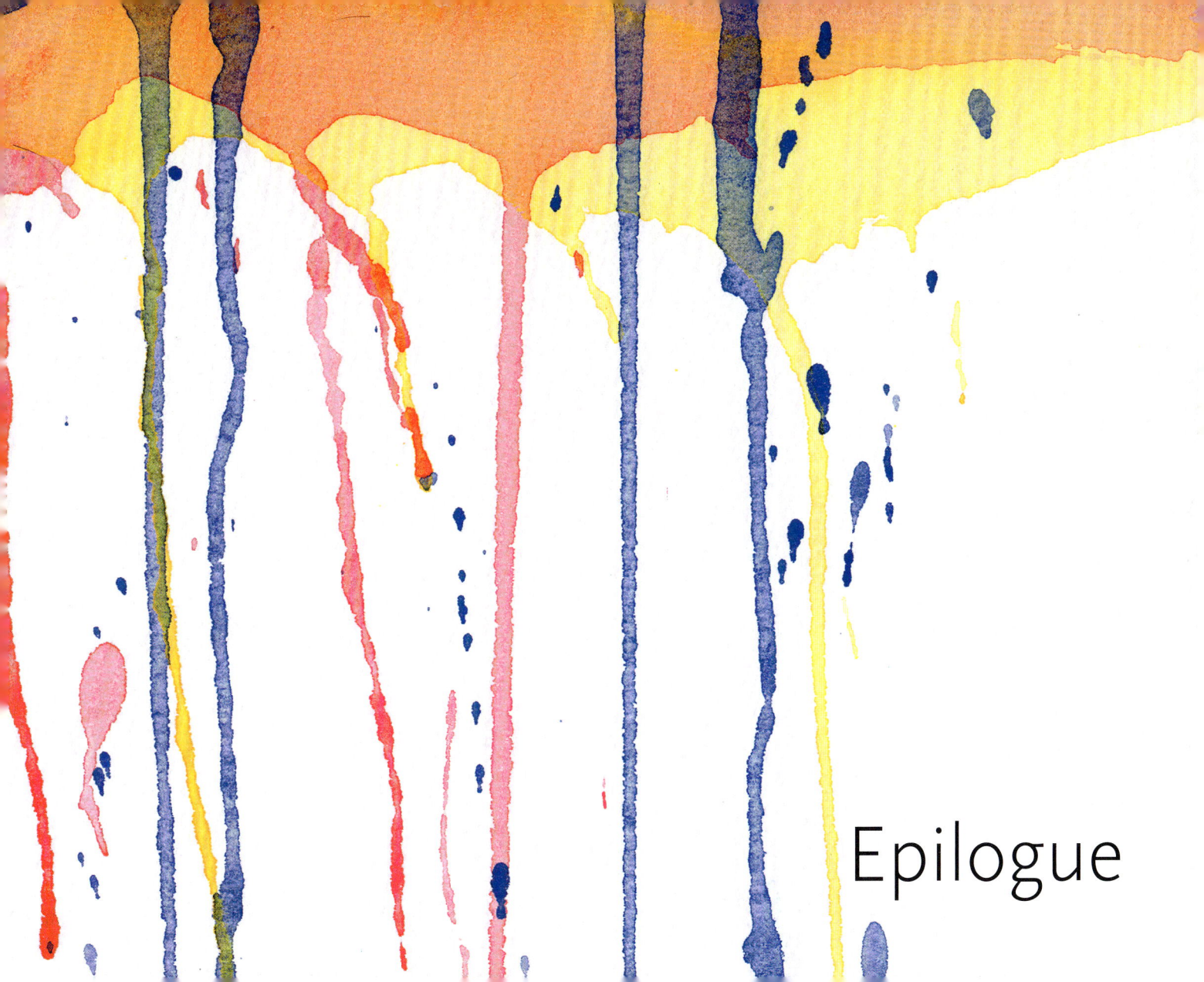

Epilogue

Painting is fun!

Painting in watercolour is an exciting challenge, and you are obviously up for it because you have reached the end of the book! Practice is everything: the more you paint, the more confident you will become. Congratulate yourself proudly when you succeed, forgive yourself quickly if you fail. Soon you will be painting in an accomplished and convincing manner, and you'll be having fun and unleashing your innate creativity along the way.

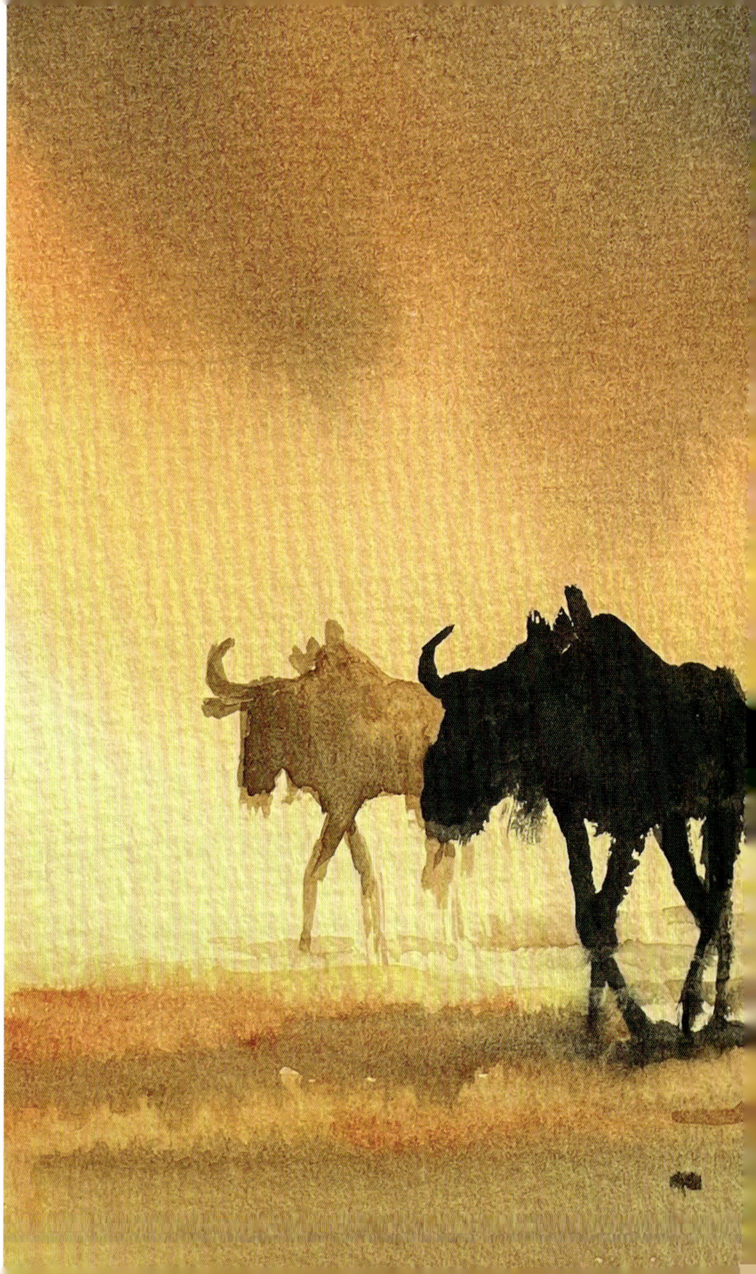

Rising Dust
18 x 28cm (7 x 11in)
Watercolour painting is a journey: each painting presents an interim destination, like the waterhole to which these wildebeest are headed. It is an exciting adventure that can take you in any direction and to unexpected places. Best of all, it can be enjoyed throughout your whole life.

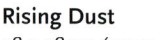

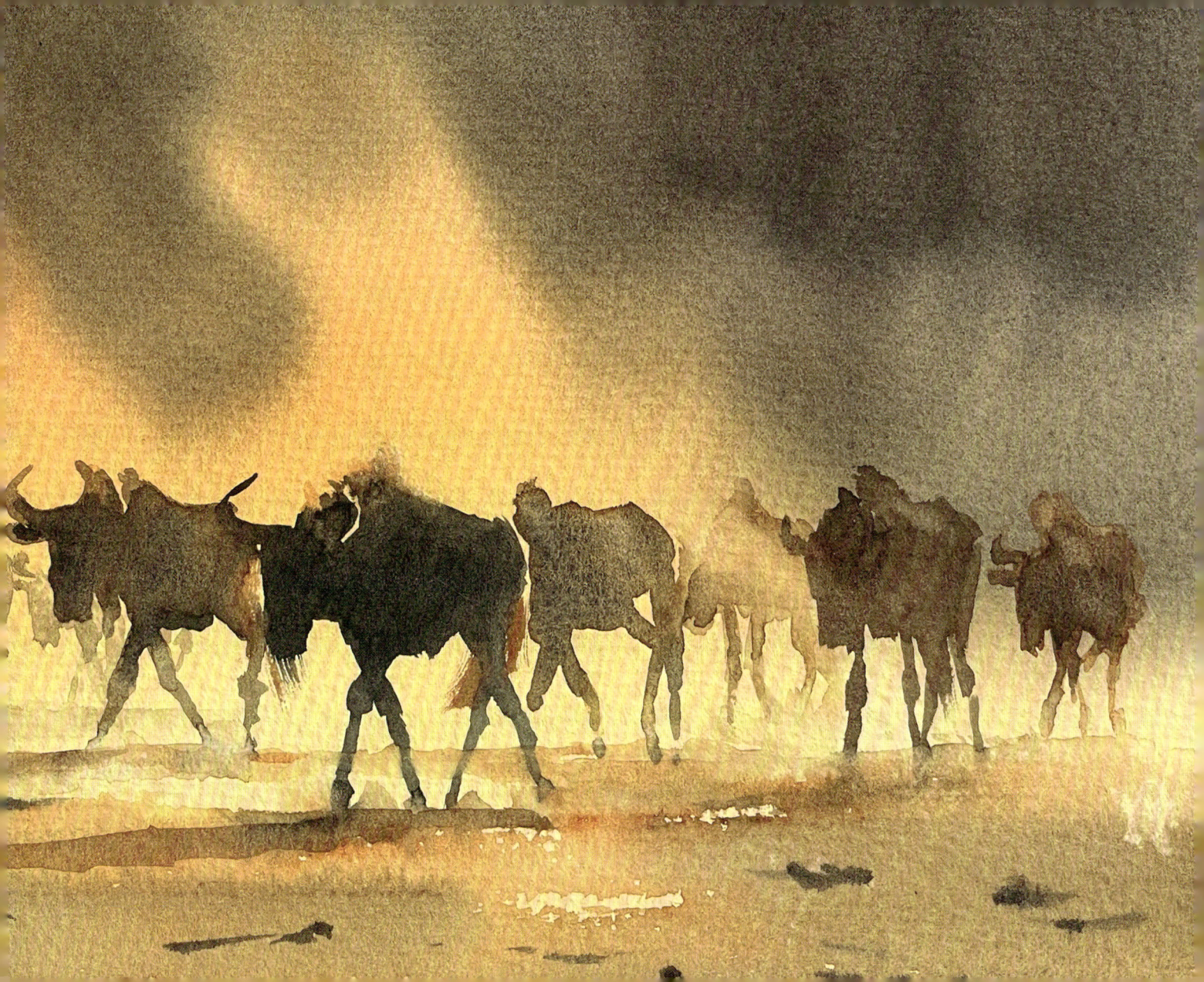

Index

positive brushstrokes 179, 205
primary colours 34–5, 38, 46, 167
profiles 243
proportion
    figures 236–47, 250
    foreshortening 247
    form 106
    size 236–41, 246–7
    subject choice 90
putty rubbers 30

rags 30
red 134, 142–3, 174–5, 209
representation, likeness 232, 242,
    274, 280
riggers 24
rivers 200–1
rough paper 29
round brushes 24, 54–5
rounded forms 100
rule of thirds 108, 109, 149
running *see* movement

salt crystals 205
scale 130–1, 140, 157, 213, 246
scratching off 87, 191
sea 206–7
secondary colours 36–7,
    38

shade/shadow
    balance 152–3
    faces 242–3
    light source 163, 260
    paint compared to light of
      paper 15
    proximity shadow 254–5, 296
    space and depth 102
    subject choice 90, 96–7
shape
    brushmarks 233
    figures, movement 253
    subject choice 90, 92–4
shoreline 206–7
silhouettes 93, 270
sitting 252
skies 62, 182–3, 196–9
space 102, 128–9, 226, 256–7
spattering paint 71
speed painting 68–9
splattering paint 71
splaying hairs 70
sponges 30, 71
sponging off 190
standing 239–40, 251
storms 198–9
streams 200–1
street life 293
structure 146–7

subject choice 90–106, 150–1, 194–5
subject rather than paint 6, 16,
    122, 194
sunlight 163, 263
sunsets 218–19
surface texture, paper 29
symmetry, proportion 244–5

techniques
    general 58–87
    landscapes 178–91
temperature bias 44–5, 134–5, 172
tertiary colours 38–41
texture, paper 29
third dimension 90, 98, 122, 124,
    232–3, 263, 265
thirds, rule of 108, 109, 149
tints 42, 60
tone
    assessing 194
    counterchange 138, 262
    silhouettes 270
    skin 275
    strength and depth 132–3, 140
torso 240
transparency 42, 60, 84, 168
trees 202–3

value *see* tone

variegated washes 81
viewfinders 150

walking *see* movement
warm colours 44, 46
washes
    brushes 56
    layering colours 62, 184
    negative space 178
    techniques 77–83, 182–5, 197,
      198
water 30, 51
watercolour pans 50
wax resist 189
weather 198–9
wet into wet 58, 64–9, 100, 180,
    186, 241, 282
wet on dry 58, 60–3, 101, 180, 186
white paint 84–5, 191
white paper, reserving 15, 72–4,
    188–9, 271
wilderness 216–17
wood pulp paper 29

yellow 142, 172–3